ORDER OF BATTLE

OF THE

GERMAN ARMY

APRIL 1943

MILITARY INTELLIGENCE SERVICE
WASHINGTON, D. C.

Published by Books Express Publishing
Copyright © Books Express, 2011
ISBN 978-1-780390-81-9

Books Express publications are available from all good retail and online booksellers. For publishing proposals and direct ordering please contact us at: info@books-express.com

FOREWORD

Order of Battle intelligence consists of carefully sifted and evaluated information received from a great variety of sources on the organization, strength, and disposition of enemy forces. This information, if complete and accurate, not only facilitates the planning of military operations but helps commanders in the field to judge the enemy's local capabilities and to make their decisions accordingly.

The purpose of this text is to furnish intelligence officers with a clear and detailed picture of the German Army in all its aspects, from the organization of the High Command to the functions of small units and auxiliary services, and to furnish specific data on individual units and commanders. It will serve both for the basic orientation of those to whom it is addressed and for ready reference in particular situations. It cannot, however, cover the entire field thoroughly and should therefore be used in conjunction with the following other War Department publications:

    TM 30–450 Handbook on German Military Forces
    TM 30–255 Miltary Dictionary (English-German, German-English)
    German Military Symbols
    Dictionary of German Military Abbreviations.

The book may be considered as divided into two parts: a basic description of the German military establishment (secs. I to V, inclusive) and specific information on the composition of German units and on German commanders (secs. VI to VIII, inclusive). To these are added a brief glossary of abbreviations used in the text (sec. IX) and an index of names (sec. X). Since much of the information in sections VI to VIII, inclusive, is of a transitory character, sectional revisions will be issued at suitable intervals.

It will be noted that German designations of rank are used throughout the text and that German military terms and abbreviations are frequently alternated with their English equivalents. This is done in order to familiarize the readers of the book with German usages as these are likely to be encountered in documents.

The study of this text will acquaint intelligence officers with the types of information desired by the Eur-African Order of Battle Branch of the Military Intelligence Service. They are urgently requested to report promptly all such intelligence data coming to their notice, and in particular any facts or evidence appearing to deviate from or to amplify the information already contained in the book. Since speed is important, such reports should be addressed direct to the Eur-African Order of Battle Branch, Military Intelligence Service, War Department, Washington, D. C.

TABLE OF CONTENTS

	Page
Section I. THE GERMAN HIGH COMMAND	01
1. INTRODUCTION	01
2. HIGH COMMAND OF THE ARMED FORCES (OKW)	02
3. ARMY HIGH COMMAND (OKH)	04
a. Advanced echelon	04
b. Rear echelon	06
II. THE BASIC STRUCTURE OF THE GERMAN ARMY	0234
4. INTRODUCTION	0234
5. THE REGIONAL ORGANIZATION	0234
6. DRAFT OF PERSONNEL	0236
7. REPLACEMENT TRAINING SYSTEM	0238
a. The original plan	0238
b. Subsequent developments	0240
c. Replacement training units in occupied territory	0244
d. Recapitulation	0246
8. LIST OF MILITARY DISTRICTS	0246
9. ARMY ADMINISTRATION IN OCCUPIED COUNTRIES	0262
a. Austria	0262
b. Czechoslovakia	0262
c. Memel District	0263
d. Poland	0263
e. Danzig Free State	0264
f. Norway	0264
g. Denmark	0264
h. Holland	0265
i. Luxemburg	0265
j. Belgium	0265
k. France	0266
l. Italy	0267
m. Rumania	0267
n. Bulgaria	0267
o. Hungary	0268
p. Yugoslavia	0268
q. Greece	0268
r. Finland	0269
s. U. S. S. R.	0269
10. ARMY ORGANIZATION IN THE COMMUNICATIONS ZONE	0269

TABLE OF CONTENTS

	Page
SECTION III. TYPES OF SMALL UNITS	0270
11. INTRODUCTION	0270
12. INFANTRY	0270
a. Organic units	0270
b. GHQ units	0271
c. Distinguishing color	0273
d. Tactical signs	0273
13. CAVALRY	0273
a. Organic units	0273
b. GHQ units	0273
c. Distinguishing color	0274
d. Tactical signs	0274
14. PANZER TROOPS	0274
a. Organic units	0274
b. GHQ units	0274
c. Distinguishing color	0275
d. Tactical signs	0275
15. ARTILLERY	0275
a. Organic division artillery	0275
b. Artillery commanders	0277
c. GHQ artillery	0278
d. Distinguishing color	0279
e. Tactical signs	0280
16. CHEMICAL WARFARE TROOPS	0280
a. Organic units	0280
b. GHQ units	0280
c. Distinguishing color	0281
d. Tactical signs	0281
17. ENGINEERS	0281
a. Organic units	0281
b. GHQ units	0281
(1) Combat engineer units	0281
(2) Fortress engineer units	0282
(3) Railway engineer units	0283
c. Distinguishing color	0284
d. Tactical signs	0284
18. SIGNAL TROOPS	0284
a. Organic units	0284
b. GHQ units	0284
c. Distinguishing color	0286
d. Tactical signs	0286

TABLE OF CONTENTS

Section III. TYPES OF SMALL UNITS—Continued.

	Page
19. TRANSPORT AND SUPPLY TROOPS	0286
a. Organic units	0286
b. GHQ units	0287
(1) Transport units	0287
(2) Supply units	0288
(3) Railway units	0289
c. Distinguishing color	0289
d. Tactical signs	0289
20. MEDICAL UNITS	0289
a. Organic units	0289
b. GHQ units	0289
c. Distinguishing color	0291
d. Tactical signs	0291
21. VETERINARY UNITS	0291
a. Organic units	0291
b. GHQ units	0291
c. Distinguishing color	0291
d. Tactical signs	0291
22. MILITARY POLICE UNITS	0291
a. Organic units	0291
b. GHQ units	0291
c. Distinguishing color and insignia	0292
d. Tactical signs	0292
23. LOCAL DEFENSE UNITS	0292
a. Organic units	0292
b. GHQ units	0292
c. Distinguishing color	0294
d. Tactical signs	0294
24. CONSTRUCTION UNITS	0294
a. Organic units	0294
b. GHQ units	0294
c. Distinguishing color	0295
d. Tactical signs	0295
25. ADMINISTRATIVE UNITS	0295
a. Organic units	0295
b. GHQ units	0295
(1) Administration of supplies	0295
(2) Administration of ordnance stores	0296
(3) Administration of occupied territory	0297
(4) Administration of PW camps	0298

TABLE OF CONTENTS

SECTION III. TYPES OF SMALL UNITS—Continued.   Page
- 26. SPECIAL MISSION UNIT 0298
- 27. ANTIAIRCRAFT UNITS OF THE AIR FORCE 0299
- 28. OTHER AIR FORCE UNITS 0300
  - a. Parachute troops 0300
  - b. Reconnaissance squadrons 0301
  - c. Air signal units 0301
  - d. Auxiliary units 0301

IV. OTHER MILITARIZED AND AUXILIARY ORGANIZATIONS 08
- 29. INTRODUCTION 08
- 30. SS AND POLICE 08
  - a. The SS organization 08
  - b. The police 010
  - c. The Waffen-SS 012
- 31. SEMI-MILITARY SERVICES 013
  - a. Todt organization 013
  - b. Nazi Party Motor Transport Corps 014
  - c. Reich Labor Service 014
  - d. Technical Emergency Corps 015
- 32. PARTY ORGANIZATIONS 015
  - a. The party as such 015
  - b. Storm troops 015
  - c. Nazi Party Aviation Corps 016
  - d. Hitler Youth 016

V. THE GERMAN FORCES IN ACTION 016

VI. GLOSSARY OF LARGE UNITS 019
- 33. INTRODUCTION 019
- 34. ARMY GROUPS 022
- 35. ARMIES 024
- 36. PANZER ARMIES 027
- 37. INFANTRY CORPS 028
- 38. PANZER CORPS 037
- 39. MOUNTAIN CORPS 040
- 40. CORPS COMMANDS AND RESERVE CORPS 040
- 41. INFANTRY AND MISCELLANEOUS DIVISIONS 044
- 42. CAVALRY DIVISIONS 0107
- 43. MOTORIZED DIVISIONS 0107
- 44. LIGHT DIVISIONS 0112
- 45. PANZER DIVISIONS 0114

		Page
Section VI. GLOSSARY OF LARGE UNITS—Continued.		
	46. MOUNTAIN DIVISIONS	0125
	47. SICHERUNGS DIVISIONS	0128
	48. SS FORMATIONS	0132
	49. DIVISIONAL EMBLEMS	
VII. TABLES OF IDENTIFIED UNITS		0302
	50. INTRODUCTION	0302
	51. ARMIES AND PANZER ARMIES	0302
	52. CORPS AND CORPS COMMANDS	0303
	53. INFANTRY, MOTORIZED, LIGHT, AND MISCELLANEOUS DIVISIONS	0303
	54. CAVALRY DIVISIONS	0312
	55. PANZER DIVISIONS	0313
	56. MOUNTAIN DIVISIONS	0314
	57. WAFFEN-SS UNITS	0315
	58. BRIGADES	0317
	59. INFANTRY REGIMENTS	0318
	60. CAVALRY REGIMENTS	0324
	61. MOTORCYCLE BATTALIONS	0325
	62. PANZER REGIMENTS AND BATTALIONS	0326
	63. RECONNAISSANCE BATTALIONS	0327
	64. ARTILLERY REGIMENTS, BATTALIONS AND BATTERIES	0329
	65. ARTILLERY OBSERVATIONS BATTALIONS AND BATTERIES	0338
	66. ANTITANK BATTALIONS	0339
	67. MOTORIZED MACHINE GUN AND ANTIAIRCRAFT BATTALIONS	0342
	68. ENGINEER REGIMENTS, BATTALIONS, ETC	0343
	69. SIGNAL REGIMENTS, BATTALIONS, AND COMPANIES	0347
	70. SMALL UNITS	0352
	71. AAA REGIMENTS, BATTALIONS, AND BATTERIES	0355
VIII. ROSTERS OF SENIOR OFFICERS		0136
	72. INTRODUCTION	0136
	a. German surnames	0136
	b. German titles	0137
	c. German military ranks	0137
	d. Ranks in the Army Medical and Veterinary Services	0140

TABLE OF CONTENTS

	Page
SECTION VIII. ROSTERS OF SENIOR OFFICERS—Continued.	
73. ARMY GENERALS	0141
a. Generalfeldmarschall	0141
b. Generaloberst	0142
c. General der Infanterie, etc	0142
d. Generalleutnant	0149
e. Generalmajor	0166
74. GENERAL STAFF CORPS OFFICERS	0189
75. AIR FORCE GENERALS	0196
a. Reichsmarschall	0196
b. Generalfeldmarschall	0196
c. Generaloberst	0196
d. General der Flieger, etc	0197
e. Generalleutnant	0199
f. Generalmajor	0202
76. SS AND POLICE OFFICERS	0208
a. Reichsführer SS	0208
b. Oberstgruppenführer	0208
c. Obergruppenführer	0209
d. Gruppenführer	0211
e. Brigadeführer	0216
IX. ABBREVIATIONS	0222
X. INDEX OF NAMES	

RESTRICTED

Section I. THE GERMAN HIGH COMMAND

1. Introduction.

Under the German military system of today the basic principle is unity of command. Thus the Army, Navy, and Air Force are not regarded as separate services but as branches of a single service, the Armed Forces (die Wehrmacht). Instead of three departments or ministries, there is a single branch of the government known as the High Command of the Armed Forces (Oberkommando der Wehrmacht), the head of which has a seat in the Cabinet and represents the joint interests of the Armed Forces with respect to other governmental departments. This joint high command is responsible for the whole preparation of national defense in time of peace and for the general conduct of war; it appoints commanders for the joint task forces in the field and sees to it that the efforts of the three branches of the service are thoroughly coordinated.

Under the Oberkommando der Wehrmacht (OKW), each branch has its own high command: the Army High Command (Oberkommando des Heeres, OKH), the Navy High Command (Oberkommando der Kriegsmarine, OKM), and the Air Force High Command (Oberkommando der Luftwaffe, OKL). These are responsible for organizing in detail, under the general direction of the OKW, the military, naval, and air establishments, respectively, and for carrying out the strategic planning of the OKW in their particular spheres.

With this system it is quite usual in a task force for units of one branch of the service to come under the immediate command control of another branch, and senior officers may even be transferred from one branch to another in the same or equivalent rank. In all cases, the OKW alone decides what is most expedient in the national interest.

In time of war the OKW as well as each of the three branches of the Armed Forces is divided into two echelons. The advanced echelon (consisting of the C in C, the Chief of the General Staff, and the bulk of the General Staff) moves out to its war station, the location of which depends on the theater of operations selected for main attention. The rear echelon, under a senior officer directly responsible to the C in C, remains in Berlin to handle all basic administrative matters, procurement, mobilization, and replacement training. This separation is made in order to relieve the advanced echelon of nonoperational concerns and to leave it free to concentrate on the control of the forces in the field.

2. High command of the armed forces (OKW).

HITLER is the Supreme Commander of the Armed Forces (Oberster Befehlshaber der Wehrmacht). His deputy as such is Generalfeldmarschall Wilhelm KEITEL, Chief of the High Command of the Armed Forces (Chef des Oberkommandos der Wehrmacht). KEITEL is responsible for the smooth functioning of the High Command and for seeing that HITLER's orders are carried out, but he has comparatively little to do with major decisions of policy.

Under the OKW the functions of a joint general staff are performed by what is known as the Armed Forces Operations Staff, (Wehrmachtführungsstab, W. F. St.). The chief of this staff General der Artillerie Alfred JODL, is believed to be HITLER's principal adviser on strategy and planning. Under JODL, the W. F. St. is divided into sections entrusted with particular functions. The most important of these sections is the Joint Planning Staff, under Generalleutnant WARLIMONT, which is responsible for all strategical, executive, and future operations planning. Another section of the W. F. St. is solely concerned with interservice communications and maintains a special network of land cables and radio channels between the Army, Navy, and Air Force headquarters and the principal subordinate headquarters.

The advanced echelon of the OKW, which includes the principal sections of the Armed Forces Operations Staff, is stationed at HITLER'S headquarters in the field, known as the Führerhauptquartier. During the Polish campaign it was situated between Berlin and the Polish frontier, moving to the Rhineland for the western campaign in 1940 and to East Prussia for the early stages of the attack on the U. S. S. R.

The rear echelon of the OKW is divided into numerous sections and subsections responsible for the following matters:

(a) Joint intelligence, in a section known as Abwehr under Admiral CANARIS.

(b) Public Relations; among other things, this section issues the daily joint communiques on the course of operations.

(c) Defense economics (Wehrwirtschaft): the over-all planning of production, allocation of raw materials, and system of procurement.

(d) Military propaganda, including control of the propaganda companies which accompany combat units.

(e) Welfare, including questions of pensions, bonuses, indemnities, and rehabilitation.

(f) Prisoners of war, including relations with the protecting power and the International Red Cross.

The personnel of the OKW and its subdivisions is drawn from all three branches, but the Army naturally has the largest representation.

The name of a command, organization, or title deriving from the OKW is often prefixed by Wehrmacht- or Führungs- in order to distinguish it from a similar command, organization, or title in one of the three branches. Thus, for example, the commander in the Netherlands, General der Flieger CHRISTIANSEN, is called a Wehrmachtbefehlshaber, since he is responsible to the OKW, while the commander in Belgium is a Militärbefehlshaber, representing the Army only. The two special signal regiments which handle interservice communications are called Führungsnachrichtenregimente. The central section in the rear echelon of the OKW is known as the Allgemeines Wehrmachtamt, whereas the corresponding section of the OKH is called the Allgemeines Heeresamt.

3. Army high command (OKH).

a. Advanced echelon.—The advanced echelon of the OKH, which may be termed Army GHQ, moved from Berlin under von BRAUCHITSCH (then C in C) on mobilization in 1939. It was originally distinct both in name and in place from HITLER'S GHQ, but has been in close union with the latter since December 1941, when von BRAUCHITSCH was superseded by HITLER.

KEITEL is now Deputy C in C of the OKH as well as Chief of the OKW.

The Chief of Staff of the OKH was formerly Generaloberst Franz HALDER, regarded as an able officer and the main organizer of the German Army. He was succeeded late in 1942 by General der Infanterie Kurt ZEITZLER, formerly C of S of the First Panzer Army.

Under the C of S, the advanced echelon of the General Staff is divided into two parts, one concerned with intelligence and operations and the other with administration and supply.

The intelligence and operations part is subdivided into departments under Deputy Chiefs of General Staff (Oberquartiermeister, abbreviated OQu). OQu I is Director of Operations and OQu IV Director of Intelligence. OQu II (Training), OQu III (Organization), and OQu V (Historical), it is believed, remain with the rear echelon.

The head of the administration and supply group is known as the Generalquartiermeister (abbreviated Gen Qu). His function is to control, under the general direction of the C in C and C of S, all questions affecting the administration and supply of the armies in the field (but not of those in Germany proper, which are under the rear echelon).

Until early in 1942 General PAULUS (now a prisoner of war) was OQu I. It is not known who succeeded him as Director of Operations, but Genlt. BLUMENTRITT is believed to have taken this post early in 1943. The Director of Intelligence is Genmaj. MATZKY, formerly German Military Attaché in Tokyo, who succeeded the then Genlt. von TIPPELSKIRCH as OQu IV in the spring of 1941. The Generalquartiermeister, Gen. d. Art. Eugen MÜLLER, a former OQu III and Commandant of the Staff College, has held the post of Gen Qu since the beginning of the war.

Army GHQ is responsible for the operations of all army forces in the field under the direction of the OKW. It exercises that control through army group Hq or army Hq, not only by the normal chain of command but also through the General Staff Corps.

The General Staff at GHQ (with an echelon in Berlin) is drawn from the General Staff Corps, which consists of officers permanently transferred from their original arms of the service. This corps also supplies certain officers for the staffs of subordinate units. The Chief of the General Staff is the head of both the GHQ General Staff and the whole corps of General Staff officers, so that such officers are responsible to him wherever they may be serving.

The number of General Staff Corps officers is strictly limited (for a list of those known see paragraph 74). A GSC officer has authority over all other officers holding appointments on the same staff, even though some of them may be senior to him in rank. Thus the staff of a division may be headed by a lieutenant colonel from the General Staff Corps, while the officers subordinate to him include colonels on active duty.

The small number of GSC officers at unit Hq may be shown best by some concrete instances. In November 1941 there were only five GSC officers at Hq of the Panzer Army of Africa. The Hq of the subordinate Africa Panzer Corps included only two (Chief of Staff and G–3), and there were only five GSC officers among the three German divisions of that corps.

Not only do GSC officers look to the C of GS as the head of their corps, but they have the right, and in certain conditions the duty, to report directly to him. In particular, the chief of staff of an army corps or any higher unit is in duty bound to report to the C of GS in writing any major difference of opinion between himself and his commander. In such a case, the commander takes responsibility for the course of action decided upon and the chief of staff complies to the best of his ability, but his opinion is on record.

It follows that the C of GS at Army GHQ is kept in very close touch with the course of the war. If he thinks it necessary, however, he may send a GSC officer as special liaison officer to army group or army Hq to submit daily direct reports on the course of events.

German commanders and chiefs of staff are expected to use their initiative. Individual responsibility for action is the German precept which officers of all ranks are required to observe. But by the system outlined above, Army GHQ is enabled to keep in the closest touch with the course of operations and so to direct them with full knowledge of the situation.

b. Rear Echelon.—On moblization, when the advanced echelon of the Army High Command (OKH) moved out to its war station at Army GHQ, the rear echelon, including all non-operational branches and the whole basic structure (described in sec. II), was placed under the command of a senior general, with the title Chief of Army Equipment and Commander of the Replacement Training Army (Chef der Heeresrüstung und Befehlshaber des Ersatzheeres, commonly abbreviated Ch H Rüst u. BdE). The importance which the Germans assign to this office may be measured by the fact that its holder, Generaloberst Fritz FROMM, was promoted Genobst. and decorated with the Knight's Cross of the Iron Cross on the conclusion of the campaign in the West in 1940.

Under FROMM are the Directors of Training and Organization (OQu II and OQu III), with the portion of the General Staff which remains behind in Berlin as well as the permanent non-operational branches of the OKH.

The most important of these branches is the Allgemeines Heeresamt, abbreviated AHA (General Army Office), which handles such matters as the Army budget, training, draft of personnel, clothing, and publications within what may for convenience be termed the Home Command. It includes the inspectors of the different arms of the service similar to our former chiefs of branches. The present head of the AHA is Gen. d. Inf. Friedrich OLBRICHT.

The development and procurement of armaments and heavy equipment are handled by the Heeres-Waffenamt, abbreviated WaA (Army Ordnance Office), at present under Gen. d. Art. Emil LEEB (a young brother of Generalfeldmarschall Ritter von LEEB). The Heeresverwaltungsamt, abbreviated VA (Army Administration Office), under Genlt. OSTERKAMP, is mainly concerned with those aspects of military administration which are assigned to civilian officials (Beamten)—pay, rations, postal services, billeting, etc.

The Heeres-Personalamt, abbreviated HPA (Army Personnel Office), is headed by Genmaj. Rudolf SCHMUNDT, who is also the Chief Adjutant and one of the closest advisers of HITLER. This branch is responsible for the proper listing and promotion of officers, and for the appointment of all except GSC officers (who are appointed by the Central Department of the General Staff—Genstb. d. H/GZ), though appointments of officers to various specialist arms are made on the nomination of the heads of those arms.

As will be seen in section II, the work of the rear echelon is considerably lightened by a large degree of decentralization to the military district Hq. Policy is laid down and plans are drawn up in Berlin, but much of the detailed work is left to the district Hq.

As Chief of Army Equipment (Chef der Heeresrüstung), Genobst. FROMM is responsible for the provision and design of equipment of all kinds, both for the armies in the field and for all troops stationed within the area of the Home Command. As Commander of the Replacement Training Army (Befehlshaber des Ersatzheeres) he is responsible for the training system described in section II, and in addition he commands such organizations or units of the field army as may be sent to Germany to rest or be reorganized.

He is also partially responsible for certain areas of occupied territory in which training divisions and replacement training units are stationed (e. g. Denmark, Holland, Belgium, and eastern France). The custom which has developed of forming new divisions in France has involved a further expansion of his sphere. The military commanders in those countries, however, are not subordinate to him.

Section IV. OTHER MILITARIZED AND AUXILIARY ORGANIZATIONS

29. Introduction.

The German ground forces whose organization and composition have been outlined in Sections I to III, inclusive, of this text are supplemented to a large and increasing extent by a number of combat and service organizations outside the army proper, most of them affiliated to the Nazi Party or a faction of it. No picture of the German forces in the field would be complete without a consideration of these autonomous groups and their important roles. Their relations with the O. K. W., the O. K. H., and subordinate army commands are somewhat obscure, but it is at least clear that in practice they function in the closest harmony with the regular army and relieve it of many responsibilities, while on the other hand they absorb a large portion of its potential manpower.

30. SS and police.

The most important of the supplementary organizations outside the army is the Waffen–SS, a branch of the Schutzstaffeln or Elite Corps of the Party. Since the SS and the German police are closely integrated and the officers of one are often officers in the other, they are treated together in this section and in the index of senior officers in section VIII. Heinrich HIMMLER controls both and since 1936 has borne the official title of Reichsführer SS und Chef der Deutschen Polizei. (It should be noted that in Germany the abbreviation SS is always printed thus: ᛋᛋ).

a. The SS organization.—Originally formed in the 1920's to furnish protective squads for political meetings and bodyguards for the leaders of the Party, the SS has been vastly expanded, especially in the past few years, and is now widely employed both for internal security duties in Germany and German-occupied territories and in permanent military units. HITLER is its supreme commander, to whom unswerving loyalty is sworn. Under him, HIMMLER is the executive chief of the organization, with Hq in Berlin. This Hq is organized on the scale of a complete ministry, with branches and departments comparable to those of the three regular armed services for the recruiting, training, equipment, administration, and control of its subordinate units as well as for political and other activities.

The SS includes the following branches:

(1) *Allgemeine SS* (General SS).—Part-time volunteers (with a permanent administrative staff) employed for political purposes within Germany and forming a reserve from which personnel for the other branches is largely drawn. The men are subject to strict discipline and receive a certain amount of military training.

Waffen-SS (Armed SS).—Takes active part in military campaigns (see *c* below).

(3) *SS-Totenkopfverbände* (SS Death's Head Formations).— Guard units for concentration camps. Some of these units have been incorporated into the Waffen-SS as the SS Totenkopf Division.

(4) *SS-Sicherheitsdienst* (SS Security Service).—A political intelligence service against internal and foreign enemies of the regime, working in close collaboration and often in personal union with the Sicherheitspolizei and the Geheime Staatspolizei (see *b* below).

The SS is organized regionally into 19 Oberabschnitte (districts), coinciding in most cases with the 17 Wehrkreise of the military authorities. Each Oberabschnitt is normally subdivided into either two or three Abschnitte (areas), which carry Roman numerals. (There is also an independent Abschnitt XXXIX, with Hq at Prague.) Each Oberabschnitt is commanded by a senior SS officer, who is also HIMMLER's immediate representative at the Hq of the corresponding Wehrkreis. In the latter capacity he is described as Höherer SS and Polizeiführer (Superior SS and Police Commander) in the Wehrkreis concerned. Each Abschnitt is commanded by an SS und Polizeiführer (SS and Police Commander).

The following is a list of the SS-Oberabschnitte, with their component Abschnitte, headquarters, and corresponding Wehrkreise:

Oa. (component Abs.)	Hq	Wkr.
Alpenland (XXXV, XXXVI)	Salzburg	XVIII
Donau (VIII, XXXI)	Wien	XVII
Elbe (II, XVIII, XXXVII)	Dresden	IV
Fulda-Werra (XXVII, XXX)	Arolsen-Waldeck	IX
Lothringen-Saarpfalz (———)	Saarbrücken	XII (part)
Main (IX, XXVIII, XXXVIII)	Nürnberg	XIII
Mitte (IV, XVI)	Braunschweig	XI
Nordost (VII, XXII)	Königsberg	I
Nordsee (XIV, XV, XX)	Hamburg	X
Nordwest (Holland)	The Hague	
Ostsee (XIII, XXXIII)	Stettin	II
Rhein (XI, XXXIV)	Wiesbaden	XII (part)
Spree (III, XII, XXIII)	Berlin	III
Süd (I, XXXII)	München	VII
Südost (VI, XXI, XXIV)	Breslau	VIII
Südwest (X, XIX, XXIX)	Stuttgart	V
Warthe (XL, XLIII)	Posen	XXI
Weichsel (XXVI, XLI)	Danzig	XX
West (V, XVII, XXV)	Düsseldorf	VI

SS and police units stationed in occupied territory are commanded by a Höherer SS und Polizeiführer cooperating with the military administration but closely controlled by the SS Hq in Berlin. Within an occupied country an area may be assigned, if necessary, to an SS und Polizeiführer, corresponding to the commander of an Abschnitt in Germany. In Norway there is also a Norwegian SS organization, normally headed by Vidkun QUISLING but subordinate to the German SS.

b. The police.—The German police, like those of most European countries, are formally placed under the Ministry of the Interior, so that HIMMLER, in his capacity as chief of the police, is nominally subordinate to Reich Minister Wilhelm FRICK. Actually, of course, he acts independently and is responsible only to HITLER.

All important German police officers today are SS men, and recruits for the ranks of all branches of the police have for some years been drawn exclusively from the SS.

The German police force is normally divided into the following two main branches:

(1) *Ordnungspolizei* (Orpo), the uniformed constabulary, or regular police, including the municipal Schutzpolizei (Schupo), the rural Gendarmerie, the river police (Flusspolizei), the building inspection police (Baupolizei), the fire-fighting police (Feuerschutzpolizei), and the air raid protection services (Sicherheits- und Hilfsdienste—S. H. D.). The Chief of the Ordnungspolizei is Generaloberst der Polizei DALUEGE.

(2) *Sicherheitspolizei* (Sipo), the security police, comprising the criminal investigation police (Kriminalpolizei) and the state police (Staatspolizei). An offshoot of the latter is the secret state police (Geheime Staatspolizei or Gestapo), which has as its special task the prevention and liquidation of all activity hostile to the regime. In this it is closely associated with the Sicherheitsdienst of the SS, and its personnel is believed to be drawn wholly from the SS. Until his death in May 1942 Reinhard HEYDRICH was Chef der Sicherheitspolizei und des SS-Sicherheitsdienstes; the present chief is Ernst KALTENBRUNNER. The Sicherheitspolizei also works in close touch with the Secret Field Police (see paragraph 22), the personnel of which is largely from the Gestapo.

Police Hq is in Berlin. Within each Wehrkreis there is a unified chain of command subordinate to the Höherer SS und Polizeiführer (see *a*, above), but there is considerable variety in the local structure, which shows traces of the old federal system. There are still separate police departments for the different federal states (Prussia, Bavaria, etc.) into which the Reich is still nominally divided. Below the SS und Polizeiführer, command is exercised by Inspekteure (inspectors) and Befehlshaber (commanders); these posts may be held independently or concurrently, and the titles are qualified by d. O. or d. Sipo u. d. S. D., according to the branch of the service.

Regular German police units are used in varying degrees i[n] the occupied countries, depending on to what extent the loca[l] national police are thought strong and reliable enough to main[-]tain law and order and to cooperate with the German militar[y] and civil authorities.

Militarized units of the regular police force are formed int[o] police battalions, either fully or partially motorized, for use out[-]side Germany. A battalion consists of about 550 men organize[d] into a Hq and four companies and equipped with rifles, machin[e] guns, antitank guns, and armored cars. The personnel is draw[n] from the Ordnungspolizei. These battalions are normally use[d] for internal security or mopping up duties behind the front, bu[t] they may on occasion be employed in the line under regular arm[y] command. They are numbered in the series 1–325; about a hu[n]dred have been identified. Their uniform is field grey like tha[t] of the army, but they are distinguished by dark green collar an[d] cuffs, white metal buttons, and the police version of the nation[al] emblem (eagle and swastika enclosed in and resting on a wreat[h] of oak leaves) worn on the left sleeve and on the cap or ste[el] helmet. Police battalions may be controlled within an occupie[d] country by a regimental staff.

c. The Waffen-SS.—Ever since 1933 a portion of the SS h[as] been armed and trained along military lines and served on a ful[l] time basis, living in special barracks. These troops were know[n] as the SS-Verfügungstruppe, the name indicating that they we[re] held at the disposal of HITLER for any purpose whateve[r] They included the Leibstandarte-SS "Adolf Hitler," which wa[s] HITLER'S own bodyguard regiment, and several other reg[i]ments. Shortly before the present war they were reorganized [into] a motorized division, which took part in the Polish campaig[n] and subsequently each of the component regiments was expande[d] into a motorized division and other new units have been forme[d] almost constantly.

The Waffen-SS is at present believed to consist of at least t[en] divisions, all motorized or armored except a mountain divisio[n] a cavalry division, and a special unit known as the SS "Polic[e]

Division. (For data on those which have been identified see paragraph 48 in sec. VI.) There are also a number of independent brigades and regiments employed for security duties behind the front. Four of the motorized divisions have recently been reclassified as Panzer divisions.

The Waffen-SS as such is directly subordinate to HITLER and is now sometimes regarded as a fourth arm of the service, coordinate with the Army, Navy, and Air Force. For military operations, however, it is provisionally placed under the OKH and individual units are assigned to army groups and armies as needed, although it is believed that an effort is made to give them independent tasks wherever possible.

The uniform of the Waffen-SS is field grey as in the army, but the national emblem is worn on the upper left sleeve instead of on the right breast. The cap insignia is a skull and crossbones, and the ᛋᛋ sign is worn on the right-hand side of the steel helmet and on the collar.

31. Semimilitary services.

The following are the principal semi-military organizations which perform service duties behind the lines. They are thoroughly disciplined and are usually equipped with small arms so that they can defend themselves if necessary against scattered enemy units and guerilla groups, as in Russia.

a. Organisation Todt, O. T.—This was first formed by the late Dr. TODT in 1938 to build the western defenses known in Germany as the Westwall. It is now widely employed to assist army engineer units in road building, road repairs, bridge construction, etc., in the wake of advancing troops and for longer term work in occupied territory such as improving communications, preparing sites for airfields, building fortifications, and clearing harbors of wreckage. It is organized into battalions with a nucleus of specialist German personnel and a large amount of hired or impressed foreign labor. Its motor transport is provided mainly by the NSKK (see below) but in part by local contractors. It is now headed by Prof. Albert SPEER, who succeeded Dr. TODT after the latter's death early in 1942 and incorporated into the O. T. his own similar organization known as the Baustab Speer. The uniform of the O. T., ordinarily worn only by its German personnel, is a khaki blouse open at the neck and khaki breeches. On the left sleeve is a red armband with a black swastika set in a white circle, and immediately above the left cuff is a narrow armband with the inscription "Org. Todt" in white Gothic letters on a black background. Foreign workers employed by the organization wear civilian work-clothes and an armband displaying the Arabic number of the battalion.

b. Nationalsozialistisches Kraftfahrkorps, NSKK (Nazi Party Motor Transport Corps).—The principal functions of this organization are to assist police in traffic control duties on the line of communications and to provide motor transport units (Brigaden) to supplement the transport services of the armed forces and the O. T. Four such brigades exist, bearing the titles Heer, Luftwaffe, Speer, and Todt. Within Germany, the NSKK also trains men in its motor schools and training units for service with the army's mobile troops. Its basic unit is the motor battalion (Motorstandarte), which carries a number in the series 1–400. The Corps is headed by Korpsführer Erwin KRAUS. The uniform is a brown shirt and black breeches. The national emblem is mounted on a wheel enclosing a swastika and is worn on the cap or black crash helmet. White Arabic numerals preceded by the letter M on the right-hand collar patch give the number of the battalion.

c. Reichsarbeitsdienst, R. A. D. (Reich Labor Service).—All German men who are physically fit are normally required to perform six months' labor service in the R. A. D. before beginning their military service. In some cases members sign up for longer periods. They are organized into companies under a cadre of permanent officers and NCOs and are available for service on the line of communications and in occupied countries, often in conjunction with the work of the O. T. or the army engineers. Their leader is Reichsarbeitsführer Konstantin HIERL. The uniform is a brownish-grey blouse with dark collar and trousers. The

R. A. D. emblem (a spade-head containing the Arabic number of the company) is worn on the left sleeve, and under it a red armband with a black swastika set in a white circle.

d. Technische Nothilfe, T. N. or Teno (Technical Emergency Corps).—This organization is classified as auxiliary police but is actually used in the combat zone or in occupied territory for such tasks as the restoration of public utilities, the demolition of damaged buildings, the removal of unexploded bombs, and the reconstruction, maintenance, and guarding of installations of all kinds. In Germany it plays an important part in passive air defense. It is closely affiliated with the German police organization and is commanded by SS-Gruppenführer und Generalleutnant der Polizei Hans WEINREICH under the control of **DALUEGE** and **HIMMLER**. The uniform for service in the field is field grey with a narrow armband immediately above the left cuff with the words "Technische Nothilfe" in white. Above this is a yellow armband with "Deutsche Wehrmacht" in black. The national emblem is worn on the upper left sleeve, superimposed on a black triangle. The Teno emblem, a cog-wheel, is worn on the collar patches.

32. Party organizations.

Certain uniformed organizations of the Party in addition to those described above may also be considered as potential auxiliary units to the military forces and are likely to be encountered performing important functions in the occupied countries. The following are the principal organizations of this type:

a. NSDAP, the National-Socialist Party as such.—It is organized regionally down to the smallest local units, and its officials, known as politische Leiter, keep close control of the activities of all German civilians at home and abroad.

b. Sturmabteilungen, SA (storm troops).—These are organized, on a pattern similar to that of the SS, under Stabschef Viktor LUTZE and are now used for a great variety of purposes on the home front, including the pre-military training of men over 18 who for some reason have not yet been called to the colors. The great majority of SA men, and particularly of SA officers, are now serving in the army as regular soldiers. The only known example of an army unit consisting wholly of volunteers from the SA is the Infanterieregiment "Feldherrnhalle."

c. Nationalsozialistisches Fliegerkorps, NSFK (Nazi Party Aviation Corps).—This organization performs an important function in training personnel for the Air Force and particularly in developing the use of gliders. It is headed by General der Flieger Friedrich CHRISTIANSEN.

d. Hitler-Jugend, HJ (Hitler Youth Organization).—All German youths up to their 17th birthdays are comprised in this organization, which gives them a large amount of premilitary training and indoctrination. It is headed by Reichsjugendführer Arthur AXMANN.

Section V. THE GERMAN FORCES IN ACTION

Sections I to IV, inclusive, have described in some detail the structure of the German Army and the basic organization of its various elements. It is the purpose of the present section V to explain briefly how these elements are combined, under the exigencies of war, to form effective combat teams. The accompaying chart should be consulted in conjunction with this text.

Like the Army, the German Navy and Air Force are composed of many different types of units for the various purposes which these branches of the service must fulfill. The Navy includes battalions of coast artillery, naval antiaircraft artillery, naval aviation units, and the various types of combat ship formations. The German Air Force has, in addition to the regular aviation units, its different types of antiaircraft units, aircraft warning service organizations, civilian air defense organizations, communications, engineer, balloon barrage, and administrative units.

All these types of units in the German Army, Navy, and Air Force may be considered as groups or pools. Unit organizations are withdrawn from these pools to form task forces, which then function as combat teams for a specific purpose. In any given situation the following factors will be considered in selecting units to form a German combat team:

   a. Mission.
   b. Judgment of the commander.
   c. Availability of units.

The commander will be selected from one of the three services, normally from the one which predominates in the task force or whose interests are paramount. He will of course be of a rank commensurate with the size of the force and the importance of its mission.

Since missions and circumstances vary almost without limit, it is obvious that every German combat team engaged in combat is likely to be composed differently from any other. Standard German organizations, especially from the division upwards, should be regarded merely as basic command frameworks, with a minimum of organically assigned combat and administrative units; task forces are formed around these frameworks. Thus the only sure method of determining the composition of the larger German formations at any particular time is by aggressive reconnaissance.

An effort is always made to assign a minimum number of combat units organically to standard German formations such as the division and to retain a maximum number in the various types of GHQ pools. Consequently, when a large German unit, such as a corps or a division, is engaged in combat it will almost always be reinforced by units from the GHQ pools. When the amount of reinforcement is large, additional commanders and staffs will also be attached. The great influence which GHQ reinforcements can have on the combat power of a standard organization, such as a division, should not be overlooked.

The German system as thus outlined is both rigid and flexible. It is rigid in the sense that all the units in any single pool are as nearly alike as possible; it is flexible because the principle of combining units from the various pools is utilized to obtain any sort of combat team which may be required for a given purpose.

Every German combat team assigned a mission is tactically and administratively an independent and self-contained organization. Coordination with other units is arranged in advance. The force is never required to depend on other units to carry out its mission.

It is hardly necessary to point out that the German system of organization for combat is economical and still effective. It enables the commanders to concentrate combat power at the most vulnerable points without changing basic dispositions. The method is also deceptive to the enemy in that it is difficult to estimate German strength in any particular situation.

The German administrative organization for supply and evacuation is arranged in a manner similar to that of the combat organization and is employed in conformance with the principle that the administrative plan must support the tactical or strategical plan. Like the tactical organization, the German administrative organization will be different in almost every situation.

One of the outstanding characteristics of the German military system is unity of command. All units engaged on a single mission are under one commander, who is charged by one authority with responsibility for the success of the mission. As a corollary, two or more German commands are never assigned the same mission simultaneously. Units from the air force, the navy, and the army all serve together under a commander chosen from any of the three branches. In basic training, likewise, great emphasis is placed on cooperation among the services and among different branches of the same service. Although members of the air force, navy, and army wear different uniforms and have somewhat diverging interests, rivalry or competitive spirit among them is practically nonexistent. The three branches of the German armed forces are all combined into one universal organization, Die Wehrmacht, which would be similar in the United States to a Defense Force serving under a Department of National Defense.

To sum up, it should always be borne in mind in confronting any situation involving German forces that the predominating note in all German military thought is the combination of all arms and services necessary for any specific mission into a task force (or mission force) under a single commander.

Section VI. GLOSSARY OF LARGE UNITS
33. Introduction.

This section consists of a catalogue of large German units, from army groups down to divisions, with the names of their commanders, particulars of their composition, and brief notes on their origin and the campaigns in which they have taken part. Divisional components are included whose numbers can be surmised with virtual certainty, even though they may not yet have been actually identified. No attempt is made to give exact or last-minute locations, and it should be remembered that these as well as the commanders change at frequent intervals. The ages shown in parentheses after the names of commanders are usually those reached in 1943.

All SS units are listed separately in paragraph 48 and are given their German designations.

Under the German system the higher command is extremely fluid, and units from the division upwards may be transferred from one larger formation to another without warning, in accordance with the needs of the immediate situation. Thus there is no permanent allocation of divisions to corps, corps to armies, or armies to army groups and there is no standard equation such as 2 divisions=1 corps or 2 corps=1 army. The following outline shows the chain of command and the various types of armies, corps, and divisions:

a. Army groups (Heeresgruppenkommandos).—These are the highest command frameworks below the Army High Command itself and are formed for particular campaigns to control two or more armies in a single theater of operations or in an important and more or less self-contained sector of such a theater. Each army group has a special signal regiment (Heeresnachrichtenregiment) at its disposal and includes a staff to deal with the many administrative and operational matters within its territory, including the rear area. Since the beginning of the Russian campaign the total number of army groups has been between four and seven.

b. Armies (Armeeoberkommandos).—These are more permanent command frameworks than army groups and are not formed only for a specific campaign, although several have been disbanded since the war began. They consist of staffs to which one or more corps are allotted in a particular sector with a particular objective, whether offensive or defensive. Each one has a signal regiment (Armeenachrichtenregiment) and certain administrative units permanently assigned to it. They are of two types: ordinary armies, of which about twelve now exist, and Panzer armies, of which there are six. The latter do not necessarily have only Panzer corps under them, but usually the Panzer element predominates.

c. Corps.—These are permanent staffs to which groups of divisions as well as GHQ artillery and other units are temporarily allotted for specific missions. Each one has a signal battalion and various services permanently assigned to it. The following types exist, all numbered in the same series from I to XC:

(1) Infantry corps (Armeekorps) to control a group of divisions in which infantry divisions predominate.

(2) Panzer corps (Panzerkorps) to control a group of divisions in which Panzer divisions usually predominate.

(3) Mountain corps (Gebirgskorps) to control a group of divisions in which mountain divisions predominate.

(4) Corps command (Höheres Kommando z. b. V.) to control an area in occupied territory in which certain defensive units are located. It may, however, be brought up to establishment and sent into action as an infantry corps.

(5) Reserve corps (Reservekorps) to control a group of reserve divisions.

d. Divisions.—These are the basic large units of the German Army having permanent military establishments. They include the following types:

(1) Infantry division (Infanteriedivision). Standard organization with some variation, especially in recently formed series.

(2) Motorized division (Infanteriedivision (mot.)). One less infantry regiment than the infantry division and including a motorcycle battalion. Recently there has been a tendency to add a Panzer battalion, suggesting that these divisions are to be made equivalent in efficiency to normal Panzer divisions.

(3) Light division (Jägerdivision). Varying organization; usually motorized and highly mobile.

(4) Light Africa division (Leichte Afrika-Division). A new designation for the light divisions of unique composition operating in Africa.

(5) Panzer division (Panzerdivision). Varying organization, tending to become more compact in recent formations.

(6) Mountain division (Gebirgsdivision). Standard organization; specialized for use in mountains and forests but effective anywhere.

(7) Cavalry division (Kavalleriedivision). The only one which existed in the German Army has been converted into a Panzer division. The Waffen-SS contains one cavalry division.

(8) "Security" division (Sicherungsdivision). Specially designed for mopping up duties in the rear areas and along the lines of communication.

(9) Frontier guard division (Grenzwachdivision). A division staff controlling frontier guard battalions only.

(10) Special duty division (Divisionskommando z. b. V.). A division staff controlling certain miscellaneous units in Germany or occupied territory.

(11) Area command (Oberfeldkommandantur). A regional administrative command in occupied territory having divisional status. (Only the ones in Poland have this status.)

(12) Reserve division (Reservedivision). A new type, formed in the autumn of 1942 from existing depot divisions of the same number to give recruits combined training while at the same time undertaking a limited amount of internal security duty in occupied territory and available as defensive reserves.

(13) Mobilization division (Div. Nr. . . . .) A division staff within the Wehrkreis to administer the permanent regional mili-

tary structure and to receive recruits and convalescents and assign them to field or training units.

All the above types with the exception of the Panzer and mountain divisions are numbered in the same series ranging from 1 to 719. The Panzer divisions are numbered separately in a series from 1 to 27 and the mountain divisions in a series from 1 to 8.

Two types of "divisions" belonging to the German Air Force but serving as ground troops have recently been identified. These are the Air Force field divisions (Luftwaffenfelddivisionen), which have appeared in Russia and consist of units of not more than 3,000 to 5,000 men each and believed to total the equivalent of five full defensive divisions; and the Division Hermann Göring and Division Broich, which have appeared in Tunisia and are classified as a Panzer and an offensive infantry division, respectively.

The divisions of the Waffen-SS are treated here under a separate heading, but they are classified as Panzer, infantry, cavalry, and mountain divisions respectively.

e. Special task forces formed for specific missions.—These are of varying size and composition and are called either Armeegruppe (usually an army plus miscellaneous units) or Kampfgruppe (combat group) if smaller. The designation usually includes the name of the commander, as Kampfgruppe Scherer. They may be controlled by any unit from an army group down to a regiment, depending on their size.

34. Army groups (as constituted in March 1943).

Army Group A

Commander: Generalfeldmarschall Ewald v. KLEIST (62)
C of S:

Formed at the start of the German offensive in June 1942 by subdivision of the old Army Group South, to control the armies advancing into the North Caucasus. May have been recombined with Army Groups Don and B.

Army Group Don

Commander: Generalfeldmarschall Fritz Erich v. LEWINSKI gen. v. MANSTEIN (56)
C of S:

Formed probably to counter the Russian offensive starting in November 1942. May have been recombined with Army Groups A and B.

Army Group B

Commander: Generalfeldmarschall Maximilian Frhr. v. WEICHS (62)
C of S: Gen. d. Inf. Georg v. SODENSTERN (54)

Formed at the start of the German offensive in June 1942 by subdivision of the old Army Group South, to control the armies advancing into the region between Stalingrad and Kursk. May have been recombined with Army Groups A and Don.

Army Group Center

Commander: Generalfeldmarschall Günther v. KLUGE (61)
C of S:

Formed at the inception of the Russian campaign in 1941 to control the armies advancing toward the Moscow region. Now extends approximately from Orel to Velikie Luki.

Army Group North

Commander: Generalfeldmarschall Georg v. KÜCHLER (62)
C of S:

Formed at the inception of the Russian campaign in 1941 to control the armies advancing into the Baltic states and toward Leningrad.

Army Group West

Commander: Generalfeldmarschall Gerd v. RUNDSTEDT (68)
C of S:

Formed after the French campaign to control the armies stationed in western Europe.

Army Group E

Commander: Generaloberst (Luftwaffe) Alexander LÖHR (58)
C of S: Genlt. Hermann FOERTSCH (58)

Formed early in 1943 in the Balkans by expansion of the Twelfth Army. Controls German and possibly other Axis units in the Balkan area.

35. **Armies** (for Panzer armies see sec. 36).

First Army

Commander: Generaloberst Johannes BLASKOWITZ (60)
C of S: Genmaj. RÖHRICHT

Formed on mobilization. Took part in the French campaign and has subsequently remained in France. Now in southwestern France.

Second Army

Commander: Generaloberst Hans v. SALMUTH (55)
C of S: Genmaj. HARTENECK

Formed on mobilization. Took part in the Polish, French, and Balkan campaigns. In Russia since June 1941; now in the southern sector.

Third Army

Formed on mobilization; disbanded after the Polish campaign.

Fourth Army

Commander: Generaloberst Gotthard HEINRICI (57)
C of S:

Formed on mobilization. Took part in the Polish and Western campaigns. In Russia, central sector, since June 1941.

Fifth Army

Formed on mobilization for service in the west during the Polish campaign; subsequently disbanded.

Sixth Army

Commander: Generalfeldmarschall Friedrich PAULUS (53) (Prisoner of war)
C of S: Genmaj. Arthur SCHMIDT (48) (Prisoner of war)

Formed early in 1940. Took part, under v. REICHENAU, in the Western campaign. In Russia, southern sector, from June 1941. Encircled and destroyed at Stalingrad.

Seventh Army

Commander: Generaloberst Friedrich DOLLMANN (61)
C of S:

Formed on mobilization. Took part in the Western campaign and has subsequently remained in western France.

Eighth Army

Formed on mobilization; disbanded after the Polish campaign.

Ninth Army

Commander: Generaloberst Walter MODEL (52)
C of S: Genmaj. WECKMANN

Formed in the spring of 1940. Took part in the Western campaign. In Russia, central sector, since June 1941.

Tenth Army

Formed on mobilization; disbanded after the Polish campaign.

Eleventh Army

Probably formed late in 1940. In Russia from June 1941, under v. MANSTEIN. After capture of Sevastopol moved to the northern and central sectors; probably now disbanded.

Twelfth Army

Probably formed in the spring of 1940. Took part in the Western and Balkan campaigns and has remained in the Balkans. Possibly disbanded on the formation of Army Group E.

Fourteenth Army

Formed on mobilization; disbanded after the Polish campaign.

Fifteenth Army

Commander:
C of S:

Probably formed late in 1940; subsequently in northwestern France and the Low Countries.

Sixteenth Army

Commander: Generalfeldmarschall Ernst BUSCH (58)
C of S: Genmaj. Rolf WUTHMANN

Formed in the spring of 1940. Took part in the Western campaign. In Russia, northern sector, since June 1941.

Seventeenth Army

Commander: Generaloberst Richard RUOFF (58)
C of S: Genmaj. Vinzenz MÜLLER (48)

Probably formed late in 1940. In Russia, southern sector, since June 1941.

Eighteenth Army

Commander: Generaloberst Georg LINDEMANN (59)
C of S: Genlt. Ulrich HASSE (48)

Formed in the spring of 1940. Took part in the Western campaign. In Russia, northern sector, since June 1941.

Twentieth Army

Commander: Generaloberst Eduard DIETL (53)
C of S: Genmaj. Erich BUSCHENHAGEN (48)

Formed during the winter of 1941–42, as the Army of Lapland, to control operations on the Murmansk front. In Northern Finland.

Army of Norway

Commander: Generaloberst Nikolaus v. FALKENHORST (58)
C of S: Genmaj. Rudolf BAMLER (48)

Formed on mobilization as the XXI Inf Corps, taking part as such in the Polish campaign. As Gruppe XXI organized the conquest of Norway. Expanded to an army in the summer of 1941. Until the formation of the Army of Lapland it was responsible for German operations in Finland as well as for the control of Norway.

36. Panzer armies.

First Panzer Army

Commander: Gen. d. Kav. Eberhard v. MACKENSEN (54)
C of S:

Formed on or shortly before mobilization as the XXII Inf Corps, taking part as such in the Polish campaign. Fought in the west as Gruppe Kleist and in the Balkans as Panzergruppe 1. Toward the end of 1941 became the First Panzer Army in Russia, southern sector.

Second Panzer Army

Commander: Generaloberst Rudolf SCHMIDT (57)
C of S:

Formed in May 1939 as the XIX Mtz Corps, taking part as such in the Polish campaign. Fought in the west as Gruppe Guderian and in the early stages of the campaign in Russia as Panzergruppe 2. Became the Second Panzer Army at the close of 1941. In the central sector.

Third Panzer Army

Commander: Generaloberst Georg-Hans REINHARDT (56)
C of S:

Part of the peacetime standing army as the XV Mtz Corps. Fought as such in the Polish campaign; in the west as Gruppe Hoth; in the early stages of the campaign in Russia as Panzergruppe 3. Became the Third Panzer Army at the close of 1941. In the central sector.

Fourth Panzer Army

Commander: Generaloberst Hermann HOTH (58)
C of S: Genmaj. RÖTTIGER

Part of the peacetime standing army as the XVI Mtz Corps. Fought as such in Poland and the west and as Panzergruppe 4 in the early stages of the campaign in Russia. Became the Fourth Panzer Army at the close of 1941. Moved from the central to the southern sector in the early summer of 1942 and heavily engaged at Stalingrad.

Fifth Panzer Army

Commander: Generaloberst Jürgen v. ARNIM (54)
C of S: Genlt. Heinz ZIEGLER (49)

Formed late in 1942 by expansion of the XC Inf Corps to control operations in northern Tunisia.

Panzer Army of Africa

Commander: Generalfeldmarschall Erwin ROMMEL (52)
C of S: Oberst BAYERLEIN

Formed in June 1941 as Panzergruppe Afrika to control the Africa Panzer Corps and Italian formations in Cyrenaica. Became a Panzer Army at the close of 1941. Moved to southern Tunisia in the winter of 1942–43.

37. Infantry corps.

I Infantry Corps

Commander: Gen. d. Inf. Philipp KLEFFEL (56)
C of S:
Home station: Königsberg (Wkr. I)

Part of the peacetime standing army.
Campaigns: Polish, Western, Russian.

II Infantry Corps

Commander: Gen. d. Inf. Walter Graf v. BROCKDORFF-AHLEFELDT (56)
C of S: Oberst SCHMIDT-RICHBERG
Home station: Stettin (Wkr. II)

Part of the peacetime standing army.
Campaigns: Polish, Western, Russian.

III Corps—see III Panzer Corps

IV Infantry Corps

Commander: Gen. d. Art. Max PFEFFER (58) (Prisoner of war)
C of S:
Home station: Dresden (Wkr. IV)

Part of the peacetime standing army. Probably dissolved after encirclement at Stalingrad.
Campaigns: Polish, Western, Russian.

V Infantry Corps

Commander: Gen. d. Inf. Wilhelm WETZEL (55)
C of S:
Home station: Stuttgart (Wkr. V)

Part of the peacetime standing army.
Campaigns: Western, Russian.

VI Infantry Corps

Commander: Gen. d. Inf. Bruno BIELER (55)
C of S:
Home station: Münster (Wkr. VI)

Part of the peacetime standing army.
Campaigns: Western, Russian.

VII Infantry Corps

Commander: Gen. d. Art. HELL (56)
C of S: Genmaj. KREBS
Home station: München (Wkr. VII)

Part of the peacetime standing army.
Campaigns: Polish, Western, Russian.

VIII Infantry Corps

Commander: Generaloberst Walter HEITZ (65) (Prisoner of war)
C of S:

Home station: Breslau (Wkr. VIII)

Part of the peacetime standing army. Probably dissolved after encirclement at Stalingrad.
Campaigns: Polish, Western, Russian.

IX Infantry Corps

Commander: Gen. d. Inf. Hans SCHMIDT (65)
C of S:
Home station: Kassel (Wkr. IX)

Part of the peacetime standing army.
Campaigns: Western, Russian.

X Infantry Corps

Commander: Gen. d. Art. Christian HANSEN (58)
C of S:
Home station: Hamburg (Wkr. X)

Part of the peacetime standing army.
Campaigns: Polish, Western, Russian.

XI Infantry Corps

Commander: Gen. d. Inf. STRECKER (57) (Prisoner of war)
C of S:
Home station: Hannover (Wkr. XI)

Part of the peacetime standing army. Probably dissolved after encirclement at Stalingrad.
Campaigns: Polish, Western, Russian.

XII Infantry Corps

Commander:
C of S:
Home station: Wiesbaden (Wkr. XII)

Part of the peacetime standing army.
Campaigns: Western, Russian.

XIII Infantry Corps

Commander: Gen. d. Inf. Erich STRAUBE (55)
C of S:
Home station: Nürnberg (Wkr. XIII)

Part of the peacetime standing army.
Campaigns: Polish, Western, Russian.

XIV Corps—see XIV Panzer Corps
XV Corps—see Third Panzer Army
XVI Corps—see Fourth Panzer Army

XVII Infantry Corps

Commander: Gen. d. Inf. Karl HOLLIDT (53)
C of S:
Home station: Wien (Wkr. XVII)

Part of the peacetime standing army since April 1938.
Campaigns: Polish, Western, Russian.

XVIII Corps—see XVIII Mountain Corps
XIX Corps—see Second Panzer Army

XX Infantry Corps

Commander: Gen. d. Art. Rudolf Frhr. v. ROMAN (50)
C of S:
Home station: Danzig (Wkr. XX)

Formed shortly before mobilization.
Campaigns: Polish, Russian.

XXI Infantry Corps—see Army of Norway
XXII Infantry Corps—see First Panzer Army

XXIII Infantry Corps

Commander: Gen. d. Inf. Karl HILPERT (53)
C of S:
Home station: Bonn (Wkr. VI)

Part of the peacetime standing army (as "Grenzkommando Eifel").
Campaigns: Western, Russian.

XXIV Infantry Corps—see XXIV Panzer Corps

XXV Infantry Corps

Commander:
C of S:
Home station: Baden Baden (Wkr. V)

Part of the peacetime standing army (as "Grenzkommando Oberrhein").
Campaign: Western.

XXVI Infantry Corps

Commander: Gen. d. Art. Albert WODRIG (60)
C of S:
Home station: (Wkr. I)

Formed on mobilization.
Campaigns: Polish, Western, Russian.

XXVII Infantry Corps

Commander: Gen. d. Inf. Walter WEISS (53)
C of S:
Home station: (Wkr. VII)

Formed on mobilization.
Campaigns: Western, Russian.

XXVIII Infantry Corps

Commander: Gen. d. Art. Herbert LOCH (57)
C of S:
Home station: (Wkr. III)

Formed in early summer 1940.
Campaign: Russian.

XXIX Infantry Corps

Commander: Gen. d. Inf. Hans v. OBSTFELDER (57)
C of S:
Home station: (Wkr. IV)

Formed in early summer 1940.
Campaign: Russian.

XXX Infantry Corps

Commander:
C of S:
Home station: (Wkr. XI)

Formed on mobilization.
Campaigns: Polish, Western, Balkan, Russian.

XXXI–XXXVII Corps—see XXXI–XXXVII Corps Commands

XXXVIII Infantry Corps

Commander: Gen. d. Art. Kurt HERZOG (55)
C of S:
Home station: (Wkr. VIII?)

Formed on mobilization.
Campaigns: Polish, Western, Russian.

XXXIX–XXXXI Corps—see XXXIX–XXXXI Panzer Corps

XXXXII Infantry Corps

Commander:
C of S:
Home station: (Wkr. III)

Formed on mobilization.
Campaigns: Polish, Western, Russian.

XXXXIII Infantry Corps

Commander:
C of S: Obst. Otto SCHULZ ( )
Home station: Hannover (Wkr. XI)

Formed in early summer 1940.
Campaigns: Western, Russian.

XXXXIV Infantry Corps

Commander: Gen. d. Art. Maximilian ANGELIS
C of S: Genmaj. Friedrich SIXT (48)
Home station: Dresden (Wkr. IV)

Formed in early summer 1940.
Campaigns: Western, Russian.

XXXXV Corps—see XXXXV Corps Command

XXXXVI–XXXXVIII Corps—see XXXXVI–XXXXVIII Panzer Corps

XXXXIX Corps—see XXXXIX Mountain Corps

L Infantry Corps

Commander: Gen. d. Inf. Herbert v. BÖCKMANN (56)
C of S:
Home station: (Wkr. V)

Formed late in 1940.
Campaigns: Balkan, Russian.

LI Infantry Corps

Commander: Gen. d. Art. Walter v. SEYDLITZ-KURZBACH (55)
         (Prisoner of war)
C of S:
Home station: (Wkr. XI)

Formed late in 1940. Probably dissolved after encirclement at Stalingrad.
Campaigns: Balkan, Russian.

LII Infantry Corps

Commander: Gen. d. Inf. Eugen OTT (53)
C of S:
Home station: (Wkr. III)

Formed late in 1940.
Campaign: Russian.

LIII Infantry Corps

Commander: Gen. d. Inf. Erich CLÖSSNER (57)
C of S: Genlt. Kurt WAEGER
Home station: (Wkr. XII)

Formed late in 1940.
Campaign: Russian.

LIV Infantry Corps

Commander: Gen. d. Kav. Erik HANSEN (54)
C of S:
Home station:

Formed as a corps command in 1940 and became an active corps in the spring of 1941.
Campaign: Russian.

LV Infantry Corps

Commander: Gen. d. Inf. Erwin VIEROW (53)
C of S:
Home station:

Probably formed in the spring of 1941.
Campaign: Russian.

LVI-LVII Corps—see LVI-LVII Panzer Corps

LIX Infantry Corps

Commander: Gen. d. Inf. Kurt v. d. CHEVALLERIE (52)
C of S:
Home station:
  Probably formed in the spring of 1941.
  Campaign: Russian.

LX–LXXI Corps—see LX–LXXI Corps Commands

LXXX Infantry Corps

Commander:
C of S:
Home station:
  Probably formed in early summer 1942. Location unknown.

LXXXI Infantry Corps

Commander: Gen. d. Pz. Tr. Adolf KUNTZEN (54)
C of S:
Home station:
  Formed in early summer 1942 and subsequently in France.

LXXXII Infantry Corps

Commander:
C of S:
Home station:
  Formed in early summer 1942 and subsequently in Belgium.

LXXXIII Infantry Corps

Commander: Gen. d. Inf. Hans FELBER (55)
C of S:
Home station:
  Formed in early summer 1942 and subsequently in France.

LXXXIV Infantry Corps

Commander:
C of S:
Home station:
  Formed in early summer 1942 and subsequently in France.

LXXXVIII Infantry Corps

Commander: Gen. d. Inf. Hans REINHARD (55)
C of S:
Home station:
  Formed in early summer 1942 and subsequently in Holland.

XC Infantry Corps

Commander: Genlt. Walter NEHRING (51)
C of S:
Home station:
  Formed in autumn 1942 for operations in Tunisia, but soon expanded into the Fifth Panzer Army. Probably no longer exists as a corps.

38. Panzer Corps.

III Panzer Corps

Commander:
C of S:
Home station: Berlin (Wkr. III)
  Part of the peacetime standing army as III Inf Corps. Campaigns: Polish and Western (as III Inf Corps), Russian.

XIV Panzer Corps

Commander:
C of S:
Home station: Magdeburg (Wkr. XI)
  Part of the peacetime standing army. Probably dissolved after encirclement at Stalingrad.

Campaigns: Polish and Western (as XIV Mtz Corps), Balkan, Russian.

XXIV Panzer Corps

Commander:
C of S:
Home station: Kaiserslautern (Wkr. XII)

Part of the peacetime standing army (as "Grenzkommando Saarpfalz").

Campaigns: Polish and Western (as XXIV Inf. Corps), Russian.

XXXIX Panzer Corps

Commander:
C of S:
Home station: (Wkr. IX)

Formed late in 1939.

Campaigns: Western, Russian.

XXXX Panzer Corps

Commander:
C of S: Obstlt. HESSE
Home station: (Wkr. X)

Formed late in 1939.

Campaigns: Western, Balkan, Russian.

XXXXI Panzer Corps

Commander: Gen. d. Pz. Tr. Josef HARPE (53)
C of S:
Home station:

Formed late in 1939.

Campaigns: Western, Balkan, Russian.

XXXXVI Panzer Corps

Commander: Gen. d. Inf. Hans ZORN (52)
C of S:
Home station: (Wkr. X)

Formed in early summer 1940.

Campaigns: Balkan, Russian.

XXXXVII Panzer Corps

Commander: Gen. d. Pz. Tr. LEMELSEN (55)
C of S:
Home station: Danzig (Wkr. XX)

Formed in early summer 1940.
Campaign: Russian.

XXXXVIII

Commander: Gen. d. Pz. Tr. Otto v. KNOBELSDORFF (56)
C of S:

Home station: Posen (Wkr. XXI)

Formed in early summer 1940.
Campaign: Russian.

LVI Panzer Corps

Commander:
C of S:
Home station: (Wkr. VI)

Formed late in 1940.
Campaign: Russian.

LVII Panzer Corps

Commander: Gen. d. Pz. Tr. Friedrich KIRCHNER (58)
C of S:
Home station: (Wkr. II)

Formed late in 1940.
Campaign: Russian.

Africa Panzer Corps (Pz. K. Afrika)

Commander: Gen. d. Inf. Gustav FEHN (51)
C of S: Obst. FRANZ
Home station: Berlin (Wkr. III)

Formed as the German Africa Corps in the spring of 1941.
Campaigns: Libya and Egypt; Tunisia

SS Panzer Corps—see section XV

39. Mountain Corps.

XVIII Mountain Corps

Commander: Gen. d. Inf. Franz BÖHME (58)
C of S:
Home station: Salzburg (Wkr. XVIII)

Part of the peacetime standing army since April 1938.
Campaigns: Polish, Western, Balkan. Now in Finland.

XXXVI Mountain Corps

Commander: Gen. d. Inf. Karl WEISENBERGER (53)
C of S: Genmaj. Heinrich Burggraf u. Graf zu DOHNASCHLOBITTEN (60)
Home station: (Wkr. II)

Formerly XXXVI Corps Command, probably formed shortly after mobilization. In Norway from summer 1940 until June 1941. Moved to northern Finland as an infantry corps and subsequently converted to a mountain corps.

XXXXIX Mountain Corps

Commander: Gen. d. Geb. Tr. Rudolf KONRAD (52)
C of S:
Home station: Prague (Protectorate).

Formed in early summer 1940.
Campaigns: Balkan, Russian.

Norway Mountain Corps (Geb. K. Norwegen)

Commander: Gen. d. Geb. Tr. Ferdinand SCHÖRNER (49)
C of S:
Home station:

Formed in summer 1940 in northern Norway.
Campaigns: Murmansk front.

40. Corps Commands and Reserve Corps.

XXXI Corps Command

Commander: Gen. d. Inf. v. HANNEKEN (53)
C of S:
Home station: (Wkr. X?)

Probably formed shortly after mobilization.
Since April 1940 at Copenhagen, Denmark.

XXXII Corps Command

Commander:
C of S: Obstlt. v. STEUBEN
Home station:

Probably formed shortly after mobilization. Identified in France but now possibly dissolved.

XXXIII Corps Command

Commander: Gen. d. Kav. Erwin ENGELBRECHT (52)
C of S:
Home station: (Wkr. VI)

Probably formed shortly after mobilization.
Since summer 1940 at Trondhjem, Norway.

XXXIV Corps Command

Commander:
C of S:
Home station: (Wkr. III)

Probably formed shortly after mobilization.
In Poland from late in 1939 until June 1941; thereafter operating as an infantry corps in Russia.

XXXV Corps Command

Commander: Gen. d. Art. Rudolf KAEMPFE (60)
C of S:
Home station: (Wkr. VIII)

Probably formed shortly after mobilization.

In Poland from late in 1939 until June 1941; thereafter operating as an infantry corps in Russia.

XXXVI Corps Command—see XXXVI Mountain Corps

XXXVII Corps Command

Commander: Gen. d. Kav. Günther v. POGRELL (64)
C of S:
Home station: Wien (Wkr. XVII)

Probably formed shortly after mobilization.
Identified in France but now possibly dissolved.

XXXXV Corps Command

Commander: Gen. d. Inf. Kurt v. GREIFF (65)
C of S: Obst. Ritter v. HEITERER-SCHALLER
Home station: (Wkr. XIII)

Probably formed early in 1940.
In France.

LX Corps Command

Commander: Gen. d. Art. BEHLENDORFF (54)
C of S:
Home station:

Probably formed late in 1940.
Identified in France but now possibly dissolved.

LXI Reserve Corps

Commander: Gen. d. Art. Edgar THEISEN (54)
C of S:
Home station:

Date of formation uncertain.
Location unknown.

LXII Reserve Corps

Commander: Gen. d. Inf. Ferdinand NEULING (57)
C of S:
Home station:

    Date of formation uncertain.
    Location unknown. Possibly in the Government General.

LXIII Corps Command

Commander:
C of S:
Home station:

    Probably formed late in 1940.
    Location unknown.

LXIV Reserve Corps

Commander:
C of S:
Home station:

    Date of formation uncertain.
    In former unoccupied France.

LXV Corps Command

Commander: Gen. d. Art. Paul BADER (58)
C of S:
Home station: (Wkr. II)

    Probably formed early in 1941.
    At Belgrade, Serbia, since May 1941.

LXVI Reserve Corps

Commander:
C of S:
Home station:

    Date of formation uncertain.
    In former unoccupied France.

LXVII Corps Command

Commander:
C of S:
Home station:

Existence uncertain.

LXX Corps Command

Commander: Gen. d. Geb. Tr. Valentin FEURSTEIN (58)
C of S:
Home station:

Formed in southern Norway in autumn 1941.
At Oslo, Norway.

LXXI Corps Command

Commander: Gen. d. Inf. Emmerich NAGY (61)
C of S:
Home station:

Formed in northern Norway in spring 1942.
At Alta, Norway.

41. Infantry and miscellaneous divisions.

1st Infantry Division

Commander: Genlt. Martin GRASE (52)
Composition: 1st Inf Regt, 22d Inf Regt, 43d Inf Regt, 1st Arty Regt, 1st Rcn Bn, 1st AT Bn, 1st Engr Bn, 1st Sig Bn
Auxiliary unit number:* 1
Home station: Insterburg (Wkr. I)

Active division. Personnel partly East Prussian, partly from the Rhineland. Fought well in Poland, less actively engaged in France. Engaged on the Northern Russian front since June, 1941.

---

*This is the number carried by the auxiliary units such as the med bn, vet co, and other services.

3d Infantry Division see 3d Mtz Div

4th Infantry Division see 14th Pz Div

5th Infantry Division see 5th L Div

6th Infantry Division

Commander: Genlt. GROSSMAN (51)
Composition: 18th Inf Regt, 37th Inf Regt, 58th Inf Regt, 6th Arty Regt, 6th Rcn Bn, 6th AT Bn, 6th Engr Bn, 6th Sig Bn
Auxiliary unit number: 6
Home station: Bielefeld (Wkr. VI)

Active division. Personnel from Westphalia and, in part, East Prussia. Fought with distinction throughout the French campaign. Engaged in Russia, central sector, since the beginning of the campaign.

7th Infantry Division

Commander: Genlt. Hans TRAUT (48)
Composition: 19th Inf Regt, 61st Inf Regt, 62d Inf Regt, 7th Arty Regt, 7th Rcn Bn, 7th AT Bn, 7th Engr Bn, 7th Sig Bn
Auxiliary unit number: 7
Home station: München (Wkr. VII)

Active division. Personnel Bavarian. Heavily engaged in southern Poland. Fought against the British in Belgium, but took no part in the French campaign. A good fighting division. Continuously engaged in Russia, central sector, since the beginning of the campaign. (The 638th Inf Regt, composed of French volunteers, is believed to have operated under its command.)

8th Infantry Division see 8th L Div

9th Infantry Division

Commander:
Composition: 36th Inf Regt, 57th Regt, 116th Inf Regt, 9th Arty Regt, 9th Rcn Bn, 9th AT Bn, 9th Engr Bn, 9th Sig Bn
Auxiliary unit number: 9
Home station: Giessen (Wkr. IX)

Active division. Personnel from Hessen-Nassau. On the Saar front for a time. Fought well in France. Engaged in Russia, on the Southern Front, since the beginning of the campaign.

10th Infantry Division see 10th Mtz Div

11th Infantry Division

Commander: Genlt. Siegfried THOMASCHKI (49)
Composition: 2d Inf Regt, 23d Inf Regt, 44th Inf Regt, 11th Arty Regt,
    11th Rcn Bn, 11th AT Bn, 11th Engr Bn, 11th Sig Bn
Auxiliary unit number: 11
Home station: Allenstein (Wkr. I)

Active division. Personnel from East Prussia and from the Rhineland. Fought well in Poland. Not identified during the French campaign. Engaged in Russia from the beginning of the campaign in the northern sector, but now possibly in the center.

12th Infantry Division

Commander: Genlt. Hans Jürgen Frhr. v. LÜTZOW (50)
Composition: 27th Inf Regt, 48th Inf Regt, 89th Inf Regt, 12th Arty Regt,
    12th Rcn Bn, 12th AT Bn, 12th Engr Bn, 12th Sig Bn
Auxiliary unit number: 12
Home station: Schwerin (Wkr. II)

Active division. Personnel mainly Prussian. Fought with distinction in Poland and in France. Identified in Russia on the northern sector, but so far has played an inconspicuous part.

14th Infantry Division see 14th Mtz Div

15th Infantry Division (See 27th Pz Div.)

16th Infantry Division see 16th Pz Div and 16th Mtz Div

17th Infantry Division

Commander: Genlt. Gustav v. ZANGEN (52)
Composition: 21st Inf Regt, 55th Inf Regt, 95th Inf Regt, 17th Arty Regt,
    17th Rcn Bn (Bicycle), 17th AT Bn, 17th Engr Bn, 17th Sig Bn

Auxiliary unit number: 17
Home station: Nürnberg (Wkr. XIII)

Active division. Personnel Bavarian. Distinguished alike in Poland and in France. A good fighting division. Engaged in Russia from the beginning of the campaign in the central sector. Transferred to France in the summer of 1942 and returned to Russia in February 1943, possibly reorganized as a motorized division.

18th Infantry Division see 18th Mtz Div

19th Infantry Division see 19th Pz Div

21st Infantry Division

Commander: Genlt. Wilhelm BOHNSTEDT (53)
Composition: 3d Inf Regt, 24th Regt, 45th Inf Regt, 21st Arty Regt, 21st Rcn Bn, 21st AT Bn, 21st Engr Bn, 21st Sig Bn
Auxiliary unit number: 21
Home station: Elbing (Wkr. XX)

Active division. Personnel from East Prussia and from the Rhineland. Fought well in Poland. Played an inconspicuous part in the French campaign. Engaged in Russia in the northern sector since the beginning of the campaign.

22d Infantry Division

Commander: Genmaj. Friedrich-Wilhelm MÜLLER
Composition: 16th Inf Regt, 47th Inf Regt, 65th Inf Regt, 22d Arty Regt, 22d Rcn Bn, 22d AT Bn, 22d Mtz Engr Bn, 22d Sig Bn
Auxiliary unit number: 22
Home station: Oldenburg (Wkr. X)

Active division. Personnel mainly from East Prussia and Oldenburg. Employed as an air-borne division in Holland. Played a valuable part in the capture of Fortress Holland. Engaged continuously in Russia in the southern sector. Transferred from the Crimea to Salonika in the late summer of 1942; subsequently partly in Crete and partly in Tunisia.

23d Infantry Division see 26th Pz Div

24th Infantry Division

Commander: Genlt. Hans v. TETTAU (54)
Composition: 31st Inf Regt, 32d Inf Regt, 102d Inf Regt, 24th Arty Regt, 24th Rcn Bn, 24th AT Bn, 24th Engr Bn, 24th Sig Bn
Auxiliary unit number: 24
Home station: Chemnitz (Wkr. IV)

Active division. Personnel Saxon. Morale and fighting value very high, to judge by the Polish campaign. Less prominent during the French campaign. Engaged in Russia from the beginning of the campaign, on the southern front and in the Crimea. Now possibly in northern sector.

25th Infantry Division see 25th Mtz Div

26th Infantry Division

Commander: Genlt. Friedrich WIESE (51)
Composition: 39th Inf Regt, 77th Inf Regt, 78th Inf Regt, 26th Arty Regt, 26th Rcn Bn, 26th AT Bn, 26th Engr Bn, 26th Sig Bn
Auxiliary unit number: 26
Home station: Köln (Wkr. VI)

Active division. Personnel mainly from the Rhineland, partly from East Prussia. Took a minor part in the French campaign. Continuously engaged in Russia in the central sector from the beginning of the campaign. Transferred to the southern sector early in 1943.

27th Infantry Division see 17th Pz Div

28th Infantry Division see 28th L Div

29th Infantry Division see 29th Mtz Div

30th Infantry Division

Commander:
Composition: 6th Inf Regt, 26th Inf Regt, 46th Inf Regt, 30th Arty Regt, 30th Rcn Bn (Bicycle), 30th AT Bn, 30th Engr Bn, 30th Sig Bn (Mtz)

Auxiliary unit number: 30
Home station: Lübeck (Wkr. X)

Active division. Recruited mainly in Schleswig-Holstein. Earned special distinction in northern Poland. Fought in Belgium, but took no part (so far as is known) in the French campaign. Engaged in Russia in the northern sector, since the beginning of the campaign.

31st Infantry Division

Commander:
Composition: 12th Inf Regt, 17th Inf Regt, 82d Inf Regt, 31st Arty Regt, 31st Rcn Bn, 31st Engr Bn, 31st Sig Bn
Auxiliary unit number: 31
Home station: Braunschweig (Wkr. XI)

Active division. Recruited mainly in the Braunschweig area. Took little part in the Polish campaign, but fought hard in Belgium and throughout the French campaign. Continuously engaged in Russia in the central sector since the beginning of the campaign.

32d Infantry Division

Commander: Genlt. Wilhelm WEGENER (48)
Composition: 4th Inf Regt, 94 Inf Regt, 96th Inf Regt, 32d Arty Regt, 32d Rcn Bn, 32d AT Bn, Engr Bn, 32d Sig Bn
Auxiliary unit number: 32
Home station: Köslin (Wkr. II)

Active division. Personnel Prussians from Pomerania. Fought well in Poland and in France. A good attacking division. Engaged in Russia, northern sector since the beginning of the campaign.

33d Infantry Division see 15th Pz Div

34th Infantry Division

Commander:
Composition: 80th Inf Regt, 107th Inf Regt, 253d Inf Regt, 34th Arty Regt, 34th Rcn Bn, 34th AT Bn, 34th Engr Bn, 34th Sig Bn
Auxiliary unit number: 34
Home station: Heidelberg (Wkr. XII)

Active division. Personnel mainly from the Rhineland. On the Saar front for some months and later took part in the French campaign, without winning special distinction. Continuously engaged in Russia, central sector, since the beginning of the campaign.

35th Infantry Division

Commander: Genmaj. MERKER
Composition: 34th Inf Regt, 109th Inf Regt, 111th Inf Regt, 35th Arty Regt, 35th Rcn Bn, 35th AT Bn, 35th Engr Bn, 35th Sig Bn
Auxiliary unit number: 35
Home station: Karlsruhe (Wkr. V)

Active division. Personnel from Baden and Württemberg. Fought against the British in Belgium; otherwise saw little active fighting prior to the Russian campaign. Continuously engaged in Russia, central sector; transferred to the southern sector in the winter of 1942–43.

36th Infantry Division—see 36th Mtz Div

38th Infantry Division

Commander:
Composition: 68th Inf Regt, 106th Inf Regt, Inf Regt, 138th Arty Regt, Rcn Bn, AT Bn, Engr Bn, Sig Bn
Auxiliary unit number: 138
Home station:

Formed in summer 1942. Believed to be on the Finnish front.

39th Infantry Division

Commander:
Composition: 113th Inf Regt, 114th Inf Regt, Inf Regt, 139th Arty Regt, 139th Rcn Bn, AT Bn, 139th Engr Bn, Sig Bn
Auxiliary unit number: 139
Home station:

Formed in the summer of 1942. Identified in Holland, in the Flushing area, in the autumn of 1942.

44th Infantry Division

Commander: Genlt. Heinrich DEBOI (50) (Prisoner of war)
Composition: 131st Inf Regt, 132d Inf Regt, 134th Inf Regt, 96th Arty Regt, 44th Rcn Bn, 46th AT Bn, 80th Engr Bn, 64th Sig Bn
Auxiliary unit number: 44
Home station: Wien (Wkr. XVII)

Active division. Personnel mainly Austrian. Sustained heavy casualties in Poland. Saw little fighting but marched great distances in France. Morale less high than that of the other Austrian active divisions. Engaged in Russia on the southern front from the beginning of the campaign. Virtually destroyed at Stalingrad.

45th Infantry Division

Commander: Genlt. KÜHLWEIN (50)
Composition: 130th Inf Regt, 133d Inf Regt, 135th Inf Regt, 98th Arty Regt, 45th Rcn Bn, 45th AT Bn, 81st Engr Bn, 65th Sig Bn
Auxiliary unit number: 45
Home station: Linz (Wkr. XVII)

Active division. Personnel mainly Austrian. Fought well in southern Poland and in the French campaign. Continuously engaged in Russia, in the central sector, where it appears to have sustained considerable casualties. Subsequently transferred to the southern sector.

46th Infantry Division

Commander: Genlt. SCHNECKENBURGER (51)
Composition: 42d Inf Regt, 72d Inf Regt, 97th Inf Regt, 114th Arty Regt, 46th Rcn Bn, 52d AT Bn, 88th Engr Bn, 76th Sig Bn
Auxiliary unit number: 46
Home station: Karlsbad (Wkr. XIII)

Active division, formed at the close of 1938. Personnel partly Bavarian, partly Sudeten German. Saw comparatively little active fighting before the Russian campaign where it has been engaged on the southern front, in the Crimea, and in the Caucasus.

50th Infantry Division

Commander:
Composition: 121st Inf Regt, 122d Inf Regt, 123d Inf Regt, 150th Arty Regt, 150th Rcn Bn, 150th AT Bn, 150th Engr Bn, 150th Sig Bn
Auxiliary unit number: 150
Home station: Posen (Wkr. XXI)

Active division as "Grenzkommando Küstrin" (Küstrin Frontier Command). Personnel Prussian. Had little fighting to do in Poland, but took an active part in the French campaign. Continuously engaged on the Southern Russian front, in the Crimea, and later in the Caucasus.

52d Infantry Division

Commander:
Composition: 163d Inf Regt, 181st Inf Regt, 205th Inf Regt, 152d Arty Regt, 152d Rcn Bn, 152d AT Bn, 152d Engr Bn, 152d Sig Bn
Auxiliary unit number: 152
Home station: Kassel (Wkr. IX)

Reserve division formed on mobilization. Personnel mainly from Hessen. On the Saar front for some months. Some units fought in France, but the division may have been sent to Norway. Engaged in Russia, in the central sector, from the beginning of the campaign.

56th Infantry Division

Commander: Genlt. Karl v. OVEN (54)
Composition: 171st Inf Regt, 192d Inf Regt, 234th Inf Regt, 156th Arty Regt, 156th Rcn Bn, 156th AT Bn, 156th Engr Bn, 156th Sig Bn
Auxiliary unit number: 156
Home station: Naumburg (Wkr. IV)

Reserve division formed on mobilization. Personnel Saxon. Took part in the Polish Campaign. Fought well against the British in Belgium. Identified in the central sector of the Russian front in November 1941, where it has since remained.

57th Infantry Division

Commander: Genlt. Friedrich SIEBERT (55)
Composition: 179th Inf Regt, 199th Inf Regt, 217th Inf Regt, 157th Arty Regt, 157th Rcn Bn, 157th AT Bn, 157th Engr Bn, 157th Sig Bn
Auxiliary unit number: 157
Home station: Bad Reichenhall (Wkr. VII)

Reserve division formed on mobilization. Personnel mainly Bavarian. Distinguished itself in southern Poland and in the operations on the lower Somme. A good fighting division. Continuously engaged in Russia on the southern front since the beginning of the campaign.

58th Infantry Division

Commander:
Composition: 154th Inf Regt, 209th Inf Regt, 220th Inf Regt, 158th Arty Regt, 158th Rcn Bn, 158th AT Bn, 158th Engr Bn, 158th Sig Bn
Auxiliary unit number: 158
Home station: Rendsburg? (Wkr. X)

Reserve division formed on mobilization. Personnel from northern Germany. On the Saar front in April 1940. Identified in the northern sector of the Russian front in December 1941, but little evidence that it has seen much action.

60th Infantry Division see 60th Mtz Div

61st Infantry Division

Commander:
Composition: 151st Inf Regt, 162d Inf Regt, 176th Inf Regt, 161st Arty Regt, 161st Rcn Bn, 161st AT Bn, 161st Engr Bn, 161st Sig Bn
Auxiliary unit number: 161
Home station: Königsberg (Wkr. I)

Reserve division formed on mobilization. Personnel mainly from East Prussia. Fought well against the British in Belgium. Identified on the northern sector of the Russian front but little evidence that it has seen much action.

62d Infantry Division

Commander:
Composition: 164th Inf Regt, 183d Inf Regt, 190th Inf Regt, 162d Arty Regt, 162d Rcn Bn, 162d AT Bn, 162d Engr Bn, 162d Sig Bn
Auxiliary unit number: 162
Home station: Glatz (Wkr. VIII)

Reserve division formed on mobilization with Silesian personnel. Fought well in Poland and in Flanders. Identified on the Southern Russian front and suffered casualties on withdrawal from Stalingrad.

65th Infantry Division

Commander:
Composition: 145th Inf Regt, 146th Inf Regt,   Inf Regt, 165th Arty Regt, 165th Mtrcl Bn, 165th combined Rcn and AT Bn, Engr Bn, 165th Sig Bn
Auxiliary unit number: 165
Home station:

Formed in the summer of 1942.
First identified in Holland, in the Flushing area, late in 1942.

68th Infantry Division

Commander:
Composition: 169th Inf Regt, 188th Inf Regt, 196th Inf Regt, 168th Arty Regt, 168th Rcn Bn, 168th AT Bn, 168th Engr Bn, 168th Sig Bn
Auxiliary unit number: 169
Home station: Guben (Wkr. III)

Reserve division formed on mobilization. Took part in the operations in France without earning special distinction. Engaged since the beginning of the Russian campaign in the southern sector.

69th Infantry Division

Commander:
Composition: 159th Inf Regt, 193d Inf Regt, 236th Inf Regt, 169th Arty Regt, 169th Rcn Bn, 169th AT Bn, 169th Engr Bn, 169th Sig Bn
Auxiliary unit number: 169
Home station: Soest (Wkr. VI)

Reserve division formed on mobilization and recruited mainly from the Ruhr area. Fought well against weak Norwegian forces. Remained in Norway on occupational and defense duties until early in 1943, when it was transferred to the central sector in Russia. (The 193d Inf Regt has been detached and may be under the control of the 210th Inf Div.)

71st Infantry Division

Commander:
Composition: 191st Inf Regt, 194th Inf Regt, 211th Inf Regt, 171st Arty Regt, 171st Rcn Bn, 171st AT Bn, 171st Engr Bn, 171st Sig Bn
Auxiliary unit number: 171
Home station: Hildesheim (Wkr. XI)

Reserve division formed on mobilization and recruited mainly from the Hannover area. On the Saar front for a period. Fought with distinction in the Sedan area and in the advance on Verdun. Fought in Russia in the southern sector for the first four months of the campaign, then returned to France and left again for the Eastern front during April 1942. Virtually destroyed at Stalingrad.

72d Infantry Division

Commander: Genlt. Alfred MÜLLER-GEBHARD (54)
Composition: 105th Inf Regt, 124th Inf Regt, 266th Inf Regt, 172d Arty Regt, 172d Rcn Bn, 172d AT Bn, 172d Engr Bn, 172d Sig Bn
Auxiliary unit number: 172
Home station: Trier (Wkr. XII)

Formed on mobilization in Wkr. IX and XII, incorporating two active infantry regiments and one reserve. Mainly Rhinelanders and Bavarians. Originally known as "Grenzkommando Trier" (Trier Frontier Command). On the Saar front for many months. Not an aggressive division during the early part of the war. Took part in the Balkan campaign and was continuously engaged in Russia on the Southern front and in the Crimea. Transferred to the central sector in the autumn of 1942.

73d Infantry Division

Commander: Genlt. Rudolf v. BÜNAU (53)
Composition: 170th Inf Regt, 186th Inf Regt, 213th Inf Regt, 173d Arty Regt, 173d Rcn Bn, 173d AT Bn, 173d Engr Bn, 173d Sig Bn
Auxiliary unit number: 173
Home station: Würzburg (Wkr. XIII)

Reserve division formed on mobilization. Bavarian personnel. Saw little fighting in Poland, less on the Saar front, and was not distinguished during the campaign in France. Took part in the Balkan campaign and has been continuously engaged on the Southern Russian front, in the Crimea, and later in the Caucasus.

75th Infantry Division

Commander: Genmaj. DIESTEL
Composition: 172d Inf Regt, 202d Inf Regt, 222d Inf Regt, 175th Arty Regt, 175th Rcn Bn, 175th AT Bn, 175th Engr Bn, 175th Sig Bn
Auxiliary unit number: 175
Home station: Neustrelitz (Wkr. II)

Reserve division formed on mobilization. Personnel Prussian, mainly from Schwerin area. On the Saar front for several months and in France in June 1940. Identified in the southern sector of the Russian front.

76th Infantry Division

Commander: Genlt. Karl RODENBURG (49) (Prisoner of war)
Composition: 178th Inf Regt, 203d Inf Regt, 230th Inf Regt, 176th Arty Regt, 176th Rcn Bn, 176th AT Bn, 176th Engr Bn, 176th Sig Bn
Auxiliary unit number: 176
Home station: Berlin (Wkr. III)

Reserve division formed on mobilization. Prussian personnel. Fought well in France. Engaged in Russia in the southern sector from the beginning of the campaign. Virtually destroyed at Stalingrad.

78th Infantry Division

Commander: Genlt. Paul VÖLCKERS (52)
Composition: 195th Inf Regt, 215th Inf Regt, 238 Inf Regt, 178th Arty Regt, 178th Rcn Bn, 178th AT Bn, 178th Engr. Bn, 178th Sig Bn
Auxiliary unit number: 178
Home station: Tübingen (Wkr. V)

Reserve division formed on mobilization. Personnel mainly from Württemberg. Took part in the French campaign where its fighting value was indeterminate. Continuously engaged since the beginning of the Russian campaign in the central sector.

79th Infantry Division

Commander:
Composition: 208th Inf Regt, 212th Inf Rgt, 226th Inf Regt, 179th Arty Regt, 179th Rcn Bn, 179th AT Bn, 179th Engr Bn, 179th Sig Bn
Auxiliary unit number: 179
Home station: Koblenz (Wkr. XII)

Reserve division formed on mobilization. Personnel mainly from the Rhineland. On the Saar front for a period, but took little part in active operations. Identified on the southern sector of the Russian front. Virtually destroyed at Stalingrad.

81st Infantry Division

Commander: Genlt. v. LOEPER (55)
Composition: 161st Inf Regt, 174th Inf Regt, 189th Inf Regt, 181st Arty Regt, 181st Rcn Bn, 181st AT Bn, 181st Engr Bn, 181st Sig Bn
Auxiliary unit number: 181
Home station: (Wkr. VIII)

Reserve division formed on mobilization. Took part in the French campaign without winning special distinction. Apparently arrived on the northern sector of the Russion front from France in January 1942 and has remained there.

82d Infantry Division

Commander: Genlt. Alfred BAENTSCH (48)
Composition: 158th Inf Regt, 166th Inf Regt, 168th Inf Regt, 182d Arty Regt, 182d Rcn Co, 182d AT Bn, 182d Engr Bn, 182d Sig Bn
Auxiliary unit number: 182
Home station: Frankfurt/Main (?) (Wkr. IX)

Reserve division formed on mobilization. Not identified during the French campaign. Identified in Holland late in 1941 but left for Russia in May 1942, where it has since operated on the southern sector.

83d Infantry Division

Commander: Genlt. Theodor SCHERER (54)
Composition: 251st Inf Regt, 257th Inf Regt, 277th Inf Regt, 183d Arty Regt, 183d Rcn Bn, 183d AT Bn, 183 Engr Bn, 183d Sig Bn
Auxiliary unit number: 183
Home station: Hamburg (Wkr. X)

Reserve division formed on mobilization. Took part in the Polish and French campaigns without winning special distinction. Left France for Russia early in 1942 and has fought on the central sector since April 1942.

86th Infantry Division

Commander: Genlt. Helmuth WEIDLING (52)
Composition: 167th Inf Regt, 184th Inf Regt, 216th Inf Regt, 186th Arty Regt, 186th Rcn Bn, 186th AT Bn, 186th Engr Bn, 186th Sig Bn
Auxiliary unit number: 186
Home station: (Wkr. VI)

Reserve division formed on mobilization. Personnel mainly Westphalian. On the Saar front for two months. Took part in the French campaign. Continuously engaged in Russia, in the central sector, since the beginning of the campaign.

87th Infantry Division

Commander: Genmaj. Gerhard (?) RICHTER
Composition: 173d Inf Regt, 185th Inf Regt, 187th Inf Regt, 187th Arty Regt, 187th Rcn Bn, 187th AT Bn, 187th Engr Bn, 187th Sig Bn
Auxiliary unit number: 187
Home station: (Wkr. IV)

Reserve division formed in Wkr. IV and Wkr. IX on mobilization. Personnel mainly Saxon or Thuringian. First in action during French campaign, when it fought well. Continuously engaged in Russia, in the central sector, since the beginning of the campaign.

88th Infantry Division

Commander: Genlt. Friedrich GOLLWITZER (54)
Composition: 245 Inf Regt, 246th Inf Regt, 248th Inf Regt, 188th Arty Regt, 188th Rcn Bn, 188th AT Bn, 188th Engr Bn, 188th Sig Bn
Auxiliary unit number: 188
Home station: (Wkr. VII)

Reserve division, formed in autumn 1939. Played an inconspicuous part in the French campaign. Left France for Russia early in 1942 and has fought on the southern front.

93d Infantry Division

Commander: Genlt. TIEMANN (55)
Composition: 270th Inf Regt, 271st Inf Regt, 272d Inf Regt, 193d Arty Regt, 193d Rcn Bn, 193d AT Bn, 193d Engr. Bn, 193d Sig Bn
Auxiliary unit number: 193
Home station: Berlin (Wkr. III)

Reserve division formed in September 1939. Personnel Prussian, with some previous military training. On the Saar front for several months without distinguishing itself. Identified on the northern sector of the Russian front, where it has remained. (The 271st Inf Regt has been given the honorary title of "Infanterieregiment Feldherrnhalle" and is composed entirely of volunteers from the Party storm troops.)

94th Infantry Division

Commander: Genlt. Georg PFEIFFER (52) (?)
Composition: 267th Inf Regt, 274th Inf Regt, 276th Inf Regt, 194th Arty Regt, 194th Rcn Bn, 194th AT Bn, 194th Engr Bn, 194th Sig Bn
Auxiliary unit number: 194
Home station: (Wkr. IV)

Reserve division formed in September 1939. Personnel mainly Saxon or Sudeten German, with some previous military training. Took some part in the French campaign. Engaged in Russia in the southern sector, where it suffered heavy casualties on the withdrawal from Stalingrad.

95th Infantry Division

Commander:
Composition: 278th Inf Regt, 279th Inf Regt, 280th Inf Regt, 195th Arty Regt, 195th Rcn Bn, 195th AT Bn, 195th Engr Bn, 195th Sig Bn
Auxiliary unit number: 195
Home station: (Wkr. IX)

Reserve division formed in September 1939. Personnel mainly Westphalian and partly Thuringian, with some previous military training. Showed initiative and dash on the Saar front. Not indentified during the French campaign. Continuously engaged in Russia, on the southern front, until it was transferred to the central sector, probably late in 1942.

96th Infantry Division

Commander: Genlt. Siegmund Frhr. v. SCHLEINITZ (53)
Composition: 283d Inf Regt, 284th Inf Regt, 287th Inf Regt, 196th Arty Regt, 196th Rcn Bn, 195th AT Bn, 196th Engr Bn, 196th Sig Bn
Auxiliary unit number: 196
Home station: (Wkr. XI)

Reserve division formed in September 1939. Personnel mainly with some previous military training. Took part in the French campaign. Engaged in Russia in the northern sector.

98th Infantry Division

Commander: Genlt. Martin GAREIS (51)
Composition: 282d Inf Regt, 289th Inf Regt, 290th Regt, 193th Arty Regt, 198th Rcn Bn, 198th AT Bn, 198th Engr Bn, 198th Sig Bn
Auxiliary unit number: 198
Home station: (Wkr. XIII)

Reserve division formed in September 1939. Personnel Bavarian, mainly with some previous military training. Fought well in the French campaign. Identified in the central sector of the Russian front in November 1941, where it has since remained.

102d Infantry Division

Commander:
Composition: 232d Inf Regt, 233d Inf Regt, 235th Inf Regt, Arty Regt, 102d Rcn Bn, 102d AT Bn, 102d Engr Bn, 102d Sig Bn
Auxiliary unit number: 102
Home station: (Wkr. VIII)

Formed in December 1940. First identified in action on Central Russian front in August 1941. Constantly engaged until February 1942, when it may have been withdrawn to Germany to rest. Returned to the central front in mid-April, where it is still located.

106th Infantry Division

Commander:
Composition: 239th Inf Regt, 240th Inf Regt, 241st Inf Regt, 107th Arty Regt, 106th Rcn Bn, 106th AT Bn, 106th Engr Bn, 106th Sig Bn
Auxiliary unit number: 106
Home station: (Wkr. VI)

Formed in December 1940. First identified in action on the Central Russian front in August 1941. Fought in the central sector throughout the winter, sustaining heavy casualties, particularly in the latter half of January 1942. Has subsequently returned to France for rest and refit.

110th Infantry Division

Commander:
Composition: 252d Inf Regt, 254th Inf Regt, 255th Inf Regt, 120th Arty Regt, 110th Rcn Bn, 110th AT Bn, 110th Engr Bn, 110th Sig Bn
Auxiliary unit number: 110
Home station: Oldenburg (Wkr. X)

Formed in December 1940. First identified in action on the Russian front in August 1941, where it has been heavily engaged in the central sector.

111th Infantry Division

Commander: Genmaj. Hermann RECKNAGEL (49)
Composition: 50th Inf Regt, 70th Inf Regt, 117th Inf Regt, 117th Arty Regt, 117th Rcn Bn, 111th AT Bn, 111th Engr Bn, 111th Sig Bn
Auxiliary unit number: 111
Home station: (Wkr. III)

Formed in December 1940. Has been in action in Russia in the southern sector, where it took part in the fighting for Mozdok.

112th Infantry Division

Commander: Genlt. MIETH (56)
Composition: 110th Inf Regt, 256th Inf Regt, 258th Inf Regt, 86th Arty Regt, 120th Rcn Bn, 112th AT Bn, 112th Engr Bn, 112th Sig Bn
Auxiliary unit number: 112
Home station: Darmstadt (Wkr. XII)

Formed in December 1940. Engaged on the Russian front, central sector, since August 1941.

113th Infantry Division

Commander: Genlt. Hans Heinrich SIXT v. ARMIN (54) (Prisoner of war)
Composition: 260th Inf Regt, 261st Inf Regt, 268th Inf Regt, 87th Arty Regt, 113th Rcn Bn, 113th AT Bn, 113th Engr Bn, 113th Sig Bn

Auxiliary unit number: 113
Home station: (Wkr. XIII)

Formed in December 1940. Was in the Balkans on occupational duties during November and December 1941. Later transferred to the southern sector of the Russian front, where it was finally virtually destroyed at Stalingrad.

121st Infantry Division

Commander:
Composition: 405th Inf Regt, 407th Inf Regt, 408th Inf Regt, 121st Arty Regt, 121st Rcn Bn, 121st AT Bn, 121st Engr Bn, 121st Sig Bn
Auxiliary unit number: 121
Home station: (Wkr. X)

Formed in Wehrkreis X in October 1940. In action in the northern sector since the outset of the Russian campaign.

122d Infantry Division

Commander:
Composition: 409th Inf Regt, 411th Inf Regt, 414th Inf Regt, 122d Arty Regt, 122d Rcn Bn, 122d AT Bn, 122 Engr Bn, 122d Sig Bn
Auxiliary unit number: 122
Home station: (Wkr. II)

Formed in October 1940. In action on the Northern Russian front since the outset of the campaign.

123d Infantry Division

Commander:
Composition: 415th Inf Regt, 416th Inf Regt, 418th Inf Regt, 123d Arty Regt, 123d Rcn Bn, 123d AT Bn, 123d Engr Bn, 123d Sig Bn
Auxiliary unit number: 123
Home station: (Wkr. III)

Formed in October 1940. In action on the Northern Russian front, where it appears to have been fairly heavily engaged.

125th Infantry Division

Commander:
Composition: 419th Inf Regt, 420th Inf Regt, 421st Inf Regt, 125th Arty Regt, 125th Rcn Bn, 125th AT Bn, 125th Engr Bn, 125th Sig Bn
Auxiliary unit number: 125
Home station: (Wkr. V)

Formed in October 1940. Engaged on the Southern Russian front since July 1941.

126th Infantry Division

Commander:
Composition: 422d Inf Regt, 424th Inf Regt, 426th Inf Regt, 126th Arty Regt, 126th Rcn Bn, 126th AT Bn, 126th Engr Bn, 126th Sig Bn
Auxiliary unit number: 126
Home station: (Wkr. VI)

Formed in October 1940. In action on the Northern Russian front since the outset of the campaign, where it appears to have been fairly continuously engaged.

129th Infantry Division

Commander: Genmaj. PRAUN
Composition: 427th Inf Regt, 428th Inf Regt, 430th Inf Regt, 129th Arty Regt, 129th Rcn Bn, 129th AT Bn, 129th Engr Bn, 129th Sig Bn
Auxiliary unit number: 129
Home station: Fulda (Wkr. IX)

Formed in October 1940, and has been continuously engaged on the Central Russian front since the beginning of the campaign.

131st Infantry Division

Commander: Genlt. Heinrich MEYER-BUERDORF (54)
Composition: 431st Inf Regt, 432d Inf Regt, 434th Inf Regt, 131st Arty Regt, 131st Rcn Bn, 131st AT Bn, 131st Engr Bn, 131st Sig Bn
Auxiliary unit number: 131
Home station: (Wkr. XI)

Formed in October 1940. Has fought on the Central Russian front since August 1941.

132d Infantry Division

Commander: Genlt. Fritz LINDEMANN (51)
Composition: 436th Inf Regt, 437th Inf Regt, 438th Inf Regt, 132 Arty Regt, 132d Rcn Bn, 132d AT Bn, 132d Engr Bn, 132 Sig Bn
Auxiliary unit number: 132
Home station: (Wkr. XII)

Formed in Wehrkreis VII in October 1940. Subsequently transferred to Wkr. XII. Engaged on the Southern Russian front and in the Crimea from July 1941. Now believed to be in the northern sector.

134th Infantry Division

Commander: Genlt. Dipl. Ing. Hans SCHLEMMER (50)
Composition: 439th Inf Regt, 445th Inf Regt, 446th Inf Regt, 134th Arty 134th Rcn Bn, 134th AT Bn, 132d Engr Bn, 132 Sig Bn
Auxiliary unit number: 134
Home station: (Wkr. IV)

Formed in Wehrkreis XIII in October 1940. Subsequently transferred to Wkr. IV. Continuously and heavily engaged on the Central Russian front since the beginning of the campaign.

137th Infantry Division

Commander: Genlt. KAMECKE (52)
Composition: 447th Inf Regt, 448th Inf Regt, 449th Inf Regt, 137th Arty Regt, 137th Rcn Bn, 137th AT Bn, 137th Engr Bn, 137th Sig Bn
Auxiliary unit number: 137
Home station: (Wkr. XVII)

Formed in October 1940. Identified on the Central Russian front in August 1941, where it appears to have been fairly heavily engaged.

141st Mobilization Division

Commander:
Home station: Königsberg (Wkr. I)

143d Reserve Division

Commander: Genlt. WINDECK (54)
Home station: Frankfurt/Oder (Wkr. III)

Now stationed in Poland.

147th Mobilization Division

Commander: Genlt. HELD (61)
Home station: Augsburg (Wkr. VII)

148th Reserve Division

Commander: Genlt. BOETTCHER (57)
Home station: Metz (Wkr. XII)

Now stationed in former unoccupied France in the Toulouse area.

151st Mobilization Division

Commander:
Home station: Allenstein (Wkr. I)

152d Depot Division

Commander: Genlt. Arthur BOLTZE (65)
Home station: Stettin (Wkr. II)

153d Reserve Division

Commander: Genlt. Rene de l'HOMME de COURBIÈRE (56)
Home station: Potsdam (Wkr. III)

Now stationed in southern Russia.

154th Reserve Division

Commander: Genmaj. Dr. Friedrich ALTRICHTER (52)
Home station: Dresden (Wkr. IV)

Recently stationed in Poland; may have moved to France.

155th Mobilization Division

Commander:
Home station: Ulm (Wkr. V)

156th Reserve Division

Commander: Genlt. BALTZER (56)
Home station: Köln (Wkr. VI)

Now stationed in Belgium in the Spa area.

157th Reserve Division

Commander: Genmaj. Karl PFLAUM (53)
Home station: München (Wkr. VII)

Now stationed in former unoccupied France in the Besançon area.

158th Reserve Division

Commander: Genlt. Ernst HAECKEL (53)
Home station: Strassburg (Wkr. V)

Now stationed in former unoccupied France in the Nimes area.

159th Reserve Division

Commander: Gen. d. Pion. SACHS (58)
Home station: Frankfort/Main (Wkr. IX)

Now stationed in France.

160th Mobilization Division

Commander:
Home station: Copenhagen

161st Infantry Division

Commander: Genlt. RECKE (53)
Composition: 336th Inf Regt, 364th Inf Regt, 371st Inf Regt, 241st Arty Regt, 241st Rcn Co, 241st AT Bn, 241st Engr Bn, 241st Sig Bn
Auxiliary unit number: 241
Home station: (Wkr. I)

Formed in January 1940. Continuously engaged on the Central Russian front, where it has recently suffered heavy losses.

162nd Infantry Division

Commander: Genmaj. Prof. Dr. Ritter v. NIEDERMAYER
Composition: 303d Inf Regt, 314th Inf Regt, 329th? Inf Regt, 236th Arty Regt, 236th Rcn Bn, 236th AT Bn, 236th Engr Bn, 236th Sig Bn
Auxiliary unit number: 236
Home station: Rostock? (Wkr. II)

Formed in January 1940. Continuously engaged on Central Russian front from the beginning of the campaign until the late summer of 1942, when it was transferred to the southern sector.

163rd Infantry Division

Commander: Genlt. Anton DOSTLER (52)
Composition: 307th Inf Regt, 310th Inf Regt, 324th Inf Regt, 234th Arty Regt, 234th Rcn Co, 234th AT Bn, 234th Engr Bn, 234th Sig Bn
Auxiliary unit number: 234
Home station: Berlin (Wkr. III)

Formed in January 1940. Personnel mainly Prussian. Fought well in the Gudbransdal during the Norwegian campaign. Transferred to Finland at the beginning of the Russian campaign, where it has fought fairly continuously.

165th Reserve Division

Commander: Genlt. Siegmund Frhr. v. SCHACKY auf SCHÖNFELD (57)
Home station: Epinal

Now stationed in former unoccupied France in the Vesoul area.

166th Mobilization Division

Commander: Genlt. Justin v. OBERNITZ (59)
Home station: Bielefeld (Wkr. VI)

167th Infantry Division

Commander:
Composition: 315th Inf Regt, 331st Inf Regt, 339th Inf Regt, 238th Arty Regt, 238th Rcn Bn, 238th AT Bn, 238th Engr Bn, 238th Sig Bn
Auxiliary unit number: 238?
Home station: (Wkr. VII)

Formed in January 1940. Personnel Bavarian. First in action during the French campaign. Continuously engaged on the Central Russian front from the beginning of the campaign. Transferred to Holland in the summer of 1942. Returned to the Southern Russian front early in 1943.

168th Infantry Division

Commander:
Composition: 417th Inf Regt, 429th Inf Regt, 442nd Inf Regt, 248th Arty Regt, 248th Rcn Bn, 248th AT Bn, 248th Engr Bn, 248th Sig Bn
Auxiliary unit number: 248
Home station: (Wkr. VIII)

Formed in January 1940. Identified on the Southern Russian front in July 1941, where it has since remained.

169th Infantry Division

Commander: Genlt. Hermann TITTEL (54)
Composition: 378th Inf Regt, 379th Inf Regt, 392d Inf Regt, 230th Arty Regt, 230th Rcn Bn, 230th AT Bn, 230th Engr Bn, 230th Sig Bn
Auxiliary unit number: 230
Home station: (Wkr. IX)

Formed in January 1940. First in action during the French campaign. Apparently arrived in Finland from Norway during the early stages of the Russian campaign and has been in action on the Kandalaksha front.

170th Infantry Division

Commander: Genlt. Erwin SANDER (52)
Composition: 391st Inf Reg, 399th Inf Regt, 401st Inf Regt, 240th Arty Regt, 240th Rcn Bn, 240th AT Bn, 240th Engr Bn, 240th Sig Bn
Auxiliary unit number: 240
Home station: Bremen (Wkr. X)

Formed in January 1940. Fairly continuously engaged on the Southern Russian front and in the Crimea from the beginning of the campaign. Transferred to the northern sector in the late summer of 1942.

171st Reserve Division

Commander:
Home station: Hannover (Wkr. XI)

Now stationed in France in the Epinal area.

172d Mobilization Division

Commander:
Home station: Mainz (Wkr. XII)

173rd Mobilization Division

Commander: Genlt. PFLUGRADT (53)
Home station: Würzburg (Wkr. XIII)

174th Reserve Division

Commander:
Home station: Leipzig (Wkr. IV)

Now stationed at Prague (Prot.)

177th Mobilization Division

Commander:
Home station: Wien (Wkr. XVII)

178th Mobilization Division

Commander:
Home station: Liegnitz (Wkr. VIII)

179th Mobilization Division

Commander:
Home station: Weimar (Wkr. IX)

180th Mobilization Division

Commander:
Home station: Bremen (Wkr. X)

181st Infantry Division

Commander: Genlt. BAYER (56)
Composition: 334th Inf Regt, 349th Inf Regt, 359th Inf Regt, 222d Arty
    Regt, 222d Rcn Bn, 222d AT Bn, 222d Engr Bn, 222d Sig Bn
Auxiliary unit number: 222
Home station: (Wkr. XI)

Formed in January 1940. Employed in Norway (Trondhjem-Dombaas area) since April 1940.

182d Reserve Division

Commander: Genlt. Franz KARL (55)
Home station: Nancy (Wkr. XII)

183d Infantry Division

Commander: Genlt. DETTLING (52)
Composition: 330th Inf Regt, 343d Inf Regt, 351st Inf Regt, 219th Arty
    Regt, 219th Rcn Bn, 219th AT Bn, 219th Engr Bn, 219th
    Sig Bn
Auxiliary unit number: 219
Home station: (Wkr. XIII)

Formed in January 1940. Identified on Central Russian front late in 1941, where it has since remained.

187th Reserve Division

Commander: Genlt. Josef BRAUNER
Home station: Linz (Wkr. XVII)

Now at Agram (*Zagreb*), Croatia.

188th Mobilization Division

Commander: Genlt. Wilhelm v. HÖSSLIN (65)
Home station: Salzburg (Wkr. XVIII)

Now stationed at Marburg (*Maribor*), Slovenia.

189th Reserve Division

Commander: Genmaj. v. NEINDORFF
Home station: Kassel? (Wkr. IX)

May have moved from France, Besançon area, to Greece early in 1943.

190th Mobilization Division

Commander:
Home station: Neumünster (Wkr. X)

191st Reserve Division

Commander: Genmaj. v. DEWITZ gen. v. KREBS
Home station: Braunschweig (Wkr. XI)

Now possibly stationed in France.

192d Mobilization Division

Commander:
Home station: Rostock (Wkr. II)

193d Mobilization Division

Commander:
Home station: Regensburg (Wkr. XIII)

Now stationed at Pilsen (Prot.)

196th Infantry Division

Commander: Genmaj. Dr. Friedrich FRANEK (52)
Composition: 340th Inf Regt, 345th Inf Regt, 362d Inf Regt, 233d Arty Regt, 233d Rcn Co, 233d AT Bn, 233d Engr Bn, 233d Sig Bn
Auxiliary unit number: 233
Home station: Bielefeld (Wkr. VI)

Formed early in 1940. Fought well during Norwegian campaign and stayed on as a garrison division in Central Norway.

197th Infantry Division

Commander:
Composition: 321st Inf Regt, 332d Inf Regt, 347th Inf Regt, 229th Arty Regt, 229th Rcn Bn, 229th AT Bn, 229th Engr Bn, 229th Sig Bn
Auxiliary unit number: 229
Home station: Speyer (Wkr. XII)

Formed early in 1940. Identified on the Central Russian front in August 1941, where it has since remained.

198th Infantry Division

Commander: Genmaj. Ludwig MÜLLER
Composition: 305 Inf Regt, 308th Inf Regt, 326th Inf Regt, 235th Arty Regt, 235th Rcn Bn, 235th AT Bn, 235th Engr Bn, 235th Sig Bn
Auxiliary unit number: 235
Home station: (Wkr. V)

Formed early in 1940. Indentified on the Southern Russian front in July, 1941, where it appears to have been fairly continuously engaged.

199th Infantry Division

Commander: Genlt. Hans v. KEMPSKI (58)
Composition: 341st Inf Regt, 357th Inf Regt, 410th Inf Regt, 199th Arty Regt, 199th Rcn Co, 199th AT Bn, 199th Engr Bn, 199th Sig Bn
Auxiliary unit number: 199
Home station: Düsseldorf (Wkr. VI)

Formed on mobilization. In southern Norway from the end of 1940 until the middle of May 1941, when it was moved to northern Norway. During the latter half of 1941 it may have been for a time in Finland but did not do any fighting. Since December 1941 in Norway (Tromsö area).

205th Infantry Division

Commander: Genlt. RICHTER (54)
Composition: 335th Inf Regt, 353d Inf Regt, 358th Inf Regt, 205th Arty Regt, 205th Rcn Co, 205th AT Bn, 205th Engr Bn, 205th Sig Bn

Auxiliary unit number: 205
Home station: Ulm (Wkr. V)

Formed on mobilization with a high proportion of Landwehr personnel, from Baden and Württemberg. Indentified in France in August 1941 and left for Russia early in 1942. Subsequently in action in the central sector. Personnel now more uniformly distributed in age groups.

206th Infantry Division

Commander: Genlt. Huge HÖFL (65)
Composition: 301st Inf Regt, 312th Inf Regt, 413 Inf Regt, 206th Arty Regt, 206th Rcn Co, 206th AT Bn, 206th Engr Bn, 206th Sig Bn
Auxiliary unit number: 206
Home station: Gumbinnen (Wkr. I)

Formed on mobilization. Personnel mainly East Prussian, of the Landwehr age group. Fairly continuously engaged on the Central Russian front since the beginning of the campaign. Personnel now of normal age groups.

207th Infantry Division—See 207th Sicherungs Division

208th Infantry Division

Commander: Genlt. Hans Karl v. SCHEELE (52)
Composition: 309th Inf Regt, 337th Inf Regt, 338th Inf Regt, 208th Arty Regt, 208th Rcn Co, 208th AT Bn, 208th Engr Bn, 208th Sig Bn
Auxiliary unit number: 208
Home station: Cottbus (Wkr. III)

Formed on mobilization. Personnel Prussian, originally mainly Landwehr. Identified in France in April 1941 and was transferred to Russia, probably in December, where it has been continuously engaged in the central sector since January 1942. Personnel age groups now normal.

209th Infantry Division

Landwehr division formed on mobilization in Wkr. IV with Saxon personnel. Disbanded after the French campaign, in the summer of 1940.

210th Infantry Division

Commander:
Composition: 193d (?) Inf Regt, 388th Inf Regt,   Inf Regt,   Arty Regt,   Rcn Bn,   AT Bn,   Engr Bn,   Sig Bn
Auxiliary unit number:
Home station:

Identified in northern Finland late in 1942. Apparently controls infantry regiments detached from the 69th and 214th Inf Divs.

211th Infantry Division

Commander:
Composition: 306th Inf Regt, 317th Inf Regt, 365th Inf Regt, 211th Arty Regt, 211th Rcn Bn, 211th AT Bn, 211th Engr Bn, 211th Sig Bn
Auxiliary unit number: 211
Home station: Köln (Wkr. VI)

Formed on mobilization. Personnel mainly from the Köln area and of the Landwehr age group. In southwestern France during most of 1941. Moved east at the beginning of 1942 and has fought on the central front. Personnel now normal.

212th Infantry Division

Commander:
Composition: 316th Inf Regt, 320th Inf Regt, 323d Inf Regt, 312th Arty Regt, 212th Rcn Co, 212th AT Bn, 212th Engr Bn, 212th Sig Bn
Auxiliary unit number: 212
Home station: München (Wkr. VII)

Formed on mobilization, with personnel mainly from southern Bayern and of the Landwehr age group. On the Saar front for a time, later in France. Left France for Russia late in 1941 where it was identified in the central sector and subsequently in the northern sector.

213th Infantry Division—see 213th Sicherungs Division

214th Infantry Division

Commander: Genlt. Max HORN (54)
Composition: 355th Inf Regt, 367th Inf Rgt, 388th Inf Regt, 214th Arty Regt, 214th Rcn Bn, 214th AT Bn, 214th Engr Bn, 214th Sig Bn
Auxiliary unit number: 214
Home station: Hanau (Wkr. IX)

Formed on mobilization with personnel from the Frankfurt area. On the Saar front until December 1939. In southern Norway from May 1940. Since September 1941, the 388th Inf Regt has been detached for service in northern Finland, and may now be under the control of the new 210th Inf Div.

215th Infantry Division

Commander:
Composition: 380th Inf Regt, 390th Inf Regt, 435th Inf Regt, 215th Arty Regt, 215th Rcn Bn, 215th AT Bn, 215th Engr Bn, 215th Sig Bn
Auxiliary unit number: 215
Home station: Heilbronn (Wkr. V)

Formed on mobilization. Personnel mainly Landwehr from Baden and Württemberg. On the Saar front in May 1940. In Central France during the summer of 1941, but left for Russia late in that year and has been identified subsequently in the northern sector. Personnel age groups now normal.

216th Infantry Division

Commander: Genlt. Werner Frhr. v. u. zu GILSA (54)
Composition: 348th Inf Regt, 396th Inf Regt, 398th Inf Regt, 216th Arty Regt, 216th Rcn Bn, 216th AT Bn, 216th Engr Bn, 216th Sig Bn
Auxiliary unit number: 216
Home station: Hameln (?) (Wkr. XI)

Formed on mobilization. Personnel mainly Landwehr from

the Hannover area. Fought in Holland and Belgium. Apparently arrived on the Central Russian front from France early in January 1942, where it has since remained. Personnel now normal.

217th Infantry Division

Commander:
Composition: 311th Inf Regt, 346th Inf Regt, 389th Inf Regt, 217 Arty Regt, 217th Rcn Bn, 217th AT Bn, 217th Engr Bn, 217th Sig Bn
Auxiliary unit number: 217
Home station: Allenstein (Wkr. I)

Formed on mobilization. Personnel mainly East Prussian of the Landwehr age group. Fought in Poland and in Flanders. Identified on the northern Russian front in July 1941, where it has been employed on coastal defense duties. Personnel now normal.

218th Infantry Division

Commander: Genmaj. Horst Frhr. v. UCKERMANN (51)
Composition: 323d Inf Regt, 386th Inf Regt, 397th Inf Regt, 218th Arty Regt, 218th Rcn Bn, 218th AT Bn, 218th Engr Bn, 218th Sig Bn
Auxiliary unit number: 218
Home station: Spandau (Wkr. III)

Formed on mobilization. Personnel mainly of the Landwehr age group. Distinguished itself both in Poland and France, but has been reorganized since those campaigns with younger men. In Denmark from May 1941 till January 1942, when it left for the Eastern front and has since fought in the northern sector.

221st Infantry Division—see 221st Sicherungs Division

223d Infantry Division

Commander:
Composition: 344th Inf Regt, 385th Inf Regt, 425th Inf Regt, 223d Arty Regt, 223d Rcn Co, 223d AT Bn, 223d Engr Bn, 223d Sig Bn
Auxiliary unit number: 223
Home station: Bautzen (Wkr. IV)

Formed on mobilization. Personnel Saxon, mainly Landwehr. No evidence for active operations prior to the Russian campaign. Identified in southwestern France in May 1941, where it remained until transferred to Russia at the end of the year. Has subsequently fought in the northern sector. Personnel now normal.

225th Infantry Division

Commander:
Composition: 333d Inf Regt, 376th Inf Regt, 337th Inf Regt, 225th Arty Regt, 225th Rcn Bn, 225th AT Bn, 225th Engr Bn, 225th Sig Bn
Auxiliary unit number: 225
Home station: Hamburg (Wkr. X)

Formed in the greater Hamburg district on mobilization. Personnel mainly of Landwehr age groups. Arrived on the Northern Russian front from France in January 1942, and has since remained there. Personnel now normal.

227th Infantry Division

Commander:
Composition: 328th Inf Regt, 366th Inf Regt, 412th Inf Regt, 227th Arty Regt, 227th Rcn Bn, 227th AT Bn, 227th Engr Bn, 227th Sig Bn
Auxiliary unit number: 227
Home station: Düsseldorf (Wkr. VI)

Formed on mobilization. Personnel mainly of the Landwehr age group. Took part in active operations in Belgium. In northeastern France in the latter part of 1941. Transferred to the Northern Russian front in April 1942, where it has since remained. Personnel now normal.

228th Infantry Division

Landwehr division formed in Wkr. I on mobilization. Distinguished itself in northern Poland; later in action in Holland and Belgium. Disbanded in the late summer of 1940.

230th Infantry Division

Probably formed in the summer of 1942 as a coastal defense division in northern Norway.

231st Infantry Division

Landwehr division formed in Wehrkreis XIII on mobilization. No evidence of any active operations: Disbanded in the late summer of 1940.

233d Depot Division (Mtz)

Commander:
Home station: Frankfurt/Oder (Wkr. III)

Serves as a depot division for Panzer and motorized troops.

239th Infantry Division

Formed on mobilization. No evidence of any active operations prior to the Russian campaign. In the Protectorate during the winter of 1940–41. Engaged in the southern sector at the beginning of the Russian campaign. Disbanded late in 1941.

246th Infantry Division

Commander:
Composition: 313th Inf Regt, 352d Inf Regt, 404th Inf Regt, 246th Arty Regt, 246th Rcn Co, 246th AT Bn, 246th Engr Bn, 246th Sig Bn
Auxiliary unit number: 246
Home station: Trier (Wkr. XII)

Formed on mobilization. On the Saar front for a time. In southwestern France from August 1941 until January 1942, when it left for Russia. Has since operated in the central sector.

250th Infantry Division (Blue Division)

Commander: (Spanish) Gen. Estaban INFANTES
Composition: 262d Inf Regt, 263d Inf Regt, 269th Inf Regt, 250th Arty Regt, 250th Rcn Bn, AT Bn, Engr Bn, Sig Bn
Auxiliary unit number: 250

Formed in August 1941 from Spanish volunteers, at Grafenwöhr (Wkr. XIII). Originally destined for the Southern Russian front, it was eventually sent to the northern sector, where it has been since late in 1941. Has suffered considerable casualties.

251st Infantry Division

Commander:
Composition: 451st Inf Regt, 459th Inf Regt, 471st Inf Regt, 251st Arty Regt, 251st Rcn Bn, 251st AT Bn, 251st Engr Bn, 251st Sig Bn
Auxiliary unit number: 251
Home station: Hanau (Wkr. IX)

Formed on mobilization from men already serving in Ergänzungs units in Hessen and Thüringen. First identified on the Central Russian front in July 1941, where it has been fairly heavily and continuously engaged.

252d Infantry Division

Commander:
Composition: 452d Inf Regt, 461st Inf Regt, 472d Inf Regt, 252d Arty Regt, 252d Rcn Bn, 252d AT Bn, 252d Engr Bn, 252d Sig Bn
Auxiliary unit number: 252
Home station: Neisse (Wkr. VIII)

Formed on mobilization from Silesians already serving in Ergänzungs units. On the Saar front for several months. Later distinguished itself in the attack on the Maginot Line. Morale high. Continuously and heavily engaged on the Central Russian front since the beginning of the campaign.

253d Infantry Division

Commander:
Composition: 453d Inf Regt, 464th Inf Regt, 473d Inf Regt, 253d Arty Regt, 253d Rcn Bn, 253d AT Bn, 253d Engr Bn, 253d Sig Bn
Auxiliary unit number: 253
Home station: Aachen (Wkr. VI)

Formed on mobilization from men already serving in Westphalian Ergänzungs units. Took part in the French campaign. First identified on the Northern Russian front in July 1941, but subsequently transferred to the central sector.

254th Infantry Division

Commander: Genlt. Walter BEHSCHNITT (58)
Composition: 454th Inf Regt, 474th Inf Regt, 484th Inf Regt, 254th Arty Regt, 254th Rcn Bn, 254th AT Bn, 254th Engr Bn, 254th Sig Bn
Auxiliary unit number: 254
Home station: Dortmund (Wkr. VI)

Formed on mobilization from men already serving in Westphalian Ergänzungs units. Took part in active operations in Holland, Belgium, and Northern France. Identified on the Northern Russian front in July 1941, where it has since remained.

255th Infantry Division

Commander: Genlt. POPPE (50)
Composition: 455th Inf Regt, 465th Inf Regt, 475th Inf Regt, 255th Arty Regt, 255th Rcn Bn, 255th AT Bn, 255th Engr Bn, 255th Sig Bn
Auxiliary unit number: 255
Home station: Löbau (Wkr. IV)

Formed on mobilization from men already serving in Saxon Ergänzungs units. Also contains a proportion of Sudeten Germans. Took an inconspicuous part in the French campaign. Identified on the Central Russian front in August 1941, where it has since remained.

256th Infantry Division

Commander: Genmaj. Paul DANHAUSER (50)
Composition: 456th Inf Regt, 476th Inf Regt, 481st Inf Regt, 256th Arty Regt, 256th Rcn Bn, 256th AT Bn, 256th Engr Bn, 256th Sig Bn
Auxiliary unit number: 256
Home station: Meissen (?) (Wkr. IV/XIII)

Formed in Wkr. IV and XIII on mobilization from men already serving in Ergänzungs units. Personnel Saxon, Bavarian, and Sudeten German. Fought in Holland and Belgium. Continuously engaged in Russia, central sector, since the beginning of the campaign.

257th Infantry Division

Commander: Genmaj. PÜCHLER
Composition: 457th Inf Regt, 466th Inf Regt, 477th Inf Regt, 257th Arty Regt, 257th Rcn Bn, 257th AT Bn, 257th Mtz Engr Bn, 257th Sig Bn
Auxiliary unit number: 257
Home station: Frankfurt/Oder (Wkr. III)

Formed on mobilization from men already serving in Ergänzungs units. Personnel Prussian. On the Saar front for a time. Identified on the Southern Russian front in July 1941, where it has been continuously and heavily engaged.

258th Infantry Division

Commander:
Composition: 458th Inf Regt, 478th Inf Regt, 479th Inf Regt, 258th Arty Regt, 258th Rcn Bn, 258th AT Bn, 258th Engr Bn, 258th Sig Bn
Auxiliary unit number: 258
Home station: Rostock (Wkr. II)

Formed in Wkr. II and III on mobilization from men already serving in Ergänzungs units. Personnel Prussian. On the Saar front for some months and took part in the attack on the Maginot Line. Continuously engaged on the Central Russian front since the beginning of the campaign.

260th Infantry Division

Commander: Genlt. HAHM (49)
Composition: 460th Inf Regt, 470th Inf Regt, 480th Inf Regt, 260th Arty Regt, 260th Rcn Bn, 260th AT Bn, 260th Engr Bn, 260th Sig Bn
Auxiliary unit number: 260
Home station: Karlsruhe (Wkr. V)

Formed on mobilization from men already serving in Ergänzungs units in Baden and Württemberg. No evidence of active operations prior to the Russian campaign. Continuously and heavily engaged on the central front until transferred to France in the summer of 1942. Subsequently returned to Russia, central sector.

262d Infantry Division

Commander: Genmaj. KARST
Composition: 462d Inf Regt, 482d Inf Regt, 486th Inf Regt, 262d Arty Regt, 262d Rcn Bn, 262d AT Bn, 262d Engr Bn, 262d Sig Bn
Auxiliary unit number: 262
Home station: Wien (Wkr. XVII)

Formed on mobilization from men already serving in Ergänzungs units in Austria. On the Saar front for several months. Identified on the Central Russian front in September 1941, where it has since remained.

263d Infantry Division

Commander:
Composition: 463d Inf Regt, 483d Inf Regt, 485th Inf Regt, 263d Arty Regt, 263d Rcn Bn, 263d AT Bn, 263d Engr Bn, 263d Sig Bn
Auxiliary unit number: 263
Home station: Ida-Oberstein (Wkr. XII)

Formed on mobilization from men already serving in Ergänzungs units. Personnel mainly Bavarians from the Palatinate. Fought with distinction during the French campaign. Identified on the Central Russian front in July 1941, where it has since remained.

267th Infantry Division

Commander: Genlt. Friedrich Karl v. WACHTER (54)
Composition: 467th Inf Regt, 487th Inf Regt, 497th Inf Regt, 267th Arty Regt, 267th Rcn Bn, 267th AT Bn, 267th Engr Bn, 267th Sig Bn
Auxiliary unit number: 267
Home station: Hannover (?) (Wkr. XI)

Formed on mobilization from men already serving in Ergänzungs units in the Hannover-Braunschweig area. Identified on the Central Russian front in July 1941, where it has been fairly continuously engaged.

268th Infantry Division

Commander:
Composition: 468th Inf Regt, 488th Inf Regt, 499th Inf Regt, 268th Arty regt, 268th Rcn Bn, AT Bn, 268th Engr Bn, 268th Sig Bn
Auxiliary unit number: 268
Home station: München (Wkr. VII)

Formed in Wehrkreise VII and XVII on mobilization from men already serving in Ergänzungs units. On the Saar front for several months. Continuously engaged since the beginning of the Russian campaign on the central front.

269th Infantry Division

Commander: Genmaj. Kurt BADINSKI (48)
Composition: 469th Inf Regt, 489th Inf Regt, 490th Inf Regt, 269th Arty Regt, 269th Rcn Bn, 269th AT Bn, 269th Engr Bn, 269th Sig Bn
Auxiliary unit number: 269
Home station: Delmenhorst (Wkr. X)

Formed on mobilization from men already serving in Ergänzungs units. Personnel North German. Fought in northern France. Transferred to Denmark in the late summer of 1940, where it remained until May 1941. Engaged in Russia, northern sector, until early in 1943, when it was transferred to Norway.

270th Infantry Division

Probably formed in the summer of 1942 as a coastal defense division in central Norway.

271st Infantry Division

Formed and disbanded in the summer of 1940.

273d Infantry Division

Formed and disbanded in the summer of 1940.

276th Infantry Division

Formed and disbanded in the summer of 1940.

277th Infantry Division

Formed and disbanded in the summer of 1940.

280th Infantry Division

Probably formed in the summer of 1942 as a coastal defense division in southern Norway.

290th Infantry Division

Commander: Genlt. Theodor Frhr. v. WREDE (55)
Composition: 501st Inf Regt, 502d Inf Regt, 503d Inf Regt, 290th Arty Regt, 290th Rcn Bn, 290th AT Bn, 290th Engr Bn, 290th Sig Bn
Auxiliary unit number: 290
Home station: (Wkr. X)

Formed in March/April 1940 from newly trained personnel. First in action in June 1940 during the French campaign. Heavily engaged on the Northern Russian front since July 1941.

291st Infantry Division

Commander: Genlt. GOERITZ (52)
Composition: 504th Inf Regt, 505th Inf Regt, 506th Inf Regt, 291st Arty Regt, 291st Rcn Bn, 291st AT Bn, 291st Engr Bn, 291st Sig Bn
Auxiliary unit number: 291
Home station: Insterburg (Wkr. I)

Formed in March/April 1940 from newly trained Prussian personnel. First in action during the French campaign, but did little fighting. Identified on the Northern Russian front in July 1941, where it remained until transferred to the Velikie Luki area early in 1943.

292d Infantry Division

Commander: Genmaj. SEEGER (52)
Composition: 507th Inf Regt, 508th Inf Regt, 509th Inf Regt, 292d Arty Regt, 292d Rcn Bn, 292d AT Bn, 292d Engr Bn, 292d Sig Bn
Auxiliary unit number: 292
Home station: (Wkr. II)

Formed in March/April 1940 from newly trained Prussian personnel. Experience in the French campaign similar to that of the 291st Division. Identified on the Central Russian front in August 1941, where it has since remained.

293d Infantry Division

Commander: Genlt. Werner FORST (48)
Composition: 510th Inf Regt, 511th Inf Regt, 512th Inf Regt, 293d Arty Regt, 293d Rcn Bn, 293d AT Bn, 293d Engr Bn, 293d Sig Bn
Auxiliary unit number: 293
Home station: (Wkr. III)

Formed in March/April 1940 from newly trained Prussian personnel. Experience in the French campaign similar to that of the 291st Division. Identified on the Central Russian front in July 1941, where it has since remained.

294th Infantry Division

Commander: Genlt. Johannes BLOCK
Composition: 513th Inf Regt, 514th Inf Regt, 515th Inf Regt, 294th Arty Regt, 294th Rcn Bn, 294th AT Bn, 294th Engr Bn, 294th Sig Bn
Auxiliary unit number: 294
Home station: (Wkr. IV)

Formed in March/April 1940 from newly trained Saxon personnel. First identified in action during the Balkan campaign and has fought on the Russian front, southern sector, since September 1941. Suffered heavy losses on withdrawal from Stalingrad.

295th Infantry Division

Commander: Genmaj. Dr. Otto KORFES (Prisoner of war)
Composition: 516th Inf Regt, 517th Inf Regt, 518th Inf Regt, 295th Arty Regt, 295th Rcn Bn, 295th AT Bn, 295th Engr Bn, 295th Sig Bn
Auxiliary unit number: 295
Home station: (Wkr. XI)

Formed in March/April 1940 from newly trained personnel. Not identified in action prior to the Russian campaign, where it was continuously engaged on the southern front from July 1941. Virtually destroyed at Stalingrad.

296th Infantry Division

Commander: Genlt. Friedrich KRISCHER (52)
Composition: 519th Inf Regt, 520th Inf Regt, 521st Inf Regt, 296th Arty Regt, 296th Rcn Bn, 296th AT Bn, 296th Engr Bn, 296th Sig Bn
Auxiliary unit number: 296
Home station: Nürnberg(?) (Wkr. XIII)

Formed in March/April 1940 from newly trained men from northern Bayern and western Sudetenland. Not identified in action prior to the Russian campaign, where it has operated in the central sector.

297th Infantry Division

Commander: Genmaj. Moritz v. DREBBER (Prisoner of war)
Composition: 522d Inf Regt, 523d Inf Regt, 524th Inf Regt, 297th Arty Regt, 297th Rcn Bn, 297th AT Bn, 297th Engr Bn, 297th Sig Bn
Auxiliary unit number: 297
Home station: Wein (Wkr. XVII)

Formed in March/April 1940 from newly trained Austrian personnel. Not identified in action prior to the Russian campaign where it operated in the southern sector from July 1941. Virtually destroyed at Stalingrad.

298th Infantry Division

Commander: Genlt. SZELINSKI (52)
Composition: 525th Inf Regt, 526th Inf Regt, 527th Inf Regt, 298th Arty Regt, 298th Rcn Bn, 298th AT Bn, 298th Engr Bn, 298th Sig Bn
Auxiliary unit number: 298
Home station: (Wkr. VIII)

Formed in March/April 1940 from newly trained Silesian personnel. Not identified in action prior to the Russian campaign, where it has operated with the Southern Group since July 1941.

299th Infantry Division

Commander:
Composition: 528th Inf Regt, 529th Inf Regt, 530th Inf Regt, 299th Arty Regt, 299th Rcn Bn, 299th AT Bn, 299th Engr Bn, 299th Sig Bn
Auxiliary unit number: 299
Home station: Weimar (Wkr. IX)

Formed in March/April 1940 from newly trained men from Hessen and Thüringen. First in action during the French campaign in June 1940. Continuously engaged in Russia, on the southern front.

302d Infantry Division

Commander: Genlt. Conrad HAASE (55)
Composition: 570th Inf Regt, 571st Inf Regt, 572d Inf Regt, 302d Arty Regt, 302d Rcn Co, 302d AT Bn, 302d Engr Bn, 302d Sig Co
Auxiliary unit number: 302
Home station: Schwerin (?) (Wkr. II)

Formed late in 1940, but not reliably identified until early in 1942 in northern France, where it remained until it was transferred to the Russian front, southern sector, early in 1943.

304th Infantry Division

Commander: Genlt. Heinrich KRAMPF (55)
Composition: 573d Inf Regt, 574th Inf Regt, 575th Inf Regt, 304th Arty Regt, 304th Rcn Co, 304th AT Bn, 304th Engr Bn, 304th Sig Co
Auxiliary unit number: 304
Home station: (Wkr. IV)

Formed late in 1940. From April 1942 in Belgium. Transferred to the southern sector in Russia early in 1943.

305th Infantry Division

Commander:
Composition: 576th Inf Regt, 577th Inf Regt, 578th Inf Regt, 305th Arty Regt, 305th Rcn Co, 305th AT Bn, 305th Engr Bn, 305th Sig Co
Auxiliary unit number: 305
Home station: Konstanz (?) (Wkr. V)

Formed late in 1940. In western France from the end of 1941 until the beginning of May 1942, when it left for the Russian front, southern sector. Virtually destroyed at Stalingrad.

306th Infantry Division

Commander:
Composition: 579th Inf Regt, 580th Inf Regt, 581st Inf Regt, 306th Arty Regt, 306th Rcn Co, 306th AT Bn, 306th Engr Bn, 306th Sig Co
Auxiliary unit number: 306
Home station: (Wkr. VI)

Formed late in 1940. In Belgium from late 1941. Transferred to the Russian front southern sector, in December 1942.

311th Administrative Division

Commander: Genlt. Albrecht BRAND (55)
Composition:
Home station: (Wkr. I)

Classification uncertain. Stationed in the Warsaw area, Poland.

319th Infantry Division

Commander: Genlt. Erich MÜLLER (53)
Composition: 582d Inf Regt, 583d Inf Regt, 584th Inf Regt, 319th Arty Regt, 319th Rcn Co, 319th AT Bn, 319th Engr Bn, 319th Sig Co
Auxiliary unit number: 319
Home station: (Wkr. IX)

Formed late in 1940. In Brittany from August 1941. Transferred to Russia early in 1943.

320th Infantry Division

Commander: Genlt. Karl MADERHOLZ (58)
Composition: 585th Inf Regt, 586th Inf Regt, 587th Inf Regt, 320th Arty Regt, 320th Rcn Co, 320th AT Bn, 320th Engr Bn, 320th Sig Co
Auxiliary unit number: 320
Home station: (Wkr. X)

Formed late in 1940. Moved early in January 1942 from Belgium to Brittany. Transferred early in April to northeastern France and to the southern sector in Russia early in 1943.

321st Infantry Division

Commander:
Composition: 588th Inf Regt, 589th Inf Regt, 590th Inf Regt, 321st Arty Regt, 321st Rcn Co, 321st AT Bn, 321st Engr Bn, 321 Sig Co
Auxiliary unit number: 321
Home station: (Wkr. XI)

Formed late in 1940. In northeastern France from the end of 1941 until it was transferred to the central sector in Russia early in 1943.

323d Infantry Division

Commander: Genmaj. Johann BERGEN (52)
Composition: 591st Inf Regt, 592d Inf Regt, 593d Inf Regt, 323d Arty Regt, 323d Rcn Co, 323d AT Bn, 323d Engr Bn, 323d Sig Co

Auxiliary unit number: 323
Home station: (Wkr. XIII)

Formed late in 1940. In northwestern France from the end of 1941 until early in May 1942, when it left for Russia, southern sector.

326th Infantry Division

Commander:
Composition: Inf Regt, Inf Regt, Inf Regt, Arty Regt, Rcn Co. AT Bn, Engr Bn, Sig Co
Auxiliary unit number:
Home station:

Probably formed late in 1942. In former unoccupied France.

327th Infantry Division

Commander:
Composition: 595th Inf Regt, 596th Inf Regt, 597th Inf Regt, 327th Arty Regt, 327th Rcn Co, 327th AT Bn, 327th Engr Bn, 327th Sig Co
Auxiliary unit number: 327
Home station: (Wkr. XVII)

Formed late in 1940. In eastern France in the latter half of 1941 and in southwestern France from January 1942. Took part in the occupation of former unoccupied France and transferred to Russia, southern sector, early in 1943.

328th Infantry Division

Commander: Genmaj. Joachim v. TRESCKOW (49)
Composition: 547th Inf Regt, 548th Regt, 549th Inf Regt, 328th Arty Regt, 328th Rcn Co, 328th AT Bn, 328th Engr Bn, 328th Sig Co
Auxiliary unit number: 328
Home station: (Wkr. IX)

Formed late in 1941. First identified in March 1942 in the central sector in Russia. Transferred to former unoccupied France in November 1942 and back to Russia, southern sector, early in 1943.

329th Infantry Division

Commander: Genmaj. Dipl. Ing. Helmut CASTORF (52)
Composition: 551st (?) Inf Regt, 552d (?) Inf Regt, 553d Inf Regt, 329th Arty Regt, 329th Rcn Co, 329th AT Bn, 329th Engr Bn, 329th Sig Co
Auxiliary unit number: 329
Home station: (Wkr. VI)

Formed late in 1941. First identified in May 1942, in the northern sector of the Russian front, where it has since remained.

330th Infantry Division

Commander: Genlt. Edwin Graf v. ROTHKIRCH u. TRACH (55)
Composition: 554th Inf Regt, 555th Inf Regt, 556th Inf Regt, 330th Arty Regt, 330th Rcn Bn, 330th AT 330th Engr Bn, 330th Sig Co
Auxiliary unit number: 330
Home station: (Wkr. V)

Formed late in 1941. First identified in February 1942 and has subsequently been in action on the Central Russian front.

331st Infantry Division

Commander: Genlt. Dr. BEYER (53)
Composition: 557th Inf Regt, 558th Inf Regt, 559th Inf Regt, 331st Arty Regt, 331st Rcn Co, 331st AT Bn, 331st Engr Bn, 331st Sig Co
Auxiliary unit number: 331
Home station: (Wkr. XVII)

Formed late in 1941. First identified in February 1942 and has operated on the Central Russian front.

332d Infantry Division

Commander:
Composition: 676th Inf Regt, 677th Inf Regt, 678th Inf Regt, 332d Arty Regt, 332d Rcn Co, 332d AT Bn, 332d Engr Bn, 332d Sig Co
Auxiliary unit number:
Home station: (Wkr. VIII)

Formed in January 1941. In Normandy since August 1941.

333d Infantry Division

Commander:
Composition: 679th Inf Regt, 680th Inf Regt, 681st Inf Regt, 333d Arty Regt, 333d Rcn Co, 333d AT Bn, 333d Engr Bn, 333d Sig Co
Auxiliary unit number: 333
Home station: Berlin (Wkr. III)

Formed in January 1941. Moved in May 1941 from Wkr. III to southwestern France. Transferred to Brittany in March 1942 and to Russia, southern sector, early in 1943.

334th Infantry Division

Commander: Genmaj. Friedrich WEBER (44)
Composition: 754th Inf Regt, 755th Inf Regt, 756th Mtn R Regt, 334th Arty Regt, 334th Mobile Bn (combined Rcn and AT), 334th Engr Bn, 334th Sig Co
Auxiliary unit number: 334
Home station: (Wkr. XIII)

Formed in the autumn of 1942. Sent to Tunisia in December 1942.

335th Infantry Division

Commander: Genmaj. CASPER
Compostion: 682d Inf Regt, 683d Inf Regt, 684th Inf Regt, 335th Arty Regt, 335th Rcn Co, 335th AT Bn, 335th Engr Bn, 335th Sig Co
Auxiliary unit number: 335
Home station: (Wkr. V)

Formed in January 1941. First identified in northern France in October 1941. Moved to Brittany in February 1942. Took part in the occupation of former unoccupied France. Transferred to Russia, southern sector, early in 1943.

336th Infantry Division

Commander: Genlt. Walter LUCHT (61)
Composition: 685th Inf Regt, 686th Inf Regt, 687th Inf Regt, 336th Arty Regt, 336th Rcn Co, 336th AT Bn, 336th Engr Bn, 336th Sig Co

Auxiliary unit number: 336
Home station: Rheine (Wkr. VI)

Formed in January 1941 with cadres from the 256th Inf Div and moved to Normandy. Transferred at the end of March 1942 to Brittany. Left for the Eastern front at the end of May 1942, where it has operated in the southern sector.

337th Infantry Division

Commander:
Composition: 688th Inf Regt, 689th Inf Regt, 690th Inf Regt, 337th Arty Regt, 337th Rcn Co, 337th AT Bn, 337th Engr Bn, 337th Sig Co
Auxiliary unit number: 337
Home station: (Wkr. VII)

Formed in January 1941. In central France from August 1941 until late in 1942, when it was transferred to the central sector in Russia.

339th Infantry Division

Commander:
Composition: 691st Inf Regt, 692d Inf Regt, 693d Inf Regt, 339th Arty Regt, 339th Rcn Co, 339th AT Bn, 339th Engr Bn, 339th Sig Co
Auxiliary unit number: 339
Home station: Jena (Wkr. IX)

Formed in January 1941. In central France until it left for the Russian front at the end of 1941. Has subsequently been in action in the central sector.

340th Infantry Division

Commander: Genlt. BUTZE (52)
Composition: 694th Inf Regt, 695th Inf Regt, 696th Inf Regt, 340th Arty Regt, 340th Rcn Co, 340th AT Bn, 340th Engr Bn, 340th Sig Co
Auxiliary unit number: 340
Home station: Königsberg (Wkr. I)

Formed in January 1941, but first identified in April 1942 in northeastern France. Left in May 1942 for the Eastern front, where it has operated in the southern sector.

342d Infantry Division

Commander: Genlt. Albrecht BAIER (49)
Composition: 697th Inf Regt, 698th Inf Regt, 699th Inf Regt, 342d Arty Regt, 342d Rcn Co, 342d AT Bn, 342d Engr Bn, 342d Sig Co
Auxiliary unit number: 342
Home station: Kaiserslautern (Wkr. XII)

Formed in January 1940. Engaged in mopping up operations in Yugoslavia from late in 1941 until February 1942, when it was transferred to the central sector of the Russian front.

343d Infantry Division

Commander:
Composition: Inf Regt,   Inf Regt,   Inf Regt,   Arty Regt,
               Rcn Co,   AT Bn,   343 Engr Bn, Sig Co
Auxiliary unit number:
Home station: (Wkr. XIII)

Formed late in 1942.

344th Infantry Division

Commander:
Composition: Inf Regt,   Inf Regt,   Inf Regt,   Arty Regt,
               Rcn Co,   AT Bn,   Engr Bn,   Sig Co
Auxiliary unit number:
Home station:

Probably formed late in 1942. Identified in France, in the Bordeaux area.

347th Infantry Division

Commander:
Composition: Inf Regt,   Inf Regt,   Inf Regt,   Arty Regt,
               Rcn Co,   AT Bn, Engr Bn,   Sig Co
Auxiliary unit number:
Home station:

Probably formed late in 1942. In southern France.

358th Infantry Division

Landwehr division formed late in 1939 and disbanded after the French campaign.

365th Area Command

Landwehr division formed late in 1939. Now an Oberfeldkommandantur at Lemberg (Lwow), Poland.

369th Infantry Division

Commander: Genmaj. NEIDHOLDT
Composition: 369th Inf Regt, 370th Inf Regt, Inf Regt, Arty Regt, Rcn Co, AT Bn, Engr Bn, Sig Co

Formed in the latter part of 1942 by the expansion of the 369th Inf Regt, consisting of Croatians, which formerly operated under the 100th Light Division. Now in Croatia.

370th Infantry Division

Commander:
Composition: 666th Inf Regt, 667th Inf Regt, 668th Inf Regt, 370th Arty Regt, Rcn Co, 370th AT Bn, 370th Engr Bn, 370th Sig Co
Auxiliary unit number: 370
Home station: (Wkr. IV)

Completed formation in France in May 1942, and then transferred to the Russian front, where it has operated in the southern sector.

371st Infantry Division

Commander:
Composition: 669th Inf Regt, 670th Inf Regt, 671st Inf Regt, 371st Arty Regt, 371st Rcn Co, 371st AT Bn, 371st Engr Bn, 371st Sig Co
Auxiliary unit number: 371
Home station: (Wkr. VI)

Completed formation in France in May 1942, and then transferred to the Russian front, where it operated in the southern sector. Virtually destroyed at Stalingrad.

ORDER OF BATTLE OF THE GERMAN ARMY

372d Area Command

Landwehr division formed late in 1939. Now an Oberfeldkommandantur at Kielce, Poland.

376th Infantry Division

Commander: Genlt. Alexander Edler v. DANIELS (52) (Prisoner of war)
Composition: 672d Inf Regt, 673d Inf Regt, Inf Regt, 376th Arty Regt, 376th Rcn Co, 376th AT Bn, 376th Engr Bn, 376th Sig Co
Auxiliary unit number: 376
Home station: (Wkr. VII)

Completed formation in France in May 1942; then transferred to the Russian front, where it operated in the southern sector. Virtually destroyed at Stalingrad.

377th Infantry Division

Commander: Genmaj. Ehrich BAESSLER (51)
Composition: 768th Inf Regt, 769th Inf Regt, 770th Inf Regt, 377th Arty Regt, 377th Rcn Co, 377th AT Bn, 377th Engr Bn, 377th Sig Co
Auxiliary unit number: 377
Home station: (Wkr. IX)

Completed formation in France in May 1942; then transferred to the Russian front, where it has operated in the southern sector.

379th Area Command

Formed after mobilization. Now an Oberfeldkommandantur at Lublin, Poland.

383d Infantry Division

Commander: Genmaj. Eberhard v. FABRICE (51)
Composition: 531st Inf Regt, 532d Inf Regt, 533d Inf Regt, 383d Arty Regt, 383d Rcn Co, 383d AT Bn, 383d Engr Bn, 383d Sig Co
Auxiliary unit number: 383
Home station: (Wkr. III)

Formed in the winter of 1941-42. In action on the Southern Russian front since June 1942.

384th Infantry Division

Commander:
Composition: 534th Inf Regt, 535th Inf Regt, 536th Inf Regt, 384th Arty Regt, 384th Rcn Co, 384th AT Bn, 384th Engr Bn, 384th Sig Co
Auxiliary unit number: 384
Home station: (Wkr. IV)

Formed in the winter of 1941-42. In action on the Southern Russian front from May 1942. Virtually destroyed at Stalingrad.

385th Infantry Division

Commander:
Composition: 537th Inf Regt, 538th Inf Regt, 539th Inf Regt, 385th Arty Regt, 385th Rcn Co, 385th AT Bn, 385th Engr Bn, 385th Sig Co
Auxiliary unit number: 385
Home station: (Wkr. VI)

Formed in the winter of 1941-42. In action on the Central Russian front from May 1942; later transferred to the southern sector.

386th Infantry Division

Formed late in 1939 in Wehrkreis VI. Disbanded after the French campaign.

387th Infantry Division

Commander:
Composition: 541st Inf Regt, 542d Inf Regt, 543d Inf Regt, 387th Arty Regt, 387th Rcn Co, 387th AT Bn, 387th Engr Bn, 387th Sig Co
Auxiliary unit number: 387
Home station: (Wkr. VII)

Formed in the winter of 1941-42. On the Southern Russian front from May 1942.

389th Infantry Division

Commander: Genmaj. Martin LATTMAN (Prisoner of war)
Composition: 544th Inf Regt, 545th Inf Regt, 546th Inf Regt, 389th Arty Regt, 389th Rcn Co, 389th AT Bn, 389th Engr Bn, 389th Sig Co
Auxiliary unit number: 389
Home station: (Wkr. X?)

Formed in the winter of 1941–42. In action on the Southern Russian front from May 1942. V i r t u a l l y destroyed at Stalingrad.

393d Area Command

Formed late in 1939. Now an Oberfeldkommandantur at Warsaw, Poland.

395th Infantry Division

Formed after mobilization and disbanded in the autumn of 1940.

399th Infantry Division

Formed after mobilization and disbanded in the autumn of 1940.

401st Division z. b. V.

Commander: Genlt. v. DIRINGSHOFEN
Composition: Varying attached units
Home station: Königsberg (Wkr. I)

402d Division z. b. V.

Commander:
Composition: Varying attached units.
Home station: Stettin (Wkr. II)

403d Division z. b. V.—see 403d Sicherungs Div.

404th Division z. b. V.

Commander:
Composition: Varying attached units.
Home station: Dresden (Wkr. IV)

405th Division z. b. V.

Commander:
Composition: Varying attached units.
Home station: Stuttgart (Wkr. V)

406th Division z. b. V.

Commander: Genmaj SCHERBENING (52)
Composition: Varying attached units.
Home station: Münster (Wkr. VI)

407th Division z. b. V.

Commander:
Composition: Varying attached units.
Home station: München (Wkr. VII)

408th Division z. b. V.

Commander:
Composition: Varying attached units.
Home station: Breslau (Wkr. VIII)

409th Division z. b. V.

Commander: Genmaj. Hans EHRENBERG (53)
Composition: Varying attached units.
Home station: Kassel (Wkr. IX)

410th Division z. b. V.

Commander: Genlt. Adolf POETTER (59)
Composition: Varying attached units.
Home station: Hamburg (Wkr. X)

411th Division z. b. V.

Commander:
Composition: Varying attached units.
Home station: Hannover (Wkr. XI)

412th Division z. b. V.

Commander: Genlt. Kurt FISCHER (66)
Composition: Varying attached units.
Home station: Wiesbaden (Wkr. XII)

413th Division z. b. V.

Commander:
Composition: Varying attached units.
Home station: Nürnberg (Wkr. XIII)

416th Infantry Division

Commander: Genlt. BRABÄNDER (52)
Composition: 930th Inf Regt., 931st Inf Regt. ?
Auxiliary unit number:
Home station:

Previously 416th Div. z. b. V. In Denmark, stationed in the Silkeborg area.

417th Division z. b. V.

Commander:
Composition: Varying attached units.
Home station: Wien (Wkr. XVII)

421st Division z. b. V.

Commander:
Composition: Varying attached units.
Home station: (Wkr. I)

428th Division z. b. V.

Commander:
Composition: Varying attached units.
Home station: Danzig (Wkr. XX)

429th Division z. b. V.

Commander: Genlt. SCHARTOW (51)
Composition: Varying attached units.
Home station: Posen (Wkr. XXI)

430th Division z. b. V.

Commander:
Composition: Varying attached units.
Home station: Gnesen (Wkr. XXI)

431st Division z. b. V.

Commander: Genlt. Otto v. SCHWERIN (60)
Composition: Varying attached units.
Home station: Litzmannstadt (*Lodz*) (Wkr. XXI)

432d Division z. b. V.

Commander:
Composition: Varying attached units
Home station: Neisse (Wkr. VIII)

461st Division z. b. V.

Commander: Genlt. Hans Erich NOLTE (61)
Composition: Varying attached units
Home station:

Formerly known as Division z. b. V. Bialystok.

467th Division z. b. V.

Commander:
Composition: Varying attached units
Home station: München (Wkr VII)

526th Grenzwach Division

Commander: Genlt. Hans v. SOMMERFELD (57)
Composition: Frontier guard units
Home station: Aachen (Wkr. VI)

Now in Belgium in the Namur area.

537th Grenzwach Division

Commander:
Composition: Frontier guard units
Home station: Innsbruck (Wkr. XVIII)

538th Grenzwach Division

Commander:
Composition: Frontier guard units
Home station: Klagenfurt (Wkr. XVIII)

539th Grenzwach Division

Commander: Genlt. Dr. Richard SPEICH (59)
Composition: Frontier guard units
Home station: Prague (Prot.)

540th Grenzwach Division

Commander: Genlt. Karl TARBUK v. SENSENHORST
Composition: Frontier guard units
Home station: Brünn (Prot.)

554th Infantry Division

Formed in Wkr. IV early in 1940 and disbanded after the French campaign.

555th Infantry Division

Formed in Wkr. VI in 1940 and disbanded after the French campaign.

556th Infantry Division

Formed in Wkr. XII in 1940 and disbanded after the French campaign.

557th Infantry Division

Formed in Wkr. V in 1940 and disbanded after the French campaign.

702d Infantry Division

Commander:
Composition: 722d Inf Regt, 742d Inf Regt, 662d Arty Bn
702d Rcn Co, 702 Engr Co, 702 Sig Co
Auxiliary unit number: 702
Home station: (Wkr. II)

Formed in April and sent to southern Norway in May 1941. Moved at the end of June 1941 to northern Norway. The 742d Inf Regt has been under command of the 181st Inf Div.

704th Infantry Division

Commander: Genlt. Hans JUPPE (51)
Composition: 724th Inf Regt, 734th Inf Regt, 654th Arty Bn, 704th Rcn Co,
704th Engr Co, 704th Sig Co
Auxiliary unit number: 704
Home station: (Wkr. IV)

Formed in April 1941. Known to have been in Yugoslavia between September 1941 and April 1942. Now in Serbia, Belgrade area.

707th Infantry Division

Commander: Genmaj. SCHEFOLD (55)
Composition: 727th Inf Regt, 747th Inf Regt, 657th Arty Bn, 707th Rcn Co,
707th Engr Co, 707th Sig Co
Auxiliary unit number: 707
Home station: (Wkr. VII)

Formed in April 1941. Identified on the Central Russian front in October 1941, where it was employed on rear area duties. Transferred to the southern sector in the autumn of 1942.

708th Infantry Division

Commander: Genlt. Hermann WILCK (58)
Composition: 728th Inf Regt, 748th Inf Regt,   Arty Bn, 708th Rcn Co,
708th Engr Co, 708th Sig Co
Auxiliary unit number: 708
Home station: (Wkr. VIII)

Formed in April 1941. Probably in central France in November 1941; from December 1941 in southwestern France.

709th Infantry Division

Commander:
Composition: 729th Inf Regt, 739th Inf Regt, Arty Bn, 709th Rcn Co, 709th Engr Co, 709th Sig Co
Auxiliary unit number: 709
Home station: (Wkr. IX)

Formed in April 1941. In Brittany since November 1941.

710th Infantry Division

Commander: Genlt. PETSCH (55)
Composition: 730th Inf Regt, 740th Inf Regt, Arty Bn, 710th Rcn Co, 710th Engr Co, 710th Sig Co
Auxiliary unit number: 710
Home station: (Wkr. X)

Formed in April 1941. In southern Norway since June 1941.

711th Infantry Division

Commander: Genmaj. (?) HOFFMANN
Composition: 731st Inf Regt, 744th (?) Inf Regt, Arty Bn, 711th Rcn Co, 711th Engr Co, 711th Sig Co
Auxiliary unit number: 711
Home station: (Wkr. XI)

Formed in April 1941. From August to December 1941 in northeastern France. From January 1942 until the middle of May 1942 in Normandy. Now in France in the Rouen area.

712th Infantry Division

Commander:
Composition: 732d Inf Regt, 745th Inf Regt, 652d Arty Bn, 712th Rcn Co, 712th Engr Co, 712th Sig Co
Auxiliary unit number: 712
Home station: (Wkr. XII)

Formed in April 1941. Now in Belgium in the Zeebrugge area.

713th Infantry Division

Commander:
Composition: 733d Inf Regt, 746th Inf Regt, Arty Bn, 713th Rcn Co, 713th Engr Co, 713th Sig Co
Auxiliary unit number: 713
Home station: (Wkr. XIII)

Formed in April 1941. Part in Crete and part in southern Greece since the autumn of 1941.

714th Infantry Division

Commander: Genmaj. Josef REICHERT (51)
Composition: 721st Inf Regt, 741st Inf Regt, 661st Arty Bn, 714th Rcn Co, 714th Engr Co, 714th Sig Co
Auxiliary unit number: 714
Home station: (Wkr. I)

Formed in April 1941. Engaged in mopping-up duties in Yugoslavia since November 1941.

715th Infantry Division

Commander: Genmaj. DEUTSCH
Composition: 725th Inf Regt, 735th Inf Regt, Arty Bn, 715th Rcn Co, 715th Engr Co, 715th Sig Co
Auxiliary unit number: 715
Home station: (Wkr. V)

Formed in April 1941. Since August 1941, in southwestern France.

716th Infantry Division

Commander:
Composition: 726th Inf Regt, 736th Inf Regt, Arty Bn, 716th Rcn Co, 716th Engr Co, 716th Sig Co
Auxiliary unit number: 716
Home station: (Wkr. VI (?))

Formed in April 1941 and identified in February 1942 in Brittany. Since the beginning of April 1942 in northeastern France.

717th Infantry Division

Commander: Genlt. Benignus DIPPOLD (54)
Composition: 737th Inf Regt, 749th Inf Regt, 670th Arty Bn, 717th Rcn Co, 717th Engr Co, 717th Sig Co
Auxiliary unit number: 717
Home station: (Wkr. XVII)

Formed in April 1941. Engaged in mopping-up operations in Yugoslavia since September 1941.

718th Infantry Division

Commander: Genlt. Johann FORTNER (59)
Composition: 738th Inf Regt, 750th Inf Regt, 668th Arty Bn, 718th Rcn Co, 718th Engr Co, 718th Sig Co
Auxiliary unit number: 718
Home station: (Wkr. XVIII)

Formed in April 1941. Stationed in Yugoslavia since the summer of 1941.

719th Infantry Division

Commander:
Composition: 723d Infa Regt, 743d Inf Regt, Arty Bn, 719th Rcn Co, 719th Engr Co, 719th Sig Co
Auxiliary unit number: 719
Home station: (Wkr. III)

Formed in April 1941. Possibly now in Holland.

Division von Broich

Commander: Obst. Hasso Eccard v. MANTEUFFEL
Composition:
Auxiliary unit number:
Home station:

A composite division, probably containing the Barenthin Regiment (ground troops of the Air Force) plus miscellaneous units. Believed formed in Tunisia in November-December 1942.

SS Police Division—see paragraph 48

42. Cavalry divisions.

1st Cavalry Division—see 24th Panzer Division
SS Cavalry Division—see paragraph 48

43. Motorized divisions.

2d Motorized Division—see 12th Pz Div
3d Motorized Division

Commander:
Composition: 8th Mtz Inf Regt, 29th Mtz Inf Regt, 3d Mtz Arty Regt,

53d Pz Rcn Bn, 53d Mtrcl Bn, 3d AT Bn, 3d Mtz Engr Bn, 3d Mtz Sig Bn
Auxiliary unit number: 3
Home station: Frankfurt/Oder (Wkr. III)

Originally 3d Inf Div, an active division mainly recruited in Prussia. As such it took part in the Polish and French campaigns without winning any special distinction. Motorized in the autumn of 1940. Fought in Russia from the beginning, at first in the center and subsequently in the southern sector, where it was virtually destroyed at Stalingrad.

10th Motorized Division

Commander:
Composition: 20th Mtz Inf Regt, 41st Mtz Inf Regt, 10th Mtz Arty Regt, 10th Pz Rcn Bn, 40th Mtrcl Bn, 10th AT Bn, 10th Mtz Engr Bn, 10th Mtz Sig Bn
Auxiliary unit number: 10
Home station: Regensburg (Wkr. XIII)

Originally 10th Inf Div, an active division with personnel from northern Bavaria and western Sudetenland. As such, it was actively engaged in Poland, less so in France. Motorized in the autumn of 1940. Fought in the Balkan campaign. Has operated in Russia in the central sector from the beginning.

13th Motorized Division—see 13th Pz Div.
14th Motorized Division

Commander: Genlt. Friedrich FÜRST (52)
Composition: 11th Mtz Inf Regt, 53d Mtz Inf Regt, 14th Mtz Arty Regt, 14th Pz Rcn Bn, 54th Mtrcl Bn, 14th AT Bn, 14th Mtz Engr Bn, 14th Mtz Sig Bn
Auxiliary unit number: 14
Home Station: Leipzig (Wkr. IV)

As the 14th Inf Div, a Saxon division belonging to the peacetime army, it took part in the campaigns in Poland and France, without winning special distinction. Motorized in the autumn of 1940. Identified early in the Russian campaign in the battle for Vitebsk. Since then, continuously in action in the central sector.

16th Motorized Division

Commander:
Composition: 116th Pz Bn, 60th Mtz Inf Regt, 156th Mtz Inf Regt, 146th Arty Regt, 341st Pz Rcn Bn, 59th Mtrcl Bn, AT Bn, 146th Mtz Engr Bn, 228th Mtz Sig Bn
Auxiliary unit number: 66
Home station: Rheine (Wkr. VI)

Formed in the late summer of 1940 from elements of the 16th Inf Div. An active division with personnel mainly Westphalian but partly Prussian. On the Saar front for a period and later took part in the attack on Sedan in support of Panzer units. Engaged in the Balkan campaign and later in the Ukraine. Has since remained in the southern sector.

18th Motorized Division

Commander: Genlt. Werner v. ERDMANNSDORF (52)
Composition: 30th Mtz Inf Regt, 51st Mtz Inf Regt, 18th Mtz Arty Regt, 18th Pz Rcn Bn, 38th Mtrcl Bn, 18th AT Bn, 18th Mtz Engr Bn, 18th Mtz Sig Bn
Auxiliary unit number: 18
Home station: Liegnitz (Wkr. VIII)

Formerly 18th Inf Div, an active division with Silesian personnel. As such, fought in Poland and in northern France, winning distinction and sustaining considerable casualties. Motorized in the autumn of 1940. Fought in Russia from the beginning of the campaign, first in the central and subsequently in the northern sector.

20th Motorized Division

Commander: Genlt. Erich JASCHKE (53)
Composition: 76th Mtz Inf Regt, 90th Mtz Inf Regt, 20th Mtz Arty Regt, 20th Pz Rcn Bn, 30th Mtrcl Bn, 20th AT Bn, 20th Mtz Engr Bn, 20th Mtz Sig Bn
Auxiliary unit number: 20
Home station: Hamburg (Wkr. X)

Active division. Recruited mainly in Hamburg. Fought hard and well in Poland. In France it covered great distances but saw less action. Morale very high. First identified in Russia in the Minsk area and later in the northern sector. Recently engaged at Velikie Luki (central sector).

25th Motorized Division

Commander:
Composition: 35th Mtz Inf Regt, 119th Mtz Inf Regt, 25th Mtz Arty Regt, 25th Pz Rcn Bn, 25th Mtrcl Bn, 25th AT Bn, 25th Mtz Engr Bn, 25th Mtz Sig Bn
Auxiliary unit number: 25
Home station: Ludwigsburg (Wkr. V)

Originally 25th Infantry Division, an active division recruited in Württemberg, which took little part in active operations. Motorized in the autumn of 1940. Has fought in the central sector since the beginning of the Russian campaign.

29th Motorized Division

Commander: Genmaj. Hans Georg v. LEYSER (Prisoner of War)
Composition: 129th Pz Bn, 15th Mtz Inf. Regt, 71st Mtz Inf Regt, 29th Mtz Arty Rgt, 29th Pz Rcn Bn, 29th Mtrcl Bn, 29th AT Bn, 29th Mtz Engr Bn, 29th Mtz Sig Bn
Auxiliary unit number: 29
Home station: Erfurt (Wkr. IX)

Active division. Personnel largely Thuringian. Moved great distances and fought hard in Poland and France. Identified in the central sector in Russia in July 1941. Transferred to the southern sector in the summer of 1942 and virtually destroyed at Stalingrad.

36th Motorized Division

Commander: Genlt. Hans GOLLNICK (51)
Composition: 87th Mtz Inf Regt, 118th Mtz Inf Regt, 36th Mtz Arty Regt, 36th Pz Rcn Bn, 36th Mtrcl Bn, 36th AT Bn, 36th Mtz Engr Bn, 36th Mtz Sig Bn
Auxiliary unit number: 36
Home station: Wiesbaden (Wkr. XII)

As 36th Infantry Division (peacetime army: personnel mainly Bavarian from the Palatinate) it earned some distinction in

France, but without a great deal of fighting. Motorized in the autumn of 1940. Entered Russia via the Baltic States and has since operated in the central sector.

60th Motorized Division

Commander:
Composition: 160th Pz Bn, 92d Mtz Inf Regt, 120th Mtz Inf Regt, 160th Mtz Arty Regt, 160th Pz Rcn Bn, 160th Mtrcl Bn, 160th AT Bn, 160th Mtz Engr Bn, 160th Mtz Sig Bn
Auxiliary unit number: 160
Home station: Danzig (Wkr. XX)

Originally the 60th Infantry Division formed at Danzig in August 1939 and embodying the Danzig Heimwehr. As such took part in the attack on the Hela peninsula in September 1939 and in the French campaign. In the late summer of 1940 it provided a nucleus for the formation of the 60th Motorized Division, which fought in Yugoslavia in April 1941. Subsequently in the southern sector in Russia. Virtually destroyed at Stalingrad.

Grossdeutschland Motorized Division

Commander: Genlt. Walter HOERNLEIN (49)
Composition: Pz Bn, "Grenadier Regt Grossdeutschland", "Füsilier Regt Grossdeutschland", Mtz Arty Regt, Pz Rcn Bn, Mtrcl Bn, AT Bn, Mtz Engr Bn, Mtz Sig Bn
Home station: Berlin (Wkr. III)

Formed early in 1942 by expansion of the former independent regiment of the same name, which had been operating in the central sector in Russia. In action as a division in the southern sector from June 1942. Transferred to the central sector in September 1942 and back to the south at the time of the Russia offensive.

44. Light divisions.

5th Light Division

Commander: Genlt. Karl ALLMENDINGER (51)
Composition: 56th Jäg Regt, 75th Jäg Regt, 5th Mtz Arty Regt, 5th Bicycle Bn, 5th AT Bn, 5th Mtz Engr Bn, 5th Mtz Sig Bn
Auxiliary unit number: 5
Home station: Konstanz (Wkr. V)

Active division (as the 5th Inf Div). Recruited in Baden and Württemberg. Not actively engaged before the French campaign, where it played a minor role. Identified in Russia during the summer of 1941. After suffering heavy casualties in the Vyazma sector, withdrawn to France during December for rest and conversion to a light division. Returned to Russia, northern sector, in February 1942.

8th Light Division

Commander: Genlt Gustav HÖHNE (51)
Composition: 38th Jäg Regt, 84th Jäg Regt, 8th Arty Regt, 8th Bicycle Bn, 8th AT Bn, 8th Engr Bn, 8th Sig Bn
Auxiliary unit number: 8
Home station: Neisse (Wkr. VIII)

Active division (as the 8th Inf Div). Personnel from Silesia. Fought well in Poland and in France. Took part in the Russian campaign as an infantry division from the beginning. After suffering heavy casualties, withdrawn to France in December 1941 for rest and conversion to a light division. Returned to Russia, northern sector, in the early spring of 1942.

28th Light Division

Commander:
Composition: 49th Jäg Regt, 83d Jäg Regt, 28th Arty Regt, 28th Bicycle Bn, 28th AT Bn, 28th Engr Bn, 28th Sig Bn
Auxiliary unit number: 28
Home station: Breslau (Wkr. VIII)

Active division (as the 28th Inf Div). Personnel Silesian, with some German Poles. Actively engaged in the Polish campaign and in the operations in the west. First identified in

Russia during the late summer of 1941 in the central sector. Withdrawn to France in November for rest and conversion to a light division. Returned to Russia at the end of the winter and took part in operations in the Kerch sector during May 1942. Transferred to the northern sector in the late summer of 1942.

90th Light Africa Division

Commander: Genmaj. Graf v. SPONECK
Composition: 190th Pz Bn, 155th Pz Gren Regt, 200th Pz Gren Regt, 361st Pz Gren Regt, 190th Mtz Arty Regt, 580th Rcn Bn, 190th AT Bn, 190th AA Co, 900th Mtz Engr Bn, 190th Mtz Sig Bn
Auxiliary unit number: 190
Home station: (Wkr III)

Formed as "Afrika-Division z. b. V." early in 1941. First identified in Africa during the autumn. Renamed "90th Light Division" in November 1941. After being reorganized in March 1942, played a prominent role in operations during June. Suffered heavy losses in Africa in the autumn of 1942. Renamed 90th Light Africa Division in the latter part of 1942. Entered Tunisia early in 1943.

97th Light Division

Commander: Genlt. Rupp (50)
Composition: 204th Jäg Regt, 207th Jäg Regt, 71st Arty Regt, 97th Rcn Bn, 97th AT Bn, 97th Engr Bn, 97th Sig Bn
Auxiliary unit number: 97
Home station: (Wkr. VII)

Formed in December 1940. First identified in action on the Southern Russian front during the summer of 1941, where it has remained.

99th Light Division—See 7th Mtn Div

100th Light Division

Commander: Genlt. SANNE (53) (Prisoner of war)
Composition: 54th Jäg Regt, 227th Jäg Regt, 83d Arty Regt, 100th Rcn Bn, 100th AT Bn, 100th Engr Bn, 100th Sig Bn

Auxiliary unit number: 100
Home station: (Wkr. XVII)

Formed in December 1940. First identified in action during the summer of 1941 on the Southern Russian front. The 369th Reinforced Inf Regt (Croatian) was attached to it until late in 1942. The division was virtually destroyed at Stalingrad.

101st Light Division

Commander: Genmaj. Emil VOGEL
Composition: 228th Jäg Regt, 229th Jäg Regt, 85th Arty Regt, 101st Rcn Bn, 101st AT Bn, 101st Engr Bn, 101st Sig Bn
Auxiliary unit number: 101
Home station: (Wkr. V)

Formed in December 1940. First identified in action on the Southern Russian front during the summer of 1941, where it has remained.

164th Light Africa Division

Commander:
Composition: 125th Pz Gren Regt, 382d Pz Gren Regt, 433d Pz Gren Regt, 220th Arty Regt, 220th Rcn Bn, 220th AT Bn, 220th Engr Bn, 220th Sig Bn
Auxiliary unit number: 220
Home station: Leipzig (Wkr. IV)

Formed in January 1940 as the 164th Infantry Division. In reserve on the Western front; first identified in action in Greece. Remained in the Aegean area after the Balkan campaign, based at first at Salonika and, from early in 1942, on Crete. Transferred to the Panzer Army of Africa during the summer of 1942 and there classified as a light division. Suffered heavy losses in the autumn of 1942. Renamed 164th Light Africa Division toward the end of the year. Entered Tunisia early in 1943.

45. Panzer divisions.

1st Panzer Division

Commander: Genlt. Walter KRÜGER (52)
Composition: 1st Pz Regt, 1st Mtz Inf Brig (1st Pz Gren Regt, 113th Pz Gren Regt, 1st Mtrcl Bn), 73d Pz Arty Regt, Pz Obsn Btry, 4th Pz Rcn Bn, 37th AT Bn, 37th Pz Engr Bn, 37th Pz Sig Bn

Auxiliary unit number: 81
Home station: Weimar (Wkr. IX)

Active division. Personnel largely from Türingen and Sachsen. Fought well in Central Poland and throughout the operations of May–June 1940. Continuously engaged in Russia, at first in the North and subsequently in the Center. Transferred to France early in 1943.

2d Panzer Division

Commander: Genlt. Hans-Karl Frhr. v. ESEBECK (51)
Composition: 3d Pz Regt, 2d Mtz Inf Brig (2nd Pz Gren Regt, 304th Pz Gren Regt, 2d Mtrcl Bn), 74th Pz Arty Regt, 320th Pz Obsn Btry, 5th Pz Rcn Bn, 38th AT Bn, 38th Pz Engr Bn, 38th Pz Sig Bn
Auxiliary unit number: 82
Home station: Wien (Wkr. XVII)

Active division. Personnel largely Austrian. Fought in Southern Poland. Not so conspicuous as the other Panzer divisions during the operations in France. Fought in the Balkan campaign and has been engaged in Russia in the central sector since September 1941.

3d Panzer Division

Commander: Gen. d. Pz. Tr. Hermann BREITH (51)
Composition: 6th Pz. Regt, 3d Mtz Inf Brig (3d Pz Gren Regt, 394th Pz Gren Regt, 3d Mtrcl Bn), 75th Pz Arty Regt, 327th Pz Obsn Btry, Pz Rcn Bn, AT Bn, 39th Pz Engr Bn, 39th Pz Sig Bn
Auxiliary unit number: 83
Home station: Berlin (Wkr. III)

Active division. Personnel mainly Prussian. Fought well in Poland and in Belgium and France. Continuously engaged in Russia since the outset of the campaign, first in the Central and subsequently in the southern sector. Suffered heavy losses in the Mozdok area at the end of 1942.

4th Panzer Division

Commander: Genlt. Hans EBERBACH (47)
Composition: 35th Pz Regt, 4th Mtz Inf Brig (12th Pz Gren Regt, 33d Pz Gren Regt, 34th Mtrcl Bn), 103d Pz Arty Regt, 324th Pz

Obsn Btry, 7th Pz Rcn Bn, 49th AT Bn, 79th Pz Engr Bn, 79th Pz Sig Bn

Auxiliary unit number: 84
Home station: Würzburg (Wkr. XIII)

Active division. Personnel largely Bavarian. Fought in Poland and in Belgium and France. Continuously engaged in the Russian campaign in the central sector.

5th Panzer Division

Commander:
Composition: 31st Pz Regt, 5th Mtz Inf Brig (13th Pz Gren Regt, 14th Pz Gren Regt, 55th Mtrcl Bn), 116th Pz Arty Regt, Pz Obsn Btry, 8th Pz Rcn Bn, 53d AT Bn, 89th Pz Engr Bn, 85th (?) Pz Sig Bn
Auxiliary unit number: 85
Home station: Oppeln (Wkr. VIII)

Active division, formed late in 1938. Personnel mainly Silesian or Sudeten German. Inconspicuous in Poland but prominent in the French campaign, where it shared with the 7th Panzer Division in the advance on Le Havre. Took part in the Balkan campaign, both in Yugoslavia and Greece, and has been continuously engaged in Russia in the central sector.

6th Panzer Division

Commander:
Composition: 11th Pz Regt, 6th Mtz Inf Brig (4th Pz Gren Regt, 114th Pz Gren Regt, 6th Mtrcl Bn), 76th Pz Arty Regt, Pz Obsn Btry, 57th Pz Rcn Bn, 41st AT Bn, 57th Pz Engr Bn, 82d Pz Sig Bn
Auxiliary unit number: 57
Home station: Wuppertal (Wkr. VI)

Active division (formerly 1st Light Div). Personnel mainly Westphalian. Fought hard in Poland and in France. Has been continuously engaged in the Russian campaign, first in the North and later in the Center, where it apparently suffered serious losses. Transferred to France for rest and refit in May 1942 and subsequently back to the southern sector in Russia.

7th Panzer Division

Commander: Genlt. Hans Frhr. v. FUNCK (48)
Composition: 25th Pz Regt, 7th Mtz Inf Brig (6th Pz Gren Regt, 7th Pz Gren Regt, 7th Mtrcl Bn), 78th Pz Arty Regt, 325th Pz Obsn Btry, 37th Pz Rcn Bn, 42d AT Bn, 58th Pz Engr Bn, 83d Pz Sig Bn
Auxiliary unit number: 58
Home station: Gera (Wkr. IX)

Active division (formerly 2d Light Div). Personnel mainly Thuringian or Saxon. Fought in Poland and with outstanding dash in France, where it was mainly responsible for the successful advance to Le Havre. During these operations it was commanded by the then Genmaj. ROMMEL. Continuously engaged in Russia in the central sector, where it appears to have sustained appreciable casualties. Transferred to France for rest and refit in May 1942. Took part in the occupation of former unoccupied France. Returned to Russia, southern sector, in February 1943.

8th Panzer Division

Commander: Genlt. Erich BRANDENBERGER (51)
Composition: 10th Pz Regt, 8th Mtz Inf Brig (8th Pz Gren Regt, 28th Pz Gren Regt, 8th Mtrcl Bn), 80th Pz Arty Regt, Pz Obsn Btry, 59th Pz Rcn Bn, 43d AT Bn, 59th Pz Engr Bn, 59th Pz Sig Bn
Auxiliary unit number: 59
Home station: Cottbus (Wkr. III)

Active division (formerly 3d Light Div). Personnel mainly Prussian. Fought well in Poland and in France. In Yugoslavia during the Balkan campaign, but no evidence that it took any particular part in the operations. Continuously and heavily engaged on the Northern Russian front up to the end of 1941. Identified in the central sector in the autumn in 1942.

9th Panzer Division

Commander: Genlt. Walter SCHELLER (52)
Composition: 33d Pz Regt, 9th Mtz Inf Brig (10th Pz Gren Regt, 11th Pz Gren Regt, 9th Mtrcl Bn), 102d Pz Arty Regt, Pz Obsn Btry, 9th Pz Rcn Bn, 50th AT Bn, 86th Pz Engr Bn, 81st Pz Sig Bn

Auxiliary unit number: 60
Home station: Wien (Wkr. XVII)

Active division (formerly 4th Light Div). Personnel largely Austrian. Fought well in Poland. Continuously engaged throughout the operations in the West, covering a greater distance than any other Panzer division. Took part in the Balkan campaign, both in Yugoslavia and Greece. Continuously engaged in Russia during the advance through the Ukraine and during the offensive in the southern sector in 1942. Later transferred to the central sector.

10th Panzer Division

Commander:
Composition: 7th Pz Regt, 10th Mtz Inf Brig (69th Pz Gren Regt, 86th Pz Gren Regt), 90th Pz Arty Regt, 322d Pz Obsn Btry, 10th Mfrcl Bn, 90th AT Bn, 49th Pz Engr Bn, 90th Pz Sig Bn
Auxiliary unit number: 90
Home station: Stuttgart (Wkr. V)

Composite division, made up of active units from various parts of Germany. Fought well in Poland. Spearhead in the breakthrough at Sedan, taking only a minor part in subsequent operations. Heavily engaged in the Russian campaign in the central sector up to the end of 1941. Transferred to France for rest and refit in May 1942. Took part in the occupation of former unoccupied France. Transferred to Tunisia late in 1942.

11th Panzer Division

Commander: Genlt. Hermann BALCK (50)
Composition: 15th Pz Regt, 11th Mtz Inf Brig (110th Pz Gren Regt, 111th Pz Gren Regt, 61st Mtrcl Bn), 119th Pz Arty Regt, Pz Obsn Btry, 231st Pz Rcn Bn, AT Bn, Pz Engr Bn, 341st Pz Sig Bn
Auxiliary unit number: 61
Home station: Görlitz (Wkr. VIII)

Formation completed after the French campaign during which the 11th Mtz Inf Brig fought and distinguished itself as an independent command. Took part in the Balkan campaign. Continuously engaged in Russia, first in the advance through the

Ukraine and subsequently in the central sector. Transferred to the southern sector in the summer of 1942.

12th Panzer Division

Commander: Genlt. Walter WESSEL (51)
Composition: 29th Pz Regt, 12th Mtz Inf Brig (5th Pz Gren Regt, 25th Pz Gren Regt, 22d Mtrcl Bn), 2d Pz Arty Regt, Pz Obsn Btry, 2d Pz Rcn Bn, 2d AT Bn, 32d Pz Engr Bn, 2d Pz Sig Bn
Auxiliary unit number: 2
Home station: Stettin (Wkr. II)

Originally the 2d Motorized Division, belonging to the peacetime army, with mainly Prussian personnel. As such saw little fighting in Poland, but was actively engaged in France. Reorganized as the 12th Panzer Division in the autumn of 1940. Was continuously engaged in Russia, first in the Center and later in the North up to the end of 1941, when after sustaining considerable losses it was withdrawn to Estonia for rest and refit. Has subsequently returned to the front in the northern sector.

13th Panzer Division

Commander: Genlt. Traugott HERR (49)
Composition: 4th Pz Regt, 13th Mtz Inf Brig (66th Pz Gren Regt, 93d Pz Gren Regt, 43d Mtrcl Bn); 13th Pz Arty Regt, Pz Obsn Btry, 13th Pz Rcn Bn, 13th AT Bn, 4th Pz Engr Bn, 13th Pz Sig Bn
Auxiliary unit number: 13
Home station: Magdeburg (Wkr. XI)

Formed in the autumn of 1940 out of the former 13th Motorized Division, which had fought with great distinction in Poland and in France. Spent the winter of 1940–41 in Roumania. Continuously engaged on the Southern Russian front, where it took part in the encirclement of Kiev in 1941 and in the advance to Mozdok in 1942. Suffered heavy losses late in 1942.

14th Panzer Division

Commander:
Composition: 36th Pz Regt, 14th Mtz Inf Brig (103d Pz Gren Regt, 108th Pz Gren Regt, 64th Mtrcl Bn); 4th Pz Arty Regt, Pz Obsn Btry, 40th Pz Rcn Bn, 4th AT Bn, 13th Pz Engr Bn, 4th Pz Sig Bn
Auxiliary unit number: 4
Home station: Dresden (Wkr. IV)

Originally the 4th Infantry Division, belonging to the peacetime army, with personnel from Saxony and Sudetenland. As such fought well in Poland and in the French campaign and was reorganized as the 14th Panzer Division in the late summer of 1940. Fought in Yugoslavia in the Balkan campaign and was continuously engaged on the Southern Russian front, where it was finally encircled and virtually destroyed at Stalingrad.

15th Panzer Division

Commander: Genmaj. BOROWIETZ
Composition: 8th Pz Regt, 115th Pz Gren Regt, 33d Pz Arty Regt, 326th Pz Obsn Btry, 33d Pz Rcn Bn, 33d AT Bn, 33d Pz Engr Bn, 78th Pz Sig Bn
Auxiliary unit number: 33
Home station: Kaiserslautern (Wkr. XII)

Originally the 33d Infantry Division, belonging to the peacetime army, with Bavarian personnel from the Palatinate. As such was on the Ardennes front in January 1939 and fought well during the French campaign. Reorganized as the 15th Panzer Division in the autumn of 1940. Transferred to Libya in the spring of 1941. Suffered heavy losses in the autumn of 1942. Entered Tunisia early in 1943.

16th Panzer Division

Commander:
Composition: 2d Pz Regt, 16th Mtz Inf Brig (64th Pz Gren Regt, 79th Pz Gren Regt, 16th Mtrcl Bn); 16th Pz Arty Regt, Pz Obsn Btry, 16th Pz Rcn Bn, 16th AT Bn, 16th Pz Engr Bn, 16th Pz Sig Bn

Auxiliary unit number: 16
Home station: Münster (Wkr. VI)

Originally the 16th Infantry Division, belonging to the peacetime army, with personnel from Westphalia and some East Prussians. As such was on the Saar front for a period and later took part in the attack on Sedan in support of armored formations. Reorganized as the 16th Panzer Division in the late summer of 1940. First identified in action during the early weeks of the Russian campaign and then continuously engaged in the southern sector. Virtually destroyed at Stalingrad.

17th Panzer Division

Commander: Genmaj. LICHT (51)
Composition: 39th Pz Regt. 17th Mtz Inf Brig (40th Pz Gren Regt, 63d Pz Gren Regt, 17th Mtrcl Bn); 27th Pz Arty Regt, Pz Obsn Btry; 27th Pz Rcn Bn, 27th AT Bn, 27th Pz Engr Bn, 27th Pz Sig Bn
Auxiliary unit number: 27
Home Station: Augsburg (Wkr. VII)

Originally the 27th Infantry Division, belonging to the peacetime army, with Bavarian personnel. As such fought and marched extremely well, both in Poland and in France. Reorganized as the 17th Panzer Division in the autumn of 1940. First identified in action on the Central Russian front in late June 1941 and subsequently was continuously in action. Transferred to the southern sector at the time of the Russian offensive in November 1942.

18th Panzer Division

Commander: Genmaj. Erwin MENNY
Composition: 18th Pz Regt, 18th Mtz Inf Brig (52d Pz Gren Regt, 101st Pz Gren Regt, 18th Mtrcl Bn); 88th Pz Arty Regt, Pz Obsn Btry, 88th Pz Rcn Bn, 88th AT Bn, 209th Pz Engr Bn, 88th Pz Sig Bn
Auxiliary unit number: 88
Home station: (Wkr. IV)

Formed in the autumn of 1940. First identified in action on the Central Russian front in late June 1941. Operated in the southern sector in the summer of 1942 and subsequently transferred back to the central sector.

19th Panzer Division

Commander: Genmaj. Otto SCHMIDT
Composition: 27th Pz Regt, 19th Mtz Inf Brig (73d Pz Gren Regt, 74th Pz Gren Regt, 19th Mtrcl Bn); 19th Pz Arty Regt, Pz Obsn Btry, 19th Pz Rcn Bn, 19th AT Bn, 19th Pz Engr Bn, 19th Pz Sig Bn
Auxiliary unit number: 19
Home station: Hannover (Wkr. XI)

Originally the 19th Infantry Division, belonging to the peacetime army and recruited mainly in the Hannover area. As such fought well in Poland and against the British in Belgium. Not identified during the French campaign and was reorganized as the 19th Panzer Division in the autumn of 1940. Took part in the initial attack on Russia, and has since operated in the central sector. May have recently moved to the South.

20th Panzer Division

Commander:
Composition: 21st Pz Regt, 20th Mtz Inf Brig (59th Pz Gren Regt, 112th Pz Gren. Regt, 20th Mtrcl Bn); 92d Pz Arty Regt, 335th Pz Obsn Btry, 92d Pz Rcn Bn, 92d AT Bn, 92d Pz Engr Bn, 92d Pz Sig Bn
Auxiliary unit number: 92
Home station: Gotha (Wkr. IX)

Formed in the autumn of 1940. First identified in action on the Central Russian front at the outset of the campaign, where it has been continuously engaged ever since.

21st Panzer Division

Commander: Obst. Kurt Frhr. v. LIEBENSTEIN (48)
Composition: 5th Pz Regt, 104th Pz Gren Regt, 155th Arty Regt, Pz Obsn Btry, 3d Pz Rcn Bn, 39th AT Bn, 200th Pz Engr Bn, 200 Pz Sig Bn

Auxiliary unit number: 200
Home station: Berlin (Wkr. III)

At first known as the 5th Light Division. Formed after the French campaign partly from units of the 3d Panzer Division. Reorganized as a Panzer Division in Africa during the summer of 1941. Suffered heavy losses in the autumn of 1942. Entered Tunisia early in 1943.

22d Panzer Division

Commander: Genmaj. Wilhelm v. APELL (50)
Composition: 204th Pz Regt, 22d Mtz Inf Brig (129th Pz Gren Regt, 140th Pz Gren Regt); 140th Pz Arty Regt, Pz Obsn Btry, 24th Mtrcl Bn, 140th AT Bn, 140th Pz Engr Bn, 140th Pz Sig Bn
Auxiliary unit number: 140
Home station:

Formed in France in October 1940. Transferred to Russia (southern sector) early in 1942 and thrown immediately into action, subsequently suffering heavy casualties both in the Crimea and at Stalingrad.

23d Panzer Division

Commander:
Composition: 201st Pz Regt, 23d Mtz Inf Brig (126th Pz Gren Regt, 128th Pz Gren Regt); 128th Pz Arty Regt, Pz Obsn Btry, 23d Mtrcl Bn, 128th AT Bn, 128th Pz Engr Bn, 128th Pz Sig Bn
Auxiliary unit number: 128
Home station:

Formed in France in October 1940. Transferred to Russia in the spring of 1942 and identified in action in the Kharkov area. Later fought at Mozdok and then transferred to the Stalingrad area at the time of the Russian breakthrough.

24th Panzer Division

Commander: Genlt. Arno v. LENSKI (50) (Prisoner of war)
Composition: 24th Pz Regt, 24th Mtz Inf Brig (21st Pz Gren Regt, 26th Pz Gren Regt), 89th Pz Arty Regt, Pz Obsn Btry, Mtrcl Bn, 40th AT Bn, 40 Pz Engr Bn, Pz Sig Bn
Auxiliary unit number:
Home station: (Wkr. I)

Formed in France in February 1942 largely from the former 1st Cavalry Division, which had fought as a brigade in Poland and as a division in France and in the early stages of the Russian campaign. Transferred to the Southern Russian front in the summer of 1942 and virtually destroyed at Stalingrad.

25th Panzer Division

Commander: Genlt. HAARDE (54)
Composition: Pz Regt, 25th Mtz Inf Brig (146th Pz Gren Regt, Pz Gren (Regt); 91st Pz Arty Bn, Pz Obsn Btry, Mtrcl Bn, AT Bn, Pz Engr Bn, Pz Sig Bn
Auxiliary unit number:
Home station: (Wkr. VI)

Reported forming in Norway early in 1942. May possess only one Pz Gren Regt. Not yet identified in action.

26th Panzer Division

Commander: Genmaj. Frhr. v. LÜTTWITZ
Composition: 202d Pz Regt, 9th Pz Gren Regt, 67th Pz Gren Regt, 23d Pz Arty Regt, Pz Obsn Btry, Mtrcl Bn, 23d AT Bn, 23d Pz Engr Bn, 23d Pz Sig Bn
Auxiliary unit number: 23
Home station: Potsdam (Wkr. III)

Formerly the 23d Infantry, an active division. As such heavily engaged in Poland, less so in France. Engaged continuously in the central sector in Russia until its transfer to France in the spring of 1942, where it has since been reorganized as a Panzer division.

27th Panzer Division

Commander:
Composition:	Pz Regt, 71st Pz Gren Regt, 88th Pz Gren Regt, 15th Pz Arty Regt, Pz Obsn Btry, Mtrcl Bn, 15th AT Bn, 15th Pz Engr Bn, 15th Pz Sig Bn
Auxiliary unit number: 15
Home Station: (Wkr. IX)

Formerly the 15th Infantry, an active division, recruited largely in the Frankfurt area and partly in Austria. As such on the Saar front for some months and later in the Luxemburg area. Engaged on the Central Russian front until April 1942, when it was transferred to France for reorganization as a Panzer division. Returned to Russia early in 1943.

Division Hermann Göring

Commander: Genmaj. (Luftwaffe) Dipl. Ing. Gerhard CONRAD
Composition: Pz Regt, Jäger Regt, Inf Regt (?), Guard Regt (?), Arty Regt, AA Regt, Pz Rcn Bn, Pz Engr Bn
Auxiliary unit number:
Home station:

Formed during the summer of 1942 by expansion of the Hermann Göring Brigade. All components bear the name Hermann Göring. Appeared in Tunisia early in 1943.

For SS Panzer formations see paragraph 48

46. Mountain divisions.

1st Mountain Division

Commander: Genmaj. KRESS
Composition: 98th Mtn Inf Regt, 99th Mtn Inf Regt, 79th Mtn Arty Regt, 54th Bicycle Bn, 44th AT Bn, 54th Mtn Engr Bn, 54th Mtn Sig Bn
Auxiliary unit number: 54
Home station: Garmisch (Wkr. VII)

Active division. Personnel mainly Bavarian, with some Austrians. Fought with great distinction in southern Poland. Less prominent during the French campaign. Played a minor role in the Yugoslavian campaign of 1941. Has operated throughout the Russian campaign in the southern section.

2d Mountain Division

Commander: Genlt. Ritter v. HENGL
Composition: 136th Mtn Inf Regt, 137th Mtn Inf Regt, 111th Mtn Arty Regt, 67th Bicycle Bn, 47th AT Bn, 82d Mtn Engr Bn, 67th Mtn Sig Bn
Auxiliary unit number: 67
Home station: Innsbruck (Wkr. XVIII)

Active division. Personnel Austrians from the Tirol. Fought well in southern Poland and during the Norwegian campaign. Part of the Mountain Corps in northern Norway (later expanded to the Lapland Army) at the opening of the Russian campaign. After suffering casualties in operations on the Murmansk front was withdrawn to northern Norway and held in reserve during the winter of 1941–42. Since then operating in northern Finland.

3d Mountain Division

Commander: Genlt. Hans KREYSING (53)
Composition: 138th Mtn Inf Regt, 139th Mtn Inf Regt, 112th Mtn Arty Regt, 68th Bicycle Bn, 48th AT Bn, 83d Mtn Engr Bn, 68th Mtn Sig Bn
Auxiliary unit number: 68
Home station: Graz (Wkr. XVIII)

Active division. Personnel Austrian. Fought with distinction in southern Poland and in Norway. Part of the Mountain Corps (later expanded to the Lapland Army) at the opening of the Russian campaign. Probably partly in Norway and partly in Finland during the winter of 1941–42. Transported from Norway to the Baltic states in the autumn of 1942. Transferred to the southern sector early in 1943.

4th Mountain Division

Commander: Obst. Stettner Ritter v. GRABENHOFEN
Composition: 13th Mtn Inf Regt, 91st Mtn Inf Regt, 94th Mtn Arty Regt, 94th Bicycle Bn, 94th AT Bn, 94th Mtn Engr Bn, 94th Mtn Sig Bn
Auxiliary unit number: 94
Home station: Ulm (Wkr. V)

Formed in the autumn of 1940. Personnel mainly South Germans. First identified during the Balkan campaign where it played a minor role. Has operated in the southern sector in Russia since the beginning of the campaign.

5th Mountain Division

Commander: Genlt. Julius RINGEL
Composition: 85th Mtn Inf Regt, 100th Mtn Inf Regt, 95th Mtn Arty Regt, 95th Bicycle Bn, 95th AT Bn, 95th Mtn Engr Bn, 95th Mtn Sig Bn
Auxiliary unit number: 95
Home station: Salzburg (Wkr. XVIII)

Formed in the autumn of 1940. Personnel mainly Bavarian, with some Austrians. First identified in Greece, where it fought well during the Balkan campaign. Subsequently took part in the air-borne attack on Crete. Remained in the Aegean area during 1941. Transferred to the Leningrad front early in 1942, where it has remained.

6th Mountain Division

Commander: Genmaj. Lothar PHILIPP (?)
Composition: 141st Mtn Inf Regt, 143d Mtn Inf Regt, 118th Mtn Arty Regt, Bicycle Bn, 55th AT Bn, 91st Mtn Engr Bn, 91st Mtn Sig Bn
Auxiliary unit number: 91
Home station: Klagenfurt ? (Wkr. XVIII)

Formed in winter of 1939–40. Took part in the later stages of the French campaign. In Greece it played a leading part in the advance on Salonika. Elements took part in the attack on Crete. Transferred in the late summer of 1941 from Greece to

Finland, where it has since operated as part of the Twentieth (Lapland) Army.

7th Mountain Division

Commander: Genmaj. KRAKAU
Composition: 206th Mtn Inf Regt, 218th Mtn Inf Regt, 82d Mtn Arty Regt, 99th Bicycle Bn, 99th AT Bn, 99th Mtn Engr Bn, 99th Mtn Sig Bn
Auxiliary unit number: 99
Home station: (Wkr. XIII)

Formed during the winter of 1941–42, mainly by conversion of the former 99th Light Division (formed in December 1940), which had operated for a time on the Southern Russian front. First in action in Finland in the late spring of 1942, where it has since remained.

8th Mountain Division

Commander:
Composition: 142d Mtn Inf Regt, 144th Mtn Inf Regt, Mtn Arty Regt, Bicycle Bn, AT Bn, Mtn Engr Bn, Mtn Sig Bn
Auxiliary unit number:
Home station: (Wkr. XVIII?)

Probably formed late in 1942. Possibly in Finland.

For SS mountain divisions see paragraph 48

47. Sicherungs divisions.

201st Sicherungs Division

Commander: Genmaj. JACOBI
Composition:
Auxiliary unit number:
Home station:

Expanded from the 201st Sicherungs Brigade during the summer of 1942. Employed in the rear area of the northern sector in Russia.

203d Sicherungs Division

Commander:
Composition:
Auxiliary unit number:
Home station:

Expanded from the 203d Sicherungs Brigade during the summer of 1942. Employed in the rear area of the central sector in Russia.

207th Sicherungs Division

Commander: Genlt. Karl v. TIEDEMANN (65)
Composition: 322d Reinf Inf Regt, 368th Reinf Inf Regt, 207th Rcn Co, 207th AT Bn, 207th Engr Bn, 207th Sig Bn
Auxiliary unit number: 207
Home station: Stargard (Wkr. II)

Formed on mobilization as the 207th Infantry Division with Prussian personnel from Pomerania. Fought with distinction in Poland. Converted in the winter of 1940–41, when it lost one infantry regiment and its artillery staff. Employed in rear area duties on the Northern Russian front since the outset of the campaign.

213th Sicherungs Division

Commander:
Composition: 318th Reinf Inf Regt, 354th Reinf Inf Regt, 213th Rcn Co, 213th AT Co, 213th Engr Bn, 213th Sig Bn
Auxiliary unit number: 213
Home station: Glogau (Wkr. VIII)

Formed on mobilization as the 213th Infantry Division in the Breslau area. Converted in the winter of 1940–41, when it lost one infantry regiment and its artillery staff. No evidence for its part in active operations prior to the Russian campaign, where it appears to have been employed on rear area duties in the southern sector.

221st Sicherungs Division

Commander: Genmaj. LENDLE (51)
Composition: 350th Reinf Inf Regt, 360th Reinf Inf Regt, 221st Rcn Bn, 221st AT Bn, 221st Engr Bn, 221st Sig Bn
Auxiliary unit number: 221
Home station: Breslau (Wkr. VIII)

Formed on mobilization as the 221st Infantry Division with Silesian personnel. Saw active fighting in Poland. Converted in the winter of 1940–41, when it lost one infantry regiment and its artillery staff. Employed first on the Central Russian front and subsequently in the south.

281st Sicherungs Division

Commander: Genmaj. Dipl. Ing. v. STOCKHAUSEN
Composition:
Auxiliary unit number:
Home station:

Probably formed in the summer of 1942. On rear area duties in the northern sector in Russia.

285th Sicherungs Division

Commander: Genmaj. Gustav ADOLPH-AUFFENBERG-KOMAROW
Composition:
Home station:

Date of formation uncertain. On rear area duties in the northern sector in Russia since early in 1942.

286th Sicherungs Division

Commander: Genmaj. RICHERT (51)
Composition:
Home station:

Date of formation uncertain. In the rear area of the central sector since the autumn of 1942.

403d Sicherungs Division

Commander: Genlt. Wilhelm RUSSWURM (55)
Composition:
Home station: Berlin (Wkr. III)

Formed in the spring of 1940 as a z. b. V. division staff. Given security functions during the Russian campaign and employed in the rear area of the central sector from November 1941, later moving to the south.

442d Sicherungs Division

Commander:
Composition:
Home station:

Formed early in 1940. In Russia in the rear area of the central sector.

444th Sicherungs Division

Commander: Genlt. AULEB (54)
Composition:
Home station: (Wkr. XII)

Formed early in 1940. In the rear area of the southern sector in Russia since the autumn of 1941.

454th Sicherungs Division

Commander:
Composition:
Home station: (Wkr. IV?)

Date of formation uncertain. In the rear area of the southern sector in Russia since the autumn of 1941.

455th Sicherungs Division

Commander:
Composition:
Home station:

Date of formation uncertain. In the rear area of the southern sector in Russia from the autumn of 1941. Believed disbanded.

48. SS formations.

SS-Panzerkorps

Commander: SS General Paul HAUSSER (62)
C of S:
Home station: (Wkr. XI)

Formed in 1941. Took part in the occupation of former unoccupied France in November 1942. Subsequently moved to the southern sector in Russia.

SS-Panzer-Grenadier-Division Leibstandarte "Adolf Hitler"

Commander:
Composition: Pz Regt, SS Regt Wisch, SS Regt Witt, SS Arty Regt, Mtrcl Bn, AT Bn, Engr Bn, Sig Bn
Home station: Berlin (Lichterfelde)

Formed in 1934 as a bodyguard regiment for Hitler. Took part in the Polish and western campaigns as an independent motorized regiment and was expanded into a division by the spring of 1941. As a motorized division fought in the Balkan campaign and was subsequently heavily engaged on the Southern Russian front. Moved to France in the autumn of 1942 and was there reorganized as a Panzer division. Returned to the southern sector in Russia in February 1943.

SS-Panzer-Grenadier-Division Das Reich

Commander:
Composition: Pz Regt, SS Regt Deutschland, SS Regt Der Führer, SS Regt Langemarck, SS Arty Regt, Mtrcl Bn, AT Bn, Engr Bn, Sig Bn
Home station: SS Regt Deutschland: München
SS Regt Der Führer: Wien

Formed in the winter of 1940–41 from two regiments of the former SS Verfügungs Division, to which a third regiment containing "Germanic" volunteers has been added. Fought in the Balkans and heavily engaged on the Central Russian front from the outset of the campaign. Transferred to France in July 1942 and there reorganized as a Panzer division. Took part in the occupation of former unoccupied France. Returned to Russia, southern sector, in February 1943.

SS-Panzer-Grenadier-Division Theodor Eicke

Commander:
Composition: Pz Regt, SS Totenkopf Inf Regts 1 and 3, SS Totenkopf Arty Regt, Mtrcl Bn, AT Bn, Engr Bn, Sig Bn
Home station: Berlin (Oranienburg)

Hitherto known as the Totenkopf Division, but renamed after its former commander when he was killed in action in March 1943. Formed in October 1939, mainly from existing concentration camp guard units. Hotly engaged in Flanders and France. Fought on the Northern Russian front from the outset of the campaign until September 1942, when it was transferred to France. Took part in the occupation of former unoccupied France, where it was reorganized as a Panzer division. Subsequently returned to Russia, southern sector.

SS-Panzer-Grenadier-Division Wiking

Commander: SS Genlt. Felix STEINER (47)
Composition: Pz Bn, SS Regt Germania, SS Regt Nordland, SS Regt Westland, SS Arty Regt, Mtrcl Bn, AT Bn, Engr Bn, Sig Bn
Home station: SS Regt Germania: Hamburg
SS Regt Nordland: Klagenfurt
SS Regt Westland: Klagenfurt

Formed in the winter of 1940–41 from one regiment of the former SS Verfügungs Division and from Scandinavian and Flemish volunteers. Continuously engaged on the Southern Russion front. Designated as a Panzer division in the autumn of 1942, but believed not yet reorganized as such.

SS Gebirgsdivision Nord

Commander: SS Genmaj. Matthias KLEINHEISTERKAMP (50)
Composition: 6th SS Mtn Inf Regt (Reinhardt Heydrich), 7th SS Mtn Inf Regt, SS Mtn Arty Regt, Rcn Bn, AT Bn, Engr Bn, Sig Bn
Home station: Trautenau

Formed during the summer of 1941 and has taken part in the Russian campaign on the Finnish front.

SS-Division Prinz Eugen

Commander: SS Genlt. PHLEPS
Composition:
Home station:

Formed in the spring of 1942 as a mountain division. Contains a large proportion of "racial" Germans whose homes are in Hungary and the Balkans. In Serbia since the summer of 1942.

SS Polizeidivision

Commander: SS Genlt. Alfred WÜNNENBERG (51)
Composition: 1st Police Inf Regt, 2d Police Inf Regt, 3d Police Inf Regt, SS Police Arty Regt, Rcn Bn, AT Bn, Engr Bn, Sig Bn
Home station:

Formed in October 1939 from members of police units in all parts of Germany. Training completed in February 1940. Took part in the French campaign and has operated in the northern sector in Russia, where it has sustained heavy casualties.

SS Kavalleriedivision

Commander: SS Genmaj. Willi BITTRICH (49)
Composition:
Home station: Debica (Government General)

In action as a division in the central sector of the Russian front in the autumn of 1942. Subsequently transferred to the southern sector.

SS Division 9

Commander:
Composition:
Home station:

In process of formation in northeastern France. Character and composition uncertain, but believed to include Panzer elements.

SS Division 10

Commander:
Composition:
Home station:

In process of formation in southwestern France. Character

and composition uncertain, but believed to include Panzer elements.

1. SS Infanteriebrigade

Commander: SS Genmaj. HARTENSTEIN
Composition: SS Inf Regt 8, SS Inf Regt 10
Home station:

Formed probably late in 1941. Includes the Danish "Free Corps". Operating in the central sector in Russia.

2. SS Infanteriebrigade

Commander: SS Genmaj. Gottfried KLINGEMANN (58)
Composition:
Home station:

Formed in January 1942. Consists of Flemish and Netherlands "legions". Operating in the northern sector in Russia.

Section VIII. Rosters of Senior Officers

72. Introduction.

This section comprises lists of generals in the German Army and Air Force, arranged alphabetically by rank, of officers in the General Staff Corps from Hauptmann to Oberst, and of senior SS and police officers. In most cases additional data are given on their age, command, seniority, origin, and arm, but the following points should be observed in consulting these lists:

The ages given are usually those reached in 1943, but in some cases they are only approximate.

The command or appointment shown is that which the officer is believed to have at the time of publication, but if it has not been confirmed since the beginning of 1942 the year of most recent confirmation is given.

Seniority is the date of promotion to the present rank.

Provincial origin in Germany is shown only when it is other than Prussian.

The data on Air Force officers is believed to be considerably less accurate than that on the Army officers.

The ranks of General Staff Corps officers are usually those which were held some time ago and hence may have changed.

a. German surnames.—Since the use of German surnames is sometimes confusing to the uninitiated, the following aids are given for understanding the method of their alphabetical listing:

(1) Hyphenated names: listed under first element. Example: KOCH-ERPACH, Rudolf.

(2) Compound names connected by und: listed under first element. Example: von ROTHKIRCH und PANTHEN, Friedrich Wilhelm.

(3) Compound names connected by von: usually listed under first element, provided this is a surname and not a title (such as Ritter) or a Christian name. Example: FISCHER von WEIKERSTHAL, Walter.

(4) Compound names connected by zu or auf: same as in (3) above.

(5) Double names connected by gennant (abbreviated gen., meaning "called"): may be listed under either of the two names according to which is more commonly used. Examples: von LEWINSKI gen. von MANSTEIN, Fritz Erich—listed under M; but von HARTLIEB gen. WALSPORN, Maximilian, listed under H.

Christian names are seldom if ever used in signatures. Officers sign orders with family name and rank only. It is therefore difficult, at times, to discover an officer's Christian name or initials (neither of which is shown in any official document, except in the original registration, or when two men of the same name and rank must be distinguished from each other), so that in a few cases in the following lists there is a possibility of confusion between officers having the same surname.

b. German titles.—The principal German titles of nobility occurring in the following lists are, in descending sequence:

Graf—count.

Freiherr (abbreviated Frhr.)—baron. The title Baron also exists.

Ritter—knight.

Elder—noble.

von (abbreviated v.)—when used alone denotes the lowest rank of nobility and corresponds to the French de. Also used in combination with all the above titles. Variants are: vom, von der, vom dem, von und zu, van. (All such particles are ignored in the alphabetical arrangement of names.)

Academic degrees, such as Dr., Dr. Ing., Dr. h. c., Dr. habil., Dr. phil., Dipl. Ing., Dipl. Wirtsch., are considered more important in German than in English. They are regularly shown before the surname both in official documents and in signatures, and are therefore included in the following lists.

c. German Military Ranks

Literal translations of ranks above that of colonel are deceptive. In the following table the corresponding American rank is given for each German rank. It should be noted, however, that the appointments held by officers of any given rank may vary widely in status, and no appointment carries or presupposes specific rank; for example:

A Generalmajor may command an infantry regiment, a division, or on occasions an army corps.

An infantry regiment may be commanded by a Generalmajor, an Oberst, an Oberstleutnant or, on occasions, a Major.

A "First General Staff Officer" (Ia) (our G-3) may be a Hauptmann, Major, Oberstleutnant, or Oberst.

German Rank	*Corresponding American Rank*
Reichsmarschall	None (Reich Marshal)
Generalfeldmarschall	None (Field Marshal)
Generaloberst	General
General (der Infanterie—Gebirgstruppen—Kavallerie—Panzertruppe—Nachrichtentruppen; der Flieger—Flakartillerie—Luftnachrichtentruppen—Luftwaffe).	Lieutenant General
Generalleutnant	Major General
Generalmajor	Brigadier General
Oberst	Colonel
Oberstleutnant	Lt Colonel
Major	Major
Hauptmann	Captain
Rittmeister	Captain (Cavalry)
Oberleutnant	Lieutenant
Leutnant	Second Lieutenant
Fahnenjunker	None

In the German Army, acting or temporary rank is not granted; hence the variety in rank to be found among officers holding similar commands. But two qualifications of rank may occur:

Ernennung (approximately the equivalent of brevet rank): An Oberstleutnant may be ernannt Oberst, or an Oberst ernannt Generalmajor, in order to obtain the higher rank sooner than his seniority in the lower rank would permit (promotion is usually according to seniority up to the rank of Genlt. inclusive). Such officers receive the pay of the higher rank, but do not obtain a specific seniority (Rangdienstalter, abbreviated R. D. A.) until their actual promotion.

Charakterisierung (honorary rank): An officer may be charakterisiert to a higher rank (e.g. Major to Oberstleutnant). Such officers do not receive the pay of the higher rank until their actual promotion, but they obtain a specific seniority in a separate charakterisiert list. The qualification is regularly shown in titles of rank: e.g. char. Oberst.

Officers are listed separately, according to their status, as follows:

Regular officers on the active list.—An aktiv officer is distinguished by the title of his rank without qualification: e.g., Oberst.

Regular officers on the supplementary list.—During the period of maximum expansion of the German Army (1934–1939), large numbers of additional officers were required, particularly for administrative appointments. To meet this special demand, an Ergänzungs (supplementary) list was formed on which ex-officers were recommissioned after undergoing suitable courses. An Ergänzungs officer is distinguished by the addition of (Erg.) or (E) to the title of his rank: e.g. Oberst (Erg.). Officers on this list take precedence after those holding the same rank on the active list.

Reserve officers.—Retired officers from the active or Ergänzungs list may be transferred to the reserve list, to which suitable candidates may also be commissioned directly. Commissions on this list correspond to some extent, in peace time, to commissions in our Organized Reserve Corps. A reserve officer takes precedence immediately after Ergänzungs officers of the same rank and is distinguished by the addition of der Reserve, d. Res., or d. R. to the title of his rank: e.g. Oberst d. R.

Landwehr officers.—Reserve officers may be transferred to the Landwehr list because of age or relative unfitness. Such officers are distinguished by the addition of der Landwehr, d. Landw., or d. L. to the title of rank: e.g. Major d. L.

Over-age officers.—Officers who have passed the age limit for their rank and classification but remain fit and willing to serve are transferred to the zur Verfügung (i.e., available) list and are distinguished by the addition of z. V. to the title of rank: e.g. Maj. d. R. z. V.

Unemployable retired officers.—Retired officers who are no longer fit or suitable for military service of any kind are described as ausser Dienst (out of service) or a. D.: e.g. Oberst a. D.

Officers on the emergency list.—For the duration of the war, emergency commissions (auf Kriegsdauer, abbreviated a. K,) are granted to suitable candidates. Such commissions rank immediately below those on the active list.

d. Ranks in the army medical and veterinary services.—The names of officers of the German Army Medical and Veterinary Services are not included in the following lists. The ranks in these services of the German Army, with the appointments normally held, are as follows:

Medical Officers	Ranking as	Normal appointment
Generaloberstabsarzt	General	Chief Inspector of Army Medical Services or Surgeon General
Generalstabsarzt	Generalleutnant	Chief Med O of an army group or army
Generalarzt	Generalmajor	Chief Med O of a corps or Wehrkreis
Oberstarzt	Oberst	Chief Med O of a division
Oberfeldarzt	Oberstleutnant	Chief Med O of a regiment, station hospital, or medical battalion
Oberstabsarzt	Major	Senior Med O of a battalion, or Comdr of a medical company
Stabsarzt	Hauptmann	In a hospital, medical unit, etc., or attached to a combat unit
Oberarzt	Oberleutnant	
Assistenzarzt	Leutnant	
Feldunterarzt		

Veterinary Officers	Ranking as	Normal appointment
Generaloberstabsveterinär	General	Chief Inspector of Army Veterinary Service
Generalstabsveterinär	Generalleutnant	Chief Vet O of an army group or army
Generalveterinär	Generalmajor	Chief Vet O of a corps or Wehrkreis
Oberstveterinär	Oberst	Chief Vet O of a division, CO of a veterinary hospital
Oberfeldveterinär	Oberstleutnant	
Oberstabsveterinär	Major	Senior Vet O of a battalion or regt, CO of a veterinary company
Stabsveterinär	Hauptmann	In a veterinary unit or attached to a veterinary unit
Oberveterinär	Oberleutnant	
Veterinär	Leutnant	

73. Army generals.

a. GENERALFELDMARSCHALL (Field Marshal)

Name (age)	Appointment	Seniority	Origin	Arm
BOCK, Fedor v. (63)		19/VII/40		Inf
BRAUCHITSCH, Walther v. (62)	Retired (XII/41)	19/VII/40		Arty
BUSCH, Ernst (58)	16th Army	1/II/43	Westphalia	Inf
KEITEL, Wilhelm (61)	Chief of O. K. W.	19/VII/40		Arty
KLEIST, Ewald v. (62)	Army Group A	1/II/43		Cav
KLUGE, Günther v. (61)	Army Group Center	19/VII/40		Arty
KÜCHLER, Georg. v. (62)	Army Group North	30/VI/42		Arty
LEEB, Wilhelm Ritter v. (67)	Retired (I/42)	19/VII/40	Bavaria	Arty
LIST, Wilhelm (63)	Retired (?)	19/VII/40	Württemberg	Inf
MANSTEIN, Fritz Erich v. LEWINSKI gen. v. (56)	Army Group Don	1/VII/42		Inf
PAULUS, Friedrich (53)	Prisoner of War (II/43)	31/I/43	Baden	Tks
ROMMEL, Erwin (52)	Panzer Army of Africa	22/VI/42	Württemberg	Tks
RUNDSTEDT, Gerd v. (68)	Army Group West	19/VII/40		Inf
WEICHS, Maximilian Frhr. v. (62)	Army Group B	1/II/43	Bavaria	Cav
WITZLEBEN, Erwin v. (62)	Retired (1940)	19/VII/40	Silesia	Inf

b. GENERALOBERST (corresponds roughly to U. S. General).

Name (age)	Appointment	Seniority	Origin	Arm
ARNIM, Jürgen v. (54)	Fifth Panzer Army	3/XII/42	Silesia	Tks
BLASKOWITZ, Johannes (60)	First Army	1/X/39	Baden	Inf
DIETL, Eduard (53)	Twentieth Army	5/VI/42	Bavaria	Mtn
DOLLMANN, Friedrich (61)	Seventh Army	19/VII/40	Bavaria	Arty
FALKENHORST, Nikolaus v. (58)	Army of Norway	19/VII/40	Silesia	Inf
FROMM, Fritz (55)	Ch H Rü u. BdE	19/VII/40		Arty
GUDERIAN, Heinz (55)	Insp Gen of Pz Tr	19/VII/40		Tks
HALDER, Franz (59)	Formerly Chief of General Staff, German Army	19/VII/40	Bavaria	Arty
HEINRICI, Gotthard (57)	Fourth Army	1/I/43		Inf
HEITZ, Walter (65)	Prisoner of War (II/43)	31/I/43		Arty
HOEPNER, Erich (57)	Retired (1942)	19/VII/40		Cav
HOTH, Hermann (58)	Fourth Panzer Army	19/VII/40		Inf
LINDEMANN, Georg (59)	Eighteenth Army	1/VII/42		Cav
MODEL, Walter (52)	Ninth Army	1/II/42		Tks
REINHARDT, Georg-Hans (56)	Third Panzer Army	1/I/42	Saxony	Tks
RUOFF, Richard (58)	Seventeenth Army	1/IV/42	Württemberg	Inf
SALMUTH, Hans v. (55)	Second Army	1/I/43		Inf
SCHMIDT, Rudolf (57)	Second Panzer Army	1/III/42		Tks
STRAUSS, Adolf (64)	Retired (1942)	19/VII/40		Inf

c. GENERAL d. INFANTERIE, KAVALLERIE, etc. (corresponds roughly to U. S. Lieutenant General).

Name (age)	Appointment	Seniority	Origin	Arm
ANGELIS, Maximilian	XXXXIV Inf Corps	1/III/42	Austria	Arty
BADER, Paul (58)	LXV Corps Command and CG Serbia	1/VII/41		Arty
BEHLENDORFF (54)	LX Corps Command	1/X/41		Arty
BIELER, Bruno (55)	VI Inf Corps	1/X/41		Inf

ORDER OF BATTLE OF THE GERMAN ARMY 0143

c. GENERAL d. INFANTERIE, KAVALLERIE, etc. (corresponds roughly to U. S. Lieutenant General)—Continued.

Name (age)	Appointment	Seniority	Origin	Arm
BOCK (61)	Retired (III/43)	1/XII/40		Inf
BÖCKMANN, Herbert v. (56)	L Inf Corps	1/IV/42	Baden	Inf
BÖHME, Franz (58)	XVIII Mtn Corps	1/VIII/40	Austria	Inf
BOETTICHER, Friedrich v. (62)	Retired (?)	1/IV/40	Saxony	Arty
BOTH, v. (59)		1/VI/40		Inf
BRAEMER, Walter (60)	CG Ostland	1/IX/42		Cav
BRAND, Fritz (55)	A Corps (1941)	1/VIII/40		Arty
BRANDT, Georg (67)	Retired (?)	1/VIII/41		Cav
BREITH, Hermann (51)	3rd Pz Div	1/III/43		Tks
BRENNECKE, Kurt (52)	An Inf Corps	1/II/42		Inf
BROCKDORFF-AHLEFELDT, Walter Graf v. (56)	II Inf Corps	1/VIII/40		Inf
CHEVALLERIE, Kurt v. der (52)	LIX Inf Corps	1/III/42		Inf
CLÖSSNER, Erich (57)	LIII Inf Corps	1/I/42	Hesse	Inf
COCHENHAUSEN, Friedrich v. (64)	Retired (1942)	1/XII/40		Arty
CRUEWELL, Ludwig (51)	Prisoner of War (1942)	1/XII/41		Tks
DALWICK zu LICHTENFELS Franz, Frhr. v. (67)	Wkr. III (1941)	1/XII/40		Inf
DEHNER, Ernst (54)		1/XII/42		Inf
EBERT, Karl (64)			Bavaria	Arty
ENGELBRECHT, Erwin (52)	XXXIII Corps Comd	1/IX/42	Silesia	Cav
ERFURTH, Waldemar (64)	Mil Mission to Finland (1940)	1/IV/40		Inf
FAHRMBACHER, Wilhelm (55)		1/XI/40	Bavaria	Arty
FALKENHAUSEN, Alexander v. (65)	CG Belgium and Northern France		Silesia	Inf
FEHN, Gustav (51)	Africa Panzer Corps (I/43)	1/XI/42		Tks
FEIGE, Hans (63)	Retired (1942)			Inf
FELBER, Hans (55)	LXXXIII Inf Corps	1/VIII/40		Inf
FELLGIEBEL, Erich (56)	Insp Gen of Sig Trs	1/VIII/40		Sig C
FESSMANN, Ernst (62)	Retired (1942)	30/IX/37	Bavaria	Tks
FEURSTEIN, Valentin (58)	LXX Corps Comd	1/IX/41	Austria	Mtn
FISCHER v. WEIKERSTHAL, Walter (53)		1/XII/41	Württemberg	Inf
FÖRSTER, Otto (58)		1/IV/381		Pion

c. GENERAL d. INFANTERIE, KAVALLERIE, etc. (corresponds roughly to U. S. Lieutenant General)—Continued.

Name (age)	Appointment	Seniority	Origin	Arm
FRETTER-PICO, Maximilian (52).		1/VI/42	Baden	Arty
FRIDERICI, Erich (58)	Rear Area, former Army Group South	1/IV/39	Saxony	Inf
GALLENCAMP, Curt (54)		1/IV/42		Arty
GEIB, Theodor (58)	Director General of Supply	1/XII/41	Bavaria	Arty
GERCKE, Rudolf (58)	Director of Army Transport	1/IV/42		Inf
GEYER, Hermann (61)	Retired (VII/42)	1/VIII/36	Württemberg	Inf
GEYR v. SCHWEPPENBURG, Leo Frhr. (57)	Retired (X/42)	1/IV/40	Württemberg	Tks
GIENANTH, Frhr. v. (64)	CG Govt Gen	1/IV/36		Cav
GLOKKE, Gerhard (59)	Wkr. VI (1941)	1/XII/40		Inf
GRAESSNER (51)		1/VI/42		Inf
GREIFF, Kurt v. (65)	XXXXV Corps Comd	27/VIII/39	Württemberg	Inf
GRÜN, Otto (60)	Insp of Arty		Bavaria	Arty
HALM, Hans (64)	Retired (VI/42)			Inf
HANNEKEN v. (53)	XXXI Corps Comd and CG Denmark	1/XII/41		Inf
HANSEN, Christian (58)	X Inf Corps	1/VI/40		Arty
HANSEN, Erik (54)	LIV Inf Corps	1/VIII/40		Cav
HARPE, Josef (53)	XXXXI Pz Corps	1/VI/42		Tks
HARTMANN, Otto (59)		1/IV/40	Bavaria	Arty
HELL (56)	VII Inf Corps	1/III/42		Arty
HENRICI, Sigfrid (55)		1/I/43	Hesse	Tks
HERZOG, Kurt (55)	XXXVIII Inf Corps	1/VII/42	Saxony	Arty
HILPERT, Karl (55)	XXIII Inf Corps	1/IX/42	Bavaria	Inf
HOLLIDT, Karl (54)	XVII Inf Corps	1/II/42	Hessen	Inf
HUBE, Hans (53)		1/X/42	Anhalt	Tks
HUBICKI, Dr. Alfred (56)		1/X/42	Austria	Tks
JACOB, Alfred (60)	Insp Gen of Engineers and Fortifications	1/VI/40	Bavaria	Pion
JAENECKE, Erwin (53)		1/XI/42		Pion
JODL, Alfred (53)	Chief of W. F. St	1/VII/40	Bavaria	Arty
JORDAN, Hans (51)	A Corps	1/I/43	Anhalt	Inf

c. GENERAL d. INFANTERIE, KAVALLERIE, etc. (corresponds roughly to U. S. Lieutenant General)—Continued.

Name (age)	Appointment	Seniority	Origin	Arm
KAEMPFE, Rudolf (60)	XXXV Corps Comd	1/VII/41		Arty
KAUPISCH, Leonard (65)	Retired (VI/42)			Arty
KEINER, Walter (53)		1/I/43		Arty
KEITEL, Bodewin (54)	Wkr. XX	1/IV/41		Inf
KEMPF, Werner (57)		1/IV/41		Tks
KIENITZ, Werner (58)	Wkr. II	1/IV/38		Inf
KIRCHNER, Friedrich (58)	LVII Pz Corps	1/II/42	Saxony	Tks
KLEFFEL, Philipp (56)	I Inf. Corps	1/III/42		Inf
KNIESS, Baptist (58)	Landwehr Comd Heilbronn Wkr. V (1939).	1/XII/42	Bavaria	Inf
KNOBELSDORFF, Otto v. (56)	XXXXVIII Pz Corps	1/VIII/42		Tks
KOCH, Friedrich (64)	Retired (V/42)			Inf
KOCH-ERPACH, Rudolf (57)	Wkr. VIII	1/XII/40	Bavaria	Cav
KÖSTRING, Ernst (67)	With Army Group A	1/IX/40		Cav
KONRAD, Rudolf (52)	XXXXIX Mtn Corps	1/III/42	Bavaria	Mtn
KORTZFLEISCH, Joachim v. (58)		1/VIII/40		Inf
KÜBLER, Ludwig (54)		1/VIII/40	Bavaria	Tks
KUNTZE, Walter (60)	Chief of Training in Repl Tng Army	1/III/38		Pion
KUNTZEN, Adolf (54)	LXXXI Inf Corps	1/IV/41		Tks
LANZ, Hubert (47)	A Corps	28/I/43	Württemberg	Mtn
LAUX, Paul (55)		1/XII/42	Saxony	Inf
LEEB, Emil (62)	Army Ordnance Office	1/IV/39	Bavaria	Arty
LEMELSEN (55)	XXXXVII Pz Corps	1/VIII/40		Tks
LEYSER, v. (55)		1/XII/42		Inf
LICHEL, Walter (58)		1/XII/42		Inf
LIEBMANN, Curt (62)	Retired (1939)	1/IV/35		Inf
LOCH, Herbert (57)	XXVIII Inf Corps	1/X/41	Bavaria	Arty
LÜDKE, Erich (61)	Retired (?)	1/XII/40		Inf
LÜTERS, Rudolf (60)	An Inf Div	1/I/43	Hesse	Inf
LUTZ, Oswald (67)	Retired (1942)	1/X/35	Bavaria	Tks
MACKENSEN, Eberhard v. (54)	First Panzer Army	1/VIII/40		Cav

c. GENERAL d. INFANTERIE, KAVALLERIE, etc. (corresponds roughly to U. S. Lieutenant General)—Continued.

Name (age)	Appointment	Seniority	Origin	Arm
MARCKS, Erich (52)		1/X/42		Arty
MARTINEK, Robert (59)		1/I/43	Austria	Arty
MATERNA, Friedrich (58)	Wkr. XVIII	1/XI/40	Austria	Inf
MATTENKLOTT, Franz (59)	CG Crimea	1/X/41	Silesia	Inf
METZ, Hermann (64)	Retired (1942)	/41		Inf
MOSER, Willi (56)		1/XII/42		Arty
MÜLLER, Eugen (52)	Gen. Qu	1/VI/42	Bavaria	Arty.
MUFF, Wolfgang (63)	Retired (III/43)	1/XII/40	Württemberg	Inf
NAGY, Emmerich (61)	LXXI Corps Comd	1/VIII/42	Austria	Inf
NEHRING, Walter (51)	XC Inf Corps	1/VII/42		Tks
NEULING, Ferdinand (57)	LXII Reserve Corps	1/X/42	Saxony	Inf
NIEBELSCHÜTZ, Günther v. (61)	An O. F. K			Inf
OBSTFELDER, Hans v. (57)	XXIX Inf Corps (1941)	1/VI/40	Thuringia	Inf
OLBRICHT, Friedrich (55)	General Army Office, O. K. H.	1/VI/40	Saxony	Inf
OSSWALD, Erwin (61)	Wkr. V	1/XII/40	Würtemberg	Inf
OTT, Eugen (52)	LII Inf Corps	1/X/41		Inf
OTTENBACHER, Otto (55)		/42		Inf
OTTO, Paul (62)	Wkr. IX	1/XII/40		Inf
PETRI, Hans (65)	Retired (V/42)			Inf
PETZEL, Walter (60)	Wkr. XXI	1/X/39		Arty
PFEFFER, Max (58)	Prisoner of War (II/43)	22/1/43		Arty
POGRELL, Günther v. (64)	XXXVII Corps Comd (1941)	1/X/36		Cav
PRAGER, Karl Ritter v. (65)	Retired (VI/42)	1/IX/40	Bavaria	Inf
RABENAU, Dr. phil. h. c. Friedrich v. (59)	Army Archives, O. K. H.	1/IX/40		Inf
RASCHICK, Erich (Walther) (61)	Wkr. X	1/IV/39		Inf
REINECKE, Hermann (55)	General Office, O. K. W.	1/VI/42		Inf
REINHARD, Hans (55)	LXXXVIII Inf Corps	1/XI/40	Saxony	Inf

c. GENERAL d. INFANTERIE, KAVALLERIE, etc. (corresponds roughly to U. S. Lieutenant General)—Continued.

Name (age)	Appointment	Seniority	Origin	Arm
RENDULIC, Dr. Lothar (56)		1/XII/42	Austria	Inf
RINTELEN, Enno v. (52)	Head of Military Mission and M/A, Rome	1/VII/42		Inf
ROESE, Franz v. (65)	Retired (VII/42)	1/II/42		Inf
ROMAN, Rudolf Frhr. v. (50)	XX Inf Corps	1/XI/42	Bavaria	Arty
ROQUES, Franz v. (65)	Rear Area, Army Group North	1/VII/42		Inf
SACHS (58)	159th Res Div	1/X/42		Pion
SCHAAL, Ferdinand (54)		1/X/41	Baden	Tks
SCHALLER-KALIDE, Hubert (61)	Retired (II/43)	1/XII/40		Inf
SCHENCKENDORFF, Max v. (66)	Rear Area, Army Group Center	1/XII/40 ?		Inf
SCHMIDT, Hans (65)	IX Inf Corps	1/XII/42	Württemberg	Inf
SCHNIEWINDT, Rudolf (64)	Retired (VI/42)	1/IX/40		Inf
SCHÖRNER, Ferdinand (49)	Norway Mountain Corps	1/VI/42	Bavaria	Mtn
SCHROTH, Walther (61)	Wkr. IV	1/II/38		Inf
SCHUBERT, Albrecht (57)	Wkr. XI	1/VI/41	Silesia	Inf
SCHWANDNER, Maximilian (62)	A Corps (1941)	1/XII/40	Bavaria	Inf
SCHWEDLER, Viktor v. (58)		1/II/38		Inf
SEYDLITZ-KURZBACH, Walter v. (55)	Prisoner of War (II/43)	1/VI/42		Arty
SODENSTERN, Georg v. (54)	C of S, Army Group B	1/VIII/40		Inf
STAPF, Otto (53)		1/X/42	Bavaria	Inf
STEMMERMANN, Wilhelm (53)		1/XII/42	Baden	Arty
STEPPUHN, Albrecht (66)	Wkr. XII (1941)	27/VIII/39		Inf
STRAUBE, Erich (55)	XIII Inf Corps	1/VI/42	Silesia	Inf
STRECCIUS, Alfred (64)	Wkr. XVII			Inf
STRECKER (57)	Prisoner of War (II/43)	1/IV/42		Inf
STÜLPNAGEL, Heinrich v. (56)		1/IV/39		Inf

c. GENERAL d. INFANTERIE, KAVALLERIE, etc. (corresponds roughly to U. S. Lieutenant General)—Continued.

Name (age)	Appointment	Seniority	Origin	Arm
STÜLPNAGEL, Otto v. (64)	CG Occupied France	1/I/32		Inf
THEISEN, Edgar (54)	LXI Reserve Corps	1/X/42		Arty
THOMA, Wilhelm Ritter v. (52)	Prisoner of War (XI/42)	1/XI/42	Bavaria	Tks
THOMAS, Georg (53)	Mil Economics & Armaments Office, O. K. W.	1/VIII/40		Inf
TIPPELSKIRCH, Kurt v. (52)	A Corps	27/VIII/42		Inf
ULEX, Wilhelm (63)	Retired (1942)	1/X/36		Arty
UNRUH, Walter v. (65)	Chief of Special Duties Staff, O. K. W. (Total Mobilization)	1/VII/42		
VEIEL, Rudolf (60)	Retired?	1/IV/42	Württemberg	Tks
VIEBAHN, Max v. (55)	Retired (IX/42)	1/III/41		Inf
VIEROW, Erwin (53)	LV Inf Corps (1941)	1/I/41		Inf
VIETINGHOFF gen. SCHEEL, Heinrich v. (55)		1/VI/40		Tks
VOGL, Oskar (62)	Head of Armistice Commission	/41	Bavaria	Arty
VOLLARD-BOCKELBERG v. (69)	Retired (1942)	1/X/33		Arty
WACHENFELD, Edmund (65)	Retired (III/43)			Arty
WÄGER, Alfred (60)	Retired (?)	1/XI/38	Bavaria	Inf
WANDEL (53)		1/I/43	Silesia	Arty
WEISENBERGER, Karl (53)	XXXVI Mtn Corps	1/IV/41	Bavaria	Inf
WEISS, Walter (53)	XXVII Inf Corps	1/IX/42		Inf
WETZEL, Wilhelm (55)	V Inf Corps	1/III/42		Inf
WEYER, Peter (64)	Wkr. I	1/XII/40		Arty
WIETERSHEIM, Gustav v. (59)	Retired ?	1/II/38		Inf
WIKTORIN, Mauriz (60)	Wkr. XIII (?)	1/XI/40	Austria	Inf
WITTHÖFT (56)		1/III/42	Thuringia	Inf
WODRIG, Albert (60)	XXVI Inf Corps	1/X/39		Arty
WÖLLWARTH, Erich (71)	Retired (VI/42)	1/IX/40	Württemberg	Inf
ZEITZLER, Kurt (48)	C of S, German Army	25/IX/42		Inf
ZORN, Hans (52)	XXXXVI Pz Corps	1/VI/42	Bavaria	Inf

ORDER OF BATTLE OF THE GERMAN ARMY

d. GENERALLEUTNANT (corresponds roughly to U. S. Major General)

Name (age)	Appointment	Seniority	Origin	Arm
ADAM, WILHELM (66)	Insp of Transport Troops.			H-Dr T.
AGRICOLA, Kurt (53)	580th Army Rear Area		Saxony	Inf
ALLMENDINGER, Karl (51)	5th Light Div	1/VIII/42	Württemberg	Inf
AMANN v. (62)	Retired (VI/42)			Inf
ANDREAS (58)		1/IV/41		Inf
ANGERN, Günther (50)		I/XII/42		Cav
ANSAT, (51)		1/VIII/42		Arty
APELL v. (57)		1/VI/38		Inf
AULEB (54)	444th Sich Div	1/XII/40	Hessen	Inf
BAENTSCH, Alfred (48)	82nd Inf Div	1/I/43		Inf
BAIER, Albrecht (49)	342nd Inf Div	1/I/43		Arty
BALCK, Hermann (50)	11th Pz Div	1/I/43		Cav
BALTZER (56)	156th Res Div	1/X/39		Inf
BARCKHAUSEN, Franz (61)	Mil Economics & Armaments Staff, France	1/III/38		Arty
BASSE, Hans v. (54)		1/IV/42		Inf
BAYER (56)	181st Inf Div	1/X/40		Inf
BEHR, v. (53)		1/XI/42		Inf
BEHSCHNITT, Walter (58)	254th Inf Div (1941)	1/IX/40	Silesia	Inf
BERG, Ludwig v. (61)	Insp of Recruiting Area, Koblenz, Wkr. XII (1939)	1/XI/40	Baden	Arty
BERLIN, (53)	Artillery School, Jüterbog, Wkr. III (1941)	1/III/42	Baden	Arty
BERNARD, Kurt (56)		1/X/39	Silesia	Tks
BERNHARD, Friedrich Gustav (53)		1/VIII/42		Sig C
BERTRAM, Georg (58)		1/VIII/39		Cav
BEUTTEL (56)	O. F. K. Lemberg	1/III/41		Inf
BEYER, Dr. (53)	331st Inf Div	1/I/43		Inf
BIELFELD (54)	Cmdt of Posen (Wkr. XXI)	1/II/42		Inf

ORDER OF BATTLE OF THE GERMAN ARMY

d. GENERALLEUTNANT (corresponds roughly to U. S. Major General)—Continued.

Name (age)	Appointment	Seniority	Origin	Arm
BLOCK, Johannes	294th Inf Div	1/I/43		Inf
BLÜMM, Oskar (59)	An Inf Div	1/III/40	Bavaria	Inf
BLUMENTRITT (50)	Director of Operations, (OQuI)	1/XII/42	Thuringia	Inf
BOCK v. WÜLFINGEN, Ferdinand (60)	Insp of Recruiting Area Berlin, Wkr. III	1/IV/38		Arty
BOEGE, Ehrenfried (48)		1/I/43	Silesia	Inf
BOEHM-BEZING, Diether v. (63)	Retired (?)	1/IV/35		Cav
BOETTCHER (57)	148th Res Div	1/XI/39		Inf
BÖTTCHER, Karl (53)		1/III/42	Silesia	Arty
BOHNSTEDT, Wilhelm (53)	21st Inf Div	1/IV/42		Inf
BOINEBURG-LENGSFELD, Wilhelm, Frhr. v. (54)		1/XII/42		Cav
BOLTENSTERN, Walter v. (52)		1/VIII/42		Inf
BOLTZE, Arthur (65)	Div. No. 152		Saxony	Arty
BORDIHN (54)	Insp of Fortress Engineers, Wkr. IV (1939)	1/XI/42		Pion
BOTZHEIM, Erich Frhr. v. (72)			Bavaria	Arty
BOYSEN, Wolf (59)		1/IX/42		Inf
BRABÄNDER, (52)	416th Inf Div	1/I/43		Inf
BRAND, Albrecht (55)	311th Admin Div (1940)	1/X/39	Silesia	Arty
BRANDENBERGER, Erich (51)	8th Pz Div (1941)	1/VIII/42	Bavaria	Arty
BRAUNER, Josef	187th Res Div	1/III/41	Austria	Inf
BREMER (56)		1/X/38		Arty
BRODOWSKI, Fritz v. (57)		1/II/41		Cav
BÜCHS (57)	307th Higher Arty Comd	1/X/39		Inf?
BÜNAU, Rudolf v. (53)	73d Inf Div	1/IX/42	Württemberg	Inf
BUHLE (49)	Head of a Section, O. K. H. (1939)	1/IV/42	Württemberg	Inf
BURCKHARDT (52)		1/III/42		Sig C
BURDACH, Karl (49)	Head of a section O. K. H. (1939)	1/XI/42	Saxony	Arty
BUSCHMANN (54)		1/XI/41		Arty

ORDER OF BATTLE OF THE GERMAN ARMY 0151

d. GENERALLEUTNANT (corresponds roughly to U. S. Major General)—Continued.

Name (age)	Appointment	Seniority	Origin	Arm
BUTZE, (52)	340th Inf Div	1/I/43		Inf
CANTZLER, Oskar (53)	Chief Engineer, former Army Group South.	1/VIII/42	Bavaria	Pion
CARP, Georg (56)	Insp of Recruiting Area Kattowitz, Wkr. VIII (1941).	1/VI/41	Hesse	Arty
CHOLTITZ, Dietrich v.		1/II/43		
COURBIERE, Rene de l'Homme de (56).	153d Res Div	1/VI/40		Inf
CRAMER, Hans (47)	Africa Panzer Corps (II/43)	22/I/43		Tnks
CURTZE, Heinrich (67)	Retired (VI/42)			Arty
DANIELS, Alexander Edler v. (52).	Prisoner of War (II/43).	1/XII/42		Inf
DEBOI, Heinrich (50)	Prisoner of War (II/43).	1/XII/42	Bavaria	Inf
DEHMEL (55)		1/VI/41	Silesia	Pion
DENECKE, Erich (51)	Cmdt of Smolensk (1941)	1/XII/39	Saxony	Inf
DENNERLEIN, Max (58)		1/III/40	Bavaria	Pion
DETMERING (56)	Insp of Recruiting Area Frankfurt/Main, Wkr. IX (1939).	1/VI/41	Bavaria	Inf
DETTLING (52)	183d Inf Div	1/I/43	Württemberg	Inf
DIHM, Friedrich (63)	Chief Supply O, Wkr. VII (1939).	1/X/42	Bavaria	Arty
DIPPOLD, Benignus (54)	717th Inf Div	1/X/41	Bavaria	Inf
DIRINGSHOFEN, v	401st Div z. b. V	1/III/43		Cav
DITFURTH, v	Retired (VII/42)			
DITTMAR (53)	Public Relations, O. K. H.	1/IV/42		Pion
DOEHLA, Heinrich (62)			Bavaria	Inf
DOSTLER, Anton (52)	163d Inf Div	1/I/43	Bavaria	Inf
DRABICH-WAECHTER, Viktor v. (52)	Head of a Dept., Army Personnel Office (1941)	1/VIII/42		Inf
DROGAND (60)	Inspector of Welfare, O. K. W. (1941)	1/VII/41		Inf
DÜMLEIN, Friedrich (64)	Retired (VI/42)			Inf
DÜVERT, Walther (51)		1/I/43		Arty
EBERBACH, Hans (47)	4th Pz Div	1/I/43	Württemberg	Tks

d. GENERALLEUTNANT (corresponds roughly to U. S. Major General)—Continued.

Name (age)	Appointment	Seniority	Origin	Arm
EBERHARDT (52)		1/II/41		Cav
ECKSTEIN (53)		1/VI/42		Pion
EGLSEER, Karl		1/II/43	Austria	Mtn
ENDRES, Theodore (67)		3/IX/31	Bavaria	Arty
ERDMANNSDORFF, Werner v. (52)	18th Mtz Div	1/IV/42	Saxony	Inf
ESEBECK, Hans-Karl Frhr. v. (51)	2d Pz Div	1/XII/42		Cav
FABER du FAUR, Moritz v. (57)	Cmdt of Bordeaux	1/IV/39	Württemberg	Cav
FAULENBACH (51)		1/I/43		Inf
FEICHTMEIR, Joseph (65)	PW camps, Poltava			Inf
FELDT, Kurt (54)		1/II/42		Inf
FETT, Albert (69)				Cav
FISCHER, Herbert (61)		1/I/36	Württemberg	Inf
FISCHER, Kurt (66)	412th Div z. b. V			Inf
FÖRSTER, Sigismund v. (56)	Staff of Rear Area Command, former Army Group South (1941)	1/IV/38	Thuringia	Inf
FOERTSCH, Hermann (48)	C of S Army Group E	1/I/43		Inf
FOLTTMANN (54)		1/II/41	Silesia	Inf
FORST, Werner (48)	293d Inf Div	1/I/43		Arty
FORTNER, Johann (59)	718th Inf Div	1/XI/42	Bavaria	Inf
FRANKE, Hermann (65)	Retired (VI/42)			Inf
FRIEDRICH, Rudolf (52)		1/IV/42	Saxony	Arty
FRIESSNER, Johannes (51)		1/X/42	Saxony	Inf
FÜRST, Friedrich (52)	14th Mtz Div	1/X/42	Bavaria	Inf
FUNCK, Hans Frhr. v. (48)	7th Pz Div	1/IX/42		Cav
GABLENZ, Eccard, Frhr. v		1/VIII/40		Inf
GAREIS, Martin (51)	98th Inf Div	1/I/43		Inf
GERHARDT, Paul (62)		1/II/41		Inf
GERKE, Ernst (53)	C Sig O, former Army Group South (1941)	1/I/43	Saxony	Sig O
GILBERT, Martin (54)	An Inf Div	1/I/42	Saxony	Inf
GILSA, Werner Frhr. v. u. zu (54)	216th Inf Div	1/X/42		Inf

d. GENERALLEUTNANT (corresponds roughly to U. S. Major General)—Continued.

Name (age)	Appointment	Seniority	Origin	Arm
GIMBORN, Hermann v. (63)				Inf
GINKEL, Oskar van (61)	Insp of Recruiting Area München, Wkr. VII (1941)		Bavaria	Arty
GLAISE-HORSTENAU, Dr. h. c. Edmund v. (61)	German general in Agram—Mil Mission to Croatia		Austria	
GOERITZ (52)	291st Inf Div	1/I/43	Baden	Inf
GOETTKE (59)		1/XI/41	Silesia	Arty
GOLLNICK, Hans (51)	36th Mtz Div (1941)	1/I/43		Inf
GOLLWITZER, Friedrich (54)	88th Inf Div	1/X/41	Bavaria	Inf
GRAF, Karl (60)	Deputy Cmdr, Wkr. VII		Bavaria	Inf
GRAFFEN, Karl v. (50)	An Inf Div	1/I/43		
GRASE, Martin (52)	1st Inf Div	1/I/43		Inf
GRASSER, Anton (50)		1/I/43		Inf
GREIFFENBERG, Hans v. (50)		1/IV/42		Inf
GREINER, Heinz (48)		1/I/43	Bavaria	Cav
GROPPE, Theodor (60)		1/XI/39		Arty
GROSCHUPF (61)	Potsdam I, Wkr. III (Admin) (1939)	1/VII/42		Arty
GROSSMAN (51)	6th Inf Div	1/I/43		Inf
GROTE, Waldemar Frhr. (65)	Retired (1942)	1/XI/39		Cav
GUDOWIUS	Retired (III/42)			Inf
GÜMBEL, Karl (55)		1/I/43		Inf
GUHL	Retired (V/42)			Art
GULLMANN, Otto (53)		1/I/43	Bavaria	Art
GUNZELMANN, Emil (56)	Insp of Recruiting Area Graz, Wkr. XVIII (1939)	1/X/41	Bavaria	Inf
HAARDE (54)	25th Pz Div	1/X/41		Tks
HAASE, Conrad (55)	302d Inf Div	1/I/42	Saxony	Inf
HACCIUS, Ernst (46)	Staff of Wkr X (1939)	1/I/43		Inf
HAECKEL, Ernst (53)	158th Res Div	1/X/42	Bavaria	Inf
HAENICKE, Siegfried (65)		27/VIII/39		Inf
HAGEN, Heinrich v. dem (70)	PW camps, Wkr VI			Inf

d. **GENERALLEUTNANT** (corresponds roughly to U. S. Major General)—Continued.

Name (age)	Appointment	Seniority	Origin	Arm
HAHM (49)	260th Inf Div	1/I/43	Silesia	Inf
HAMMER, Karl (60)		1/XI/40	Hesse	Inf
HAMMERSTEIN-EQUORD, Günther Fhrh. v. (65)	Oberfeldkdtr. 672, Brussels			Inf
HANSEN	Retired (V/42)			
HARTLIEB gen. WALSPORN, Maximilian v. (60)		1/IV/39	Württemberg	Tks
HARTMANN, Walter (50)	390th Field Training Div	1/II/43	Saxony	Arty
HASE, Paul v. (58)	Cmdt of Berlin, Wkr III	1/IV/40		Inf
HASSE, Ulrich	C of S 18th Army	1/I/43		Inf
HAUFFE (51)	Mil Mission to Rumania (1941)	1/I/43		Inf
HEBERLEIN, Hans (55)	Grafenwöhr Training Area (Wkr XIII)	1/IV/41	Bavaria	Inf
HEIM, Ferdinand (48)		1/XI/42		Art
HEINECCIUS v. (61)	Retired ?	1/II/41	Thuringia	Inf
HEINEMANN, Erich (62)				Arty
HEINRICHS (51)	An Inf Div	1/II/43		Inf
HEINZ, v. (56)		3/XII/42		Inf
HELD (61)	Div. Nr. 147, Wkr. VII			Inf
HELLMICH, Heinz (51)	An Inf Div (1941)	1/IX/41		Inf
HEMMERICH, Gerlach (61)	Topographical section, O. K. H. (1939)	1/XII/41		Inf
HENGEN, Fritz (56)	Insp of Recruiting Area Chemnitz, Wkr. IV (1941)	1/II/41	Bavaria	Arty
HENGL, Ritter v.	2d Mtn Div	1/I/43	Bavaria	Inf
HERR, Traugott (49)	13th Pz Div	1/XII/42		Inf
HERRGOTT, Adolf (71)	PW camps, Wkr. V			
HERRLEIN, Friedrich (53)	Inf Gen, O. K. H.	1/IX/42		Inf
HEUNERT (55)		1/X/40		Cav
HEUSINGER (48)		1/I/43		Inf
HINGHOFER, Dr. Walter		1/VII/41	Austria	Inf
HÖBERTH, Eugen v.	Cmdt of Cracow		Austria	Cav

d. GENERALLEUTNANT (corresponds roughly to U. S. Major General)—Continued.

Name (age)	Appointment	Seniority	Origin	Arm
HÖCKER, Erich (60)	Landwehr Training O, Oppeln 2, Wkr. VIII (1939)	1/XI/42		Inf
HÖCKER (50)		1/XI/42		Inf
HÖFL, Hugo (65)	206th Inf Div (XII/41)	1/VII/41	Bavaria	Inf
HOEGNER, Hermann (58)	1st Supply Group (1941)	1/II/41		H-DrT
HÖHNE, Gustav (51)	8th Light Div	1/VIII/42		Inf
HOERNLEIN, Walter (49)	Grossdeutschland Mtz Div	1/I/43		Inf
HÖSSLIN, Wilhelm v. (65)	Div. Nr. 188, Wkr. XVIII (1941)		Bavaria	Inf
HOPFF, Hermann (67)				Pion
HORN, Max (54)	214th Inf Div	1/X/41	Saxony	Inf
HÜHNER, Werner (49)		1/I/43		Inf
HÜTTMANN (63)	Retired (VI/42)			Inf
JAGOW, v.	Retired (VII/42)			Cav
JAHN (51)		1/XI/40	Thuringia	Arty
JASCHKE, Erich (53)	20th Mtz Div	1/I/43		Inf
JUPPE, Hans (51)	704th Inf Div	1/VIII/42		Sig C
KAMECKE (52)	137th Inf Div	1/I/43		Inf
KARL, Franz (55)	182d Res Div	1/III/41	Bavaria	Inf
KASPAR, Johann (64)	Retired ?			Cav
KAUFFMANN (52)		1/IV/41		Inf
KEMPSKI, Hans v. (58)	199th Inf Div	1/II/41		Inf
KERN, Emil (51)	Chief Engineer Fourth Army (1941)	1/X/41	Austria	Pion
KERSTEN	C Sig O, Wkr. X (1939)	1/X/42	Saxony	Sig C
KESSEL, Hans (52)	Cmdt of Maierhofen, Wkr. XIII (1940)	1/XI/42		Inf
KIEFFER, Friedrich Ritter v. (62)	Cmdt of München, Wkr. VII (1941)	1/VI/42	Bavaria	Inf
KIESLING auf KIESLINGSTEIN, Bruno Edler v. (65)	Insp of Recruiting Area, Regensburg, Wkr. XIII (1939)	1/XI/41	Bavaria	Inf
KIRCHHEIM, Heinrich (60)	Staff of Africa Panzer Army	1/VII/42		Inf
KLEIST v. (56)		1/IV/41		Cav

d. GENERALLEUTNANT (corresponds roughly to U. S. Major General)—Continued.

Name (age)	Appointment	Seniority	Origin	Arm
KLINGBEIL, Erich (62)	Insp of GHQ Labor Units (1941)			Pion
KLUTMANN (63)	Retired (1942)	1/IV/41		Cav
KNESEBECK, v. dem (66)	Insp of Recruiting Area Münster, Wkr. VI (1939)	1/II/41		Cav
KOBUS		1/VII/42		Inf
KOCH, Hellmuth (62)	Landwehr Training O, Glatz, Wkr. VIII (1939)	1/XI/42		Arty
KÖCHLING, Friedrich (50)		1/I/43		Inf
KÖRNER, Willy (65)	Insp of Recruiting Area Mannheim, Wkr. XII	1/XI/39	Saxony	Inf
KOHL, Otto (55)		1/IX/41		Inf
KOREUBER (53)	Zossen Training Area, Wkr. III (1941)	1/I/43		Tks
KRAISS, Dietrich (53)	A Silesian Inf Div	1/X/42	Württemberg	Inf
KRAMPF, Heinrich (55)	304th Inf Div	1/XII/41	Bavaria	Inf
KRATZERT, Hans (60)	303d Higher Arty Comd (1941)	1/I/38	Saxony	Arty
KRENSKI, Kurt v. (56)	Feldkdtr. 808, Salonika			Inf
KREYSING, Hans (53)	3d Mtn Div	1/VII/42	Oldenburg	Inf
KRIEBEL, Kurt (55)	Wkr. VII	1/VIII/40	Bavaria	Inf
KRISCHER, Friedrich (52)	296th Inf Div	1/XII/41	Austria	Arty
KRÜGER, Walter (52)	1st Pz Div	1/X/42	Saxony	Cav
KUBENA, Johann (61)				Arty
KUCKEIN	Retired (VII/42)			Pion
KÜHLENTHAL, Erich (63)		1/X/33		Arty
KÜHLWEIN (50)	45th Inf Div (1941)	1/I/43		Inf
KÜHN, Friedrich (54)	Retired (VII/42)	1/VII/42		Tks
KÜHNE, Fritz (60)		1/IV/36	Silesia	Inf
KURZ	Insp of Recruiting Area Danzig, Wkr. XX (1941)	1/III/42		Inf
LAHODE, Kurt (54)		1/VII/42	Saxony	Inf
LANDGRAF, Franz (55)		1/IX/42	Bavaria	Tks
LANG, Viktor (51)		1/I/43		Inf

d. GENERALLEUTNANT (corresponds roughly to U. S. Major General)—Continued.

Name (age)	Appointment	Seniority	Origin	Arm
LECHNER, Adolf (59)	112th Arty Comd (1941)	1/III/42	Bavaria	Arty
LEHMANN, Joseph (55)	Oberfeldkdtr. 398	1/VI/41	Bavaria	Inf
LEISTER (55)		1/I/41		Arty
LEISTNER, v.	Retired (VI/42)			Inf
LENSKI, Arno v. (50)	Prisoner of War (II/43)	1/I/43		Tks
LEYEN, Ludwig v. der (57)		1/VI/38		Inf
LEYKAUF, Hans (58)	Insp of Armaments, Wkr. VIII	1/II/41	Saxony	Inf
LIEBER, Hans (60)	Head of Army Archives, Prague			Arty
LINDEMANN, Fritz (51)	132d Inf Div	1/I/43		Arty
LINDIG, Max (55)	Head of a section, O. K. H. (1939)	1/XII/42		Arty
LINN	Insp of Transport Engineering	1/I/42		Inf
LOEPER v. (55)	81st Inf Div (1941)	1/IX/40		Inf
LÖWENBECK, Ludwig (55)		1/II/41	Bavaria	Sig C
LOHMANN, Hans (61)	Insp of Armaments, Wkr. XII	1/II/41		Arty
LUCHT, Walter (61)	336th Inf Div	1/XI/42		Arty
LÜTZOW, Hans Frhr. v. (50)	12th Inf Div	1/I/43		Inf
MACHOLZ (53)	An Inf Div	1/VI/42		Inf
MADERHOLZ, Karl (58)	320th Inf Div	1/X/41	Bavaria	Inf
MAJEWSKI, v. (53)		1/XII/42		Pion
MANTELL (62)		1/X/42		Arty
MATTERSTOCK, Otto (54)	Cmdt of Würzburg, Wkr. XIII	1/XI/42	Bavaria	Inf
MAYER, Dr. Dr.-Ing., Johannes (47)		1/II/43		Inf
MEHNERT, Karl (55)	Cmdt of Dresden, Wkr. IV	1/XI/40	Saxony	Sig C
MEISE, Dr. Wilhelm (52)		1/IX/42	Bavaria	Pion
MEISSNER, Robert		1/X/42		Inf
MENGE, v.		1/I/43		
MEYER-BUERDORF, Heinrich (54)	131st Inf Div (1941)	1/IX/41		Arty

d. GENERALLEUTNANT (corresponds roughly to U. S. Major General)—Continued.

Name (age)	Appointment	Seniority	Origin	Arm
MEYER-RABINGEN, Hermann (54)	Judge Advocate's Dept.	1/XI/41		Inf
MIETH (56)	112th Inf Div (1941)	1/III/40		Inf
MIKULICZ, Adalbert		1/III/43	Austria	Inf
MITTELBERGER, Hilmer Ritter v. (65)	Retired ?	1/I/32	Bavaria	Inf
MITTERMAIER, Wilhelm (53)	Ortskdtr. Vyazma	1/XII/42		Inf
MOLO, Louis Ritter v. (62)	An Inf Div (1941)	1/VII/42	Württemberg	Inf
MOYSES, Karl (59)	Insp of Recruiting Area Köslin, Wkr. II (1939)	1/II/41	Austria	Pion
MÜHLMANN, Max (54)		1/IX/41	Saxony	Arty
MÜLLER, Erich (53)	319th Inf Div	1/VI/42		Cav
MÜLLER, Ferdinand (61)				Pion
MÜLLER, Hermann	Retired (V/42)			
MÜLLER, Ludwig	Retired (VI/42)			
MÜLLER, Richard (51)		1/I/43		Pion
MÜLLER-GEBHARD, Alfred (54)	72d Inf Div	1/I/42	Saxony	Inf
MUNDT, Dr. habil		1/IX/40		Inf
NAUMANN (53)		1/IV/42		Tks
NEUBRONN v. EISENBURG, Alexander Frhr. v. (66)	Army Control Inspectorate (Armistice Commission) (1940)	1/XII/42		Inf
NEUMANN, Friedrich-Wilhelm (63)		1/II/42		Inf
NEUMANN-NEURODE, Karl (63)			Silesia	Inf
NOLTE, Hans Erich (61)	461st Div z. b. V	1/X/42		Cav
OBERHÄUSSER, Eugen (54)	C Sig O, Army Group Center	1/XI/42	Bavaria	Sig C
OBERNITZ, Justin v. (59)	Div Nr. 166	1/VI/40		Cav
ONDARZA, Herbert v. (63)	305th Higher Arty Comd	1/XI/42	Mecklenburg	Arty
ORTNER, Bruno		1/X/42	Austria	Inf
OSTERKAMP (51)	Army Administration Office, O. K. H. (1941)	1/IV/41		Arty

d. GENERALLEUTNANT (corresponds roughly to U. S. Major General)—Continued.

Name (age)	Appointment	Seniority	Origin	Arm
OSTERROHT (62)	Retired (VII/42)	1/II/41		Inf
OVEN, Karl v. (54)	56th Inf Div	1/VII/41		Inf
PELLENGAHR, Richard (60)		1/VI/40	Westphalia	Arty
PELTZ, Joachim (59)		1/IV/41	Saxony	Inf
PERFALL, Gustav Frhr. v. (60)	Retired	1/VIII/39	Bavaria	Cav
PETSCH (55)	710th Inf Div (1941)	1/XI/42		Inf
PFEIFFER, Dr. phil Georg (53)	94th Inf Div (?)	1/VI/42		Arty
PFLIEGER (53)		1/X/42		Arty
PFLUGBEIL, Johann (61)	388th Field Training Div	1/X/39	Saxony	Inf
PFLUGRADT (53)	Div. Nr. 173, Wkr. XIII	1/IV/42		Inf
PHILIPP, Christian		1/I/43		Inf
PICHLER	Retired (VII/42)			
PILZ		1/II/42		Inf
PINCKVOSS (57)	Insp of Recruiting Area Kassel, Wkr. IX (1939)	1/II/42		Inf
PLOTHO, Wolfgang Edler Herr u. Frhr. v. (64)	With Army Group A			Inf
POETTER, Adolf (59)	410th Div. z. b. V. (1941)			Inf
POPPE (50)	255th Inf Div	1/I/43	Thuringia	Inf
PRAETORIUS, Robert (61)	Inspector of Recruiting Area Dresden, Wkr. IV	1/II/38	Silesia	Arty
PRAGER, Karl (55)	309th Higher Arty Comd	1/II/42	Bavaria	Arty
PRONDYZYNSKI v. (62)	Insp of Recruiting Area, Prague (1941).	1/IV/42		Arty
PUTTKAMER, Alfred v. (58)	An Army Rear Area	1/VIII/39		MT
RADLMAIER, Ludwig Ritter v. (55)		1/IV/42	Bavaria	Tks
RATHKE (54)	Prisoner of War (II/43)	1/X/42		Arty
RAUCH, Erwin (54)	An Inf Div	1/XI/42		Inf
RAUS, Erhard	A Mtz Inf Brig (1941)	1/I/43	Austria	Inf
RECKE (53)	161st Inf Div	1/VI/42		Inf
REICHE v. (58)	Insp. of Recruiting Area Oppeln, Wkr. VIII (1939)	1/IV/38		Cav

d. GENERALLEUTNANT (corresponds roughly to U. S. Major General)—Continued.

Name (age)	Appointment	Seniority	Origin	Arm
RENNER, Theodor (56)		1/VII/40	Saxony	Inf
RENZ, Maximilian (59)	An Inf Div (1941)	31/X/38	Bavaria	Cav
RICHTER (54)	205th Inf Div (1940)	1/X/39	Baden	Inf
RICHTER, Werner (50)		1/III/43	Saxony	Inf
RIEBESAM, Ludwig (55)	Insp of Recruiting Area Linz, Wkr. XVII (1939)	1/VI/41	Austria	Inf
RINGEL, Julius	5th Mtn Div	1/XII/42	Austria	Mtn
RODENBURG, Karl (49)	Prisoner of War (II/43)	1/XII/42	Baden	Inf
ROEDER v. DIERSBURG, Kurt Frhr. (57)	Insp of Recruiting Area Cologne, Wkr. VI (1940)	1/II/41	Baden	Arty
ROETTIG, Otto (53)	With Army Group Center	1/VI/41		Inf
ROHDE, Hans (50)	MA, Ankara	1/I/43		Inf
ROSENBUSCH (53)	Chief Engineer, Army of Norway (1941)	1/IV/42	Silesia	Pion
ROSSUM (53)	O. F. K., Warsaw	1/XII/42		Inf
ROTBERG, Frhr. v. (67)	Retired (VI/42)	1/I/42?		Inf
ROTHKIRCH u. PANTHEN, Friedrich Wilhelm v. (59)		1/VIII/40	Hesse	Cav
ROTHKIRCH u. TRACH, Edwin Graf. v. (55)	330th Inf Div	1/III/42		Cav
RÜHLE v. LILIENSTERN, Alexander (63)	Insp of Recruiting Area Königsberg, Wkr. I (1939)	1/II/41		Inf
RUPP (50)	97th Light Div	1/I/43		Inf
RUPPRECHT, Wilhelm (53)	An Inf Div (1941)	1/XI/42	Bavaria	Inf
RUSSWURM, Josef (55)	Insp of Sig Tr in Repl Tng Army	1/IX/40	Württemberg	Sig C
RUSSWURM, Wilhelm (55)	403d Sich Div	1/IX/40	Württemberg	Sig C
SANDER, Erwin (52)	170th Inf Div	1/I/43		Arty
SANNE (53)	Prisoner of War (II/43)	1/IV/42	Hessen	Inf
SATOW (55)	Insp of Recruiting Area Frankfurt/Oder, Wkr. III (1940)	1/XI/41	Baden	Cav
SAUER, Otto Ritter v. (67)			Bavaria	Inf
SCHACKY auf SCHÖNFELD, Siegmund Frhr. v. (57)	165th Res Div	1/VIII/40	Bavaria	Inf

d. GENERALLEUTNANT (corresponds roughly to U. S. Major General)—Continued.

Name (age)	Appointment	Seniority	Origin	Arm
SCHAEFER, Hans (51)		1/I/43		Inf
SCHAEWEN, Dr. v. (56)	Chief Engineer, Wkr. III (1939)	1/II/41		Pion
SCHARTOW (51)	429th Div z. b. V	1/III/43		Inf
SCHAUMBURG, Ernst (63)	Comdt of Paris	1/II/38		Inf
SCHAUROTH, Athos v. (57)	Insp of Recruiting Area Breslau, Wkr. VIII (1941)	1/IV/38		Inf
SCHEDE, Wolfgang (55)		1/VII/40	Baden	Inf
SCHEELE, Hans Karl v. (52)	208th Inf Div	1/I/43		Inf
SCHELL, Adolf v. (49)	Insp of Army Motorization	1/IV/42		MT
SCHELLBACH, Oskar (65)	Retired (V/42)			Arty
SCHELLER, Walter (52)	9th Pz Div	1/I/43	Hesse	Inf
SCHELLERT (56)		1/I/41		Inf
SCHERER, Theodor (54)	83d Inf Div	1/XI/42	Bavaria	Inf
SCHIMPF (54)		1/XII/40	Württemberg	Pion
SCHINDLER, Maximilian (61)	Insp of Armaments, Govt Gen	1/II/34	Bavaria	Inf
SCHIRMER, Georg (53)		1/I/43		Inf
SCHLEINITZ, Siegmund Frhr. v. (53)	96th Inf Div (1940)	1/IX/42		Inf
SCHLEMMER, Ernst (54)		1/XII/42	Bavaria	MT
SCHLEMMER, Dipl Ing. Hans (50)	134th Inf Div	1/I/43	Bavaria	Arty
SCHLENTHER (65)	An Inf Div	1/III/38		Inf
SCHLIEPER (52)	Mil Mission to Slovakia	1/XI/41		Arty
SCHLÖMER, Helmut (50)	Prisoner of War (II/43)	1/XII/42		Inf
SCHMETZER, Rudolf (58)	Insp of Fortifications in the West	1/II/41	Bavaria	Pion
SCHMID-DANKWARD, Walter (56)		1/XII/40	Thuringia	Arty
SCHMIDT, Arthur (47)	Prisoner of War (Russian) (II/43)	17/I/43		Inf
SCHMIDT, August (50)		1/I/43		Inf
SCHMIDT, Curt (53)		1/X/42		Inf
SCHMIDT, Gustav (50)		1/I/43		Inf

d. GENERALLEUTNANT (corresponds roughly to U. S. Major General)—Continued.

Name (age)	Appointment	Seniority	Origin	Arm
SCHMIDT-LOGAN, Wolfgang (59)			Württemberg	Arty
SCHMITT, Artur	Prisoner of War (British)	1/I/43		Inf
SCHNECKENBURGER (51)	46th Inf Div	1/VII/42	Württemberg	Inf
SCHNEIDER	Retired (IV/42)			
SCHNEIDER, Ernst (60)		1/VII/42		Pion
SCHÖNBERG, Wilhelm (70)	Retired (VI/42)			Arty
SCHONHÄRL, Hans (65)	Retired?	1/XII/40	Bavaria	Inf
SCHOPPER (51)		1/II/43		Arty
SCHRADER, Rudolf (54)	Chief Sig O, Army Group West	1/VII/42		Sig C
SCHREIBER (66)	Cmdt of Hannover, Wkr. XI (1941)		Hesse	Inf
SCHROECK (54)		1/VI/41		Inf
SCHROEDER (61)	Retired (VII/42)			Arty
SCHUBERT, Artur (67)	Retired (?)	1/II/30 (?)	Saxony	Arty
SCHÜNEMANN, Otto (60)	Retired (VI/42)	1/VIII/37	Hesse	Inf
SCHWARZNECKER (59)	Insp of Recruiting Area Vienna, Wkr. XVII (1941)	1/III/38		Inf
SCHWERIN, Otto v. (60)	431st Div z.b.V. (1941)			Cav
SCHWERIN, Richard v. (48)		1/XII/42		Inf
SCOTTI, v. (56)		1/II/41		Arty
SEIFERT, Ernst (59)		1/VIII/38		Inf
SELLERT, v.	113th Arty Comd	1/I/42		Arty
SEYFFARDT (49)		1/I/43		Inf
SIEBERT, Friedrich (55)	57th Inf Div	1/IV/41	Bavaria	Inf
SINNHUBER (56)		1/IV/41		Arty
SINTZENICH, Rudolf (54)		1/XII/41	Bavaria	Inf
SINZINGER, Adolf		1/I/43	Austria	Inf
SIRY, Maximilian (52)	An Inf Div	1/I/43	Bavaria	Arty
SIXT v. ARMIN, Hans Heinrich (54)	Prisoner of War (II/43)	1/III/40		Inf
SODAN (62)		1/XII/42		Cav

d. GENERALLEUTNANT (corresponds roughly to U. S. Major General)—Continued.

Name (age)	Appointment	Seniority	Origin	Arm
SOMMERFELD, Hans v. (57)	526th Grenzwach Div (1940)	1/IX/41		Inf
SORSCHE, Konrad (58)	Insp of Recruiting Area Liegnitz, Wkr. VIII	1/III/38	Silesia	Arty
SPANG, Karl (57)		1/IV/40	Württemberg	Arty
SPEEMANN, Kurt (66)	An Army Rear Area			Arty
SPEICH, Dr. Richard (59)	539th Grenzwach Div (1941)			Pion
SPONECK, Graf. v. (54)	Retired (V/42)	1/II/40		Inf
SPONHEIMER, Otto (57)	An Inf Div (1941)	1/VII/41	Bavaria	Inf
STAHL, Friedrich (53)		1/IX/42		Tks
STEINBAUER, Gerhard (54)	311th Higher Arty Comd	1/X/42	Bavaria	Arty
STENGEL, Hans (63)	Landwehr Comd Chemnitz, Wkr. IV (1939)	1/IV/41	Saxony	Cav
STEPHAN, Friedrich (51)		1/I/43		Inf
STEPHANUS (62)	Retired (?)			Inf
STEVER (55)		1/VI/41		Cav
STIELER v. HEYDEKAMP (62)	Insp of Armaments, Wkr. III	1/II/41		Inf
STIMMEL (57)	An Inf Div (1940)	1/VI/41	Baden	Inf
STOEWER, Paul (54)	An Inf Div (1941)	1/II/42		Inf
STRACK, Heinrich (56)	Cmdt of Danzig, Wkr. XX (1941)	1/IX/41		Inf
STUD (54)	Head of a Dept, Army Ordnance Office (1941)	1/II/40		Arty
STÜMPFL, Heinrich (60)	Comdt. of Vienna, Wkr. XVII	1/VI/40	Austria	Inf
STUMPFF, Horst (56)		1/II/41		Tks
SUTTNER (57)		1/IV/40	Württemberg	Inf
SZELINSKI (52)	298th Inf Div	1/I/43		Inf
TARBUK v. SENSENHORST, Karl	540th Grenzwach Div		Austria	Inf
TESCHNER (70)	Retired (VII/42)			Inf
TETTAU, Hans v. (54)	24th Inf Div (1940)	1/III/42	Saxony	Inf

d. GENERALLEUTNANT (corresponds roughly to U. S. Major General)—Continued.

Name (age)	Appointment	Seniority	Origin	Arm
THOFERN, Wilhelm	Gross-Born Tng Area, Wkr. II (1941)	1/IX/42		Inf
THOMASCHKI, Siegfried (49)	11th Inf Div	1/I/43		Arty
THÜNGEN, Karl Frhr. v. (50)	A division	1/I/43	Bavaria	Cav
TIEDEMANN, Karl v. (65)	207th Sich Div	1/XI/39		Inf
TIEMANN (55)	93d Inf Div	1/X/39		Pion
TITTEL, Hermann (54)	169th Inf Div	1/IX/41		Arty
TOUSSAINT, Rudolf (52)	CG, Protectorate	1/X/42	Bavaria	Inf
TRAUT, Hans (48)	7th Inf Div	1/I/43	Alsace	Inf
TRIERENBERG (53)		1/XI/42	Bavaria	Inf
TSCHERNING, Otto (62)	Insp of Recruiting Area Stuttgart, Wkr. V (1941)	1/IX/35	Württemberg	Arty
UTHMANN, Bruno v. (52)	MA, Stockholm	1/IX/41		Inf
VAERST, Gustav v. (50)		1/XII/42	Hesse	Cav
VEITH, Richard (53)	With an Army Group	1/VIII/42	Bavaria	Inf
VÖLCKERS, Paul (52)	78th Inf Div	1/IX/42		Inf
VOLK, Erich (59)	Insp of Recruiting Area, Eger, Wkr. XIII (1940)	1/II/41	Thuringia	Cav
VOSS, Hans v.	Retired (VII/42)			Inf
WACHTER, Friedrich Karl v. (54)	267th Inf Div (1941)	1/IV/42	Hesse	Inf
WAEGER, Kurt	C of S, LIII Inf Corps	1/I/43		
WAGNER, August (59)		1/VIII/40	Bavaria	Tks
WAGNER, Eduard (49)		1/IV/42	Bavaria	Arty
WALDENFELS, Wilhelm Frhr. v. (59)	Insp of Recruiting Area Innsbruck, Wkr. XVIII (1941)	1/II/41	Saxony	Inf
WALDOW v. (62)	Retired (V/42)			Inf
WANGER, Rudolf (53)	An Inf Div (1941)	1/II/42	Bavaria	Inf
WARLIMONT, Walter (49)	Joint Planning Staff	1/IV/42		Arty
WEDDERKOP, Magnus v. (61)	Retired (VII/42)	1/II/41		Inf
WEGENER, Wilhelm (48)	32d Inf Div	1/II/43		Inf
WEIDINGER, Wilhelm (53)	Inspector of Army AA	1/X/42		Arty
WEIDLING, Helmuth (52)	86th Inf Div	1/I/43		Arty

d. GENERALLEUTNANT (corresponds roughly to U. S. Major General)—Continued.

Name (age)	Appointment	Seniority	Origin	Arm
WEINGART, Erich (56)	Insp of H-DrT (1939)	1/VIII/40	Bavaria	H-DrT
WESSEL, Walter (51)	12th Pz Div	1/I/43		Inf
WESSELY, Marian			Austria	Inf
WICKEDE, Emil v. (50)		1/I/43		Inf
WIESE, Friedrich (51)	26th Inf Div	1/I/43		Inf
WILCK, Hermann (58)	708th Inf Div	/42	Thuringia	Inf
WILL, Otto (52)	Insp of Railway Troops, O. K. H.	1/XII/42	Bavaria	Pion
WILLICH, Fritz (61)			Württemberg	Inf
WILMOWSKY, Friedrich Frhr. v. (62)	Insp of Recruiting Area Potsdam, Wkr. III (1939)	1/VIII/35		Cav
WINDECK (54)	143d Res Div (1941)	1/IV/42		Inf
WINTZER, Heinz (53)	Chief of Mil Economics and Armaments Staff, Norway	1/X/41		Arty
WITTKE, Walter (55)	With Army Group South (?)	1/VIII/41		Inf
WÖHLER (49)		1/X/42		Inf
WOLFF, Ludwig (50)	Chief of Army Educational Dept	1/XII/42	Saxony	Inf
WOLFF	Prisoner of War (II/43)	1/I/43		Inf
WOLLMANN (53)		1/VI/40		Pion
WOSCH (53)		1/I/43		Inf
WOYTASCH, Kurt (62)	Retired (VI/42)	1/VIII/41		Inf
WREDE, Theodor Frhr. v. (55)	290th Inf Div (1941)	1/III/41		Cav
ZANGEN, Gustav v. (52)	17th Inf Div	1/I/43		Inf
ZEHLER, Albert (55)	304th Higher Arty Comd	1/XII/41	Bavaria	Arty
ZEPELIN, Ferdinand v. (57)	Retired (VII/42)	1/VI/41		Inf
ZICKWOLFF, Friedrich (54)		1/X/41	Württemberg	Inf
ZIEGLER, Heinz (49)	C of S, Fifth Panzer Army	3/XII/42		Arty
ZIMMERMANN, Georg (64)	Retired (?)			Inf
ZÜLOW, Alexander v. (53)		1/X/41	Silesia	Inf
ZUKERTORT, Johannes (58)	306th Higher Arty Comd	1/II/41	Saxony	Arty
ZWENGAUER, Karl (61)	Special duties with Insp of Arty	1/II/41	Bavaria	Arty

e. GENERALMAJOR (corresponds roughly to U. S. Brigadier General)

Name (age)	Command	Seniority	Origin	Arm
ABT (51)	C Sig O, IX Inf Corps (1939)	1/IV/42		Sig C
ADLHOCH		1/XI/42		Inf
ADOLPH (66)	Cmdt of Dnepropetrovsk			Inf
ADOLPH-AUFFENBERG-KOMAROW, Gustav	285th Sich Div	1/IX/42	Austria	
ALDRIAN, Eduard		1/IX/42	Austria	
ALTEN, Viktor v. (55)		1/II/41		Inf
ALTRICHTER, Dr. Friedrich (52)	154th Res Div	1/IV/41		Inf
ALTROCK, Wilhelm v. (53)	379th Area Comd (Lublin)	1/IV/40	Saxony	Inf
AMMON, Carl v. (61)	Insp of Recruiting Area Stettin, Wkr. II (1941)			Cav
ANGER (54)		1/X/39		Arty
APELL, Wilhelm v. (50)	22d Pz Div	1/IV/41		Inf
ARNIM v.		1/XI/42		
ARNOLD (53)	Insp. of Munitions, SE Area (1939)	1/VI/41		Inf
ASCHEBERG, Percy Baron v. (61)	Wesel, Wkr. VI (admin) (1939)	1/VI/42		Sig C
ASCHENBRANDT, Henrich (58)	Area Comd, NE Estonia	1/XII/41	Bavaria	Arty
AUER, Franz (64)			Bavaria	Arty
BAARTH (52)	Remount School, Beeskow, Wkr. III (1939)	1/IV/42		Cav
BACHER		1/XII/42		
BADINSKI, Kurt (48)	269th Inf Div	/42		Inf
BAESSLER, Erich (51)	377th Inf Div	1/I/42		Inf
BAESSLER, Hans (47)		1/II/42	Silesia	Tks
BALDENSTEIN, Frhr. Rinck v.		1/III/43		
BALTZER, Martin (52)	C Sig O, XII Inf Corps (1939)	1/IV/41	Saxony	Sig C
BALTZER, Robert (52)		1/IV/41		Sig C
BAMBERG, Dr. (54)	Cmdt of Riga (1941)	1/II/41	Saxony	Inf

e. GENERALMAJOR (corresponds roughly to U. S. Brigadier General)—Continued.

Name (age)	Appointment	Seniority	Origin	Arm
BAMLER, Rudolf (45)	C of S, Army of Norway	1/IV/42		Arty
BARENDS (61)	Neustrelitz, Wkr. II (admin) (1939)	1/VI/41		Inf
BARTON, Gottfried	Cavalry School, Schlosshof, Wkr. XVII (1939)	1/II/42	Austria	Cav
BASSE, Max v. (58)	Army Welfare Office, Wkr. XII	1/IV/42		Inf
BAUER, Franz				
BAUMGARTNER, Richard		1/XII/39	Austria	Pion
BAZING		1/XI/42		
BECHT, Dipl. Wirtsch. (48)	Chief of a section, Mil. Economics and Armaments Office	1/IV/42		Arty
BECHTOLSHEIM, Anton Frhr. v. MAUCHENHEIM gen.		1/VII/42		Arty
BECHTOLSHEIM, Gustav Frhr. v. MAUCHENHEIM gen. (53)		1/VIII/41	Bavaria	Inf
BECKE		1/XII/42		
BECKER		1/VIII/42		
BECKER, Fritz		1/IV/42		Inf
BECKMANN, Alfred (66)				
BEEREN v. (51)	270th Inf Div	1/II/42		Inf
BEHRENS, Wilhelm (51)		1/I/42		Inf
BEININGER		1/VIII/41		
BERG, v		1/III/38	Baden	Arty
BERGEN, Johann (52)	323d Inf Div (1942)	1/X/41	Bavaria	Inf
BERKA (62)	Neisse, Wkr. IV (admin) (1939)	1/III/41		Inf
BERTHOLD				Inf
BESCH, Helmut	Heuberg Tng Area, Wkr. V	1/XI/42		
BESSEL, v	Landwehr Training O Karlsruhe, Wkr. V. (1939)	1/VI/41		Inf
BEUKEMANN, Helmuth		1/XI/42		Inf
BIERMANN (66)	In O. K. H	1/IV/41		Pion

e. GENERALMAJOR (corresponds roughly to U. S. Brigadier General)—Continued.

Name (age)	Appointment	Seniority	Origin	Arm
BIESS, Paul (72)	PW Camps, Wkr. IX			
BILHARZ, Eugen (55)	3d Supply Group (1941)	1/II/41	Saxony	Inf
BLOCK, Lothar v. (51)	Psychological Tests Dept. Wkr. XX (1939)	1/II/42		Inf
BLÜCHER, Johann Albrecht v.		1/VIII/42		Cav
BOECKH-BEHRENS		1/VII/42		Inf
BOEHRINGER, Gustav (51)	Head of a Section, O. K. H. (1939)	1/II/42	Württemberg	Pion
BÖMERS, Hans (49)		1/IV/42		Arty
BOESSER (63)		1/IV/42		Arty
BÖTTGER, Karl (52)	Head of a Section O. K. W. (1939)	1/IV/41	Saxony	Inf
BOGEN, v.		1/II/43		Inf
BOIE		1/XII/42		Inf
BORCHERS		1/XII/42		
BOROWIETZ	15th Pz Div	1/I/43		Tks
BOROWSKI (61)		1/IV/41		Arty
BRAUMÜLLER, Hans (59)	Psychological Tests Dept, Wkr. IX	1/VI/41		Arty
BRAUSE		1/VIII/42		
BREHMER, Walter		1/III/43		Cav
BREITH, Friedrich (50)		1/IV/42	Bavaria	Arty
BRENKEN (62)	Koblenz, Wkr. XII (admin)	1/VI/42		Cav
BRIESEN v.		1/X/42		
BROICH, Frhr. v.		1/I/43		Cav
BRUNS (52)		1/IV/42		Pion
BRUNS, Walter	MA Madrid (1941)	1/IV/42		Inf
BÜLOW, Cord v. (51)	10th Mtz Inf Brig (10th Pz Div)	1/II/42		Cav
BÜLOWIUS, Karl (52)	Chief Fortress Engineer, Wkr. X (1939)	1/IV/42		Pion
BURGDORF	Deputy Chief of HPA	1/X/42		
BUSCHENHAGEN, Erich (48)	C of S, 20th Army	1/VIII/41		Inf

e. GENERALMAJOR (corresponds roughly to U. S. Brigadier General)—Continued.

Name (age)	Appointment	Seniority	Origin	Arm
BUSICH, Rudolf		1/V/42	Austria	Pion
CABANIS, Horst	C of S of a Wkr	1/I/43		
CASPER	335 Inf Div	1/X/42		
CASTORF, Dipl. Ing. Helmut (52)	329th Inf Div	1/II/42	Thuringia	Inf
CHEVALLERIE, v. der		1/XI/42		
CHILL		1/XII/42		
CLAER, Bernhard v. (54)	4th Inf Regt., (32d Inf Div) (1939)	1/IV/42		Inf
CONRADI, Siegfried (54)		1/I/40	Saxony	Arty
CRAMOLINI (61)	Leipzig III, Wkr. IV. (admin)	1/VI/41		Cav
CRATO (61)	Düsseldorf, Wkr. VI (admin) (1939)	1/VI/42		Arty
CZETTRITZ, u. NEUHAUS, Konrad v.		1/II/43		Cav
DAHLMANN (52)	Chief Supply O, Wkr. I. (1939)	1/VII/40		Inf.
DANHAUSER, Paul (50)	256th Inf Div	1/IV/42	Bavaria	Inf
DANNEEL		1/II/43		Inf
DASER, Wilhelm		1/VII/42		
DAUBER, Julius		1/VII/42		
DECKMANN		1/IX/42		Cav
DEDEK, Emil		1/VII/42	Austria	Pion
DEGENER		1/XI/42		Cav
DEINDL, Otto (32)	Rear Area, Pz Army of Africa	1/II/42	Bavaria	Tks
DEININGER	Army Welfare Office, Wkr. IX.			
DEMOLL (61)	Ludwigshafen, Wkr. XII (admin) (1939)	1/VI/41		Arty
DETTEN, Gustav v	Psychological Tests Dept., Wkr. V (1939)	1/XI/41		
DEUTSCH	715th Inf Div	1/VII/42		Inf
DICKMANN (62)	Dortmund I, Wkr. VI (admin) (1939)	1/VI/42		Inf
DIESTEL	75th Inf Div	1/VIII/42		
DIGEON v. MONTETON, Baron Albrecht	391st Field Training Div	1/IV/42		Cav

ORDER OF BATTLE OF THE GERMAN ARMY

e. **GENERALMAJOR** (corresponds roughly to U. S. Brigadier General)—Continued.

Name (age)	Appointment	Seniority	Origin	Arm
DINTER		1/II/43		
DOHREN, v. (57)	Landwehr Training O, Wiesbaden, Wkr. XII (1939)	1/VII/41		Inf
DOHNASCHLOBITTEN, Heinrich Burggraf u. Graf z. (61)	C of S XXXVI Mtn Corps	1/VI/42		Cav
DONAT, Dipl. Ing. v. (51)	3d Ry Engr Regt (1941)	1/XI/41		Pion
DREBBER, Moritz v.	Prisoner of War (II/43)	1/I/43		
DREES	Head of a Dept, Army Ordnance (1940)	1/VII/41		Arty
DRESSLER		1/I/43		
DROBNIG (55)		1/VII/41		Arty
DYBILASZ, Dipl.-Ing		1/VIII/42		Pion
EBELING, Curt (51)		1/IV/42		Arty
EBELING, Fritz (55)		1/VI/41		Inf
EBERLE, Rene (51)		1/IV/41	Austria	Inf
EBNER, Karl (57)		1/IV/39	Austria	Arty
ECKARDT, Eduard	Army Welfare Office, Wkr. III (1940)	1/IV/41		Inf
EDELMANN, Karl (51)	103d Inf Regt (4th Inf Div) (1939)	1/XI/41	Saxony	Inf
EHRENBERG, Hans (53)	409th Div z. b. V. (1940)	1/VIII/40	Saxony	Inf
EHRIG, Richard (59)	Staff of Wkr. IV (1939)	1/VI/41	Saxony	Inf
EISENHART-ROTHE, Hans-Georg v. (52)		1/IV/42		Cav
EISENSTUCK	381st Field Training Div	1/IX/42		Inf
ELFELDT		1/I/43		Arty
ELSTER, Botho		1/III/43		Arty
ENGELHARDT, Alfred		1/XI/42		Inf
ERDMANN, Kurt		1/I/43		
ERDMANNSDORFF, v.		1/XII/42		
ERTEL, Theodor (69)	Chief Supply O, Wkr. VII (1941)	1/IX/41	Bavaria	Arty
FABRICE, Eberhard v. (51)	383d Inf Div	1/III/42		Inf
FAECKENSTEDT, Ernst Felix		1/VII/42		Cav
FALKENSTEIN, Erich Frhr. v. (63)	Chief Supply O, Wkr. VII (1939)	1/IV/41		Inf

e. GENERALMAJOR (corresponds roughly to U. S. Brigadier General)—Continued.

Name (age)	Appointment	Seniority	Origin	Arm
FANGOHR		1/II/43		Inf
FEHN, Franz (59)	Cmdt. of Augsburg, Wkr. VII	1/VI/41	Bavaria	Cav
FICHTNER		1/VIII/42		MT
FIEDLER, Erich		1/VII/42		
FISCHER, Hermann (48)	340th Inf Regt (196th Inf Div) (1941)	1/IV/42	Thuringia	Inf
FISCHER, Karl		1/IV/42		Inf
FISCHER, Karl (60)	Staff of Wkr. VII (1939)	1/III/42		Arty
FISCHER, Theodor		1/VIII/42		
FITZLAFF		1/I/43		Arty
FORSTER		1/VII/42		
FRANEK, Dr. Friedrich (52)	196th Inf Div	1/IV/42	Austria	Inf
FREMEREY, Max (52)	An Inf Div	1/VI/41		Cav
FRANKEWITZ		1/I/43		Arty
FRETTER-PICO		1/III/43		Tks
FREYE		1/VII/42		
FREYTAG, Walter		1/VIII/42		
FRIEDRICHS, Walter (58)	Landwehr Comd, Munich, Wkr. VII (1939)	1/X/37	Bavaria	Inf
FRIEMEL, Georg (51)	Prisoner of War	1/II/41		Inf
FUCIK, Karl		1/VII/41	Austria	Inf
FÜCHTBAUER, Ritter v. Heinrich (63)	Feldkdtr. 568 (1941)	1/IX/41	Bavaria	Inf
GALL		1/I/43		
GAUL, Hans (66)	Comdr. PW Area G		Bavaria	Inf
GAUSE (50)	104th Arty Comd (under Pz. Army Africa).	1/VI/41		Pion
GEBAUER, Artur		1/VI/42	Austria	Inf
GENEE, Paul (62)				MT
GENTHE, Friedrich (70)	A PW Camp		Saxony	Cav
GERBER, Alexander		1/IX/42	Austria	
GERMAR v. (64)	Stolp. Wkr. II (admin) (1940)	1/III/41		Inf

e. GENERALMAJOR (corresponds roughly to U. S. Brigadier General)—Continued.

Name (age)	Appointment	Seniority	Origin	Arm
GEROCK		1/III/43		
GERSDORFF, Gero v		1/I/43		Cav
GESCHWANDTNER		1/X/42		Arty
GEYSO, v		1/X/42		Inf
GIEHRACH (60)	Staff of Wkr. XVII (1939)	1/VIII/41		Arty
GIMMLER (53)	Head of Section, Army Ordnance (1940)	1/IV/41		Sig C
GLODKOWSKI, Erich (62)	Insp of Recruiting Area, Essen, Wkr. VI (1941)	1/IV/41		Inf
GOECKEL, Hans v. (54)	Ohrdruf Training Area, Wkr. IX (1939)	1/II/41	Thuringia	Inf
GOELDEL, v. (53)	Judge Advocate's Dept (1939)	1/II/41		Inf
GOESCHEN (54)	Comdt of Bamberg, Wkr. XIII (1940)	1/VIII/41		Cav
GRACHEGG, Gustav	PW Camps, Wkr. VIII		Austria	
GRÄSER, Fritz Hubert (55)	An Inf Regt (1940)	1/X/41		Inf
GRAEVENITZ, Hans v. (49)	Head of a Section, O. K. W. (1941)	1/II/42	Württemberg	Inf
GRASSMANN		1/III/43		Arty
GRIMMEISS	Liaison with German Air Force			Arty
GROBHOLZ, Dr		1/X/42		MT
GRODDECK, v		1/VIII/42		
GROENEVELD (62)			Baden	Inf
GÜNDELL, Walther v. (51)	Camp Cmdt, Army GHQ (1941)	1/XII/41		Inf
GUHR (70)			Silesia	Inf
GUTKNECHT		1/VII/42		
HABENICHT (52)		1/VI/41	Hesse	Inf
HAGL, August (53)		1/XII/40	Bavaria	Inf
HAMANN, Adolf	327th Inf Regt (239th Inf Div) (1941)	1/VI/42		Inf
HANSTEIN, Hans v		1/VIII/42		Inf
HARTENECK	ccrd Army	1/IV/42		Cav

e. GENERALMAJOR (corresponds roughly to U. S. Brigadier General)—Continued.

Name (age)	Appointment	Seniority	Origin	Arm
HARTMANN, Wilhelm Dipl. Ing.	In Ministry of Munitions	1/VIII/42		
HASELOFF		1/I/43		Inf
HAUENSCHILD, Ritter v. (49)		1/IV/42	Bavaria	Tks
HAUGER, Dipl. Wirtsch		1/VIII/42		Inf
HAUSER, Wolfgang		1/XII/42		
HAVERCAMP, Wilhelm (51)		1/VIII/41	Bavaria	Inf
HEDERICH, Hans (63)	Chief Supply O, Wkr. II (1939)	1/IV/41		Arty
HEDERICH, Willy (63)	Feldkdtr. 520, Antwerp	1/II/42		
HELLWIG, Georg		1/VI/42		Pion
HENKE, Gerhard		1/II/43		
HENRICI, Rudolf	140th Arty Comd	1/VIII/42		Arty
HERNEKAMP, Dipl. Ing. Karl (47)	105th Arty Comd	1/VI/42		Arty
HERRMANN, Paul		1/X/42		
HEYL, Friedrich (61)	Munich II, Wkr. VII (admin) (1939)	1/X/41	Bavaria	Arty
HIEPE, Hellmuth (51)	17th Arty Regt (17th Inf Div) (1939)	1/II/42		Arty
HILDEBRANDT, Hans Georg	21st Pz Div (I/43)	1/III/43		Tks
HILDEMANN (51)		1/XI/41		Pion
HILLERT, Dipl. Ing Walter	Insp. of Armaments Wkr. IX	1/I/42		Inf
HINDENBURG, Oskar v. (58)				Cav
HINTZE		1/VII/42		
HITTER	An Arty Regt	1/VIII/42		Arty
HOCHBAUM, Friedrich		1/I/43		Inf(?)
HOCKER (50)		1/IV/42		Inf
HÖRAUF, Franz Ritter v. (64)			Bavaria	Inf
HÖRMANN, Dr. Maximilian (50)		1/IV/42	Bavaria	Sig C
HOFERT, Johannes (58)	Munich I, Wkr. VII (admin) (1941)			Arty
HOFFMANN, Dr. Heinrich		1/XII/42		Inf
HOFFMANN, Kurt (51)		1/II/42		Inf

e. GENERALMAJOR (corresponds roughly to U. S. Brigadier General)—Continued.

Name (age)	Appointment	Seniority	Origin	Arm
HOFFMANN, Max		1/I/42		Sig C
HOFFMAN, Paul		1/VI/41		
HOFFMAN, Paul	Allenstein, Wkr. I (admin) (1939)	1/VI/42		Inf
HOFMANN, Erich	Staff of Wkr. XVIII (1939)	1/IX/41	Austria	
HOFMANN, Friedrich		1/XI/42		
HOFMANN, Rudolf (47)		1/IV/42	Bavaria	Inf
HOFMANN, Frhr. v (51)		1/VI/42		Inf
HOLZHAUSEN		1/IX/42		Arty
HOPPE, Arthur		1/XII/42		Inf
HORSTIG gen. d'AUBIGNY v. ENGELBRUNNER, Dr. Ing. Ritter v. (49).		1/III/42		Arty
HOSSBACH, Friedrich (48)		1/III/42	Hesse	Inf
HOSSFELD		1/VIII/42		Inf
HOTZY, Dr. Otto	239th Inf Ers Regt (1941)	1/IV/42	Austria	Inf
HÜBNER, Kurt (51)		1/IV/42	Bavaria	Cav
HÜHNLEIN, Friedrich (69)			Bavaria	Inf
HÜNERMANN, Dipl. Ing. Rudolf (49).	C of S, Mil Economics and Armaments Office, O. K. W.	1/IV/42		Arty
HUFFMANN		1/X/42		
IHSSEN (56)	Chief Supply O, Wkr. III (1941)	1/X/40		Arty
ILGEN, Max		1/II/43		Arty
JACOBI	201st Sich Div	1/XII/41		Tks
JACOBI, Alfred (58)	Feldkdtr. 549, Rennes (1941)	1/VII/41		Inf
JAEHN		1/I/43		
JAIS		1/X/42	Bavaria	Inf
JANSEN (61)	Insp of Armaments, Ostland	1/XI/41		Sig C
JANSSEN, Adolf Wilhelm (65)				Cav
JATZOW (62)	Schwerin, Wkr. II (admin) (1939)	1/X/41		Inf

e. GENERALMAJOR (corresponds roughly to U. S. Brigadier General)—Continued.

Name (age)	Appointment	Seniority	Origin	Arm
JESSER		1/XII/42		
JODL		1/II/42		Arty
JOHN, Dipl. Ing. Friedrich-Wilhelm.		1/XI/42		
JORDAN, Gerhard (48)	Chief Engineer, Panzer Army of Africa (1941)	1/IV/42	Hesse	Pion
JUST		1/X/42		Arty
KALDRACK, Otto (62)				Inf
KALM, Otto v. (52)		1/II/41	Hesse	Arty
KANITZ, Graf v.		1/XII/42		CW
KARL		1/IX/42		Inf
KARST	262d Inf Div	1/X/42		Inf
KEIL		1/VII/42		
KEIM (62)	Cmdt of Liege		Hesse	Inf
KELTSCH		1/XI/42		Arty
KEPER		1/III/43		
KESSEL, v.		1/XI/42		Cav
KINSEL		1/I/43		Inf
KIRCHBACH, Harry v.		1/VII/42		Inf
KIRCHENPAUER u. KIRCHDORFF.		1/I/43		
KITTEL, Heinrich (50)		1/I/42	Bavaria	Inf
KLEEMANN, Werner (50)		1/XI/41	Baden	Cav
KLEIST (57)		27/VIII/39		Arty
KLEPP, Dr. Ernst		1/IV/42	Austria	Inf
KLISZCZ, Ing. Otto	Staff of VI Inf Corps (1939)	1/IX/41	Austria	Pion
KLUGE, v.		1/X/42		Arty
KNOERZER, Hans		1/VII/42		
KOCH, Dipl. Ing. Walter (51)		1/IV/42		Arty
KOEHLER, Carl-Erich (49)	General Staff	1/IV/42		Cav
KOHL, Gustav (55)	Cmdt of Linz, Wkr. XVII (1940)	1/II/41	Bavaria	Inf
KOHLERMANN		1/VII/42		MT

e. **GENERALMAJOR** (corresponds roughly to U. S. Brigadier General)—Continued.

Name (age)	Appointment	Seniority	Origin	Arm
KOHNKE		1/XII/42		Arty
KOPP		1/II/43		Inf
KORFES, Dr. Otto	Prisoner of War (II/42)	1/I/43		
KORTE, Heinz (51)	102d Arty Comd (1941)	1/IV/42	Hesse	Arty
KOSSACK, Walter (60)		1/VI/42		Arty
KRATZER, Franz	359th Inf Regt (181st Inf Div) (1939)	1/VI/42	Austria	Inf
KRAKAU, August (49)	7th Mtn Div	1/VIII/42	Bavaria	Inf
KRAPPE		1/XI/42		Cav
KRAUSE, Fritz		1/VII/42		
KRAUSE, Walter (51)	Lehr-Regt 900 (1941)	1/I/42		Inf
KRAUSE, Johannes		1/II/43		Inf
KREBS	C of S, VII Inf Corps	1/II/42?		Inf
KREBS, v. DEWITZ gen. v.	191st Res Div	1/VII/42		
KREBS, v. DEWITZ gen. v.		1/VIII/41		Inf
KRECH, Franz (52)	Insp. of Munitions, W. Area (1939)	1/IV/42		Inf
KRESS	1st Mtn Div	1/IX/42		
KRETSCHMER		1/VII/42		
KRIEBEL, Ritter v.		1/II/41		
KRIEGER, Hans (50)		1/VI/42		Inf
KROPFF, v. (55)		1/III/39		Inf
KRUMMEL		1/XII/42		
KRUSE, Hermann		1/II/41		Arty
KÜBLER, Josef		1/I/43		Inf
KÜPPER		1/XI/42		Cav
KULLMER		1/I/43		Inf
KUMMER, v.	Cmdt of Weimar, Wkr. IX (1941)	1/IX/41		
KUNZE, Friedrich (62)		1/IV/40		Arty
KURNATOWSKI, v. (62)	Feldkdtr. 605, La Roche/Yon	1/II/42		Inf
KUROWSKI, Eberhard v. (47)		1/VI/42		Inf

ORDER OF BATTLE OF THE GERMAN ARMY

e. GENERALMAJOR (corresponds roughly to U. S. Brigadier General)—Continued.

Name (age)	Appointment	Seniority	Origin	Arm
LASCH		1/VIII/42		
LATTMANN, Martin	Prisoner of War (II/43)	1/I/43		Arty
LECHNER, Heinrich		1/VII/41	Austria	Inf
LEDEBUR, Frhr. v. (62)				Inf
LEEB		1/IX/41		
LEMKE, Herbert (53)		1/VIII/41		Inf
LENDLE (51)	221st Sich Div	1/IV/42	Württemberg	Tks
LEOPRECHTING, Waldemar Frhr. v.		1/VII/42		Pion
LETTOW (51)		1/IV/42		Inf
LEUZE, Walter (51)	687th Inf Regt (336th Inf Div) (1941)	1/IV/42	Bavaria	Cav
LEYERS, Dr. Ing		1/I/43		MT
LEYSER, Hans Georg	Prisoner of War (II/43)	1/XI/42		Inf
LEYTHAUSER, Hermann (58)	Elsenborn Training Area, Wkr. VI (1939)	1/IV/40	Bavaria	Cav
LICHT (51)	17th Pz Div	1/II/42		Inf
LIEB (52)	27th Inf Regt (12th Inf Div) (1939)	1/VI/41	Württemberg	Inf
LIEGMANN, Wilhelm (53)		1/VI/41	Saxony	Inf
LINDE, v. der (51)	Chief ATO, Wkr. IV (1939)	1/III/42		Cav
LINDENAU (61)	Cmdt of Flensburg, Wkr. X (1940)	1/VIII/41		Inf
LINKENBACH (53)		1/VIII/41		Cav
LINNARZ	In Army Personnel Office	1/I/43		MT
LOCHAU, Axel v. der (59)		1/VII/41		Inf
LOEHNING (53)		1/IV/40		Inf
LONTSCHAR, Adalbert	Cmdt of Belgrade	1/VII/41	Austria	Inf
LORENZ, Hans (61)	Staff of Wkr. V (1939)	1/IV/41		Inf
LÜBBE		1/X/42		Inf
LUER, Hilmar (59)	Liegnitz, Wkr. VIII (admin)	1/VIII/41		Inf
LÜTKENHAUS		1/III/43		Inf
LÜTTWITZ, Frhr. v.	26th Pz Div	1/XII/42		Tks

e. GENERALMAJOR (corresponds roughly to U. S. Brigadier General)—Continued.

Name (age)	Appointment	Seniority	Origin	Arm
LÜTTWITZ, Smilo Frhr. v.		1/X/42		Cav
LUNGERSHAUSEN		1/X/42		Cav
LUS		1/V/42		
LUTZ, Ernst Frhr. v.		1/VII/42		Inf
MAERCKER				Inf
MAGNUS	Prisoner of War (II/43)	1/X/42		
MAHLMANN		1/I/43		Inf
MANN, Edler v. TIECHLER, Ferdinand Ritter v. (51)	Garrison Cmdt, Bucharest (1941)	1/IV/42	Bavaria	Inf
MARCINKIEWICZ, August		1/XII/41	Austria	Pion
MARKGRAF, Emil		1/IX/41	Austria	Inf
MARSEILLE, Siegfried (55)	Bremen I, Wkr. X (admin)	1/VII/41		Inf
MATZKY, Gerhard (50)	Director of Intelligence (Q Qu IV)	1/IV/41		Inf
MEDEM (50)	2d Engineer School (1939)	1/IX/41		Pion
MEINHOLD (52)		1/IV/42		Inf
MEISSNER, Hans (59)	C of S, Wkr. XII (1940)		Saxony	SigC
MELCHERT		1/II/43		Inf
MELTZER, Rudolf (51)		1/IV/42		SigC
MELZER		1/II/43		Inf
MENKEL		1/X/42		Inf
MENNY, Erwin	18th Pz Div	1/XI/42		Tks
MERKER	35th Inf Div	1/X/42		Inf
MERTENS (69)	Oflag II C (1941)	1/IX/41		Inf
METSCHER, Karl	Arty Ers Regt (1941)	1/VI/42		Arty
METZ		1/I/43		
METZ, Eduard	A Pz Div	1/VIII/42		
MEYER, Carl Ludwig		1/IV/42		
MEYER, Heinrich	Cmdt of Mainz, Wkr. XII (1940)			Tks
MIERZINSKY (62)	Feldkdtr. 245 (1941)	1/II/42		Inf
MORITZ		1/XII/41		Cav

e. GENERALMAJOR (corresponds roughly to U. S. Brigadier General)—Continued.

Name (age)	Appointment	Seniority	Origin	Arm
MOST	Landwehr Comd Weinsberg, Wkr. V (1939).		Württemberg	Inf
MÜLLER, Angelo (50)		1/IV/42	Bavaria	Arty
MÜLLER, Friedrich-Wilhelm	22d Inf Div	1/VIII/42		
MÜLLER, Hans Ludwig		1/XII/42		
MÜLLER, Ludwig	198th Inf Div	1/X/42		Inf
MÜLLER, Vinzenz (48)	C of S, Seventeenth Army	1/II/42	Württemberg	Pion
MUHL		1/X/42		Arty
MUMMENTHEY (55)		1/IV/37		Inf
MYLO, Walter (62)	Fulda, Wkr. IX (admin) (1940)	1/I/42		Inf
NAGEL	Chief of a Dept, O. K. W.	1/IV/42		
NAKE, Albin		1/IV/42	Austria	Inf
NEIDHOLDT	369th Inf Div	1/X/42		Inf
NEINDORFF, v	189th Res Div	1/XII/42		Inf
NEUMAYR, Franz (52)		1/IV/42	Bavaria	Inf
NEWIGER		1/I/43		Tks
NICHTERLEIN (61)	Göttingen, Wkr. XI (admin) (1940)	1/IV/41		Inf
NICHKELMANN		1/II/43		
NIEBECKER (67)	A construction staff			Pion
NIEDENFÜHR, Günther (54)				Arty
NIEDERMAYER, Prof. Dr. Ritter v.	162d Inf Div	1/IX/42		
NOACK (61)				Inf
NOELDECHEN		1/XI/42		Arty
NOSTITZ-WALLWITZ, Gerhard v. (57)	Inspector of Armaments former Army Group South	1/XII/41		Inf
OCHSNER, Hermann (50)	Head of a Section O. K. H. (1939)	1/IV/42	Bavaria	CWS
OELSNER, (54)	Wandern Training Area, Wkr. III (1939)	1/II/41		Inf
OESTERREICH, v. (61)		1/III/41		Inf

e. GENERALMAJOR (corresponds roughly to U. S. Brigadier General)—Continued.

Name (age)	Appointment	Seniority	Origin	Arm
OFFENBÄCHER, Konrad (52)	Döllersheim Training Area, Wkr. XVII (1939)	1/VI/41	Hesse	Inf
OHNACKER (51)	Chief Supply O, Army Group West (1941)	1/IV/42		
OPPENLÄNDER (51)		1/XI/41	Württemberg	Inf
OSTER		1/XII/42		Inf
OTTO (55)	Eifel Fortifications (1940)	1/VIII/38	Baden	Pion
PACHMAYR	Army Mechanics School (1941)	1/IX/41		Arty
PAUER, Ernst		1/IX/41	Austria	Arty
PAWEL		1/IX/42		
PECHMANN, Albrecht Frhr. v. (63)	Feldkdtr. 598 (1941)	1/IX/41	Bavaria	Arty
PESCHEL		1/XII/42		Inf
PETERSEN, Matthias	Cmdt of Kaiserslautern, Wkr. XII (1941)	1/II/42		Inf
PETERSEN, Wilhelm (51)		1/IV/42		Pion
PETTER (62)	Cmdt of Frankfort/-Main, Wkr. IX (1940)			Inf
PFETTEN		1/XI/42		Cav
PFLAUM, Karl (53)	157 Res Div	1/X/40		Inf
PHILIPP, Ernst		1/V/42		
PHILIPP, Lothar	6 Mtn Div	1/IV/40	Austria	Inf
PHILIPPS, Dipl. Ing		1/X/41	Saxony	Tks
PITREICH, August v	Staff of CG Protectorate (1941)		Austria	
PLAMBÖCK (62)	Lötzen Fortifications, Wkr. I (1941)	1/IV/41		Arty
PLEWIG, Willy (62)	Salzbrunn, Wkr. VIII (Admin)	1/IV/41		Inf
PLOETZ, v		1/VIII/42		
POEL, Gerhard (57)	Remount School, Wkr. V. (1939)	1/VII/41		Cav
POHL, v. (68)				Arty
POSTEL	A Lt Div	1/I/43		Inf
POTEN		1/VII/42		

e. GENERALMAJOR (corresponds roughly to U. S. Brigadier General)—Continued.

Name (age)	Appointment	Seniority	Origin	Arm
PRAUN	129th Inf Div	1/VIII/42		Sig C
PRIEM, v. (59)		1/I/42		Inf
PRIESS		1/I/43		Inf
PRINNER		1/III/43		
PRITTWITZ u. GAFFRON, Max v. (67).		1/IX/41	Silesia	Inf
PRÜGEL, Dr. Karl (66)	Cmdt of Zagreb		Bavaria	Sig C
PRÜTER		1/I/43		Inf
PÜCHLER	257th Inf Div	1/VII/42		Inf
PUTTKAMER, v. (61)	Insp of Recruiting, Schwerin, Wkr. II (1940)			Inf
RAAB, Matthias		1/IV/42	Austria	Arty
RABSILBER, Friedrich (63)	Osnabrück, Wkr. XI (admin) (1939)	1/IV/41		Inf
RAESFELD, Werner v. (51)	Transport Office, Essen, Wkr. VI (1939)	1/VI/42	Silesia	Inf
RÄSSLER, Rudolf (58)	Landwehr Training O Aachen, Wkr. VI (1939)	1/VI/42	Saxony	Cav
RAITHEL (48)		1/IV/42	Bavaria	Arty
RAITZ v. FRENTZ, Maximilian Frhr. (62)	Staff of Wkr. VI (1939)	1/VI/41		Arty
RAPPARD v.		1/XI/42		Inf
RAVENSTEIN, Johann v.	Prisoner of War (1941)			Inf
RECKNAGEL, Hermann (50)	111th Inf Div	1/III/42	Hesse	Inf
REIBNITZ, v. (54)		1/VII/40		Inf
REICHER, Franz	Staff of Wkr. XVII (1941)		Austria	Inf
REICHERT, Josef (51)	714th Inf Div	1/IX/41	Bavaria	Inf
REINERSDORFF-PACZYNSKI u. TENCZYN (67) Dietrich v.	An Inf Div			
REINHARDT, Fritz (52)		1/VI/41	Saxony	Inf
REMLINGER		1/XII/42		Cav
REXILIUS		1/II/43		Inf
REYMANN, Hellmuth		1/X/42		
RIBBENTROP, Friedrich (62)	168th Arty Ers Regt (1941)	1/IV/41	Saxony	Arty

e. GENERALMAJOR (corresponds roughly to U. S. Brigadier General)—Continued.

Name (age)	Appointment	Seniority	Origin	Arm
RICHERT (51)	286th Sich Div	1/IV/42		Inf
RICHTER, Gerhard	87th Inf Div?	1/VIII/42		
RICHTER, Wilhelm		1/III/43		
RIEDEL		1/VIII/42		
RIEGER, Leopold (52)	Chief Supply O, Wkr. XIII (1939)	1/VI/41	Saxony	Arty
REIMHOFER		1/X/42		MT
RINGE, Hans		1/II/42		Cav
RISSE		1/XI/42		
RITTER, Rene		1/IV/42	Austria	Inf
RITTWEGER, Ernst (56)	Cmdt of Karlsruhe, Wkr. V. (1941)	1/II/42		Inf
RODEWALD (56)	Staff of First Army (1940)			H-Dr
RÖHRICHT	C of S, First Army	1/IV/42		Inf
ROEMER v		1/I/43		
ROESINGER, Otto (52)		1/IV/42	Bavaria	Pion
RÖTTIGER	C of S, Fourth Panzer Army	1/II/42?		Tks
ROSKE, Dipl. Ing		27/I/43		
ROSLER, Eberhard	An Inf Regt (1941)	1/IV/41	Württemberg	Inf
ROSSI		1/VII/42		
ROST, v		1/III/43		Arty
ROTH, Hans		1/VIII/42		Inf
ROTHE		1/VII/42		
RÜDIGER, Dipl. Ing		1/VI/41		Arty
RÜGAMER, Ferdinand		1/VII/41	Austria	Arty
RÜGGENMANN, Alfons (51)	Insp of Armaments Wkr. I	1/IV/42		H-Dr
RÜHLE v. LILIENSTERN		1/VII/42		
RUFF		1/XII/42		Arty
RUNGE, Wilhelm (52)	Insp of Engineer Equipment, Wkr. I (1939)	1/VI/41		Pion
RUPPERT, Hans Eberhard (51)		1/VI/42		H-Dr
RUVILLE, v		1/VII/42		

e. GENERALMAJOR (corresponds roughly to U. S. Brigadier General)—Continued.

Name (age)	Appointment	Seniority	Origin	Arm
SAGERER		1/VIII/41	Bavaria	Inf
SALITTER, Fritz	A Training Area	1/IV/41		Arty
SAUCKEN, Dietrich v. (49)	A Pz Div	1/I/42		Cav
SAUVANT (52)	Arys Training Area, Wkr. I (1939)	1/III/42		Inf
SCHACKE		1/III/43		
SCHADE		1/VIII/41		Inf
SCHAEFFER	Cmdt of Kassel, Wkr. IX (1939)	1/II/41		Inf
SCHAEFER (50)		1/IV/42	Silesia	Inf
SCHAUM (52)		1/X/41		Pion
SCHAUWECKER (61)	Insp. of Recruiting Area Schleswig Holstein, Wkr. X (1939).			Sig C
SCHEFOLD (55)	707th Inf Div		Württemberg	Arty
SCHELLER (65)	Königsberg II, Wkr. I (admin) (1939)	1/VI/42		Arty
SCHELLMANN (61)		1/IV/41		Inf
SCHELLWITZ		1/I/43		Inf
SCHERBENING	406th Div z. b. V. (1941)	1/IX/41		Inf
SCHICKFUS u. NEUDORFF, Erich v. (62).		1/II/32		Inf
SCHILLING		1/XII/42		
SCHILLING, Walter (48)		1/VI/42		Cav
SCHINDKE		1/I/43		Cav
SCHLIEBEN, Dietrich v.		1/I/43		Cav
SCHLUETER, Robert		1/III/43		
SCHMETTOW, Graf v. (51)		1/IV/42	Silesia	Cav
SCHMIDT, Friedrich (51)	72d Inf Regt (46th Inf Div) (1939)	1/III/42		Inf
SCHMIDT, Otto	19th Pz Div	1/X/41		
SCHMIDT, Otto (51)	35th Inf Regt (12th Inf Div) (1940)	1/I/42		Inf
SCHMIDT-KOLBOW (63)				Arty
SCHMUNDT, Rudolf (55)	Chief Adjutant to Hitler; chief of H.P.A.	1/X/41		Inf

e. GENERALMAJOR (corresponds roughly to U. S. Brigadier General)—Continued.

Name (age)	Appointment	Seniority	Origin	Arm
SCHNARRENBERGER		1/XI/42		Inf
SCHNEIDEMESSER, Gustav v. (51)		1/VI/42		Inf
SCHNEIDER (59)	Chief Fortress Engineer, Wkr. XI (1941)	1/IV/40		Pion
SCHNEIDER, Erich		1/I/43		
SCHNEIDER, Friedrich	Berlin VIII, Wkr. III (admin) (1939)	1/IV/41		Inf
SCHNEIDER, Otto		1/XII/41		
SCHÖNBERG, Wilhelm (69)				Arty
SCHÖNFELDER, Fritz (52)	Chief Engineer, Wkr. XVII (1939)	1/IV/41	Saxony	Pion
SCHÖNFELDER, Kurt (72)	3d Arty Ers Regt (1941)			Arty
SCHÖNHERR, Otto		1/IX/41	Austria	Inf
SCHOLZ		1/VIII/42		
SCHREIBER, Alfred (51)		1/VI/42		Inf
SCHRÖDER (60)	Army Welfare Dept., Wkr. XX (1941)			Pion
SCHROETER, v. (52)		1/I/42		Cav
SCHROETTER, Dipl. Ing. (50)		1/IV/42		Tks
SCHUBERT, Rudolf (52)		1/IV/41		Sig C.
SCHUBERTH		1/VII/42		MT
SCHÜNEMANN		1/XI/42		Inf
SCHÜTZ, v		1/VII/42		
SCHÜTZE		1/VII/42		Arty
SCHULER, Rüdiger v. (52)		1/IX/41		Inf
SCHULZ, Friedrich (46)		1/VII/42		
SCHUNCK, Theodor (53)		1/VI/41		Arty
SCHUSTER, Friedrich (61)		1/I/42	Bavaria	Inf
SCHWALBE		1/X/42		Inf
SCHWARTZ (52)	Cmdt of Hagenau	1/VIII/41		H-DrT
SCHWERIN, Graf v		1/X/42		
SCULTETUS, Bruno (61)		1/XII/41		Inf
SCULTETUS, Herbert (62)		1/XII/41		Inf

e. GENERALMAJOR (corresponds roughly to U. S. Brigadier General)—Continued.

Name (age)	Appointment	Seniority	Origin	Arm
SEEGER (52)	292d Inf Div (1941)	1/IX/41	Württemberg	Inf
SEHMSDORF, Hans (55)	3d Supply Group (1941)	1/II/41		Inf
SENGER u. ETTERLIN, Fridolin v. (51)	Liaison with Italian Armistice Commission	1/IX/41	Baden	Cav
SENSFUSS, Franz		1/X/42		Pion
SEUFFERT, Franz (53)		1/XII/40	Bavaria	Inf
SICHART, Werner v. (61)	Kiel, Wkr. X (admin)	1/IX/41	Saxony	Inf
SIEGLIN, Kurt (58)			Württemberg	Inf
SIELER		1/I/43		Inf
SIXT, Friedrich (48)	C of S, XXXXIV Corps (1940).	1/VI/42	Bavaria	Arty
SOHN (59)	Chief Supply O, Wkr. XVII (1941).	1/IX/41		Arty
SOUCHAY		1/VIII/42		Inf
SPECHT, Karl-Wilhelm		1/VIII/42		
SPEIDEL, Dr. Hans	C of S, Occupied France.	1/I/43		Inf
SPENGLER		1/III/43		Inf
SPETH		1/I/43		Arty
SPONECK, Graf v.	90th Light Div	1/XI/42		
STAHR, Wolfgang (51)	II Armorer School (1941).	1/IV/42	Saxony	Inf
STAMM		1/VII/42		
STAMMER		1/IX/42		Inf
STEIGLEHNER		1/VIII/42		
STEIN, v.	Cmdt of Leipzig	1/VII/42		Inf
STEINBACH, Paul (53)	Chief Supply O, Wkr. XX (1941)	1/X/41	Bavaria	Arty
STEINMETZ		1/I/43		Arty
STENZEL, Richard	An Arty Regt	1/IV/42	Austria	Arty
STEUDNER (63)	C of S, Wkr. II (1941)			Arty
STOCKHAUSEN, Dipl. Ing. v. (48)	281st Sich Div	1/IV/41	Hesse	Inf
STOCKHAUSEN, v. (71)	Feldkdtr. 816	1/X/41		

e. GENERALMAJOR (corresponds roughly to U. S. Brigadier General)—Continued.

Name (age)	Appointment	Seniority	Origin	Arm
STRACK, Karl (51)	253rd Inf Regt (34 Inf Div) (1940).	1/II/42		Inf
STREICH, Hans (51)		1/II/41		Tks
STUBENRAUCH, Wilhelm (57)		1/VI/41	Saxony	Cav
STÜLPNAGEL, Siegfried v. (51)	Cmdt of Stettin, Wkr. II	1/VI/42		Inf
STUMM, Berthold (51)		1/VI/42		Inf
STUMPFELD, v. (57)	Landwehr Training O, Hamburg, Wkr. X (1939)	1/X/40		Arty
STURM		1/II/43		Inf
TAEGLICHSBECK		1/II/43		Inf
TANN-RATHSAMHAUSEN, Reichsfrhr. v. u. zu der (58).	C of S, Wkr. XVIII?	1/VII/42		
TARBUK, Johann	Nikolsburg, Wkr. XVII (admin) (1939)	1/VIII/41	Austria	Inf
TESCHNER (70)			Baden	Inf
THÄTER, Maximilian (64)	Würzburg, Wkr. XIII (admin) (1939)	1/XII/41	Bavaria	Inf
THAMS	Brdy-Wald Training Area (1939)	1/III/41		Inf
THEISS, Rudolf		1/IX/41	Austria	Tks
THIELE, Fritz	Chief of Sig Comd Sec, O. K. W.	1/X/42		
THOENISSEN		1/VIII/42		
THOMA, Heinrich (52)		1/IX/41	Bavaria	Inf
THOMAS (54)	2d Engineer School, Dessau-Rosslau, Wkr. XI (1939)	1/XI/40		Pion
THOMAS, Alfred		1/XII/42		
THOMAS, Wilhelm		1/V/42		
THON, Friedrich (67)	Insp of Sig Troops			Sig C
THÜNGEN, Karl Frhr. v. (49)		1/XII/41	Bavaria	Cav
TRAUCH, Rudolf (50)	Head of a Section, O. K. H. (1940)	1/X/41	Bavaria	H-DrT
TRESCKOW, Joachim v. (49)	328th Inf Div	1/VI/42		Inf
TRÖGER		1/I/43		Cav
TSCHAMMER u. OSTEN, Eckart v. (55).	Landwehr Training O, Dortmund, Wkr. VI (1939)	1/XII/40		Inf

e. GENERALMAJOR (corresponds roughly to U. S. Brigadier General)—Continued.

Name (age)	Appointment	Seniority	Origin	Arm
TSCHUDI-JACOBSEN, Heinrich v.		1/II/43		
UBL, Bruno		1/VII/42	Austria	Inf
UCKERMANN, Horst Frhr. v. (51).	218th Inf Div	1/II/42		Inf.
UNRUH, Walter Willy Hermann v.	Cmdt of Warsaw			
USEDOM, v.		1/I/43		Cav
USINGER		1/XII/42		
VASSOLL (59)	An Arty Regt (1941)	1/VI/42		Arty
VATERRODT	Cmdt of Strassburg	1/III/41		Inf
VIEBAHN, v.		1/VII/42		Inf
VOGEL, Emil	101st Lt Div	1/X/42		
VOIGT, Adolf		1/VII/42		
VOIT, Paul (67)	C of S, Wkr. XIII (1941)	1/IV/38	Bavaria	Inf
VOLCKAMER u. KIRCHENSITTENBACH		1/IX/42		Inf
VORMANN, v.		1/I/43		Inf
VOSS, Erich	Staff of Wkr. VIII (1941)	1/VI/42		SigC
WAGNER, Georg (62)	Halberstadt, Wkr. XI (admin) (1939)	1/IV/41		Inf
WAGNER, Paul		1/I/43		
WAHLE	Military Cmdt of Hamburg	1/VII/42		Inf
WARNICKE (61)	Staff of Wkr. I (1939)	1/VIII/41		H-DrT
WARTENBURG, v.		1/I/43		
WEBER				
WEBER, Friedrich (44)	334th Inf Div	1/I/43		
WEBERN, v.		1/X/42		Arty
WECKMANN	C of S, Ninth Army	1/II/42		Inf
WEISS, Wilhelm	138th Inf Regt (2d Mtn Div) (1940)	1/X/41	Austria	Inf
WENCK, Walter (44)	With Gen Staff of Army Group Don	1/II/43		Inf
WENING, Ernst (58)	Landwehr Training O, Innsbruck, Wkr. XVIII (1939)	1/VI/41	Bavaria	Cav

e. GENERALMAJOR (corresponds roughly to U. S. Brigadier General)—Continued.

Name (age)	Appointment	Seniority	Origin	Arm
WERTHERN, Georg Thilo Frhr. v. (51).		1/VI/40		Arty
WESTHOVEN		1/VIII/42		Cav
WIEROW, Dipl. Ing		1/X/42		
WILKE, Kurt		1/XII/42		
WINKLER, Hermann (54)	Psychological Tests Dept, Wkr. II (1939)	1/VII/41	Saxony	Inf
WINTER, Paul (49)	Head of a Section, O. K. H. (1939)	1/XI/41	Bavaria	Arty
WINTERGERST, Karl (50)		1/IV/42	Bavaria	Arty
WIRTZ (51)	Chief Engineer, VII Inf Corps (1939)	1/IV/42		Pion
WISSELINCK		1/III/43		
WITZLEBEN, Hermann v. (51)		1/VI/42		Cav
WOLFSBERGER, Franz	CG Latvia (1941)	1/VII/41	Austria	Inf
WOLPERT, Johann (53)	Cmdt of Nürnberg, Wkr. XIII (1940)	1/IX/41	Bavaria	Inf
WUERST		1/I/43		
WULZ		1/XI/42		Arty
WUTHMANN, Rolf	C of S, Sixteenth Army	1/IV/42		Arty
ZAHN, Alois (52)		1/VIII/41	Württemberg	Inf
ZANTHIER, v. (52)	349th Inf Regt (181st Inf Div) (1941)	1/X/41		Inf
ZEDNICEK, Franz		1/IV/42	Austria	Pion
ZEISS		1/VII/42		H DrT
ZEITZ, Erich (55)		1/II/41	Bavaria	Cav
ZELLNER, Emil	C of S, Wkr. XVII (1941)	1/IV/41	Austria	Inf
ZELTMANN		1/I/43		
ZIEGENRÜCKER		1/II/43		
ZUKERTORT, Karl (53)	Head of Section, Army Ordnance O (1939)	1/IV/40	Saxony	MT
ZUNEHMER				Inf
ZUTAVERN (50)		1/VI/42	Baden	Arty

74. General Staff Corps Officers.

Rank	Name	Rank	Name
Obst	ADAM, Kurt	Maj	BLÜMKE
Maj	AHLEFELD, v.	Maj	BLUMRÖDER, v.
Maj	ALBEDYLL, Frhr. v.	Hptm	BOEHLES
Hptm	AMSBERG, Rik. v.	Hptm	BOEHM, Eberhard
Hptm	ANNUSS	Obst	BÖHME
Obstlt	ASSMANN	Maj	BOELTZIG, Hans Dietrich v.
Obstlt	BABEL, Ottomar	Obst	BOGEN u. SCHÖNSTEDT, v.
Obstlt	BACKHAUS	Maj	BONIN, Bogislav
Obstlt	BADER	Maj	BONTE
Hptm	BAER, v.	Obst	BORK
Hptm	BANG, Gunter	Maj	BOTH, v.
Maj	BARCHEWITZ	Maj	BRANDSTÄDTER
Hptm	BAUMANN	Maj	BRANDT, Heinz
Obst	BAUR	Hptm	BRAUN, Kurt
Obst	BAYERLEIN	Maj	BREITHAUPT
Obstlt	BEHLE, Hans	Maj	BROCKDORFF, Friedrich Baron v.
Maj	BEICHELE	Maj	BRUNN, v.
Obstlt	BEIGEL	Maj	BRUSCHKE
Maj	BELOW, Nicolaus v.	Obst	BUCHER
Maj	BENNECKE, Jürgen	Maj	BÜNAU, v.
Maj	BERGER	Obst	BÜRKER, Ulrich
Obstlt	BERGER, Claus	Obst	BUTTLAR, v.
Hptm	BERLICHINGEN-JAGSTHAUSEN, Frhr. v.	Obstlt	CLAUSIUS
Maj	BERLIN	Obst	CLAUSS, Joachim
Maj	BERLING	Maj	COELIN, v.
Maj	BERNSTORFF, v.	Obst	COLLANI, v.
Hptm	BEUCK	Maj	COLLASIUS
Obst	BEUTLER, Otto	Maj	CONRAD
Hptm	BIELITZ	Maj	CRIEGERN, Fritz v.
Obstlt	BLAUROCK	Obst	CROME
Hptm	BLEICKEN, Otto Heinrich	Maj	DAHMS, Hans-Jochen
Obst	BLOCH v. BLOTTNITZ, Johann Gottlob	Maj	DANKE

74. General Staff Corps Officers—Continued.

Rank	Name	Rank	Name
Obstlt	DAWANS, Ritter u. Edler v.	Maj	FÄHNDRICK
Obstlt	DEEGENER	Maj	FAUNER
Hptm	DEHLE, Otto	Obst	FELLER, Gustav
Obst	DEINHARDT	Maj	FINCK, Frhr. v.
Hptm	DERSCHAU, Christoph Friedrich v.	Obst	FLECK, Hans
Obst	DEUTELMOSER	Maj	FRANKENBERG u. LUDWIGSDORF, Wolf v.
Maj	DEYHLE, Willy	Obst	FRANZ
Obst	DIERMAYER	Obst	FREGE
Obst	DIESENER, Paul	Obst	FREYTAG v. LORINGHOVEN, Wessel Baron
Maj	DIETL	Obstlt	FRIEBE
Maj	DINGLER	Maj	FROVERT
Maj	DISSELL, Gerhard	Obst	GEBAUER, Hans
Hptm	DOBSCHÜTZ, v.	Obstlt	GELDERN-CRISPENDORF, Joachim v.
Hptm	DOEPNER	Obst	GERLACH, Erwin
Obst	DOERR, Hans	Maj	GIESE, Karl
Maj	DONKE	Obstlt	GITTNER, Hans
Obst	DORN, Hellmuth	Obst	GLASL, Anton
Maj	DRABICH-WAECHTER, v.	Maj	GOLDAMMER, v.
Maj	DRESCHER	Maj	GOSS, Ritter v.
Rittm	DREWS, Werner	Obst	GOTH
Hptm	DUENSING	Maj	GRABS
Maj	DÜRLING, v.	Maj	GRAEVENITZ, v.
Maj	EHLERT, Hans	Maj	GREME
Obst	EHRIG, Werner	Obstlt	GROBLER
Maj	EICHLER	Maj	GROEBEN, Peter v. der
Maj	EINBECK	Obstlt	GRÖPLER, Erich
Maj	EINEM, v.	Obstlt	GROLMANN, Helmuth v.
Maj	ELCHEPP	Maj	GROME
Obstlt	ELVERFELDT, Frhr. v.	Hptm	GRONEMANN-SCHÖNBORN
Obstlt	EMMERICH, Albert		
Maj	ENGELHORN	Hptm	GUNDELACH
Hptm	EPPENDORFF		
Hptm	ERHARDT, Kurt	Obst	GYLDENFELDT, v.

74. General Staff Corps Officers—Continued.

Rank	Name	Rank	Name
Hptm	HAACKE, v.	Maj	HUHS
Obstlt	HAAS	Obst	IRKENS
Maj	HAINRICH	Obstlt	JACOBI, Georg
Maj	HAMBERGER	Maj	JACOBI, Dr.
Hptm	HAMMERSTEIN-GESMOLD, Frhr. v.	Maj	JAIS, Franz
Obstlt	HARBOU, v.	Obst	JANK
Hptm	HARLING, v.	Hptm	JENA, Egbert v.
Obst	HAUCK	Maj	JESSEL
Maj	HAUSER	Maj	JOHN
Hptm	HAYESSEN	Obst	KAHLEN, v.
Obstlt	HEIDER	Obst	KAUFMANN, v.
Obst	HEIDKÄMPER	Hptm	KESSEL, Guido v.
Maj	HEINRICH	Maj	KIELMANSEGG, Graf v.
Obst	HEISTERMANN v. ZIEHLBERG, Gustav	Maj	KIENLE, Ritter u. Edler v.
Obst	HEITERER-SCHALLER, Ritter v.	Obstlt	KIRCHBACH, Hans Hugo Graf v.
Maj	HELBIG	Hptm	KLARHOEFER
Maj	HERBER	Maj	KLEINSCHMIT
Obstlt	HERRBERG, Friedrich	Maj	KLEIST, v.
Hptm	HERRE	Maj	KLIMKE
Hptm	HERZOG	Hptm	KLINCKOWSTROEM, Karl Heinrich Graf v.
Obstlt	HESSE	Obstlt	KLOTZ, Karl
Hptm	HESSE	Hptm	KLUGE, v.
Hptm	HEYSE	Obst	KNESCH
Hptm	HILGERT	Hptm	KNESEBECK, v. der
Hptm	HINRICH, Otto	Obstlt	KNOLL
Hptm	HOBE, Cord v.	Maj	KNÜPPEL, Wilhelm
Maj	HOEFS	Obst	KOCH
Obstlt	HÖLTER	Maj	KOEHN
Hptm	HOLZHAUSEN, v.	Obstlt	KÖLLER, v.
Obst	HORN, v.	Obstlt	KOERBLER, Dr.
Hptm	HÜBNER	Obst	KOERNER, Karl Theodor
Obst	HÜNERSDORFF, v.	Maj	KÖRNER, Gottfried

74. General Staff Corps Officers—Continued.

Rank	Name	Rank	Name
Maj	KÖSTLIN	Maj	LORENZ
Hptm	KOLLER-KRAUS	Maj	LORT
Obst	KOPECKY, Karl	Obst	LOSSBERG, Bernard v.
Maj	KRANTZ, Hans Ulrich	Obst	LUDWIGER, v.
Obst	KREMLING, Ludwig	Hptm	LÜHL
Maj	KRIEBEL, Rainer	Obstlt	LYNCKER, Julius
Obstlt	KRIEGSHEIM, v.	Obstlt	MAAS
Obst	KROSIGK, v.	Maj	MALTZAHN, Frhr. v.
Hptm	KRÜGER, Wolfgang	Maj	MARKERT
Hptm	KRUSEMANN	Obstlt	MELLENTHIN, Friedrich Wilhelm
Hptm	KUBAN	Obst	MELLENTHIN, Horst v.
Obst	KÜHL, Claus	Maj	MENGDEN v. ALTENWOGA, Baron
Hptm	KÜHLEIN		
Obstlt	KÜHNE, Gerhard	Obstlt	MENSING
Maj	KUHNEMANN	Obst	MERIDIES, Walter
Obst	KULLMER, Artur	Maj	MERKEL
Hptm	KUTZBACH, Freidrich	Obst	MERKER
Obst	LAEGLEER	Maj	MERTZ v. QUIRNHEIM, Ritter
Obst	LAHOUSEN, Erwin	Maj	METZ, Lothar
Maj	LAMPE	Maj	MEYER, Hans Gerhard
Hptm	LANGE	Maj	MEYER-DETRING
Obst	LANGE, Wolfgang	Hptm	MICHALSKY
Obstlt	LANGHAEUSER	Hptm	MOLL, Dietrich
Maj	LEUTHEUSSEN	Hptm	MOSER
Hptm	LIEBE	Maj	MÜLLER, Christian
Obst	LIEBENSTEIN, Kurt Frhr. v.	Obst	MÜLLER, Gerhard Dipl. Ing.
Hptm	LIESE	Maj	MÜLLER
Maj	LIESNER	Hptm	MÜLLER
Hptm	LINDEQUIST, Olaf v.	Hptm	MÜLLER, Hans
Hptm	LINKE, Ernst	Hptm	MÜLLER, Heinrich
Obstlt	LINSTOW, v.	Obst	MÜLLER-HILLEBRAND
Obstlt	LÖHR, Erich	Hptm	MÜNSTER, Eberhard Graf zu
Obst	LONGIN, Anton		

74. General Staff Corps Officers—Continued.

Rank	Name	Rank	Name
Maj	MÜRAU	Hptm	PLATE, Claus Henning v.
Hptm	MUSCHNER	Rittm	PLEHWE, v.
Hptm	NAGEL	Hptm	PLÜCKNER
Maj	NATZMER, Oldwig v.	Obst	POHLMANN
Hptm	NECKELMANN	Maj	PRAHST
Maj	NECKER	Maj	PREUSSE
Hptm	NEITZEL	Maj	PRITTWITZ u. GAFFRON Hans Eberhard v.
Maj	NIEMEYER	Obstlt	PRITZBUER, Dietrich v.
Hptm	NIEPOLD, Gerd	Obst	PÜCKLER, Graf v.
Maj	NIEPOLD, Horst	Obst	QUAST, August Viktor v.
Maj	NIKLAUS	Maj	RADTKE
Maj	NOLTE	Maj	RANCK, Werner
Obst	NÜRNBERG	Obst	RASP
Obst	OCHSNER, Wilhelm	Obst	RAUCHHAUPT, Wilhelm v.
Hptm	OETJEN	Obstlt	REICHELT
Hptm	OGILVIE	Obst	REINHARD, Walter
Maj	OHRLOFF	Hptm	REISSINGER
Hptm	ORLIK	Maj	REISSINGER
Obstlt	OSCHLIES	Hptm	RENVERS, Leopold v.
Rittm	OSSWALD	Maj	RICHERT
Maj	PANTOW, Heinz	Maj	RICHTER
Hptm	PAUMGARTTEN	Obst	RITTBERG, Georg Graf v.
Obst	PEMSEL, Max	Maj	ROEDENBECK, Walter
Obstlt	PETERSDORF, Dr. Fritz Julius v.	Maj	ROEDER, Wilhelm
Hptm	PETERSEN	Hptm	ROESTEL
Maj	PETRI	Maj	ROSENTHAL, Ritter u. Edler v.
Obst	PFAFFEROTT	Obstlt	ROSSMANN
Hptm	PFISTER, v.	Hptm	RUBESCH, v.
Maj	PFLANZ	Maj	RÜDEN, Heinz Friedrich
Maj	PHILIPPI	Hptm	RÜMENAPP
Maj	PICOT	Maj	SAPAUSCHKE
Hptm	PISTORIUS	Hptm	SASS
Hptm	PLANITZ, Ferdinand Edler v. d.		

74. General Staff Corps Officers—Continued.

Rank	Name	Rank	Name
Hptm	SAUERBRUCH, Peter	Obst	SERINI
Obstlt	SAUBERZWEIG	Hptm	SIEDSCHLAG
Obstlt	SCHAEWEN, v.	Obst	SIEWERT, Curt
Maj	SCHÄFER, Lothar	Hptm	SIMONS, Ulrich
Obst	SCHAFFITZEL	Maj	SITTMANN
Obstlt	SCHANZE, Ludwig	Hptm	SOBBE, v.
Hptm	SCHELLER, Heinz Eberhard	Maj	SOSNA
Obstlt	SCHERFF, Walter	Obst	SPERL
Obstlt	SCHEUERPFLUG	Maj	SPRENGER
Obst	SCHIEL	Maj	STAATS
Hptm	SCHIELE	Maj	STAEDKE
Maj	SCHILDKNECHT	Maj	STANGE
Obst	SCHIPP v. BRANITZ, Joachim	Maj	STARKE, Robert
Maj	SCHIRNICK	Maj	STAUBWASSER, Anton
Maj	SCHLEUSENER	Maj	STEETS
Maj	SCHLIEPER	Obstlt	STEFFLER
Obst	SCHMIDT, Hans	Maj	STEINSDORFF, v.
Obst	SCHMIDT-RICHBERG	Obstlt	STEUBEN, v.
Hptm	SCHMIDT v. ALTENSTADT	Maj	STIRIUS
Hptm	SCHNEIDER	Rittm	STOCKHAUSEN, Hans August v.
Obstlt	SCHNIEWIND	Maj	STORP
Obst	SCHOCH, Hans Wolfgang	Obst	STRACHWITZ, Frhr. v.
Obstlt	SCHOLL, Friedrich Wilhelm	Hptm	STRACHWITZ, Heinrich Graf
Obstlt	SCHUCHARDT	Obst	STAUDINGER, Hans Heinrich
Obst	SCHULZ, Otto	Maj	SÜSSKIND-SCHWENDI, Frhr v.
Maj	SCHUMANN		
Maj	SCHWANBECK	Obst	SUIRE, von le
Hptm	SCHWANDNER	Maj	TEIN, v.
Obst	SCULTETUS	Maj	TEMPELHOFF, Hans Georg v.
Maj	SCUPIN	Maj	TESKE
Hptm	SEEBACH, v.	Obst	THADDEN v.
Rittm	SEELE	Obstlt	THEILACKER
Hptm	SENGPIEL	Maj	THEYSOHN

74. General Staff Corps Officers—Continued.

Rank	Name	Rank	Name
Hptm	THILO	Hptm	WELCK, Frhr. v.
Obstlt	TIPPELSKIRCH, Werner v.	Obstlt	WERDER, v.
Maj	TOPPE, Alfred	Obst	WESTPHAL, Siegfried
Obstlt	TROTHA, v.	Maj	WIDEKIND, y.
Obst	TSCHIRDEWAHN	Maj	WIESE
Hptm	TUMMELEY	Obstlt	WILHELMI, Hans
Hptm	ÜBELHACK	Maj	WILLEMER
Obstlt	ULRICH, Justus	Obst	WINTER, August
Maj	UNGER, v.	Obst	WISSMANN
Obstlt	VOELTER	Hptm	WOITE
Hptm	VOLLARD-BOCKELBERG, v.	Maj	WOITE
Obst	VORMANN, Nikolaus v.	Obst	WOLF, Friedrich
Maj	VORWERCK	Hptm	WOLFF
Maj	VOSS, Hans Alexander v.	Obst	WOLFF, Erich
Hptm	VOSS, Wilhelm	Maj	WOLFF, Werner
Maj	WAGENER, Otto	Maj	WÜHLISCH, Georg v.
Hptm	WAGNER, Gunter	Obstlt	WUTHENAU, v.
Obst	WAGNER, Herbert	Obst	XYLANDER, Rudolf Ritter v.
Obstlt	WAHL	Maj	ZELTMANN
Hptm	WANGENHEIM, Horst Frhr. v.	Maj	ZERBEL, Alfred
Rittm	WANGENHEIM, Konrad Frhr. v.	Hptm	ZIEGELMANN
		Obst	ZIEGLER, Joachim
Maj	WARBURG, v.	Maj	ZIEGLER v. KLIPPHAUSEN, v.
Hptm	WEBER, Josef		
Hptm	WEDEL, v.	Maj	ZIERVOGEL
Obst	WEINKNECHT	Obstlt	ZIPP
Obst	WEISE, Hans v.	Obstlt	ZITZEWITZ, v.
Hptm	WEITZ	Maj	ZOELLER

75. Air Force Officers.

a. REICHSMARSCHALL (Marshal of the Reich)

(Name) (Age)	Command	Seniority	Origin
GÖRING, Hermann (50)	C-in-C Air Force	19/VII/40	Bavaria.

b. GENERALFELDMARSCHALL (Field Marshal)

(Name) (Age)	Command	Seniority	Origin
KESSELRING, Albert (58)	Second Air Fleet and C-in-C South.	19/VII/40	Bavaria.
MILCH, Erhard (51)	Inspector General, Air Force	19/VII/40	
RICHTHOFEN, Dipl. Ing. Wolfram Frhr. v. (48).	Fourth Air Fleet	16/III/43	
SPERRLE, Hugo (58)	Third Air Fleet	19/VII/40	Württemberg

c. GENERALOBERST (corresponds roughly to U. S. General)

(Name) (Age)	Command	Seniority	Origin
GREIM, Robert Ritter v. (51)	V Air Corps (formerly)	16/II/43	Bavaria
JESCHONNEK, Hans (44)	C of S, Air Force	1/III/42	
KELLER, Alfred (61)	First Air Fleet	19/VII/40	
LÖHR, Alexander (58)	Army Group E	/41	Austria
LOERZER, Bruno (52)	II Air Corps (formerly)	16/II/43	
RÜDEL, Günther (60)	Chief of Air Defense (RLM)	17/XI/42	Lorraine
STUMPFF, Hans Jürgen (54)	Fifth Air Fleet	19/VII/40	
WEISE, Hubert (59)	AA Command	19/VII/40	

d. GENERAL d. FLIEGER, FLAKARTILLERIE, LUFTWAFFE, LUFTNACHRICHTENTRUPPEN (corresponds roughly to U. S. Lieutenant General).

(Name) (Age)	Command	Seniority	Origin
ANDRAE, Waldemar (53)		1/VII/41	
BIENECK, Hellmuth (56)	Luftgau II	1/VII/41	
BODENSCHATZ, Karl (53)	C of S to Göring and Independent Bomber Comd.	1/VII/41	Bavaria
BOGATSCH, Rudolf (53)	Liaison w. O. K. H	1/VII/41	
CHRISTIANSEN, Friedrich (64)	C G Holland	1/I/39	
COELER, Joachim (52)	IX Air Corps	1/I/42	
DANCKELMANN (55)		1/IV/41	Bavaria
DESSLOCH, Otto (54)	II AA Corps	1/I/42	Bavaria
DOERSTLING, Egon (54)	Supply Depot, R. L. M	1/VI/42	Saxony
DRANSFELD, Eduard (60)	Insp. of MT (R. L. M.)	1/X/40	
FELMY, Helmuth (58)		1/II/38	
FIEBIG	An Air Corps	30/I/43	
FISCHER, Veit	Luftgaustab z. b. V. 2	1/VI/42	
FÖRSTER, Hellmuth (54)	I Air Corps	1/V/41	
GEISSLER, Hans (52)	X Air Corps	19/VII/40	
GOSSRAU, Karl Siegfried (62)	Admin Dept, R. L. M	1/IX/41	Württemberg
HARMJANZ, Willi (52)	Luftgau Norway	1/X/42	
HAUBOLD, Alfred (55)	Luftgau III	1/X/41	Saxony
HEILINGBRUNNER, Friedrich (52)	Luftgau XIII	1/VII/42	Bavaria
HIRSCHHAUER, Friedrich (60).	Pres Luftschutzbund and Luftgau XVII	1/VIII/39	Bavaria
HOFFMANN (52)	AA Liaison with Rumanian Air Force	1/XII/42	
DÖRING, Kurt Bertrau v. (54)	Fighter Command Second Air Fleet.	1/XI/41	
DRUM, Karl		1/I/43	Baden
EGAN-KRIEGER, v		1/XII/42	
FAHNERT, Friedrich (64)	Air Signal Tng Regt	1/I/43	Saxony
FEYERABEND, Walter (52)	AA Command, Norway	1/IV/41	
FINK, Dipl. Ing	Accidents Section, R. L. M	1/X/42	Württemberg
FRANSSEN,	Insp Armaments, Belgium	1/VIII/42	

d. GENERAL d. FLIEGER, FLAKARTILLERIE, LUFTWAFFE, LUFTNACHRICHTENTRUPPEN (corresponds roughly to U. S. Lieutenant General)—Continued.

(Name) (Age)	Command	Seniority	Origin
FRIEDENSBURG, Walter	Insp of Armaments Wkr. IV	1/XII/41	
FRÖLICH, Stephan (54)		1/I/42	Austria
GAUTIER	Insp of Armaments Wkr. XVII	1/IV/41	
HAEHNELT, Wilhelm (68)	War Science Dept (1939)	1/XII/40	
HANESSE (52)	Air Liaison Staff Occupied France	1/IV/42	Hesse
HOFFMAN v. WALDAU, Otto (46)		30/I/43	Silesia
KAMMHUBER, Josef	XII Air Corps (Night Fighter Div)	30/I/43	Bavaria
KASTNER-KIRDORF, Gustav (62)	Personnel Dept., R. L. M.	1/VII/41	
KITZINGER, Karl (58)	C G, Ukraine	1/X/39	
KLEPKE, Waldemar (61)	Insp of Reconnaissance and Photography.	1/I/39	Silesia
KORTEN, Günther	C of S, Fourth Air Fleet	30/I/43	
KÜHL, Leonhard (58)	Director of Training, R. L. M.	1/IV/39	
MARTINI, Hermann (52)	C Sig O Air Force	20/IX/41	Saxony
MAYER, Wilhelm (57)	Luftgau IV	1/II/41	
MOHR	Luftgau I	1/IV/41	
ODEBRECHT	AA Regt 8	1/XII/42	
OPITZ, Dr. Ing	In R. L. M		
PETERSEN (52)	Fliegerdiv 7	1/XI/42	
PFLUGBEIL, Kurt (53)	IV Air Corps	1/II/42	Saxony
POHL, Erich Ritter v	Air Attache, Rome, and Chief Liaison Officer with Italian Air Force	1/II/42	Bavaria
PUTZIER (52)	Staff of Second Air Fleet	1/VII/42	
QUADE, Erich (60)	Public Relations	1/IX/40	Hesse
RENZ, v. (52)	AA	1/II/43	Baden
RITTER, Hans (51)	Liaison with Navy	1/IV/42	
RUGGERA, Kamillo	AA Luftgau II	1/XII/40	Austria
SCHLEMM	Staff of XI Air Corps	30/I/43	
SCHMIDT, August	AA Luftgau VI	1/VII/41	
SCHMIDT, Hugo	Luftgau VI (?)	1/VII/41	

d. GENERAL d. FLIEGER, FLAKARTILLERIE, LUFTWAFFE, LUFTNACHRICHTENTRUPPEN (corresponds roughly to U. S. Lieutenant General)—Continued.

(Name) (Age)	Command	Seniority	Origin
SCHUBERT, Dr. (55)	Chief of Mil Economics and Armaments Staff East	1/VII/42	Saxony
SCHULZ (54)	Insp of Air Force Schools	1/XII/42	Hesse
SCHWEIKHARD, Karl (61)	Retired (?)	1/VI/38	Baden
SEIDEL, Hans Georg v. (52)	Gen Qu Air Force	1/I/42	
SIBURG, Ing Hans (50)	Luftgau, Holland	1/IV/42	
SOMME, Walter (56)	Cmdr of Flying Schools & Ersatz Bn 3, Berlin.	1/VI/42	
SPEIDEL, Wilhelm	Chief of Air Mission to Rumania.	1/I/42	Württemberg
STUDENT, Kurt (53)	XI Air Corps	30/V/40	
VIERLING, Albert (57)	Luftgaustab z. b. V. 4	1/VI/42	Bavaria
WABER	Luftgau Kiev	1/III/42	Austria
WEISSMANN, Dr. Eugen (52)	AA Luftgau XII	1/VI/42	Württemberg
WENNINGER, Rudolf (53)		1/XI/40	Bavaria
WIMMER, Wilhelm (54)	Luftgau Belgium and N France.	1/X/39	Bavaria
WITZENDORFF, Bodo v. (67)	Chief of Central Div in R. L. M.	1/II/39	
WOLFF, Ludwig (57)	Luftgau XI	1/II/41	
ZANDER, Konrad (60)	Coastal Airforce	1/IV/38	
ZENETTI, Emil (60)	Luftgau VII	1/II/41	Austria

e. GENERALLEUTNANT (corresponds roughly to U. S. Major General).

(Name) (Age)	Command	Seniority	Origin
AXTHELM, Walter v. (50)	I AA Corps	1/X/42	Bavaria
BARLEN, Karl (52)		1/IV/41	
BECKER, Hermann		1/XI/42	
BRÄUER, Bruno (51)	OG Crete		
BRUCH, Hermann (60)	KG 30 and Fliegerführer N Norway	1/XI/40	
BÜLOW, Hilmer Frhr. v.	Military Science Dept, R. L. M.	1/IV/41	

e. GENERALLEUTNANT (corresponds roughly to U. S. Major General)—Continued.

(Name) (Age)	Command	Seniority	Origin
BUFFA, Ernst (51)	A Flak Div (17/I/43)	1/II/43	
BURCHARD, Dipl. Ing. Heinrich	C of S Luftgau XII	1/VIII/42	
CARLSEN	In Luftgau IX	1/I/40	
CRANZ (55)	Training Cmd, Prague	1/XI/40	
DEINHARDT		1/I/42	
HERMANN	Cmdt of Pilsen	1/XI/40	
HIPPKE	Insp of Med Corps (LW)	22/VIII/41	
KARLEWSKI			
KEIPER	Head of Air Mission to Slovakia	1/I/43	
KESSLER (52)	Air Cmdr Atlantic	1/IV/41	
KIEFFER, Maximilian (52)	Koluft of an Army Gp	1/VI/42	Bavaria
KNAUSS, Dr. (53)		1/VIII/42	Württemberg
KOLB, Alexander (54)	AA Air Defense Command Stettin (1939)	1/X/40	
KROCKER, Viktor (54)		1/XII/41	
KÜHNE	C Sig O, Fifth Air Fleet	1/VI/42	
LACKNER, Walther (52)	Blind Flying School, Königsberg	1/XII/42	
LANGEMEYER, Otto (58)	Staff of Luftflotte 4	1/IV/42	
LECH	AA	1/XI/40	
LENTZSCH, Johannes (59)	AA (?)	1/III/38	
LINDNER	Sig School, Halle	1/VIII/41	
LORENZ, Walter	Staff of Fifth Air Fleet	1/II/43	
MACKENZEN v. ASTFELD		1/IV/41	
MAHNCKE, Alfred (55)	A Luftgau	1/XI/40	
MANN, Hermann Edler v. TIECHLER, Ritter v. (54)		1/XI/40	Bavaria
MEISTER		1/III/43	
MERTITSCH (51)	Head of a section, R. L. M. (1939)	1/X/42	
MOLL (57)		1/IV/42	
MOOYER	Pre-military Training, R. L. M.	1/IV/41	
MÜLLER, Ernst	6 Air Supply Group	1/I/42	
MUSSHOFF	Luftgaustab z. b. V. (110)	1/XI/40	

e. GENERALLEUTNANT (corresponds roughly to U. S. Major General)—Continued.

(Name) (Age)	Command	Seniority	Origin
NIEHOFF, Heinrich (60)	Oberfeldkdtr. 670, Lille	1/II/38	
OSTERKAMP, Theodor (51)	Luftgaustab z. b. V. Africa	1/VIII/42	
RAMCKE, Hermann Bernhard	Ramcke Brigade	21/XII/42	
RICHTER, Hellmuth (52)	AA at R. L. M	1/VIII/41	
RÖMER, Erwin v. (55)	Zingst Training Area	1/IV/41	Saxony
RÜDT v. COELENBERG, Kurt Frhr. (61).	Insp of Armaments, Paris and NW France	1/VII/42	
SATTIER, Otfried (57)	Hamburg Air Defense District.	1/I/40	
SCHEURLEN		1/XI/42	
SCHMIDT, Kurt (56)		1/I/40	Saxony
SCHUBERT	Staff of Second Air Fleet	1/IV/42	
SCHUBERT		1/XI/42	
SCHULTHEISS, Pavel (51)		1/I/43	Württemberg
SCHWABEDISSEN, Walter	C of S Holland	1/VIII/42	
SCHWUB, Albert (56)	Mechanics School, Halle	1/X/40	Bavaria
SEIFERT, Johann	10th AA Div	1/VI/42	Austria
SOMMER, Johannes (56)		1/III/40	Württemberg
SPANG, Willibald (56)	Head of Meteorological Services, R. L. M.	1/I/42	Württemberg
SPIESS (52)	AA Hamburg	1/VIII/41	
STEUDEMANN, Kurt (53)	AA Insp R. L. M	1/I/41	Saxony
STUBENRAUCH, Wilhelm v.	AA	1/VI/42	
SUREN (55)	C Sig O, Fourth Air Fleet	1/IV/41	
TAYSEN, Adalbert v.	Rcn Flyers School 2	1/VII/42	
WAGNER	VI AA Brigade	1/XI/42	
WALZ, Franz Josef (58)	Chief of Civil Air Office RLM (1939).	1/IV/41	Bavaria
WECKE	Air Defense Zone, Slovakia	1/VIII/40	
WEIGAND, Dipl. Volksw. Wolfgang (58).	Inspector of Armaments Army Group Center	1/XI/40	
WITTING (53)	General Insp for Raw Materials	1/II/41	
WÜHLISCH, Heinz Helmut v. (52).	Prisoner of War	1/IV/42	
ZIEGLER, Dr. Günther		1/II/43	
ZOCH, Phillip (52)	Koluft, Sixteenth Army	1/IV/42	

f. **GENERALMAJOR** (corresponds roughly to U. S. Brigadier General).

Name (age)	Command	Seniority	Origin
ADAMETZ		1/II/41	
ANGERSTEIN (53)	KG 1	1/V/42	Alsace
ANTON		1/II/42	
ARNIM, v.		1/XI/42	
ASCHENBRENNER	KG 100	1/VIII/42	
BAIER, Eberhard		1/IV/42	
BANSE	Air Supply Group, W. France	1/IV/42	
BAUR de BETAZ	(Admin)	1/VII/41	
BECKER, Dipl. Ing. Wilhelm		1/VII/41	
BEHRENDT (51)		1/X/41	
BERTHOLD	(Admin)	1/VII/41	
BERTRAM (52)	AA	1/VI/39	
BIEDERMANN, Frhr. v. (51)		1/IV/41	Saxony
BIWER (50)	Lehrgruppe II (?)	1/IX/41	
BOENICK, Oskar Frhr. v. (50)		1/II/41	Silesia
BOENICKE, Walter	I AA Corps	1/IX/41	
BOETTGE	Air Recruit Depot 31	1/X/41	
BONATZ, Ernst (50)	Head of a Section, R. L. M	1/VIII/41	
BRANDT		1/I/43	
BRUNNER, (Arthur ?)	Koluft Eighteenth Army		
BRUNNER, Josef		1/IX/41	Austria
BUCHHOLZ	KG z. b. V. 3	1/XII/41	
BÜLOWIUS, Alfred (50)	Air C-in-C, Bombers and Dive-Bombers.	1/VI/41	
CABANIS, Ernst (53)	Head of a Dept in R. L. M	1/IV/40	
CARGANICO (57)		1/XII/41	
CHAMIER-GLISCZINSKI, Wolfgang v. (49).		1/XI/41	
CHAULIN-EGERSBERG, v.	AA	1/XII/41	Hesse
CONRAD, Dipl. Ing. Gerhard	Hermann Göring Div	1/IV/41	Anhalt
CZECH		1/IV/41	
DAHLMANN, Dr. Hermann		1/XII/41	Hesse
DEWALL, Job v. (63)		1/XI/40	

f. GENERALMAJOR (corresponds roughly to U. S. Brigadier General)—Continued.

Name (age)	Command	Seniority	Origin
DÖRFFLER (53)	Air Supply Group, Kiev	1/XI/40	
DRECHSEL, Ernst		1/II/42	Bavaria
EIBENSTEIN, Rudolf	12th AA Div	1/VIII/41	Saxony
ERDMANN		1/III/43	
EXSZ (49)	Armistice Commission, Aix-en-Provence	1/IV/42	
FALKENHAYN, Erich v. (53)	(Admin)	1/XI/41	
FALKOWSKI, v.		1/XI/41	
FISCHER, Eberhard (49)	An Aerodrome Regional Command.	1/VI/42	Silesia
FRANTZ, Gotthard	C Sig O, Air Command, Center	1/IX/41	
FRANTZ, Walther	AA	1/VI/41	
FREYBERG EISENBERG-ALLMENDINGEN, Egloff Frhr. v.		1/IV/39	
FÜTTERER, Cuno Heribert	Air Attache, Budapest	1/XI/41	
FUNCKE, Heinz		1/X/41	
GALLAND, Adolf (31)	Insp of Fighters	19/XI/42	
GANDERT, Hans Eberhard (51)	Head of a Section, R. L. M	1/XII/39	
GERSTENBERG, Alfred	Air Attache, Bucharest	1/IX/41	
GOLTZ		1/IV/41	
GROSCH, Walter (53)	In R. L. M	1/VI/41	
HACHENBERG, v. (55)	(Admin)	1/XI/40	
HAENSCHKE (50)	C Sig Off, Third Air Fleet	1/II/42	
HANTELMANN (59)	An Aerodrome Regional Comd	1/II/42	
HARLINGHAUSEN, Martin	Insp Gen of Torpedoes (Fliegerführ. Tunesien)		
HARTING		1/XI/40	
HARTOG (55)	(Admin)	1/IV/41	Baden
HASSE	(Admin)	1/XI/41	
HEIDRICH, Richard	3d Parachute Regt	1/VIII/42	
HEMPEL		1/II/43	
HERWARTH v. BITTENFELD, Eberhard (54)	Aerodrome Regional Comd Warsaw.	1/IV/40	

f. GENERALMAJOR (corresponds roughly to U. S. Brigadier General)—Continued.

Name (age)	Command	Seniority	Origin
HESSE, Max	6th AA Regt	1/IV/41	
HEYDE, v. der		1/X/42	
HEYDENREICH, Leopold	Head of a Section, R. L. M	1/IV/42	
HEYKING, Rüdiger v	K. G. z. b. V. 1	1/XI/41	
HILGERS, Dipl. Ing. (51)		1/IV/41	Hesse
HINKELBEIN	(Admin)	1/IX/41	Württemberg
HOEFERT, Johannes	(Admin)	1/IV/41	Saxony
HOHNE, Otto	K. G		
HOFMANN, Hans	Staff of Fourth Air Fleet	1/VI/41	
HOLLE, Alexander	C of S of a Flieger Corps	1/II/43	
HOMBURG, Erich	General Staff	1/XI/40	
HORNUNG		1/IX/42	
HÜCKEL (52)		1/IX/41	
JAKOBY		1/II/43	
KATHMANN	General Staff	1/IV/42	
KETTEMBEIL	Air Attache, Lisbon	1/VI/41	
KETTNER (50)		1/IV/42	
KLEIN, Dipl. Ing		1/II/41	
KLEIN, Hans (52)		27/VIII/39	
KLEINRATH		1/III/43	
KÖCHY, Karl (48)		1/XI/41	
KOLLER		1/III/43	
KRAHMER, Eckart (51)	Air Attache, Madrid	1/X/41	
KRAPP	(Admin)	1/IV/41	
KRESSMANN, Erich	AA	1/II/42	Baden
KRIEGBAUM (51)	In Air Force School	1/III/39	
KREIPE		1/III/43	
KRÜGER, Otto (53)	Koluft, Twelfth Army	1/V/41	
KRUEGER	(Admin)	1/XI/41	
KRUEGER, Ernst		1/VI/41	
KRUG		1/I/43	
KUEN	Luftgau West France	1/IV/42	

ORDER OF BATTLE OF THE GERMAN ARMY 0205

f. GENERALMAJOR (corresponds roughly to U. S. Brigadier General)—Continued.

Name (age)	Command	Seniority	Origin
KUTTIG, Dipl. Ing. Hans (51)		1/XI/40	
KUTZLEBEN, v. (57)		1/I/38	
LAULE (52)	(Admin)	1/VI/41	Baden
LICHTENBERGER		1/II/43	
LOEB	Chief of Finance Bureau, R. L. M.	1/I/38	
LOHMANN (50)	Koluft, Sixth Army	1/II/42	
LORENZ, Heinrich		1/II/43	
LUCZNY, Alfons (49)	AA	1/II/42	Silesia
MAASS	Air Staff	1/VIII/41	
MÄLZER, Dipl. Ing		1/X/41	Saxony
MASSOW, Albrecht v. (57)	Air Supply Group, Luftgau VIII	1/I/41	
MEINDL, Eugen (51)	XIII Air Corps (?)	1/I/41	
MEISTAR		1/IX/42	
MENSCH (56)	Staff of Fifth Air Fleet	1/XI/40	
MENSCHING (56)		1/XI/40	
MENTZEL		1/VI/41	
MENZEL, George Adolf (57)	Air Defense Command 7	1/X/39	Saxony
METZNER		1/IV/42	
MÜLLER, Gottlob	Aerodrome Regional Command, Sicily	1/XI/41	Bavaria
MUGGENTHALER, Hermann (55)	(Admin)	1/VII/41	Bavaria
NEUFFER		1/XII/41	Bavaria
NIELSEN		1/III/43	
NITZSCHE	Staff of Luftgau VII	1/I/41	
NORDT		1/IV/41	
NOWAK		1/IX/41	
NUBER	Staff of Luftgau II	1/VII/41	Württemberg.
OLBRICH		1/IV/42	
ORTNER-WEIGAND, Bruno		1/IX/41	Austria.
PFEIFFER		1/VII/42	
PICKERT, Wolfgang	An AA Division	1/X/42	

f. GENERALMAJOR (corresponds roughly to U. S. Brigadier General)—Continued.

Name (age)	Command	Seniority	Origin
PISTORIUS		1/XII/41	
PLOCH, Dipl. Ing. August (49)	C of S, Directorate of Equipment, R. L. M.	1/VIII/40	
PLOCHER		1/III/43	
POETSCH	43d Flying Tng Regt	1/VIII/41	
PRELLBERG		1/VIII/42	
PREU		1/II/43	
PULTAR, Josef	Tng Center at Kaufbeuren	1/VII/40	Austria
PUNZERT		1/III/43	
RAITHEL, Dipl. Ing. Hans (49)		1/IV/42	Bavaria
RANTZAU v. (50)	III AA Brig	1/IV/42	Bavaria
RAUCH, Hans		1/VI/42	
RIECKHOFF, Herbert	C of S, First Air Fleet	1/III/43	
REIMANN (49)	AA	1/IV/41	
REUSS, Heinrich XXXVII Prinz v.		1/II/43	
RIBENSTEIN		1/VIII/41	
RIEKE, Georg	In R. L. M	1/IX/41	
RIESCH, Dipl. Ing	Aerodrome Regional Command, Werl	1/XI/41	Bavaria
RIVA		1/VIII/42	
ROESCH (56)	Insp of Armaments, Wkr. VII	1/XII/41	Württemberg
ROTH	Fliegerführer Lofoten	1/VIII/42	
RUDLOFF, Werner v		1/VIII/41	
RUDOLF, Viktor	Personnel Branch, R. L. M		
RÜTER, Wolfgang (51)	AA	1/XII/39	
SATTLER (48)	Sig C	1/XII/41	Baden
SCHAUER, Ludwig (55)		1/IV/39	Bavaria
SCHILFFARTH, Ludwig (50)	202d AA Regt	1/II/42	Bavaria
SCHLEICH, Ritter v. (55)	Air Cmdr, Denmark	1/II/41	Bavaria
SCHMID		1/III/43	
SCHÖBEL		1/X/41	Austria
SCHÖRGI		1/XI/42	Austria

f. GENERALMAJOR (corresponds roughly to U. S. Brigadier General)—Continued.

Name (age)	Command	Seniority	Origin
SCHROEDER, Severin		1/IV/41	
SCHROTH		1/VIII/41	
SCHÜTZE	Insp of Armaments, Prague	1/XI/41	
SCHULTZE		1/IX/41	
SCHULTZE-RHONHOF (53)	C Sig O, Luftgau XVII	1/IV/41	
SEIDEMANN	Fliegerführer Afrika		
SELDNER, Eduard (53)		19/VII/40	Baden
SEYWALD, Heinz	Bomber School, Thorn	1/XI/41	Bavaria
SIESS, Gustav (59)	Head of a Section, R. L. M	1/XI/40	Austria
SOELDNER		1/IV/41	Bavaria
SONNENBURG (52)		1/VI/41	
SPERLING (51)		1/IV/41	
SPRUNER v. MERTZ, Hermann (60)		1/VIII/40	Bavaria
STAHEL	Cmdr of a LW Kampfgruppe	2/I/43	
STAHL		1/I/43	
STARKE		1/VI/41	
STEIN	Gen Qu, Third Air Fleet	1/XI/40	
STEINKOPF		1/XI/40	
STURM, Alfred (55)	2d Parachute Regt	1/VIII/40	
STUTZER (55)		1/XII/40	
TESCHNER		1/XI/40	
THYM, Heinrich		1/XI/40	Austria
TIPPELSKIRCH, v.		1/XI/40	
TRIENDL, Theodor (54)	Air Supply Group Wiesbaden	1/III/40	Bavaria
TSCHOELTSCH, Ehrenfried (51).		1/XI/41	Saxony
UNGER (53)		1/VI/41	
VEITH		1/II/43	
VODEPP		1/II/43	
VORWALD		1/III/43	
WALLAND, Eugen		1/XI/41	Austria
WALLNER, Otto (61)		1/XI/41	Bavaria

f. GENERALMAJOR (corresponds roughly to U. S. Brigadier General)—Continued.

Name (age)	Command	Seniority	Origin
WANGENHEIM, Edgar Frhr. v.		1/XI/40	
WEESE		1/XI/40	
WICHARD		1/I/43	
WILCK	Insp of Armaments, Ukraine	1/XI/40	
WITZENDORFF, v.		1/II/43	
ZECH	Air Equipment Group Naples	1/IV/42	
ZIERVOGEL		1/I/43	

76. SS and Police Officers.

a. REICHSFÜHRER SS.

Name (age)	Office
*HIMMLER, Heinrich (43)	Reichsführer SS and Chief of German Police.

*Holds rank in General SS and in police.

b. SS-OBERSTGRUPPENFÜHRER GENERALOBERST der POLIZEI.

(Name (age)	Office
*DALUEGE, Kurt (46)	Chief of Regular Police; Acting Protector of Bohemia and Moravia
SCHWARZ, Franz Xaver (68)	Reich Treasurer of NSDAP

*Holds rank in General SS and in Waffen-SS.
No asterisk: Holds rank only in General SS.

c. SS-OBERGRUPPENFÜHRER, GENERAL der POLIZEI, GENERAL der WAFFEN-SS.

Name (age)	Office
AMANN, Max (52)	Party Press Director
*BACH-ZELEWSKY, Erich v. dem (44)	H. SS Pf. Central Sector, Russia
BACKE, Herbert (47)	Acting Minister of Agriculture
*BERKELMANN, Theodor (49)	H. SS Pf. Lothringen-Saarpfalz and Chief of SS Oa. Lothringen-Saarpfalz
BORMANN, Martin (43)	Chief of Party Chancellery
**BREITHAUPT, Franz (63)	Chief of SS Legal Dept
BUCH, Walter (60)	Chief of Party Supreme Court
BÜRCKEL, Josef (48)	Gauleiter of Westmark
**DIETRICH, Josef ("Sepp") (51)	Chief of SS Oa. Spree; traditional commander of Leibstandarte and organizer of the Waffen-SS
DIETRICH, Otto (46)	Reich and Party Press Chief
*EBERSTEIN, Friedrich Karl Frhr. v. (49)	H. SS Pf. Wkr. VII and Wkr. XIII and Chief of SS Oa. Süd.
FIEHLER, Karl (48)	Head of Reich Communal Congress; Mayor of München
FORSTER, Albert (41)	Gauleiter of Danzig-Westpreussen
FRANK, Dr. Hans (43)	Governor General (Poland)
*FRANK, Karl Hermann (45)	H. SS Pf. and State Secretary for Bohemia and Moravia
GÖRING, Hermann (50)	(Inactive member of SS)
GREISER, Arthur (64)	Gauleiter of Wartheland
**HAUSSER, Paul (62)	Cmdr SS Panzer Corps

*Holds ranks in General SS and in police.
**Holds rank in General SS and in Waffen-SS.
No asterisk: Holds rank only in General SS.

c. SS-OBERGRUPPENFÜHRER, GENERAL der POLIZEI, GENERAL der WAFFEN-SS—Continued.

Name (age)	Office
HEISSMEYER, August (46)	Chief of SS Hq Berlin
HILDEBRANDT, Friedrich (45)	Gauleiter of Mecklenburg
*HILDEBRANDT, Richard (46)	H. SS Pf. Wkr. XX and Chief of SS Oa. Weichsel
*JECKELN, Friedrich (48)	H. SS Pf. Ostland
*KALTENBRUNNER, Dr. Ernst (38)	Chief of Security Police and SS Security Service
KAUFMANN, Karl (43)	Gauleiter of Hamburg
KEPPLER, Wilhelm (61)	State Secretary, Foreign Office and Ministry of Economic Affairs
KLAGGES, Dietrich (52)	Premier of Braunschweig
KÖRNER, Paul (50)	Deputy Head of Four Year Plan
*KOPPE, Wilhelm (47)	H. SS Pf. Wkr. XXI and Chief of SS Oa. Warthe
*KRÜGER, Friedrich Wilhelm (49)	H. SS Pf. Krakau and State Secretary for Security in Govt Gen
LAMMERS, Dr. Hans Heinrich (64)	Chief of Reich Chancellery
LORENZ, Werner (52)	Director of Resettlement
*MAZUW, Emil (42)	H. SS Pf. Wkr. II and Chief of SS Oa. Ostsee
MURR, Wilhelm (55)	Gauleiter of Württemberg
**POHL, Oswald (51)	Chief of SS Administration
*PRÜTZMANN, Hans-Adolf (41)	H. SS Pf. Ukraine
*REDIESS, Wilhelm (43)	H. SS Pf. Norway
REINHARD, Wilhelm (74)	Head of Veterans' League

*Holds rank in General SS and in police.
**Holds rank in General SS and in Waffen-SS.
No asterisk: Holds rank in General SS only.

c. SS-OBERGRUPPENFÜHRER, GENERAL der POLIZEI, GENERAL der WAFFEN-SS—Continued.

Name (age)	Office
RIBBENTROP, Joachim v. (50)	Foreign Minister
ROSENBERG, Alfred (50)	Minister for Occupied Eastern Areas
SAUCKEL, Fritz (49)	Plenipotentiary for Labor
*SCHMAUSER, Ernst-Heinrich (53)	H. SS Pf. Wkr. VIII and Chief of SS Oa. Südost
SCHMITT, Walter (64)	Chief of SS Personnel Dept
SEYSS-INQUARDT, Dr. Arthur (50)	Reich Commissar for the Netherlands
*WALDECK u. PYRMONT, Erbprinz Josias zu (47)	H. SS Pf. Wkr. IX and Chief of SS Oa. Fulda-Werra
*WOLFF, Karl (43)	Chief of HIMMLER's personal staff
*WOYRSCH, Udo v. (48)	H. SS Pf. Wk. IV and Chief of SS Oa. Elbe

d. SS-GRUPPENFÜHRER, GENERALLEUTNANT der POLIZEI, GENERALLEUTNANT der WAFFEN-SS.

Name (age)	Office
AHRENS	
ALPERS, Friedrich (42)	Staff of Rf. SS; Assistant Master of Forests
*BECKER	B. d. O. Govt Gen
BECKER, Herbert (56)	Staff of SS Oa. Donau
**BERGER, Gottlob (46)	Chief of Waffen-SS Hq Berlin
BEST, Dr. Karl Rudolf Werner (40)	

* Holds rank in General SS and in police.
** Holds rank in General SS and in Waffen-SS.
No asterisk: Holds rank only in General SS.

d. SS-GRUPPENFÜHRER, GENERALLEUTNANT der POLIZEI, GENERALLEUTNANT der WAFFEN-SS—Con.

Name (age)	Office
BOHLE, Ernst Wilhelm (40)	Gauleiter of "Ausland"
*BOMHARD, Adolf Theodor Ernst v. (52)	In Police Hq Berlin
BOUHLER, Philipp (44)	Chief of Führer's Chancellery
BRACHT, Werner (55)	Staff of Rf. SS; Gauleiter of Oberschlesien
CONTI, Dr. Leonardo (43)	Reich Health Leader
**DEMMELHUBER, Karl (47)	Comdr SS Regiment Germania
EBRECHT, Georg (47)	Chief of SS Abs. XXVI, Danzig (Wkr. XX)
*EGGELING, Joachim-Albrecht (59).	Gauleiter of Halle-Merseburg
FETT	
FRITSCH, Lothar	
*GLOBOCNIK, Odilo (39)	SS Pf. Lublin
**GRAWITZ, Dr. Ernst Robert (44).	Chief Medical Office of SS and police
GREIFELT, Ulrich (46)	C of S to Reich Commissioner for the Strengthening of Germanism (HIMMLER)
GROHE, Josef	Gauleiter of Köln-Aachen
*GUTENBERGER, Karl (38)	H. SS Pf. Wkr. VI and Chief of SS Oa. West
HANKE, Karl (40)	Gauleiter of Niederschlesien
HENLEIN, Konrad	Gauleiter of Sudetenland

*Holds rank in General SS and in police.
**Holds rank in General SS and in Waffen-SS.
No asterisk: Holds rank only in General SS.

d. SS-GRUPPENFÜHRER, GENERALLEUTNANT der POLIZEI, GENERALLEUTNANT der WAFFEN-SS—Con.

Name (age)	Office
*HENNICKE, Paul (60)	Police President, Weimar (Wkr. IX), and Chief of SS Abs. XXVII, Weimar
*HENZE, Max (44)	Police President, Essen (Wkr. VI)
HILGENFELDT, Erich (46)	Head of NS Welfare Organization
**HOFMANN, Dr. Philipp (40)	Chief of SS Race and Settlement Dept
HOLZSCHUHER, Wilhelm Frhr. v. (50)	Staff of Rf. SS
*JEDICKE, Georg	K. d. Sipo u. d. SD, Ostland
JOHST, Hanns (53)	Staff of Rf. SS; President of Reich Chamber of Literature
**JÜTTNER, Hans (49)	Chief of Command Office, Waffen-SS
JUNG, Prof. Dr	Labor Plenipotentiary for Protectorate
*KAMPTZ, Jürgen v. (51)	Inspector General of Gendarmery and Local Municipal Police
*KAUL, Kurt (52)	H. SS Pf. Wkr. V and Chief of SS Oa. Südwest
**KEPPLER, Georg (49)	
**KNOBLAUCH, Kurt	Chief of Ops on Staff of Rf. SS
LAUTERBACHER, Hartmann (34)	Deputy Reich Youth Leader; Gauleiter of Südhannover-Braunschweig
MACKENSEN, Hans-Georg Viktor v. (60)	Staff of Rf. SS; German Ambassador in Rome
MARTIN, Dr. Benno (50)	Police President, Nürnberg and Fürth (Wkr. XIII) and Chief of SS Oa. Main
MAUR, Dr. v.	
MEINBERG, Wilhelm (45)	Staff of Rf. SS

*Holds rank in General SS and in police.
**Holds rank in General SS and in Waffen-SS.
No asterisk: Holds rank only in General SS.

d. SS-GRUPPENFÜHRER, GENERALLEUTNANT der POLIZEI, GENERALLEUTNANT der WAFFEN-SS—Con.

Name (age)	Office
*MEYSSNER, August (56)	Comdr German Police, Belgrade
*OELHAFEN, Otto v. (57)	B. d. O., Ukraine
*PANCKE, Günter (44)	H. SS Pf. Wkr. XI and Chief of SS Oa. Mitte
PETRI	Chief of Command Office, General SS
**PHLEPS	Comdr SS Div Prinz Eugen
*QUERNER, Rudolf (50)	H. SS Pf. Wkr. XVII and chief of SS Oa. Donau
RADOWITZ, Otto v. (63)	Staff of Rf. SS
RAINER, Dr. Friederich	Gauleiter of Kärnten
*RAUTER, Hans (48)	H. SS Pf. Nordwest (Holland)
REINHARDT, Fritz (48)	State Secretary, Ministry of Finance
*RIEGE, Paul (55)	B. d. O., Bohemia and Moravia
*RÖSENER, Erwin (41)	H. SS Pf. Wkr. XII and Chief of SS Oa. Rhein
**SACHS, Ernst (62)	Chief of Communications on Staff of Rf. SS
SCHAUB, Julius (44)	Personal Adjutant to HITLER
*SCHEEL, Dr. Gustav Adolf (34)	H. SS Pf. Wkr. XVIII and Chief of SS Oa. Alpenland; Reich Student Leader; Gauleiter of Salzburg
SCHLESSMANN, Fritz (43)	Deputy Gauleiter of Essen
*SCHREYER, Georg (58)	Inspector General of Municipal Police
SCHWERK	

*Holds rank in General SS and in police.
**Holds rank in General SS and in Waffen-SS.
No asterisk: Holds rank only in General SS.

d. SS-GRUPPENFÜHRER, GENERALLEUTNANT der POLIZEI, GENERALLEUTNANT der WAFFEN-SS—Con.

Name (age)	Office
SPORRENBERG	H. SS Pf. Wkr. I and Chief of SS Oa. Nordost
**STEINER, Felix (47)	Cmdr SS Division Wiking
*STRECKENBACH, Bruno (41)	Security Police Hq, Berlin
STUCKART, Dr. Wilhelm (41)	State Secretary, Ministry of Interior
TAUBERT, Siegfried (62)	Staff of Rf. SS
TERBOVEN, Josef (45)	Reich Commissar for Norway
*THOMAS	B. d. Sipo u. d. SD, Ukraine
TURNER, Dr. Harald (52)	Chief of Military Administration, Serbia
WAHL, Karl (51)	Gauleiter of Schwaben
WEGENER, Paul	Gauleiter of Weser-Ems
*WEINREICH, Hans (47)	Chief of Technical Emergency Corps
WIMMER, Dr	Staff of Reich Commissar for the Netherlands
WILLIKENS, Werner (50)	State Secretary, Ministry of Agriculture
*WINKELMANN, Otto (48)	In Police Hq, Berlin
***WÜNNENBERG, Alfred (51)	Cmdr SS Police Div
*ZENNER, Karl (44)	SS Pf. Minsk

*Holds rank in General SS and in police.
**Holds rank in General SS and in Waffen-SS.
***Holds rank in General SS, in police, and in Waffen-SS.
No asterisk: Holds rank only in General SS.

e. SS-BRIGADE FÜHRER, GENERALMAJOR der POLIZEI, GENERALMAJOR der WAFFEN-SS.

Name (age)	Office
*ALBERT, Dr. Wilhelm (44)	Police President, Litzmannstadt (Wkr. XXI)
*ALVENSLEBEN, Rudolf v. (42)	SS Pf. Taurien
ARNOLD	
*BASSEWITZ-BEHR, Georg Graf v. (43).	H. SS Pf. Wkr. X and Chief of SS Oa. Nordsee.
BAUER, Josef	(In Finland)
BAUR, Alfred	
**BEHR, Max v. (64)	Cmdr local SS, Wien (Wkr. XVII)
BEHRENDS, Dr. Hermann (36)	Deputy Director of Resettlement
BEHRENS, Gustav	In Reich Agrarian Bureau
*BELEK, Andreas (49)	Police President, Magdeburg (Wkr. XI)
**BITTRICH, Willi (49)	Cmdr SS Cav Div
**BLUMENREUTER	(Waffen-SS)
*BRENNER	B. d. O., Oberkrain and Südsteiermark (Wkr. XVIII)
DAUSER, Hans (66)	In Bavarian Economic Ministry
**DEBES, Lothar	
DERMIETEL, Dr. Friedrich Karl (44)	Staff of SS Hq, Berlin
*DIEHM, Christoph (51)	Police President, Saarbrücken and Metz (Wkr. XII)
*DÖRING, Hans (42)	SS Pf. Stalino
DREHER	Provincial Chief, Sigmaringen
*DUNCKERN	
EBERHARD	
ECKHARDT	Gau Economic Adviser, Hessen-Nassau

*Holds rank in General SS and in police.
**Holds rank in General SS and in Waffen-SS.
No asterisk: Holds rank only in General SS.

e. SS-BRIGADE FÜHRER, GENERALMAJOR der POLIZEI, GENERALMAJOR der WAFFEN-SS—Continued.

Name (age)	Office
FALKOWSKI, v	
FIEDLER	Chief of SS Abs. XVII, Münster (Wkr. VI)
FISCHER, Franz	
**FRANK, August (45)	In SS Administrative Hq, Berlin
**GEBHARDT, Prof. Dr. Karl (45)	Chief of SS Medical Corps
**GENZKEN, Dr. med. Karl (58)	Chief of SS Medical Hq, Berlin
GIESECKE	
**GLÜCKS, Richard (54)	Staff of Chief of Totenkopf guards and concentration camps
**GOEDICKE	Cmdr. of an SS Arty Regt
GOLTZ, Frhr. v. der	
*GROLMANN, Wilhelm	In Police Hq, Berlin
GRÜNWALD	
GRUSSENDORF	
GUTTERER, Leopold	State Secretary, Ministry of Propaganda
*HALTERMANN, Hans	SS Pf. Kiev
**HANSEN	Inspector of SS Artillery
**HARTENSTEIN	Comdr 1st SS Inf Brig
*HERFF, Maximilian v	K. d. O. Kharkov
HEWEL, Walter	Chief of RIBBENTROP's personal staff
HINKEL, Hans	Head of Reich Chamber of Culture

*Holds rank in General SS and in police.
**Holds rank in General SS and in Waffen-SS.
No asterisk: Holds rank only in General SS.

e. SS-BRIGADE FÜHRER, GENERALMAJOR der POLIZEI, GENERALMAJOR der WAFFEN-SS—Continued.

Name (age)	Office
*HÖRING (Genmaj. d. Gendarmerie)	B. d. O., Norway
HOFFMANN, Karl	
JÜRS, Heinrich	Chief of SS Abs. XXXII, Augsburg (Wkr. VII)
JUNGCLAUS, Richard (38)	Representative of Rf. SS in Flanders
KAMMLER, Dr. Ing	Chief of Section II (Building) of SS Office of Works, Berlin
*KANSTEIN, Paul	Plenipotentiary for Interior Administration in Denmark
*KATZMANN, Fritz (37)	SS Pf. Galicia
**KLEINHEISTERKAMP, Matthias (50)	Comdr SS Mtn Div Nord
KLEINMANN, Wilhelm	
**KLINGEMANN, Gottfried (58)	Comdr 2d SS Inf Brig
*KLINGER	K. d. Schupo, Berlin
*KNOFE	B. d. O. Posen (Wkr. XXI)
KOCH, Fritz	
KÖRNER, Hellmut (39)	Chief of Food and Agriculture Dept, Ukraine
*KORSEMANN	H. SS Pf. z. b. V., Ukraine
KREISSL, Dr	
KRETSCHMANN, v	
*KRUMHAAR	Police President, Kiel (Wkr. X)
*KUTSCHERA	

*Holds rank in General SS and in police.
**Holds rank in General SS and in Waffen-SS.
No asterisk: Holds rank only in General SS.

e. SS-BRIGADE FÜHRER, GENERALMAJOR der POLIZEI, GENERALMAJOR der WAFFEN-SS—Continued.

Name (age)	Office
*LANKENAU, Dr	
LEYSER, Ernst Ludwig	General Commissar, Zhitomir
*LIESSEN	K. d. Schupo, Hamburg (Wkr. X)
**LOERNER	Chief of Section I (Maintenance) of SS Office of Works, Berlin
MAACK, Berthold (45)	Chief of SS Abs. XXV, Dortmund (Wkr. VI)
*MALSEN-PONICKAU, Erasmus Frhr. v. (48)	Police President, Posen (Wkr. XXI)
MARRENBACH	
MASCUS	
MEERWALD, Dr	
MENTZEL, Dr	
MEYER, Dr. Ing	Inspector General of Fire Fighting Service
MEYER, Fritz C. C	
MÖRSCHEL, Johann (62)	C of S, SS Oa. Nordsee
*MUELLER	B. d. O. (Wkr. I)
MÜLLER, Hermann	
MUELLER, Rudolf	
*OBERG, Karl Albrecht (46)	H. SS Pf., France
PEUKERT	Plenipotentiary for Farm Labor
*PFLOMM, Karl (56)	Police President, Dresden (Wkr. IV)
*POHLMEYER	K. d. Schupo, Wien (Wkr. XVII)

*Holds rank in General SS and in police.
**Holds rank in General SS and in Waffen-SS.
No asterisk: Holds rank only in General SS.

e. SS-BRIGADE FÜHRER, GENERALMAJOR der POLIZEI, GENERALMAJOR der WAFFEN-SS—Continued.

Name (age)	Office
POPP, Emil (46)	Chief of SS Abs. II, Chemnitz (Wkr. IV)
**PÜCKLER-BURGHAUSS Carlfriedrich Graf v.	Cmdr of Waffen SS in Protectorate
*RAUNER, Adolf (63)	Bavarian State Ministry of the Interior, Police Dept.
REEDER, Eggert	Chief of Civil Administration, Belgium and Northern France
REINEFARTH, Heinz (37)	Staff of SS Abs. XII, Frankfurt/Oder (Wkr. III)
RETZLAFF, Dr	I. d. O. Wien (Wkr. XVII)
SCHÄFER	Chief of SS Abs. XLIII, Litzmannstadt (Wkr. XXI)
*SCHEER	K. d. O. Kiev
*SCHIMANA	
SCHMELT	
*SCHRÖDER	SS Pf., Latvia
SCHULZ, Erwin	
*SCHUMANN	B. d. O, West
**SCHWEDLER, Hans	(Waffen-SS)
SELZNER, Dr. Klaus (44)	General Commissar, Dnepropetrovsk
*SIEBERT	Treasurer of Technical Emergency Corps
SPICKSCHEN	
*STARCK, Wilhelm (52)	Police President, Augsburg (Wkr. VII)

*Holds rank in General SS and in police.
**Holds rank in General SS and in Waffen-SS.
No asterisk: Holds rank only in General SS.

e. SS-BRIGADE FÜHRER, GENERALMAJOR der POLIZEI, GENERALMAJOR der WAFFEN-SS—Continued.

Name (age)	Office
*STOLLE, Gustav	Chief of SS Abs. XXIII, Berlin (Wkr. III)
*TENSFIELD, Willi	(In Russia)
*THIER	Chief of SS Abs. XV, Altona (Wkr. X)
THIERACK, Dr. Otto Georg	Minister of Justice
TITTMANN, Fritz (44)	SS Pf. Nikolaev
**TREUENFELD, v	
VELLER	Police President, Oberhausen (Wkr. VI)
**VOSS, Bernhard	(Waffen-SS)
WÄCHTER	Governor of Galicia, Govt Gen
*WAPPENHANS, Waldemar (49)	SS Pf. Brest-Litovsk
WEBER, Dr. Friedrich	Chief of Dept. Ministry of Interior; Reich Veterinary leader
*WENDLER, Dr. Richard (45)	Governor of Krakau District
WENZEL, Dr. Ernst (52)	Staff of SS Hq, Berlin
WILL	
*WINKLER	B. d. O. Krakau
*WYSOCKI	SS Pf., Lithuania

*Holds rank in General SS and in police.
**Holds rank in General SS and in Waffen-SS.
No asterisk: Holds rank only in General SS.

Section IX. ABBREVIATIONS

The following list is, with few exceptions, confined to the German military abbreviations which are used in this book and to their component elements. For others which may be encountered in German documents or elsewhere, the reader should consult the Dictionary of German Military Abbreviations.

The rules for forming German abbreviations are very flexible, and several abbreviations for the same word or expression may be equally authentic and equally common. For example, Artillerie may be abbreviated A., Art., or Artl., and Abteilung may occur as A., Abt., or Abtlg. In many cases the placing of periods is optional; thus Oberkommando der Wehrmacht may be either O. K. W. or OKW.

A	Armee-, Armee	army
A	Artillerie	artillery
A	Abteilung	section; detachment; department; battalion.
A. A	Aufklärungsabteilung	reconnaissance battalion
A. Bekl. Amt	Armee-Bekleidungsamt	army clothing depot
Abs	Abschnitt	sector; section; zone
Abt	Abteilung	section; detachment; department; battalion
Abtl	Abteilung	section; detachment; department; battalion
a. D	ausser Dienst	retired
a. d	an der	on the
A. E. R	Artillerieersatzregiment	artillery replacement training regiment.
AHA	Allgemeines Heeresamt	General Army Office
A. K	Armeekorps	army corps
a. K	auf Kriegsdauer	for the duration of the war
A. K. P	Armee-Kraftfahrpark	army motor park
A. Nachr. Pk	Armee-Nachrichtenpark	army signal equipment park.

A. N. F	Armee-Nachschubführer	army supply commander
A. N. R	Armee-Nachrichtenregiment	army signal regiment
A. O. K	Armee-Oberkommando	army command
A. Pf. Laz	Armee-Pferdelazarett	army veterinary hospital
A. Pf. Pk	Armee-Pferdepark	army horse park
A. R	Artillerieregiment	artillery regiment
Arfü	Artillerieführer	divisional artillery commander.
Arko	Artilleriekommandeur	artillery commander from General Headquarters pool.
Art	Artillerie	artillery
Art. Abt	Artillerieabteilung	artillery battalion
Art. Ers. Abt	Artillerieersatzabteilung	artillery replacement training battalion.
Art. Ers. Regt	Artillerieersatzregiment	artillery replacement training regiment.
Artl	Artillerie	artillery
Art. Pk	Artilleriepark	artillery equipment park
A. San Abt	Armee-Sanitätsabteilung	army medical battalion
A. San Pk	Armee-Sanitätspark	army medical park
Astr. Messzug	Astronomischer Messzug	astronomical survey platoon
Aufkl. Abt	Aufklärungsabteilung	reconnaissance battalion
Aufkl. Ers. Abt	Aufklärungsersatzabteilung	reconnaissance replacement training battalion
B. Abt	Beobachtungsabteilung	artillery observation or survey battalion (sound and flash)
Bäck. K	Bäckereikompanie	bakery company
Ball. Bttr	Ballonbatterie	observation balloon battery
Batl	Bataillon	battalion
Battr	Batterie	battery
Bau-Btl	Baubataillon	construction battalion
Bb	Beobachtungsbatterie	observation battery
BdE	Befehlshaber des Ersatzheeres	Commander of the Replacement Training Army
B. d. G	Befehlshaber der Gendarmerie	Commander of the Gendarmery
B. d. O	Befehlshaber der Ordnungspolizei	Chief of the Regular Police

B. d. Sipo u. d. SD	Befehlshaber der Sicherheitspolizei und des Sicherheitsdienstes	Chief of Security Police and of the SS Security Service
Beob. Abt	Beobachtungsabteilung	artillery observation or survey battalion (sound and flash)
Beob. Battr	Beobachtungsbatterie	observation battery
Betr. St. Kol	Betriebsstoffkolonne	fuel column
Betr. Verw. Kp	Betriebsstoffverwaltungkompanie.	fuel administration company
Bfh	Befehlshaber	commander; commanding officer
Br. Baubtl	Brückenbaubataillon	bridge construction battalion
Brig	Brigade	brigade
Brüko	Brückenkolonne	bridge column
Btl	Bataillon	battalion
Bttr	Batterie	battery
Ch	Chef	chief
char	charakterisiert	holding honorary rank
Ch. H. Rü	Chef der Heeresrüstung	Chief of Army Equipment
D	Division	division
d	der	the
d. B	des Beurlaubtenstandes	on the retired list
d. G	des Generalstabes	on the general staff
Dinafü	Divisionsnachschubführer	commander of division supply services
Dipl. Ing	Diplomierter Ingenieur	graduate engineer
Dipl. Wirtsch	Diplomierter Wirtschaftler	graduate economist
Div. Kdo	Divisionskommando	division staff
d. L	der Landwehr	of the Landwehr; of the reserve
d. R	der Reserve	of the reserve
Dr. habil		(academic degree)
Dr. h. c	Dr. honoris causa	honorary doctor's degree
Dulag	Durchgangslager	transit camp for prisoners of war
E	Ergänzungs-	reserve; supplementary
Eisb	Eisenbahn-	railroad
Eisb. Baubtl	Eisenbahnbaubataillon	railroad construction battalion
Eisb. Betr. Kp	Eisenbahnbetriebskompanie	railway operations company

Eisb. Pf. Baukp	Eisenbahnpfeilerbaukompanie	railway pillar construction company
Eisb. Pi. Pk	Eisenbahnpionierpark	railway engineer equipment park
Eisb. Pi. Regt	Eisenbahnpionierregiment	railway engineer regiment
Eisb. Pi. Stb	Eisenbahnpionierstab	railway engineer staff
Entg. Abt	Entgiftungsabteilung	decontamination battalion
Entl. St	Entladestab	unloading crew
Erg	Ergänzungs-	reserve; supplementary
ern	ernannt	appointed to brevet rank
Ers	Ersatz	reserve; replacement training; substitute
F	Fahr-	transport
F.	Feld-	field
F	Fern-	far; distant; long-range
Feldausb. Div	Feldausbildungsdivision	field training division
Feldeisb	Feldeisenbahn	field railroad
Feld.-Ers. Btl	Feld-Ersatzbataillon	field replacement training battalion
Feld. Gen	Feldgendarm; Feldgendarmerie	military policeman; military police
Feld Kdtr	Feldkommandantur	Field administrative headquarters
Feld. Laz	Feldlazarett	field hospital
Fernspr	Fernsprech	telephone
Fest	Festung	fortification; fortress; fort
F. G. A	Feldgendarmerieabteilung	field military police unit
FhJ	Fahnenjunker	cadet; rank corresponding roughly to U. S. corporal
F. K	Feldkommandantur	Field administrative headquarters
Fl	Flieger	aviator; flyer
Fla	Fliegerabwehr	anti-aircraft defense
Flak	Fliagerabwehrkanone	anti-aircraft gun
Flivo	Fliegerverbindungsoffizier	air liaison officer
F. N. K	Feldnachrichtenkommandantur	field signal headquarters
Fp	Festungspionier	fortification engineer (soldier)
F. P. A	Feldpostamt	field post office
Frh	Freiherr	Baron
Frontstalag	Frontstammlager	forward prisoner of war camp

F. S.	Fallschirm-	parachute
Fsp	Fernsprech-	telephone
Fstgs	Festungs-	fortress
Fz	Feldzeug	field equipment; ordnance
Fü	Führer	leader; commander
Führ	Führungs-	leading; of the Armed Forces High Command
Fu. Überw. Kp	Funküberwachungskompanie	radio supervision company
Gassch. Ger. Pk	Gasschutz-Gerätepark	gas protection equipment park
Geb	Gebirgs-	mountain
Geb. J. R	Gebirgsjägerregiment	mountain rifle regiment
Geb. K	Gebirgskorps	mountain corps
Geb. Tr	Gebirgstruppe	mountain troops
Geb. Werf. Abt	Gebirgswerferabteilung	mountain mortar battalion
Gen	General	(corresponds to U. S. lieutenant general)
gen	genannt	called
Genfldm	Generalfeldmarschall	field marshal (no equivalent U. S. rank)
Gen. Kdo	Generalkommando	corps headquarters
Genlt	Generalleutnant	(corresponds to U. S. major general)
Genmaj	Generalmajor	(corresponds to U. S. brigadier general)
Genobst	Generaloberst	(corresponds to U. S. general)
GenQu	Generalquartiermeister	quartermaster general
Genstb	Generalstab	general staff
Gestapo	Geheime Staatspolizei	Secret State Police
Gf	Gruppenführer	SS or SA commander with rank corresponding to U. S. major general; squad leader (infantry)
G. F. P	Geheime Feldpolizei	secret military police
G. G	General-Gouvernement	Government General (Central Poland)
Gr	Gruppe	section; squad; group; flying formation
Gr	Grenadier	infantryman
Gr. Bäck. Kp	Grosse Bäckereikompanie	large bakery company
Gr. Kw. Kol	Grosse Kraftwagenkolonne	heavy transport train

Gr R	Grenadierregiment	infantry regiment
Grz	Grenz-	border
Grz. Sch	Grenzschutz-	frontier protective force
Grz. Wa	Grenzwacht-	frontier guard
GZ	Generalstab-Zentralabteilung	Central Section of the General Staff
H	Heer, Heeres-	army
Heim	Heimat-	zone of the interior
H. Ger. Pk	Heeresgerätepark	army equipment park
H. Gr	Heeresgruppe	army group; group of armies
HJ	Hitlerjunge; Hitlerjugend	Hitler Youth
H. K. A	Heeresküstenartillerie	army coast artillery
H. K. P	Heerskraftfahrpark	army motor transport park
Höh. Kdo	Höheres Kommando	corps command
HPA	Heerespersonalamt	Army Personnel Office
Hptm	Hauptmann	captain
H. SS Pf	Höherer SS und Polizeiführer	Superior SS and Police Commander
I	Infanterie	infantry
i	in, im	in, in the
Ia	(Pronounced "Einss-ah")	operations officer of field unit
I. D	Infanteriedivision	infantry division
I. d. O	Inspekteur der Ordnungspolizei	Inspector of Regular Police
I. E. B	Infanterieersatzbataillon	infantry replacement training battalion
I. E. R	Infanterieersatzregiment	infantry replacement training regiment
I. G	Infanteriegeschütz	infantry howitzer
i. G	im Generalstab	on the general staff
Inf	Infanterie	infantry
Insp	Inspekteur, Inspizient	inspector
I. R	Infanterieregiment	infantry regiment
	Jägerregiment	rifle regiment in a light division
Inst	Instandsetzungs-	repair
Jäg	Jäger, Jäger-	rifleman in a light division; pursuit plane; light (division)
Jagdkdo	Jagdkommando	raiding detachment

Jg	Jäger, Jäger-	same as under Jäg.
J. R.	Jägerregiment, Infanterieregiment	rifle regiment in a light division; infantry regiment
K	Kavallerie	cavalry
K	Kompanie	company
K	Korps	corps
Kav	Kavallerie	cavalry
K. d. O	Kommandeur der Ordnungspolizei	Commander of Regular Police
Kdo	Kommando	command; headquarters staff
Kdr	Kommandeur	commander
K. d. Schupo	Kommandeur der Schutzpolizei	Commander of the Municipal Police
K. d. Sipo u. d. SD	Kommandeur der Sicherheitspolizei und des Sicherheitsdienstes	Chief of the Security Police and Security Service (of the SS)
Kdt	Kommandant	commander; commandant
Kdtr	Kommandantur	administrative headquarters; commandant's office
Kf	Kraftfahr-	motor transport
Kfz	Kraftfahrzeug	motor vehicle
Kol	Kolonne	column
Koluft	Kommandeur der Luftwaffe	air force commander (attached to large unit)
Komb. Kol	Kombinierte Kolonne	combined column
Kom. Gen	Kommandierender General	commanding general (of a corps)
Korück	Kommandant des rückwärtigen Armeegibietes	Commandant of Army Rear Area
Kp	Kompanie	company
K. R	Kavallarieregiment	cavalry regiment
Krad	Kraftfahrrad	motorcycle
Krd.-S. Btl	Kradschützenbataillon	motorcycle rifle battalion
Krgf	Kriegsgefangene	prisoner of war
Krgs. Laz	Kriegslazarett	station hospital in communications zone
Kripo	Kriminalpolizei	criminal investigation police
Kr. Trsp. Abt	Krankentransportabteilung	ambulance detachment
Kw	Kraftwagen	motorcar

L	Landwehr	Reserve (men 35 to 45 years old)
Laz	Lazarett	hospital
Ldsch. Btl	Landesschützenbataillon	local defense battalion
le	leicht	light
Leit	Leiter	leader; director
L. G	Luftgau	air district
Lg. St	Luftgaustab	air district staff
LKW	Lastkraftwagen	truck
Lt	Leutnant	2nd lieutenant
Ltn	Leutnant	2nd lieutenant
Luftna. Tr	Luftnachrichtentruppen	air signal troops
Lw	Luftwaffe	air force
M	Main	the river Main
Maj	Major	major
Meckl	Mecklenburg	Mecklenburg
MG	Maschinengewehr	machine gun
Mörs	Mörser, Mörser-	mortar
mot	motorisiert	motorized
N	Nachrichten-	reports; communication; information; intelligence; signal
Na	Nachrichten-	
Nachr	Nachrichten-	
Nachsch	Nachschub-	supply
Nbl. W	Nebelwerfer	chemical projector (gas or smoke)
Neum	Neumark	Neumark
N. K. A	Nachschubkolonnenabteilung	supply column detachment
Nsch	Nachschub-	supply
NSDAP	Nationalsozialistische Deutsche Arbeiterpartei	National Socialist German Workers Party
NSFK	Nationalsozialistisches Fliegerkorps	National Socialist Flying Corps
NSKK	Nationalsozialistisches Kraftfahrkorps	National Socialist Motor Corps
O	Oder	Oder (river)
O	Ober-	upper; first; chief
Oa	Oberabschnitt	region or district of the SS
Ob. Baustb	Oberbaustab	superior construction staff (equal in status to a brigade staff)
Ob. d. H	Oberbefehlshaber des Heeres	Commander in Chief of the Army

Oberfeldkdtr	Oberfeldkommandantur	Superior Administrative Headquarters
Ob. F. K	Oberfeldkommandantur	Superior Administrative Headquarters
Oberschles	Oberschlesien	Upper Silesia
Obst	Oberst	colonel
Obstlt	Oberstleutnant	lieutenant colonel
Offz	Offizier	officer
Oflag	Offizierlager	officers prisoner-of-war camp
O. K. H	Oberkommando des Heeres	Army High Command
O. K. L	Oberkommando der Luftwaffe	Air Force High Command
O. K. M	Oberkommando der Kriegsmarine	Navy High Command
O. K. W	Oberkommando der Wehrmacht	High Command of the Armed Forces
Oldb	Oldenburg	Oldenburg
OQu	Oberquartiermeister	Army Quartermaster (Deputy Chief-of-Staff)
Org. Todt	Organisation Todt	special construction organization (named after first head, Dr. Fritz Todt)
Orpo	Ordnungspolizei	regular police
Ortskdtr	Ortskommandantur	local military administrative headquarters
Ostpr	Ostpreussen	East Prussia
O. T.	Organisation Todt	Todt Organization
PA	Personalamt	Army Personnel Office
Pak	Panzerabwehrkanone	antitank gun
Pf	Polizeiführer	Police Commander
Pfd	Pferd, Pferde-	horse
Pi	Pionier, Pionier-	engineer
P. K	Propagandakompanie	propaganda company
Pom	Pommern	Pomerania
Prot	Protektorat	Protectorate
Pz	Panzer-	armor; armor-plate
Pz. A. O. K	Panzerarmeeoberkommando	high command of a Panzer army
Pz. Gr	Panzergrenadier-	infantry in a Panzer unit
Pz. Jg	Panzerjäger-	antitank
Pz. Kw	Panzerkampfwagen	tank
Pz. Tr	Panzertruppe	Panzer troops

R	Regiment	regiment
R	Reserve	reserve
R. A. D	Reichsarbeitsdienst	Reich Labor Service
Radf	Radfahr-	cyclist
r. Ag	rückwärtiges Armeegebiet	rear area under control of an army
R. D. A	Rangdienstalter	rank and seniority
Regt	Regiment	regiment
Reichsfrhr	Reichsfreiherr	Baron of the Reich (title of nobility)
Res	Reserve	reserve
Res. K	Reservekorps	reserve corps
Rf. SS	Reichsführer SS	Reich Commander of the SS
Rgt	Regiment	regiment
Riesengeb	Riesengebirge	Giant Mountains (range)
Rittm	Rittmeister	captain (cavalry)
R. L. M	Reichsluftfahrtministerium	Reich Air Ministry
R. R	Reiterregiment	horse cavalry regiment
Rü	Rüstungs-	armaments
s	schwer	heavy
SA	Sturmabteilungen	Storm Troopers Organization of the National Socialist Party
San	Sanitäts-	medical
Schlächt	Schlächterei-	butchery, slaughter
Schles	Schlesien	Silesia
Schtz	Schutz-, Schützen	protection; cover; riflemen
Schupo	Schutzpolizei	Municipal Police
Schw	schwer	heavy
Schwdr	Schwadron	squadron; cavalry troop
SD	Sicherheitsdienst	security service
Sd	Sonder-	special
S. H. D	Sicherheits- und Hilfdienste	air-raid protection auxiliary services
Sich	Sicherungs-	security
Sipo	Sicherheitspolizei	Security Police
S. R	Schützenregiment	rifle regiment
SS	Schutzstaffeln	Elite Guard (of the National Socialist Party)
SS Oa	SS Oberabschnitt	region or district of the SS
SS Pf	SS und Polizeiführer	SS and Police Commander
St	Stab, Stabs-	staff

Stalag	Stammlager	prisoner-of-war camp for enlisted men
Stb	Stab, Stabs-	staff
Stoart	Stabsoffizier (Artillerie)	staff officer for artillery
Str	Strasse, Strassen-	street
Stu. Gesch	Sturmgeschütz	assault gun
stv	stellvertretender	deputy
Techn. Btl	Technisches Bataillon	technical battalion
Teno	Technische Nothilfe	Technical Emergency Service
Thür	Thüringen	Thuringia
tmot	teilmotorisiert	partly motorized
T. N	Technische Nothilfe	Technical Emergency Service
Tr	Trupp, Truppe, Truppen-	troop; party; detail
Trsp	Transport	transport; carrier
U	Unter-	under; below; subordinate
u	und	and
Uffz	Unteroffizier	non-commissioned officer
V	Verwaltung	administration; management
v	von	from; of
VA	Verwaltungsamt	Army Administration Office
v. d	von der, von dem	of the
Verb	Verbindungs-	connection; junction; combination; communication; contact; liaison
Verk	Verkehrs-	traffic; communication; intercourse
Verl. St	Verladestab	loading crew
Verm	Vermessungs-	survey; measurement
Verpfl	Verpflegungs-	rations; food supply; rationing
Vers	Versuchs-	attempt; experiment; trial
Verst	verstärkt	reinforced
VO	Verordnung	decree
Vo	Velocitäts-	velocity
Vomi	Volksdeutsche Mittelstelle	agency for repatriation of racial Germans
Wa	Wach-, Wacht	guard; watch; sentinel; sentry
Wa	Waffen-	arm; weapon; branch of service

WaA	Waffenamt	Army Ordnance Office
Werkst	Werkstatt	workshop
Werf	Werfer	mortar
Westf	Westfalen	Westphalia
Wett	Wetter	weather; meteorology
WeWi	Wehrwirtschaft	military economics
W. F. St	Wehrmachtführungsstab	Armed Forces Operations Staff
Wg	Wagen, Waggon	wagon; vehicle; freight car
Wkr	Wehrkreis	military district
Z	Zugkraftwagen	prime mover truck
z. b. V	zu besonderer Verwendung	for special use
Z. E. L	Zentral-Ersatzteillager	central spare parts depot
Zg	Zug	train (railroad); platoon; section; groove (ordnance); pull (mechanics)
z. V	zur Verfügung	available

Section II. THE BASIC STRUCTURE OF THE GERMAN ARMY

4. Introduction.

For practical reasons which have already been indicated, the German Army in wartime is divided into the Field Army (Feldheer) and the Replacement Training Army (Ersatzheer). The Field Army is under the direct control of the Commander in Chief and his staff at field headquarters, who are thus enabled to devote themselves primarily to military operations. All other Army matters—the drafting of personnel, the training of replacements, the procurement of equipment, and the administration of permanent military posts and installations within Germany—are entrusted to the Home Command in Berlin, and the units and men serving these purposes are comprised in the Replacement Training Army. The present section describes this permanent home structure and the manner in which it supplies replacements to the Field Army in time of war.

5. The regional organization.

Germany is divided for administrative purposes into seventeen military districts (Wehrkreis). There were fifteen at the outbreak of the war, two more having been formed from annexed Polish territory. In peacetime these contained the headquarters and components of the active infantry corps and were numbered concurrently with them. Thus the II Infantry Corps, which is now in the field, has its peacetime headquarters at Stettin in Wehrkreis II, and its original component divisions and smaller units are still thought of as "affiliated" with this Wehrkreis and normally receive replacements from it. The Wehrkreis is a territorial administrative command similar to our former corps areas. Many of its functions are identical with those of the corps areas, but in wartime it also handles administrative details for the appropriate units of the field army.

Before the war there were also four independent corps—XIV, XV, XVI, and XIX—which were, in effect, staffs to control the organization and training of Panzer and motorized units. They had no corresponding military districts, but were served, as regards personnel and supplies, by the district in which corps headquarters or subordinate units had their peace stations.

In peacetime, the commander of the infantry corps was also commander of the military district; but because he was destined to take his corps into the field, his chief concern was to develop and maintain the fighting efficiency of the troops under his command. All administrative matters, therefore, were assigned to a second-in-command or deputy Wehrkreis commander—normally a general officer whose health or age rendered him unsuited for active service in the field, while his seniority and experience qualified him for a post of responsibility. (The present average age of these officers is about ten years above that of field corps commanders.)

On mobilization, the commander of the infantry corps departed with his corps to join the field army, and the second-in-command then assumed direct command of the military district. His staff was composed of reserve officers who lived near the military district headquarters and who understudied their opposite numbers in peacetime. This new Wehrkreis command put into effect the mobilization plans worked out in Berlin, and its primary concern subsequently was to provide trained manpower to all units of the field army mobilized in its district.

These field army units include not only the active units of the peacetime army which moved out with the active infantry corps but also all units formed on or after the initial mobilization in the military district in question. To illustrate this point, a military district which contained the peace stations of three divisions under one corps staff might by now have mobilized as many as four corps staffs and twelve or fourteen divisions for the field army.

The functions of the military district commanders in wartime in supplying trained personnel and equipment to the field army are controlled by the rear echelon of the O.K.H. in Berlin through the General Army Office (AHA) and the Chief of Training in the Replacement Training Army. The detailed work is decentralized as much as possible, however, and the military districts are left a large measure of freedom in applying the policies decided in Berlin. Central control is exercised by special staffs to keep close watch over any special program (such as the conversion of infantry to motorized or Panzer divisions), as well as by inspectors of the different arms (similar to our former chiefs of branches), who supervise the training of units of those arms throughout Germany.

For purposes of the draft of personnel and replacement training, each Military District (Wehrkreis) is subdivided into Recruiting Areas (Wehrersatzbezirke) and Recruiting Sub-Areas (Wehrbezirke). Most Military Districts contain two or three recruiting areas, but Wehrkreis VI, comprising the populous Ruhr and Rhineland region, has four, while Wehrkreise VII, XX, and XXI consist of only one such area each. The number of recruiting sub-areas in each area varies between four and a dozen according to local needs. Each recruiting area is controlled by an Inspector of Recruiting Area (Wehrersatzinspekteur), for the supervision of manpower (from civil life into the armed forces, within the armed forces, and back to civil life). The inspector is usually a Generalmajor or Generalleutnant similar in his qualifications to the Deputy Military District Commander. He has the status and disciplinary authority of a division commander. (In some cases he may be a naval or air force officer, since the recruiting system operates jointly for all three branches.) Recruiting sub-areas are commanded by lieutenant colonels or colonels selected from the class of officers whose suitability for active service in the field has ceased. They have the status of regimental commanders.

6. Draft of personnel.

Universal compulsory military service has existed in Germany ever since the Napoleonic wars, with the exception of the period from 1918 to 1935 when it was prohibited by the Treaty of Versailles. In March 1935 conscription was reintroduced by law, with the period of active service fixed at one year; this was extended to two years in August 1936. The law provides that all males between the ages of 18 and 45 are subject to military service in peacetime; in wartime these age limits may be extended and in addition all citizens of both sexes are liable to "service for the Fatherland."

Before the outbreak of war military service usually began at the age of 20. The first registration (Musterung), however, took place at the age of 18 and was accompanied by a preliminary medical examination and a classification according to degree of physical fitness as well as a provisional assignment to a branch of the service (infantry, artillery, air force, navy, etc.). This procedure was carried out in small local registration areas (Musterungsbezirke) with the active collaboration of the district police and other local civil authorities. The recruits then awaited the next stage, their actual drafting (Aushebung), which involved a second physical examination, a definite assignment to an arm of the service, and a decision regarding any request for deferment. If found fit (tauglich), they were then sent home pending their call to the colors (Einberufung) and their induction (Einstellung). Between their first registration and their induction the men ordinarily performed their required period of labor service (Arbeitsdienst).

All German men over 18 (except those considered totally unfit) are classified at any given time into the following categories:

    Aktiv dienende—on active service.
    Reserve I—fully trained, under 35 years of age.
    Reserve II—partly trained, under 35.
    Ersatzreserve I—untrained, not yet called up, under 35.
    Ersatzreserve II—untrained, physically unfit, under 35.
    Landwehr I—trained, between 35 and 45.
    Landwehr II—untrained, between 35 and 45.
    Landsturm I—trained, over 45.
    Lundsturm II—untrained, over 45.

In wartime the procedure for drafting personnel for the German military forces is essentially the same as that outlined above for peacetime, except that it has been greatly accelerated and expanded. For example, the Musterung and Aushebung are now combined into a single operation. The usual age of induction has been lowered to 18, and older classes have also been called up. Members of the Ersatzreserve II and Landwehr II are subject to call, and occupational and other deferments are strictly limited. In addition, volunteers are accepted at the age of 17 for the army as well as the special arms and services, and there is evidence that even younger classes are being drafted for auxiliary duties.

The entire conscription system for the Army, Navy, and Air Force is organized under Section 3 of the General Army Office (AHA), but its operation is highly decentralized through the military districts, recruiting areas, and subareas down to the registration areas (Wehrmeldebezirke) and local registration districts. Navy and Air Force interests are represented by officers specially detailed to the army recruiting organization for this purpose.

7. Replacement training system.

Like the drafting of personnel, the replacement training system is organized regionally by military districts. Its general control is now in the hands of the Chief of Training in the Replacement Training Army (Chef des Ausbildungswesens im Ersatzheer), Gen. d. Pion. Walter KUNTZE, who is responsible to Genobst. FROMM. The basic principle is that trained replacements are supplied to field units from the Wehrkreis in which those units originated, so that there is a permanent affiliation between each field unit and its home station. Despite the radical alterations resulting from the general shift of training from Germany to the occupied countries in the autumn of 1942, it is expected that this basic principle will be maintained as far as possible.

a. The original plan.—At the outbreak of the present war, every unit of the field army normally received replacement personnel from replacement training units stationed in the military district in which it was originally formed. In general, each replacement training unit carried the same number as the field army unit to which it supplied personnel and was one degree smaller than that unit. For the regular standing army (active divisions in the series 1–50) each regiment had two replacement training battalions and each non-regimental battalion had one replacement training battalion. For newly organized divisions of the field army, on the other hand, each regiment had only one replacement training battalion and each non-regimental battalion had a replacement training company. The following examples will illustrate this point:

```
    Field army Units                    Replacement training units
Of the standing army:
    26th Inf Regt_____I/ and II/26th Inf Repl Tng Bns.
    19th Arty Regt_____I/ and II/19th Arty Repl Tng Bns.
    14th AT Bn_____14th AT Repl Tng Bn.
Of newly formed divisions:
    497th Inf Regt_____497th Inf Repl Tng Bn.
    214th Arty Regt_____214th Arty Repl Tng Bn.
    157th Engr Bn_____157th Engr Repl Tng Co.
```

Specialist subunits (such as infantry howitzer cos, infantry AT cos, mounted infantry platoons) were supplied with personnel on the basis of one replacement training subunit per division, carrying the division number and serving the corresponding subunits in all its regiments. For example, in the case of the 22d Inf Div the 22d Inf AT Repl Tng Co provided personnel for the 14th (AT) Cos of the 16th, 47th, and 65th Inf Regts.

All replacement training units serving the infantry regiments of a division were controlled by an infantry replacement training regiment which carried the same number as the division. Thus the 22d Inf Replacement Training Regt at Oldenburg controlled all infantry replacement training units of the 22d Inf Div, and the 269th Inf Repl Tng Regt was formed at Delmenhorst to control the infantry replacements for the newly organized 269th Inf Div. Artillery replacement training regiments were provided on a lower scale, one for each division of the regular army, whose number it carried, although it also supplied replacements to newly formed field army units. Thus the 22d Arty Repl Tng Regt controlled the training of personnel for both the 22d and the 269th Inf Divs.

For administrative purposes and for supervision of training, all replacement training units in a Wehrkreis were controlled by special divisional staffs, designated Div. Nr ____, of which there were usually two in each Wehrkreis. In the autumn of 1942 there were thirty-three such training divisions in Germany and occupied territory.

In general, at this stage, each unit of the field army was served by either one or two replacement training units of the same number, so that the identification of either the field unit or the replacement unit justified the assumption that the other existed. (There were a few exceptions; e. g. the 157th Inf Repl Tng Regt served the 57th Inf Div.)

b. Subsequent developments.—The above system has subsequently undergone substantial modifications culminating in a radical alteration in the whole structure of the German training command during the autumn of 1942.

The first changes took place after completion of the initial expansion program (August 1939–January 1940), when the proportion of replacement training to field army units was reduced. Some of the original replacement training units were transferred to the field army, receiving new numbers; (for example, all the thirteen infantry divisions with numbers from 161 to 198 were formed from such units). In consequence, there are now many infantry regiments without similarly numbered replacement training battalions, and one infantry training regiment will usually supply personnel to two divisions of the field army.

On the other hand, in some cases infantry regiments of the field army have been disbanded or converted into motorized infantry, but their original replacement training battalions still exist under numbers which now have no field army counterpart. Similarly there are infantry replacement regiments carrying numbers in the series 601 and upwards and so apparently corresponding to no divisions of the field army.

The following notes, however, give a general idea of the system then and now still largely in force so far as the affiliation of replacement training to field army units is concerned:

Panzer divisions.—Personnel for the motorized infantry brigade of the Panzer division is controlled by a motorized infantry replacement training regiment (Panzer-Grenadier-Ersatz-Regiment). There is one motorized infantry replacement training battalion for each pair of regiments, one motorcycle replacement battalion for each pair of Panzer divisions, and there are also specialist replacement training companies under the replacement training regiment. Thus the infantry brigades of the 5th and 11th Panzer divisions of Wehrkreis VIII have the following replacement training structure under the 85th Mtz Inf Repl Tng Regt.:

Field army units	*Replacement training units*
13th and 14th Mtz Inf Regts of 5th Pz Div	13th Mtz Inf Repl Tng Bn
110th and 111th Mtz Inf Regts of 11th Pz Div	110th Mtz Inf Repl Tng Bn
55th and 61st Mtrcl Bns	55th Mtrcl Repl Tng Bn
Specialist subunits of 5th and 11th Mtz Inf Brig	85th Sig Repl Tng Co and 85th Gun Repl Tng Co

Personnel for the artillery and other divisional units is supplied in a similar manner.

Infantry divisions.—One infantry replacement training regiment may serve one or two field army divisions. The three infantry regiments of a division are usually served by two replacement training battalions. Similarly, a smaller replacement training unit is likely to provide personnel for two units of the field army instead of only one as under the original system.

The replacement training structure for motorized, light, and mountain divisions is similar to that of infantry divisions with suitable modifications of detail.

In general, it is intended that replacement training units should be permanently affiliated with specific field army units. Thus, for example, a proportion of the officers of a replacement training regiment will have seen service at the front with the corresponding field army division, and convalescent soldiers from that division are attached to a convalescent company (Genesenden-Kompanie) of the replacement training regiment before returning to the field. In times of stress, however, the system is less rigid.

If very heavy casualties are sustained by organizations in the field, the Home Command is called on for larger replacements than can be provided without improvization. In such cases, all the available trained men from each Wehrkreis are formed into personnel replacement transfer battalions (Marschbataillone), which receive either very high numbers (e. g. 2021) or double numbers (e. g. XIII/12—the twelfth battalion of the series provided by Wehrkreis XIII). From these battalions the men may be transferred to whatever unit needs them most, even though its proper replacement training units are stationed in a different military district in Germany.

More recently, due to the unusual situation in Tunisia, some Marschbataillone have functioned as independent combat units merely attached to larger organizations for operational purposes.

The main change, however, took place during the autumn of 1942 when the whole structure of the German training command underwent a radical alteration. Although full particulars are not yet available certain details of the new system are apparent.

The chief feature is the regrouping of the existing thirty-three training divisions into some ~~sixteen~~ defensive divisions designated Reservedivisionen to control training and ~~seventeen~~ purely administrative divisional staffs to control the flow of replacements from the Wehrkreis. The latter are still designated Div. Nr. ____ ad may be referred to as mobilization divisions.

The reserve divisions are moved out into occupied territory, where they come under the control of a new type of headquarters called Reservekorps, to which the supervision of training has now been largely, if not entirely, transferred from the Wehrkreis headquarters. Here they serve the dual purpose of training recruits for subsequent service in divisions in the field army under conditions closer to those of actual field service and of performing a limited amount of internal security duty in occupied territory or occupying quiet coastal sectors in the west, possibly even in an extreme emergency to be sent into the line.

The order of battle of reserve divisions reflects the manner of their formation; the regiments normally carry the number of a division of the field army like the infantry replacement training regiments from which they were formed on conversion.

Similarly, the battalions carry the numbers of regiments of the field army, whereas normally the German battalion carries the number of its regiment preceded by the roman figure I, II, or III.

An example will illustrate this:

157th Reserve Division

(Converted from the replacement training division of the same number)

Res. Inf. Regt. 7:
- Res. Inf. Btl. 19
- Res. Inf. Btl. 61
- Res. Inf. Btl. 62

Carrying the numbers of the three infantry regiments of the 7th Inf Div of the Field Army.

Res. Inf. Regt. 157 (Serves 57th Inf Div, see last sentence of *a* above):
- Res. Inf. Btl. 179
- Res. Inf. Btl. 199
- Res. Inf. Btl. 217

Carrying the numbers of the three infantry regiments of the 57th Inf Div of the Field Army.

Res. Geb. Jäg. Regt. 1:
- Res. Geb. Jäg. Regt. 98
- Res. Geb. Jäg. Regt. 99
- Res. Geb. Jäg. Regt. 100

Carrying the numbers of the original three mountain regiments of the 1st Mtn Div of the Field Army.

There is not yet sufficient evidence to forecast the composition of any specific reserve division since only some of the infantry training regiments in each Wehrkreis will be drawn upon to form reserve infantry regiments.

It is probable that the new organization of the training command has involved the creation of some new divisional and regimental staffs to administer the remaining units in the Wehrkreis concerned, but so far the method of their numbering has not been ascertained.

The notable exception to the system outlined above is the supply of replacements for Panzer and motorized divisions, the training of which is still mainly conducted in Germany itself.

c. Reserve and replacement training units in occupied territory.—Ever since the close of the Polish campaign the Germans have in certain cases been able to effect a considerable economy in manpower in moving the replacement training units from one or more military districts into occupied territory, where they could combine training of recruits with assisting in maintaining internal security. The transfer during 1941–42 of two of the three training divisions from Wehrkreis VIII to the West, where they came under the administration of Wehrkreise V and XII and were later moved still farther west into France proper, foreshadowed the subsequent reorganization of the whole training command reviewed in the above paragraphs.

It is interesting to recapitulate the events that have led up to the present system:

1939–1940. After the close of the Polish campaign, all replacement training units from Wehrkreise V, VI, and XII were transferred to the Protectorate and to Poland (where the two new military districts XX and XXI had been formed).

1940–1941. After the French campaign, the above units returned to their original districts, and replacement training units from Wehrkreis I (East Prussia) moved into the Protectorate. About the same time, many of the replacement training units from Wehrkreis X were transferred to Denmark, where Div. Nr. 160 (one of the two training divisions of Wehrkreis X) replaced a division of the field army.

1941–1942. Once the attack on the USSR had begun, the East Prussian replacement training units were brought back to Wehrkreis I from the Protectorate, where their place was taken by units from the adjoining military districts (IV, XIII, and XVII); at the same time, most of the replacement training units from Silesia (Wehrkreis VIII) were transferred to Alsace and

Lorraine where, as stated above, they came under the administration of Wehrkreise V and XII. In each of these two Wehrkreise two reserve divisions have now been formed, and one training division remains in control of the replacement units, as follows:

(1) Wehrkreis V:
- Div. Nr. 155 _____ Controls replacement units in Wehrkreis V
- Div. Nr. 158 _____ Reorganized as 158th Res Div
- Div. Nr. 165 _____ Reorganized as 165th Res Div

(2) Wehrkreis XII:
- Div. Nr. 148 _____ Reorganized as 148th Res Div
- Div. Nr. 172 _____ Controls replacement units in Wehrkreis XII
- Div. Nr. 182 _____ Reorganized as 182d Res Div

The extent to which other Wehrkreise have formed reserve divisions is not clear, but no doubt, according to their size, each will contribute to the new Defensive reserve divisions, retaining only one of the original training divisions within the Wehrkreis to administer the remaining replacement units.

Prior to the formation of reserve divisions, in cases where the replacement training units were absent from their home district, the recruits from that district reported not at the unit depot but at a central "Wehrkreis-Ersatz-Depot," from which they were conducted in batches to their training units. However, in view of the changes that have certainly been made in the training command subsequent to the withdrawal of large elements to the reserve divisions, this method has probably been modified and a number of new infantry training regiments, or even divisional staffs, may be presumed to have been formed to control the surviving replacement and administrative units and to act as reporting centers for recruits destined for the reserve divisions now operating in occupied territory.

Trained recruits arriving in small batches from the Home Command are sent to a "Frontsammelstelle" (Front Collecting Point), which distributes them to the formations or units where they are required.

d. Recapitulation.—The basic system for supplying replacements to the field forces may be illustrated as follows:

A recruit inducted into the German Army from civilian life at the present time is first placed temporarily in an Ersatzeinheit, or Stammeinheit, in his own Wehrkreis, for the purpose of receiving his papers, his personal equipment, and probably some basic training.

From here he is sent, usually after a very short period, to an Ausbildungseinheit, which is believed in most cases to be part of a reserve division in occupied territory. This transfer is generally conducted by a Marschbataillon, which consists of a nucleus of officers and enlisted men provided by the Wehrkreis for this purpose.

After a period of training the recruit is transferred to a regular Feldeinheit, usually with a group of his fellows organized under a Marschbataillon.

A man who has been wounded, if considered capable of further field service, is placed in a Genesendeneinheit in his own Wehrkreis on his release from the hospital and is thence transferred direct to a Feldeinheit. If unfit for further service, he goes back to his Stammeinheit for discharge.

8. List of military districts.

The following section outlines the essential facts concerning the military districts of Germany, i. e. the commander, units mobilized, geographical structure, and basic training organization. American terms are employed for convenience except where place names are given in their German form as they will most commonly be encountered in German documents. Where a more familiar form exists this follows in parentheses.

Wehrkreis I (Hq: Königsberg)

Ostpreussen: Extended early in 1939 to include Memel, and, after the Polish campaign, a portion of Poland. Believed to have been further extended in 1941–42 to include the Bialystok area.
Commander: Gen. d. Art. Peter WEYER (64)
C of S:

ORDER OF BATTLE OF THE GERMAN ARMY

Corps mobilized: I and XXVI Inf
Divisions mobilized: 24th Pz (former 1st Cav); 1st, 11th, 61st, 161st, 206th, 217th, 228th (since disbanded), 291st, 340th, and 714th Inf
Recruiting Area Hq: Königsberg: Genlt. Alexander RÜHLE v. LILIENSTERN (63)
Recruiting Sub-areas: Königsberg I–II, Tilsit, Gumbinnen, Treuburg, Bartenstein, Braunsberg
Recruiting Area Hq: Allenstein:
Recruiting Sub-areas: Allenstein, Ortelsburg, Lötzen, Zichenau (*Ciechanow*)
*Replacement divisions:
  No. 141: Königsberg
  No. 151: Allenstein
Replacement Training regiments:
  Infantry:
    1st: Insterburg
    11th: Allenstein
    61st: Königsberg
    206th: Gumbinnen
    217th: Allenstein
    228th: Lötzen
  Artillery:
    1st: Insterburg
    11th: Allenstein
Training areas: Arys: Genmaj. SAUVANT (52) Stablack:
Division staffs:
  401 z. b. V.: Königsberg: Genlt. v. DIRINGSHOFEN
  421 z. b. V.:
  461 z. b. V.: Bialystok

Wehrkreis II (Hq: Stettin)

Mecklenburg and Pommern
Commander: Gen. d. Inf. Werner KIENITZ (58)
C of S: Genmaj. STEUDNER (63)
Corps mobilized: II Inf, XXXVI Mtn, LVII Pz
Divisions mobilized: 12th Pz (former 2d Mtz); 12th, 32d, 75th, 122d, 162d, 258th, 292d, 302d, and 702 Inf; 207th Sicherungs (former Inf)
Recruiting Area Hq: Stettin: Genmaj. Carl v. AMMON (61)
Recruiting Sub-areas: Stettin I–II, Swinemünde, Stargard, Greifswald, Stralsund

*From mid-1940 to mid-1941 most of the replacement training units from this military district were stationed in the Protektorat; during that period Div. Nr. 141 was at Prag and Div. Nr. 151 at Budweis.

Recruiting Area Hq: Stettin: Genmaj. Carl v. AMMON (61)
Recruiting Sub-areas: Köslin, Stolp, Kolberg, Neustettin, Deutsch Krone, Woldenberg
Recruiting Area Hq: Schwerin: Genmaj. v. PUTTKAMER (61)
Recruiting Sub-areas: Schwerin, Rostock, Parchim, Neustrelitz
Replacement division:
    No 152: Stettin: Genlt. Arthur BOLTZE (65)
    No 192: Rostock
Replacement training regiments:
    Mtz infantry: 2d Mtz: Stettin
    Infantry:
        12th: Schwerin
        32d: Kolberg
        75th: Stettin
        207th: Deutsch Krone
        258th: Rostock
    Artillery:
        2d Mtz: Stettin
        12th: Schwerin
        32d: Kolberg
Training areas:
    Altwarp:
    Gross-Born: Genlt. Wilhelm THOFERN ( )
    Hammerstein:
    Wüstrow:
Division staff: 402 z. b. V.: Stettin

Wehrkreis III (Hq: Berlin)

Brandenburg
Commander: Gen. d. Inf. Frhr. v. DALWIGK zu LICHTENFELS (67)
C of S:
Corps mobilized: III Pz, XXVIII Inf, XXXIV (Corps Comd), LII Inf, and Africa Pz
Divisions mobilized: 3d, 8th (former 3d L), 21st (former 5th L Mtz), and 26th (former 23d Inf) Pz; 3d Mtz (former Inf) and Grossdeutschland; 90th L; 50th, 68th, 76th, 93d, 111th, 123d, 163d, 208th, 218th, 257th, 293d, 333d, 383d, and 719th Inf
Recruiting Area Hq: Berlin: Genlt. Ferdinand BOCK v. WÜLFINGEN (60)
Recruiting Sub-areas: Berlin I–X
Recruiting Area Hq: Frankfurt/Oder: Genlt. SATOW (55)
Recruiting Sub-Areas: Frankfurt/Oder, Küstrin, Landsberg/Warthe, Crossen/Oder, Lübben (Spreewald), Cottbus

Recruiting Area Hq: Potsdam: Genlt. Friedrich Frhr. v. WILMOWSKY (62)
Recruiting Sub-areas: Potsdam I–II, Neuruppin, Eberswalde, Bernau b. Berlin, Perleberg
Replacement divisions:
  No 143: Frankfurt/Oder: Genlt. WINDECK (54) (Transferred as 143d Reserve Div to Poland)
  No. 153: Potsdam: Genlt. Rene de l'HOMME de COURBIERE (56) (Transferred as 153d Reserve Div to Russia)
  No. 233: Frankfurt/Oder
Replacement training regiments:
  Mtz Infantry: 83d Mtz: Eberswalde
  Infantry:
    3d Mtz: Frankfurt/Oder
    23d: Potsdam
    68th: Guben
    76th: Berlin
    208th: Cottbus
    218th: Spandau
    257th: Landsberg/Warthe
  Artillery:
    3d Mtz: Frankfurt/Oder
    23d: Potsdam
Training areas:
  Döberitz:
  Jüterbog: Obst. v. MALLINCKRODT (51)
  Wandern: Genmaj. OELSNER (54)
  Zossen: Genlt. KOREUBER (53)
Division staff: 403 z. b. V.: Berlin

Wehrkreis IV (Hq: Dresden)

Sachsen and part of Thüringen: Extended in 1939 to include the northern frontier district of Böhmen
Commander: Gen. d. Inf. Walter SCHROTH (61)
C of S:
Corps mobilized: IV, XXIX and XXXXIV Inf
Divisions mobilized: 14th (former 4th Inf) and 18th Pz; 14th Mtz (former Inf); 164th L; 24th, 56th, 87th, 94th, 134th, 209th Inf (since disbanded) 223d, 255th, 256th, 294th, 304th, 336th 370th, and 704th Inf; 454th Sich
Recruiting Area Hq: Dresden: Genlt. Robert PRAETORIUS (61)
Recruiting Sub-areas: Dresden I–III, Pirna, Bautzen, Zittau, Kamenz, Meissen, Grossenhain, Leitmeritz, Böhmisch Leipa, Reichenberg

Recruiting Area Hq: Leipzig:
Recruiting Sub-areas: Leipzig I–III, Naumburg/Saale, Halle/Saale, Altenburg, Eisleben, Bitterfeld, Wittenberg, Grimm, Döbeln
Recruiting Area Hq: Chemitz: Genlt. Fritz HENGEN (56)
Recruiting Sub-areas: Chemnitz I–II, Freiberg, Annaberg, Zwickau, Auerbach, Plauen, Glauchau, Teplitz-Schönau
Replacement divisions:
    No. 154: Dresden: Gen maj. Dr. Friedrich ALTRICHTER (51) (Transferred as 154th Reserve Div to France)
    No. 174: Leipzig (Transferred as 174th Reserve Div to Poland)
Replacement training regiments:
  Mtz infantry: 4th Mtz: Dresden
  Infantry:
    14th Mtz: Leipzig
    24th: Chemnitz
    56th: Dresden
    209th:
    223d: Dresden
    255th: Löbau
    256th: Meissen
    603d: Dresden
  Artillery:
    4th Mtz: Dresden
    24th Mtz: Chemnitz
Training areas:
  Königsbrück:
  Zeithain:
Division staff: 404 z. b. V.: Dresden

Wehrkreis V (Hq: Stuttgart)

Württenberg and part of Baden: Extended after the French campaign to include the incorporated departments of Alsace.
Commander: Gen. d. Inf. Erwin OSSWALD (61)
C of S:
Corps mobilized: V, XXV and L Inf
Divisions mobilized: 10th and 22d Pz, 25th Mtz (former Inf); 5th L (former Inf) and 101st L; 4th Mtm; 35th, 78th, 125th, 198th, 205th, 215th, 260, 305th, 330th, 335th, and 715th Inf
Recruiting Area Hq: Stuttgart: Genlt. Otto TSCHERNING (62)
Recruiting Sub-areas: Stuttgart I–II, Gmünd, Hall, Heilbronn, Esslinger-Neckar, Ludwigsburg, Horb/Neckar, Calw, Karlsruhe, Pforzheim, Rastatt, Offenburg

Recruiting Area Hq: Ulm:
Recruiting Sub-areas: Ulm, Tübingen, Ehingen, Ravensburg, Sigmaringen, Rottweil, Donaueschingen, Konstanz, Freiburg (Breisgau), Lörrach
Recruiting Area Hq: Strassburg:
Recruiting Sub-areas: The organization of sub-areas in incorporated Alsace is not yet known.

*Replacement divisions:
  No. 155: Ulm
  No. 158 (from Wkr. VIII): Strassburg: Genlt. Ernst HAECKEL (53) (transferred as 158th Reserve Div to France)
  No. 165: Epinal: Genlt. Sigmund Frhr. v. SCHACKY auf SCHÖNFELD (57) (transferred as 165th Reserve Div to France)

Replacement training regiments:
  Mtz Infantry: 86th Mtz: Stuttgart
  Infantry:
    5th: Konstanz
    25th: Mtz: Ludwigsburg
    35th: Karlsruhe
    78th: Ulm
    205th: Ulm
    215th: Heilbronn
    260th: Luneville
  Artillery:
    5th: Ulm
  25th Mtz: Stuttgart
  35th: Karlsruhe
  Infantry:
    8th: Colmar
    62d: Colmar
    213th: Mülhausen (Elsass)
    221st: Strassburg
  Artillery: 8th: Strassburg.

Training areas:
  Heuberg:
  Münsingen:
  Division staff: 405 z. b. V.: Stuttgart:

---

*From late 1939 to mid-1940 most of the replacement training units from this military district were stationed in the Protektorat; during that period Div No 155 was at Prag and Div No 165 at Olmütz.

Wehrkreis VI (Hq: Münster)

Westfalen and the Rheinland: Extended after the French campaign to include the Eupen-Malmedy district of Belgium; some replacement training units from this military district are at present stationed in Holland and East Belgium.

Commander: Gen. d. Inf. Gerhard GLOKKE (59)

C of S:

Corps mobilized: VI and XXIII Inf, XXXIII (Corps Comd), LVI Pz

Divisions mobilized: 6th Pz (former 1st L), 16th Pz (former 16th Inf) and 25th Pz; 16th Mtz; 6th, 26th, 69th, 86th, 106th, 126th, 196th, 199th, 211th, 227th, 253rd, 254th, 306th, 339th, 385th, and 716th Inf

Recruiting Area Hq: Münster: Genlt. v. dem KNESEBECK (66)

Recruiting Sub-areas: Münster (Westf.), Coesfeld, Paderborn, Bielefeld, Herford, Minden, Detmold, Lingen, Osnabruck, Recklinghausen, Gelsenkirchen

Recruiting Area Hq: Dortmund:

Recruiting Sub-areas: Dortmund I–II, Arnsberg, Soest, Iserlohn, Bochum, Herne, Hagen

Recruiting Area Hq: Düsseldorf:

Recruiting Sub-areas: Düsseldorf, Neuss, Krefeld, München Gladbach, Wuppertal, Mettmann, Solingen, Essen I–II, Duisburg, Moers, Oberhausen, Wesel

Recruiting Area Hq: Köln: Genlt. Kurt Frhr. ROEDER v. DIERSBURG (57)

Recruiting Sub-areas: Köln I–III, Bonn, Siegburg, Aachen, Jülich, Düren, Monschau

*Replacement divisions:

    No. 156: Köln: Genlt. BALTZER (56) (transferred as 156th Reserve Div to Belgium)

    No. 166: Bielefeld: Genlt. Justin v. OBERNITZ (59)

*Replacement training regiments:

    Mtz infantry: 57th Mtz.: Wuppertal

    Infantry:

        6th: Bielefeld

        16th: Rheine

        26th: Köln

        69th: Soest

        211th: Köln

        227th: Düsseldorf

---

*From late 1939 to late 1940, most of the replacement training units from this military district were stationed in Wehrkreis XX; during that period Div N 156 was at Thorn and Div N 166 at Danzig.

Replacement training regiments—Continued.
  Infantry——Continued.
    253rd: Aachen
    254th: Dortmund
  Artillery:
    6th: Münster
    16th Mtz:
    26th: Köln
Training areas:
  Deilinghofen:
  Elsenborn: Genmaj. LEYTHÄUSER (58)
  Meppen:
  Sennelager:
  Wahn: Obst. BENCZEK ( )
Division staffs:
  406th z. b. V.: Münster: Genmaj. SCHERBENING (52)
  526th Grenzwach: Aachen

Wehrkreis VII (Hq: München)

Southern Bayern.
Commander: Genlt. Kurt KRIEBEL (55)
C of S
Corps mobilized: VII and XXVII Inf
Divisions mobilized: 17th Pz (former 27th Inf); 97th L; 1st Mtn: 7th, 57th, 88th, 167th, 212th, 268th, 337th, 387th, and 707th Inf
Recruiting Area Hq.: München: Genlt. Oskar van GINKEL (61)
Recruiting Sub-areas: München I–IV, Rosenheim, Traunstein, Weilheim, Augsburg, Kempten (Allgäu), Landshut, Pfarrkirchen, Inglostadt
Replacement divisions:
  No 147: Augsburg: Genlt. HELD (61)
  No 157: München: Genmaj. Karl PFLAUM (53) (Transferred as 157th Reserve Div to France)
Replacement training regiments:
  Mtz infantry: 27th Mtz: Augsburg
  Infantry:
    7th: München
    157th: Bad Reichenhall
    212th: München
    268th: München
Mountain rifle: 110th: Garmisch
Artillery:
  7th: München
  27th Mtz: Augsburg
  79th Mtn:

Training areas:
   Hohenfels:
   Mittenwald:
Division staffs:
   407 z. b. V.: München
   467 z. b. V.: München

Wehrkreis VIII (Hq: Breslau)

Schlesien: Extended after September to include certain Sudeten districts of Böhmen and Mähren; and in autumn 1939 to include part of SW Poland.
Commander: Gen. d. Kav. Rudolf KOCH-ERPACH (57)
C of S:
Corps mobilized: VIII Inf, XXXV (Corps Comd), XXXVIII Inf?
Divisions mobilized: 5th and 11th Pz; 18th Mtz (former Inf); 8th and 28th L (former Inf); 62d, 81st, 102d, 168th, 239th (since disbanded), 252d, 298th, 332d and 708th Inf; 213th and 221st Sich (former Inf)
Recruiting Area Hq: Breslau: Genlt. Athos v. SCHAUROTH (57)
Recruiting Sub-areas: Breslau I–III, Oels, Brieg, Glatz, Waldenburg (Schles.) Schweidnitz, Mährisch-Schönberg, Zwittau, Troppau, Jägerndorf, Wohlau
Recruiting Area Hq: Liegnitz: Genlt. Konrad SORSCHE (58)
Recruiting Sub-areas: Liegnitz, Glogau, Sagan, Görlitz, Bunzlau, Hirschberg (Riesengeb.), Trautenau
Recruiting Area Hq: Kattowitz: Genlt. Georg CARP (56)
Recruiting Sub-areas: Kattowitz, Königshütte (Oberschles.), Loben, Rybnik, Teschen, Bielitz-Biala, Oppeln, Neisse, Neustadt (Oberschles.), Cosel, Gleiwitz
Replacement divisions:
   No 148: transferred to Metz (Wkr. XII) (Transferred as 148th Reserve Div to France)
   No 158: transferred to Strassburg (Wkr. V) (Transferred as 158th Reserve Div to France)
   No 178: Liegnitz
*Replacement training regiments:
   Mtz infantry: 85th Mtz: Liegnitz
   Infantry: 18th Mtz: Liegnitz
Training areas:
   Lamsdorf:
   Neuhammer: Genmaj. STAMMER ( )

---

*The remaining training regiments from this military district have been transferred for the time being to Alsace and Lorraine; see under Wkr. V and Wkr. XII.

Division staffs:
    408 z. b. V.: Breslau
    432 z. b. V.: Neisse

Wehrkreis IX (Hq: Kassel)

Part of Türingen and Hessen
Commander: Gen. d. Inf. Paul OTTO (62)
C of S:
Corps mobilized: IX Inf. XXXIX Pz
Divisions mobilized: 1st Pz, 7th Pz (former 2d L), 20th and 27th (former 15th Inf), Pz: 29th Mtz; 9th, 52d, 82d, 95th, 129th, 169th, 214th, 251st, 299th, 319th, 328th, 339th, and 709th Inf
    Recruiting Area Hq: Kassel: Genlt. PINCKVOSS (57)
    Recruiting Sub-areas: Kassel I–II, Korbach, Marburg/Lahn, Hersfeld, Siegen, Wetzlar, Fulda, Giessen
Recruiting Area Hq: Frankfurt/Main: Genlt. DETMERING (56)
    Recruiting Sub-areas: Frankfurt/Main I–II, Offenbach/Main, Aschaffenburg, Friedberg, Hanau
Recruiting Area Hq: Weimar:
Recruiting Sub-Areas: Weimar, Sangerhausen, Gera, Rudolstadt, Mühlhausen (Thür.) Erfurt, Eisenach, Gotha, Meiningen
Replacement divisions:
    No 159: Frankfurt/Main: Gen. d. tion. SACHS (58) (Transferred as 159th Reserve Div to France)
    No 179: Weimar
    No. 189: Braunschweig: Genmaj. v. NEINDORF (Transferred as 189th Reserve Div to France, possibly later to the Balkans)
Replacement training regiments:
    Mtz Infantry: 81th Mtz: Meiningen
    Infantry:
        9th: Siegen:
        15th: Kassel
        29th Mtz: Erfurt
        52d: Kassel
        214th: Hanau
        251st: Frankfurt/Main?
    Artillery:
        9th:
        15th: Kassel
        29th Mtz: Erfurt
        44th:
        52d:

Training areas:
    Ohrdruf: Genmaj. Hans von GOECKEL
    Schwarzenborn:
    Wildflecken:
Division staff: 409 z. b. V.: Kassel Genmaj. Hans EHRENBERG (53)

Wehrkreis X (Hq: Hamburg)

Schleswig-Holstein and part of Hannover
Commander: Gen. d. Inf. Erich RASCHICK (61)
C of S:
Corps mobilized: X Inf, XXXI (Corps Comd)?, XXXX and XXXXVI Pz
Divisions mobilized: 20th Mtz; 22d, 30th, 58th, 83d, 110th, 121st, 170th, 225th, 269th, 290th, 320th and 710th Inf
Recruiting Area Hq: Schleswig-Holstein (at Hamburg); Genmaj. SCHAU-WECKER (61)
Recruiting Sub-areas: Neumünster, Rendsburg, Schleswig, Kiel, Eutin, Lübeck
Recruiting Area Hq: Hamburg:
Recruiting Sub-areas: Hamburg I-VI
Recruiting Area Hq: Bremen
Recruiting Sub-areas: Bremen I-II, Stade, Wesermünde, Oldenburg (Oldb.) I-II, Aurich, Nienburg/Weser, Lüneburg
Replacement divisions:
    No. 160: transferred to Denmark; probably now a Reserve Div
    No. 180: Bremen
    No. 190: Neumünster
Replacement training regiments:
    Infantry:
        20th Mtz: Hamburg
        22d: Oldenburg
        30th: Lübeck*
        58th: Rendsburg?*
        225th: Hamburg*
        269th: Delmenhorst
    Artillery:
        20th Mtz: Hamburg
        22d: Bremen
        30th: Lübeck
Training areas:
    Munsterlager:
    Putlos:
Division staff: 410 z. b. V.: Hamburg: Genlt. Adolf POETTER (59)

---
*At present stationed in Denmark under Div N 160.

Wehrkreis XI (Hq: Hannover)

Braunschweig, Anhalt, and part of Hannover
Commander: Gen. d. Inf. Albrecht SCHUBERT (57)
C of S:
Corps mobilized: XI Inf, XIV Pz, XXX Inf, XXXXIII Inf, LI Inf
Divisions mobilized: 13th Pz (former 13th Mtz) and 19th Pz (former 19th Inf); 31st, 71st, 96th, 131st, 181st, 216th, 267th, 295th, 321st and 711th Inf
Recruiting Area Hq: Hannover:
Recruiting Sub-areas: Hannover I–II, Braunschweig, Goslar, Hildesheim, Hameln, Göttingen, Celle
Recruiting Area Hq: Magdeburg:
Recruiting Sub-areas: Magdeburg I–II, Stendal, Burg bei Magdeburg, Halberstadt, Dessau, Bernburg
Replacement divisions:
    No. 171: Hannover (transferred as 171th Reserve Div to France)
    No. 191: Braunschweig: Genmaj. v. DEWITZ gen. v. KREBS (transferred as 191st Reserve Div to France)
Replacement training regiments:
    Mtz infantry: 13th Mtz: Madgeburg
    Infantry:
        31st: Braunschweig
        71st: Hildesheim
        216th: Hameln?
        267th: Hannover?
    Artillery:
        13th Mtz: Magdeburg
        19th: Hannover
        31st: Braunschweig
Training areas:
    Altengrabow:
    Bergen:
    Hillersleben:
    Salchau:
Division staff: 411 z. b. V.: Hannover

Wehrkreis XII (Hq: Wiesbaden)

Eifel, part of Hessen, the Pfalz and the Saar area: Extended after the French campaign to comprise Lorraine (including the Nancy area), and Luxemburg.
Commander: Gen. d. Inf. Albrecht STEPPUHN (66)
C of S: Genmaj. Hans MEISSNER (59)

Corps mobilized: XII Inf, XXIV Pz, LIII Inf

Divisions mobilized: 15th Pz (former 33d Inf) and 23d Pz; 36th Mtz; 34th, 72d, 79th, 112th, 132d, 197th, 246th, 263d, 342d and 712th Inf; 444th Sicherungs

Recruiting Area Hq: Koblenz: Genlt. Ludwig v. BERG (61)

Recruiting Sub-areas: Koblenz, Trier I–II, Neuwied, Kreuznach, Wiesbaden, Limburg/Lahn, Mainz, Worms, Darmstadt

Recruiting Area Hq: Mannheim: Genlt. Willy KÖRNER (65)

Recruiting Sub-areas: Mannheim I–II, Saarlautern, Saarbrücken, St. Wendel, Zweibrücken, Kaiserslautern, Neustadt (Weinstrasse), Ludwigshafen/Rhein, Heidelberg

Recruiting Area Hq: Metz:

Recruiting Sub-areas: The organization of sub-areas in incorporated Luxemburg and Lorraine is not yet known.

*Replacement divisions:
  No. 172: Mainz:
  No. 148 (from Wkr. VIII): Metz: Genlt. BOETTCHER (transferred as 148th Reserve Div to France)
  No. 182: Nancy: Genlt. Franz KARL (55) (transferred as 182d Reserve Div to France)

Replacement training regiments:
  Mtz infantry: 12th Mtz:
  Infantry:
    34th: Heidelberg
    36th Mtz: Wiesbaden
    112th: Darmstadt
    246th: Trier
    342d: Kaiserslautern
  Artillery:
    33d Mtz: Mainz
    34th: Koblenz
  Infantry:
    28th: Metz
    79th: Nancy
    239th: Diedenhofen
    252d: Mörchingen
    263d: Nancy
  Artillery:
    28th: Metz
    263d: Nancy

---

*From late 1939 to late 1940, most of the replacement training units from this military district were stationed in Wehrkreis XXI; during that period Div N 172 was at Gnesen and Div N 182 at Litzmannstadt.

Training areas:
    Baumholder:
    Bitsch:
Division staff: 412 z. b. V.: Wiesbaden Genlt. Kurt FISCHER (66)

Wehrkreis XIII (Hq: Nürnberg)

Northern Bayern: Extended in 1938 to include part of Western Böhmen
Commander: Gen. d. Inf. Mauriz WIKTORIN (60)
C of S: Genmaj. Paul VOIT (67)
Corps mobilized: XIII Inf. XXXXV (Corps Comd) (?)
Divisions mobilized: 4th Pz, 10th Mtz (former 10th Inf); 7th Mtn (former 99th L); 17th, 46th, 73d, 98th, 113th, 183d, 296th, 323d, and 713 Inf; 231st Inf (since disbanded)
Recruiting Area Hq: Nürnberg:
Recruiting Sub-areas: Nürnberg I–II, Fürth, Bamberg, Bad Kissingen, Würzburg, Ansbach, Coburg, Bayreuth, Bad Mergentheim, Tauberbischofsheim.
Recruiting Area Hq: Regensburg: Genlt. Bruno Elder v. KIESLING auf KIESLINGSTEIN (65)
Recruiting Sub-areas: Regensburg, Passau, Straubing, Weiden, Amberg
Recruiting Area Hq: Eger (at Karlsbad): Genlt. Erich VOLK (59)
Recruiting Sub-areas: Eger, Kaaden, Karlsbad, Mies, Marktredwitz
*Replacement divisions:
    No. 173: Nürnberg: Genlt. PFLUGRADT (53)
    No. 193: Regensburg:
Replacement training regiments:
    Mtz infantry: 84: Würzburg
    Infantry:
        17th: Nürnberg
        42d:
        46th: Pilsen (Prot.)
        73d: Würzburg
        95th: Coburg (?)
        231st:
    Artillery:
        10th Mtz:
        17th: Nürnberg
Training areas:
    Grafenwöhr: Genlt. Hans HEBERLEIN (55)
    Hammelburg:
Division staff: 413 z. b. V.: Nürnberg

---

*Some of the replacement training units controlled by these divisions are now stationed in the eastern districts of the Protectorate.

Wehrkreis XVII (Hq: Wien)

Oberdonau and Niederdonau: Extended in 1939 to include the southern districts of Böhmen and Mähren.
Commander: Gen. d. Inf. Alfred STRECCIUS (64)
C of S: Genmaj. Emil ZELLNER ( )
Corps mobilized: XVII Inf, XXXVII (Corps Comd)
Divisions mobilized: 2d Pz and 9th Pz (former 4 L); 100th L; 44th, 45th, 137th, 262d, 297th, 327th, 331st, and 717th Inf
Recruiting Area Hq: Wien; Genlt. SCHWARZNECKER (59)
Recruiting Sub-areas: Wien I–IV, Melk, Zwettl, St. Pölten, Krems/Donau, Znaim, Wiener Neustadt, Baden, Nikolsburg
Recruiting Area Hq: Linz: Genlt. Ludwig RIEBESAM (55)
Recruiting Sub-areas: Linz, Steyr, Wels, Ried im Innkreis, Krummau
Replacement divisions:
    No. 177*: Wein:

    No 187: Linz: Genlt. Josef BRAUNER. (Transferred as 187th Reserve Div to the Balkans)
Replacement training regiments:
    Mtz infantry: 82d Mtz: Wien
    Infantry:
        45th: Krummau Moldau
        130th: Linz
        131st: Wien
        462d:
    Artillery:
        96th: Wien
        98th: Linz
Training areas: Bruck/Leitha:
    Döllerscheim: Genmaj. Konrad OFFENBÄCHER (52)
Division staff: 417 z. b. V.: Wien

Wehrkreis XVIII (Hq: Salzburg)

Stiermark, Kärnten, Tirol: Extended in 1941 to include the northern districts of Slovenia
Commander: Gen. d. Inf. Friedrich MATERNA (58)
C. of S.: Genmaj. Reichsfrhr. v. u. zud TANN-RATHSAMHAUSEN (58)
Corps mobilized: XVIII and Norway Mtn
Divisions mobilized: 2d, 3d, 5th, 6th, and 8th Mtn; 718th Inf

---

*Some of the replacement training units controlled by these divisions are now stationed in the eastern districts of the Protectorate.

Recruiting Area Hq: Innsbruck: Genlt. Wilhelm Frhr. v. WALDENFELS (59)
Recruiting Sub-areas: Bregenz, Innsbruck, Salzburg
Recruiting Area Hq: Graz: Genlt. Emil GUNZELMANN (56)
Recruiting Sub-areas: Spittal, Klagenfurt, Judenburg, Leoben, Graz, Leibnitz, Fürstenfeld, Marburg (*Maribor*), Cilli (*Celje*), Krainburg (*Kranj*)
Replacement division: No. 188: Salzburg: Genlt. Wilhelm v. HÖSSLIN (65) (65)
Replacement training regiments:
  Mountain rifle:
    136th: Landeck
    137th: Innsbruck (?)
    138th: Leoben
    139th: Klagenfurt
  Artillery:
    110th:
    112th:
Training areas:
  Dachstein:
  Seethaler Alpe:
  Strass i. Steiermark:
  Wattener Lizum:
Division staff:
  537th Grenzwach: Innsbruck
  538th Grenzwach: Klagenfurt

Wehrkreis XX (Hq: Danzig)

Formed after the Polish campaign, comprising the areas of Danzig Free State, the Polish Corridor, and the western part of Ostpreussen.
Commander: Gen. d. Inf. Bodewin KEITEL
C of S:
Corps maintained: XX Inf, XXXXVII Pz
Divisions maintained: 60th Mtz; 21st Inf
Recruiting Area Hq: Danzig: Genlt. KURZ
Recruiting Sub-areas: Danzig, Neustadt, Pr. Stargard, Marienwerder, Graudenz, Bromberg (*Bydgoszcz*), Thorn (*Torun*).
Replacement training regiments:
  Infantry:
    21st: Elbing
    60th Mtz: Danzig
Training areas: Thorn (*Torun*):
Division staff: 428 z. b. V.: Danzig

Wehrkreis XXI (Hq: Posen) (*Poznan*).

Formed after the Polish campaign, comprising western Poland.
Commander: Gen. d. Art. Walter PETZEL (60)
C of S:
Corps maintained: XXXXVIII Pz
Divisions maintained: None
Recruiting Area Hq: Posen (*Poznan*):
Recruiting Sub-areas: Posen (*Poznan*), Lissa, Hohensalza, Leschnau (*Leszno*), Kalisch (*Kalisz*), Litzmannstadt (*Lodz*)
Replacement training regiments:
   Infantry: 50th: Posen (*Poznan*):
Training areas:
   Sieradsch (*Sieratz*):
   Warthelager:
Division staffs:
   429 z. b. V.: Posen (*Poznan*): Genlt. SCHARTOW (52)
   430 z. b. V.: Gnesen (*Gniezno*):
   431 z. b. V.: Litzmannstadt (*Lodz*): Genlt. Otto v. SCHWERIN (60)

9. Army administration in occupied countries.

In the following pages the German-occupied and German-allied countries are set out in historical sequence. The essential structure of German commands and missions therein is shown under separate headings.

a. Austria.—Occupied in March 1938 and absorbed into the Reich as Wehrkreise XVII and XVIII.

b. Czechoslovakia.—First partitioned in September, 1938, when the Sudetenland was detached and incorporated into Wehrkreise IV, VIII, and XIII. The remaining territory (except the parts which went to Hungary and Poland was occupied in March, 1939, and was divided into the Protektorat Böhmen-Mähren and the protected state of Slovakia.

(1) *Protektorat* (Hq: Prag).—This area is in effect though not in name an additional military district (Wehrkreis).

Commander (Wehrmachtbevollmächtigter): Genlt. Rudolf TOUSSAINT (52)
C of S: Obst. Anton LONGIN
Corps mobilized: XLIX Mtn
Divisions mobilized:
Recruiting Area Hq: Prag: Genlt. v. PRONDZYNSKI (62)
Recruiting Sub-areas: Prag, Budweis, Brünn, Olmütz

Training areas:
  Brdy Wald: Genmaj. THAMS
  Hohenelbe:
  Milowitz:
  Wischau:
Division staffs:
  539th Grenzwach: Prag: Genlt. Dr. Richard SPEICH (59)
  540th Grenzwach Brünn: Genlt. Karl TARBUK v. SENSENHORST

(2) *Slovakia* (Hq: Pressburg (*Bratislava*)).—This is nominally an independent country with its own army, and its own defense ministry (Minister of Defense and C in C: General CATLOS). It is, however, under complete German domination and the Germans not only have a military mission there but garrison and train their own troops in the territory.

Head of Military Mission (Chef der Heeresmission): Genlt. SCHLIEPER (52)
C of S:
Commandant of the Protected Area (Kommandant der Schutzzone):
Replacement training area: Malacky.

c. Memel District.—Occupied in March 1939 and incorporated into Wehrkreis I.

d. Poland.—Occupied after the campaign of September 1939. Western and northern portions incorporated into Wehrkreise I and VIII and into the newly formed Wehrkreise XX and XXI. Central Poland established as the Government General (General-Gouvernement).

              Government General (Hq: Krakau)

Commander: (Militärbefehlshaber): Gen. d. Kav, Frhr. von GIENANTH (64)
C of S:
Area Hq (Oberfeldkommandanturen having divisional status): The following have been identified:
  365th Lemberg (*Lwow*): Genlt. BEUTTEL (56)
  372 Kielce:
  379th Lublin: Genmaj. Wilhelm v. ALTROCK (53)
  393 Piaseczno: Genmaj. Kurt SIEGLIN (58)
City Hq (Stadtkommandanturen): The following have been identified:
  Krakau: Genlt. Eugen v. HÖBERTH
  Warschau: Genlt. ROSSUM (53)

e. Danzig Free State.—Occupied in September 1939 and incorporated subsequently into the newly formed Wehrkreis XX.

f. Norway.—Occupied after a brief campaign in April 1940, and subsequently governed by the Quisling regime under a German civilian commissar (TERBOVEN).

GERMAN FORCES IN NORWAY (Hq: Oslo)

Commander (Wehrmachtsbefehlshaber*): Genobst. Nikolaus v. FALKENHORST (58)
C of S: Genmaj. Rudolf BAMLER (48)
Areas:
    North (Hq: Alta): Gen. d. Inf. Emmerich NAGY (61) (LXXI Corps Comd) Sub-areas: **Kirkenes, Alta, Narvik
    Center (Hq: Trondhjem): Gen. d. Kav. Erwin ENGELBRECHT (52) (XXXIII Corps Comd.)
        Sub-areas: Mo, Dombaas
    South (Hq: Oslo): Gen. d. Geb. Tr. Valentin FEURSTEIN (58) (LXX Corps Comd)
        Sub-areas: Bergen, Stavanger or Christiansand South, Oslo

NOTE.—The administrative areas are corps commands, each having two or three sub-areas which are division commands. These in turn are each subdivided into three sectors, each under control of an infantry regiment. The commanders of areas and sub-areas are described as Territorial-Befehlshaber, and the commanders of sectors as Abschnittskommandeure.

g. Denmark.—Occupied almost without resistance in April 1940 and subsequently allowed a degree of autonomy in internal affairs.

GERMAN TROOPS IN DENMARK (Hq: Copenhagen)

Commander (Befehlshaber d. deutschen Truppen): Gen. d. Inf. v. HANNEKEN (53) (XXXI Corps Comd.)
C of S:
Area Hq: Copenhagen
    Sub-areas: Jutland:
        Aalborg:
        Viborg: 225th Infantry Replacement Training Regiment
        Kolding:
        Zeeland:
        Ringsted: 58th Infantry Replacement Training Regiment
Replacement division: No. 160: Copenhagen: (probably now a Reserve Div)

---

*Also commanding the Army of Norway.
**In the communications zone of the Twentieth Army.

h. Holland.—Occupied in May 1940 and subsequently governed by a German civilian commissar (Seyss-Inquart), with the help of the existing Dutch administrative agencies.

GERMAN FORCES IN HOLLAND (Hq: The Hague)

Commander (Wehrmachtsbefehlshaber): Gen. d. Flieger Friedrich CHRISTIANSEN (64)
C of S: Genlt. Walter SCHWABEDISSEN
Area Hq: The Hague
    Sub-areas: The following has been identified:
        674th: Rotterdam

i. Luxemburg.—Occupied in May 1940 and incorporated into Wehrkreis XII.

j. Belgium.—Occupied in May 1940 subsequently governed by the German military commander with the help of the existing Belgian administrative agencies. For military administration purposes it is combined with coastal northern France above the River Somme into the unified command "Belgien-Nordfrankreich."

Belgian-Nordfrankreich (Hq: Brussels)

Commander (Militärbefehlshaber): Gen. d. Inf. Alexander v. FALKENHAUSEN (65)
C of S: Obstlt. v. HARBOU
Administrative Hq*: The following have been identified:
    178th: Bruges:
    510th: Bruges:
    520th: Antwerp: Genmaj. Willy HEDERICH (63)
    611th: Ghent:
    672d: Brussels: Genlt. Günther Frhr. v. HAMMERSTEIN-EQUORD (65)
    681st: Louvain:
    701st: Antwerp:
    ——: Liege: Genmaj. KEIM (62)
Areas:
    Brabant (Hq?)
    Commander:
    C of S:
    Flanders-Artois (Hq: Tourcoing).
    Commander: Gen. d. Kav. Günther v. POGRELL (64) (XXXVIII Corps Comd)
    C of S:

---

*Including Oberfeldkommandanturen, Feldkommandanturen, Ortskommandanturen, Kreiskommandanturen. (See paragraph 25b(3).)

Landesschützen Regimental Staffs: The following have been identified:
  115th: Marais
  Wachregiment CLÜWER

k. France.—Partially occupied after the capitulation of June, 1940; allowed a degree of autonomy in matters of local government throughout the occupied area, with the exception of Alsace and Lorraine which, in fact, though not in name, have been incorporated into the Reich. Divided for purposes of military administration into the areas "France" and "Northern France" (included in Belgium). The remainder of metropolitan France was occupied in November 1942; at the time of printing this text the mode of the administration and military organization was unknown.

        France (Hq: Paris—Reported moved to Nancy)

Commander (Militärbefehlshaber): Gen. d. Inf. Otto v. STÜLPNAGEL (64)
C of S: Genmaj. Dr. Hans SPEIDEL
Military districts (of the former occupied zone):
  Northern France (SW of the River Somme):
  Southwestern France:
  Southern France: Genmaj. Heinrich Ritter v. FÜCHTBAUER (63)
  Northwestern France:
  Greater Paris: Genlt. Ernst SCHAUMBURG (61)
Administrative Hq*: The following have been identified:
  515th: Channel Islands
  529th: Amiens
  523d: Nancy
  541st: Biarritz
  549th: Rennes: Genmaj. Alfred JACOBI (58)
  568th: Dijon
  575th: Paris
  588th: Tours
  590th: Bar-le-Duc
  591st: Nancy
  592d: Laon
  602d: Laon
  605th: La Roche s/Yon: Genmaj. v. KURNATOWSKI (62)
  670th: Lille: Genlt. Heinrich NIEHOFF (60)

---

*Including Oberfeldkommandanturen, Feldkommandanturen, Ortskommandanturen, Kreiskommandanturen. (See paragraph 25b(3).)

677th: Poitiers
678th: Arras
680th: Melun: Obst. Rudolf Ritter v. XYLANDER
723d: Caen
734th: Paris area
754th: Flers
755th: Le Mans

Areas:
    Normandy East (Hq: Rouen): Commander:
        (XXXII Corps Comd)
    Burgundy (Hq: Dijon): Commander: Gen. d. Inf. Kurt v. GREIFF (65)
        (XXXXV Corps Comd)

Normandy West (Hq: Caen): Commander: Gen. d. Art. BEHLENDORFF (54)
    (LX Corps Comd)
Brittany (Hq: Angers): Commander:
    (? Corps Comd)
Guyenne-Gascony (Hq: Bordeaux): Commander:
    (? Corps Comd)
Landesschützen regimental staffs: The following have been identified:
    64 z. b. V.: Angers
    65th: Viroflay
    113th: Rouen
    122d: Troyes
    125th: Besancon
    137th: Lure
    138th: Tours

l. Italy.—Entered the war on 11 June, 1940, since which date German infiltration has continued with growing intensity.

Head of Military Mission and Military Attache: Gen. d. Inf. Enno v. RINTELEN (52)
C of S:

m. Rumania.—Under German domination since November 1940.

Head of Military Mission: Genlt. HAUFFE (51)
C of S:

n. Bulgaria.—Passively associated with Germany since March 1941.

Head of Military Mission:
C of S:

o. Hungary.—Allied to Germany since summer, 1940. Since the autumn of that year German domination has increased. The Hungarians retain, however, a much greater degree of independence than do the Rumanians.

Head of Military Mission:
C of S:

p. Yugoslavia.—Occupied in April 1941. Portions of the country annexed by Germany, Italy, Hungary, and Bulgaria, the rest divided into German and Italian spheres of influence. Part of Slovenia incorporated into Wkr. XVIII.

(1) *Serbia* (Hq: Belgrad).

Commander (Militärbefehlshaber): Gen. d. Art. Paul BADER (58)
C of S:
Corps Command: LXV
    Commander: Gen. d. Art. Paul BADER (58)
    C of S:

(2) *Croatia* (Hq: Agram) (*Zagreb*).

Head of Military Mission: Genlt. Edmund v. GLAISE-HORSTENAU (61)
Administrative Hq: The following has been identified:
735th: Agram (*Zagreb*)
Commander: Genmaj. Dr. Karl PRÜGEL (66)

q. Greece.—Occupied in April and May 1941. Portions annexed by Bulgaria and the rest divided into German and Italian spheres of influence.

(1) *Northern Greece* (Hq: Salonika).

Commander: (Feldkommandant): Genlt. Kurt v. KRENZKI (56)
C of S:
Administrative Hq: The following has been identified:
  808th: Salonika: Genlt. Kurt v. KRENZKI (56)

(2) *Southern Greece* (Hq: Athens).

Commander (Befehlshaber):
C of S:

(3) *Crete* (Hq: Heraklion.—Divided into German and Italian spheres under a military administration independent of the mainland.

Commander: Genlt. Bruno BRÄUER (51)
C of S:
Administrative Hq: The following has been identified:
  606th: Heraklion

r. Finland.—Allied to Germany since June 1941. The Twentieth Army controls German forces in northern Finland; any German forces in southern Finland come under the Finnish High Command, to which a German Military Mission is accredited.

Head of Military Mission: Gen. d. Inf. Waldemar ERFURTH (64)
C of S. Obstlt. HÖLTER

s. U. S. S. R.—Attacked in June 1941: the Baltic States and White Russia (collectively termed the Ostland) and the western Ukraine have since been placed under German civilian administrations (Rosenberg); the occupied regions farther east are under German military administration. The province of Galicia has been placed under the Government General.

   (1) *Ostland.*—Governed by a German civilian commissar (Lohse).

Commander: Gen. d. Kav. Walter BRAEMER (60)
C of S:

   (2) *Ukraine.*—Governed by a German civilian commissar (Koch).

Commander Befehlshaber): Gen. d. Flieger Karl KITZINGER (58)
C of S:

10. Army organization in the communications zone.

In the communications zone of the theater of operations the place of the military district organization is to some extent taken by the rear area command. Each army group has a Commander of Army Group Rear Area (Befehlshaber des rückwärtigen Heeresgebiets), and each army has a Commandant of Army Rear Area (Kommandant des rückwärtigen Armeegebiets) whose main task is to supervise the administration of the communications zone so that the army group or army commander can concentrate exclusively on the course of operations.

The Commander of Army Group Rear Area has the additional charge over Sicherungs (security) units—specially organized divisions and regiments formed to undertake mopping-up operations in the rear of the combat zone. He is also in charge of such administrative headquarters as may be set up within the area assigned to him, and of all guard units and supply organizations of the GHQ pool stationed within the area.

His functions, therefore, correspond very closely to those of the military commanders of occupied countries, and on the close of active operations he may in fact remain as military commander over the country or portion of a country which he has hitherto commanded as a rear area.

The functions of the Commandant of an Army Rear Area are less extensive, and his status compares more closely with that of the area commander within an occupied country.

Section III. TYPES OF SMALL UNITS

11. Introduction.

This section describes the various types of units of the German ground forces likely to be encountered in the field, arranged according to their respective arms and services. They are subdivided into organic units and GHQ units, and in each case information is given regarding their distinguishing colors and tactical signs. Units from the division upwards are not included here but are listed in section VI.

12. Infantry.

a. Organic units.

(1) *Grenadierregiment* (regular infantry regiment).—Usually three to an infantry division.

(2) *Grenadierregiment* (*mot.*) (motorized infantry regiment).—Similar in organization and armament to regular infantry, but transported in organic motor vehicles, usually two to a motorized division.

(3) *Panzer-Grenadier-Regiment.*—A motorized infantry regiment in a Panzer division (also in 90th and 164th Light Di-

visions); two battalions instead of three; somewhat more heavily armed than regular infantry.

(4) *Gebirgsjägerregiment* (mountain infantry regiment).—Similar in organization to regular infantry except that it lacks the infantry howitzer company (Infanterie-Geschütz-Kompanie); two to a mountain division.

(5) *Kradschützen-Bataillon* (motorcycle battalion).—Infantry battalion mounted on motorcycles; found in the infantry brigade of old Panzer divisions, but acting separately as a reconnaissance unit in those which have been formed or reorganized since 1941. Also found in motorized divisions.

b. *GHQ units.*

(1) *Infanterie-Lehr-Regiment* (Infantry Instruction Regiment).—A single regiment, normally stationed at the Infantry School at Döberitz (Wkr. III), where it demonstrates tactics and performs experiments with new infantry weapons. It performs the same function as our 29th Infantry in connection with the Infantry School and Infantry Board. It is possible that it may be found, in whole or in part, on active service in the field.

(2) *Sonderverband 287* (Special Unit 287).—A small self-contained group, probably of battalion strength.

(3) *Sonderverband 288* (Special Unit 288).—A small self-contained group originally consisting of a headquarters company and eight companies. It was formed in the summer of 1941 and has served with the Africa Panzer Army. It is now designated Panzer-Grenadier-Regiment Afrika.

(4) *Führerbegleitbataillon* (Führer's Escort Battalion).—A special unit formed from picked personnel to serve as Hitler's escort in the field. It is fully motorized, contains a supply column, and consists of a heaquarters and at least three companies as follows:

1st Co—Wachkompanie (Guard Company).
2d Co—Schnelle Kompanie (Mobile Company).
3d Co—Schwere Sicherungskompanie (Heavy Security Company).

(5) *Infanteriebataillon z. b. V.* (special duty infantry battalion).—An independent, fully motorized infantry battalion for special duty (not at present definable); may be attached to army headquarters. Units of this type thus far identified carry the numbers 100 and 500.

(6) *Sicherungsregiment* (*mot.*) (motorized security regiment).—A special mopping-up regiment, controlled either by a Sicherungs division staff or by a special brigade staff. Commanders of army group rear areas may have at their disposal these special units in addition to a number of converted infantry divisions. These regiments are numbered in a separate series and have certain special units such as bicycle companies and motor transport echelons. Identification: Latin "S" with an Arabic number on the shoulder strap. For Sicherungs battalions see paragraph 23.

(7) *Jagdkommando* (raiding detachment).—A special type of unit formed during the winter of 1941–42 for service on the Russian front; numbered in a separate series (7 is the highest number so far reported).

(8) *Maschinengewehrbataillon* (*mot.*) (motorized machine gun battalion).—May be incorporated into an infantry division, or may be employed as GHQ troops.

(9) *Heeresinfanteriegeschützkompanie* or schwere I. G. Kp. (heavy infantry howitzer company).—Most commonly found attached to the motorized infantry brigade of a Panzer division; ten or twelve units of this type, numbered in the series 701–, identified; equipped with 150-mm guns mounted on Pz. Kw. II chassis.

(10) *Fla-Einheiten* (antiaircraft MG units).—Units having light antiaircraft cannon in addition to their machine guns; used for both antitank and antiaircraft defense. Two series exist:

(*a*) Nos 22–66 (ten identified).—Consist of six companies (the company is the tactical unit; no battalion staff has been identified since the outbreak of the war). One company is often incorporated into a Panzer division, being attached for administrative purposes to the division AT battalion, but retaining its original number.

(*b*) Nos. 601–620 (eighteen identified).—Battalions of three companies each. The battalion is the tactical unit, but its companies may be found operating independently. Identification: Gothic letters "Fl" on the shoulder strap.

(11) *Versuchsbataillon* (Experimental Battalion).—Details of composition and station of this unit are not yet available.

(12) *Sonderbataillon* (Special Battalion).—A disciplinary unit to which soldiers found to be consistently insubordinate may be transferred temporarily. Service in it is rigorous and dangerous, usually near the front line in Russia.

(13) *Infanteriepark* (infantry equipment park).—One for each army; numbered at random from the series 501–. The officers wear the color of their arm, but other ranks wear light blue, in each case with the Arabic number of the park. This applies as well for all other parks except for the medical and veterinary services.

c. Distinguishing color.—White is the distinguishing color of the infantry, except that Gebirgsjäger wear bright green, and infantry personnel in the Panzer division (Panzer-Grenadier regiments and motorcycle battalions) wear grass green.

d. Tactical signs.—The following figures show the tactical signs for infantry units:

13. Cavalry (Kavallerie).

a. Organic units.

(1) *Aufklärungsabteilung* (reconnaissance battalion).—Two main types: one type found in the regular infantry division; the other is found in motorized, light, and Panzer divisions. The type found in the infantry division normally consists of three companies: one mounted, one cyclist, and one heavy weapons. The other type is completely motorized. Some divisional reconnaissance units have recently been reorganized as cyclist battalions.

(2) *Reiterzug* (mounted platoon).—One type; one per normal infantry regiment.

b. GHQ units.

(1) *Kavallerie-Lehr-Abteilung* (Cavalry Instruction Battalion).—Stationed at the Cavalry School at Hannover (Wkr. XI), but potentially available for service in the field.

(2) *Aufklärungs-Lehr-Abteilung* (Reconnaissance Instruction Battalion).—Likewise stationed at the Cavalry School.

(3) *Kavalleriebrigade* (cavalry brigade).—Two in the former 1st Cavalry Division, each probably of two cavalry regiments. It is possible that there still may be a number of independent cavalry brigades in the GHQ pool.

(4) *Kavallerieregiment* (cavalry regiment, part mechanized) and *Reiterregiment* (cavalry regiment, horse).—Normal size cavalry regiments. For a list of identifications see section VII.

(5) *Radfahrabteilung* (cyclist battalion).—Some reorganized reconnaissance units; others numbered in the series 401–, in the GHQ pool. The cyclist battalion normally includes a motorcycle company, hence motorcyclists may still be seen wearing yellow.

(6) *Heeresgerätepark* (heavy transport equipment park).—One with each army (excluding Panzer armies) serving its heavy transport columns as well as cavalry units; numbered the same as infantry parks.

c. Distinguishing color.—Gold yellow is the distinguishing color of the cavalry except for reconnaissance units of Panzer and motorized divisions, which wear copper-brown.

d. Tactical signs.—The following figures show the tactical signs for cavalry units:

14. **Panzer troops** (Panzertruppe).

a. Organic units.

(1) *Panzerregiment* (tank regiment).—One per Panzer division; consists of three tank battalions; may also operate independently in the GHQ pool.

(2) *Panzerabteilung* (tank battalion).—Progressively assigned to motorized divisions since the summer of 1942.

(3) *Panzerjägerabteilung*, formerly *Panzerabwehrabteilung* (antitank battalion)—ordinarily one to a division; usually equipped with 37-mm or 50-mm antitank guns; independent battalions may be assigned to GHQ pool (these are equipped with 47-mm gun on self-propelled mount).

b. GHQ units.

(1) *Panzer-Lehr-Regiment* (Tank Instruction Regiment).—Regiment stationed at the Tank School at Wünsdorf (Wkr. III);

consists of I and II (Tank) and III (Antitank) Bns. Like other demonstration units, it is potentially available for service in the field.

(2) *Panzerabteilung* (*Flammenwerfer*) (tank flame thrower battalion).—Independent flame thrower tank battalions (series 100–) normally found employed under Panzer corps in the spearhead of the attack.

(3) *Panzerabteilung* (tank battalion).—Independent battalion assigned to GHQ pool; like GHQ Panzerregiment, it may be found either under Panzer corps or Panzer brigade staffs, or on occasion supporting infantry divisions.

(4) *Schwere Panzerjägerabteilung* (heavy antitank battalion).—Assigned to GHQ; equipped with either 75-mm antitank guns (self-propelled mount), or 88-mm antiaircraft-antitank guns (tractor drawn, or on self-propelled mount).

(5) *Eisenbahn-Panzerzug* (armored train).—Numbered in series 1–50. Identification: letter "E" on the shoulder strap.

c. *Distinguishing color.*—Pink is the distinguishing color of these units. Panzerjäger units wear a Gothic "P" on the shoulder strap. Tank crews wear black uniforms.

d. *Tactical signs.*—The following figures show the tactical signs for units in this category:

15. Artillery (*Artillerie*).—In the German Army, all artillery apart from the relatively small divisional allotment belongs to the GHQ pool (*Heerestruppen*). Units are allotted from this pool to army groups or armies according to the estimated needs. They may be sub-allotted to divisions or as corps troops (in both cases usually placed under the immediate control of special artillery commanders and staffs, also provided from the GHQ pool). With the exception of artillery commanders and staffs and artillery observation units, all types of artillery carry numbers allotted from a single series.

a. *Organic division artillery.*—The division artillery regiment varies in composition according to the type and manner of employment of the division, as follows:

(1) *In Panzer divisions.*—One regiment consisting of three battalions (I and II equipped with 105-mm gun-howitzers, III with 150-mm howitzers). In some cases the III Bn was previously an independent battalion in the GHQ pool carrying a number in the series 401-450 or 601-650, thus documents from the battalion files may sometimes lead to an obsolete identification. In a task force, the artillery regiment may be reinforced by one or more units of GHQ artillery or other arms (Heeresflak or Nebeltruppen).

(2) *In motorized divisions.*—Nearly identical with organization in the Panzer division.

(3) *In light divisions.*—Artillery organization believed to be similar to that of infantry divisions.

(4) *In mountain divisions.*—One regiment consisting of four battalions (I, II, and III equipped with 75-mm mountain howitzers, the IV with 105-mm mountain howitzers); may be reinforced from the GHQ pool.

(5) *In infantry divisions.*—One regiment consisting of four battalions (I, II, and III equipped with 105-mm gun-howitzers, the IV with 150-mm howitzers). At the time of mobilization, the infantry divisions in the series 1-46 (regular divisions of the standing army) received their medium battalions from the peacetime medium regiments; therefore, these battalions are not designated as the fourth battalion of the present regiment but as the first battalion of their former medium regiment. Thus, in the 1st-36th Divisions they carry the Roman numeral I followed by the division number plus 36; for example, in the 33d Arty Regt the medium battalion was known as the I Bn, 69th Arty Regt (I./Art. Rgt. 69). In the case of the 44th, 45th, and 46th Divisions the system is the same except that the regimental number of the medium battalion is one higher than that of the artillery regiment in the division. As in the other divisions, the division artillery regiments may be reinforced from the GHQ pool.

(6) *In infantry divisions in defensive sectors.*—Artillery may be modified to suit local conditions. For example, part of the division regiment may be transferred for service in the field; or

one or more units of coast defense or railway artillery from the GHQ pool may be attached to the division. In such cases the units concerned retain their original numbers but do not display division insignia. Thus shoulder straps and vehicles will not serve to identify the unit.

b. Artillery commanders.—When the division artillery regiment is not reinforced from the GHQ pool, its commander is known as Artillerieführer (Arfü) and he is the division artillery commander. When GHQ artillery units are attached to the division the Arfü is usually subordinated to an artillery commander (Artilleriekommandeur, abbreviated Arko) whose small special staff is supplemented in action by the larger staff of the organic artillery regiment. An Arko may also be assigned to command an allotment of artillery to a corps. In this case a GHQ artillery regimental staff and an artillery observation unit are normally included in the allotment. The following echelons in the chain of artillery command exist:

(1) *At GHQ.*—GHQ artillery general (OKH/Gen. d. Art.) is the principal adviser on artillery employment; units from the GHQ pool are probably allotted to army groups and armies on his recommendation.

(2) *At army group and army Hq.*—Artillery general (a Stoart; in a coastal sector, General der Küstenartillerie) advises the commander on artillery matters and recommends the sub-allotment of GHQ artillery units to lower units.

(3) *Within army group and army.*—One senior artillery commander (Höherer Artilleriekommandeur, abbreviated Höh. Arko) and staff probably available for command over GHQ artillery units operating in an area larger than that of a single army corps.

(4) *Corps.*—Artillery may be commanded by an Arko; but a corps not in action may have only a junior artillery staff officer (Stoart).

(5) *Division.*—Artillery may be commanded by an Arko or an Arfü.

The Höh. Arkos are numbered in series 301–; the Arkos are numbered in two series 1–44 and 101–. There is no apparent connection between any of these numbers and that of the unit with which the commander concerned is operating.

c. GHQ artillery.

(1) *Artillery regimental staffs.*—Staffs of the peacetime division medium regiments (Nos 37–72, 97, 99, and 115) and special staffs formed on or after mobilization (numbered above 500). The latter are chiefly independent staffs with no battalions carrying the same number. All GHQ artillery regimental staffs except coast defense staffs are fully motorized.

(2) *Battalion staffs.*—Independent staffs controlling independent GHQ medium, heavy, and super-heavy batteries (motorized or railway), or coast defense batteries.

(3) *Battalions and batteries.*—Light, medium, heavy, and super-heavy units which may be horse-drawn, motorized, tractor-drawn, self-propelled, railway, or fixed. Numbers allotted to them are not necessarily connected with their particular type. Motorized medium battalions formerly belonging to peacetime medium regiments consist of three batteries of four guns each, but many of the battalions formed on or after mobilization may have three-gun batteries, and heavy or super-heavy batteries may have only two guns, or only one.

(4) *Artillery observation battalions (Beobachtungsabteilung).*—Part of the GHQ pool, but an armored artillery observation battery (Pz. Beob.-Battr.) is normally organically assigned to the division artillery regiment of the Panzer division and carries a number in the series 320–350.

(5) *Sturmgeschützabteilung* (armored assault gun battalion).—Headquarters battery and three six-gun batteries equipped with 75-mm guns on self-propelled mounts; numbered in the main artillery series (sixteen identified numbered between 177 and 249).

(6) *Sturmgeschützbatterie* (armored assault gun battery).—Similar to batteries described in (5) above; numbers 665 and 667 identified.

(7) *Artillerie-Lehr-Regimente* (artillery instruction regiments).—Three regiments stationed at the Artillery School at Jüterbog Wkr. III). No. 1 is horse-drawn, No. 2 is motorized (including an armored assault artillery battery), No. 3 consists of artillery observation, survey and mapping, range-finding, and balloon battalions. Portions of one or more of these regiments may be found in the field.

(8) *Heeresflak-Lehrabteilung* (Army AAA Instruction Bn).—Stationed at the Army AAA School in Wkr. II; available for service in the field.

(9) *Heeresflakabteilung*.—Consists of three 88-mm gun batteries and two 20-mm gun batteries; fully motorized. Numbered in the same series as Luftwaffe antiaircraft units; twelve identified.

(10) *Vermessungs- und Kartenabteilung* (survey and mapping units).—In GHQ pool but may be allocated to army groups or armies. Three in the series 501– and approximately twelve others in the series 601–, have been identified.

(11) *Ballonbatterie* (observation balloon battery).—Independent balloon batteries numbered in series 100–.

(12) *Velocitäts-Messzug* (velocity measurement platoon).—Numbered in series 501–.

(13) *Astronomischer Messzug* (astronomical survey platoon).—Numbered in series 701–.

(14) *Wetter-Peilzug* (meteorological platoon).—Numbered in series 501–.

(15) *Armeekartenlager* (army map depot).—Numbered arbitrarily in series 501–.

(16) *Artilleriepark* (artillery equipment park).—One per army; numbered arbitrarily in series 501–.

d. Distinguishing color.—The distinguishing color of the artillery is bright red. There are three types of special artillery units wearing distinctive letters on the shoulder straps: observation units wear a Gothic "B", survey and mapping units wear a Gothic "V", and horse artillery wear a Gothic "R".

e. Tactical signs.—The following figures show the tactical signs for artillery units:

16. Chemical warfare troops (Nebeltruppen).

a. Organic units.—There are no organic units of this arm.

b. GHQ units.—All units belong to the GHQ pool. So far they have been employed as integral parts of the artillery and have been used only for smoke projection, but they are also equipped and trained for chemical projection. Some units which were originally designated as "Nebelwerfer" (smoke projector) units to conform with the provisions of the Versailles Treaty are now called merely "Werfer" (projection) units. This does not necessarily indicate an intention to resort to gas warfare.

(1) *Nebel-Lehr-Regiment* (CWS Instruction Regiment).—Stationed at the Army Chemical Warfare School at Celle (Wkr. XI), but may be found serving at the front.

(2) *Nebelwerferregiment z. b. V.* (special regimental staff).—May also be known as Regimentsstab der Nebeltruppen; regimental staffs controlling projection battalions in action; numbered in series 1–.

(3) *Werferregiment* (projection regiment).—Formerly called Nebelwerferregiment; regiment consists of headquarters and three battalions; No 14, series 51–54, and No 70 identified.

(4) *Schweres Werferregiment* (heavy projection regiment).—Also probably consists of a headquarters and three battalions; Nos 1 and 2 are the only ones identified.

(5) *Werferabteilung* (projection battalion).—Formerly known as Nebelwerferabteilung; independent battalions, controlled in action by special regimental staffs; series 1–13 identified.

(6) *Werferbatterie* (150 mm Werfer 41) (heavy projection battery).—Independent batteries equipped with 150-mm chemical projector. No 151 has been identified.

(7) *Gebirgswerferabteilung* (mountain chemical projection battalion).—A unit of this type is known to exist, but no identification has been made.

(8) *Entgiftungsabteilung* (decontamination battalion).—Also equipped for service as a contamination battalion; series 101–103 identified.

(9) *Strassenentgiftungsabteilung* (road decontamination battalion).—Similar to the preceding unit; No 132 identified.

(10) *Gasschutzgerätepark* (gas defense equipment park).—One per army; numbered at random in the series 501–.

c. Distinguishing color.—The distinguishing color of Nebeltruppen is maroon.

d. Tactical signs.—The following figures show the tactical signs for these units:

17. Engineers (Pioniere).

a. Organic units.—Pionierbataillon (combat engineer battalion).—One per division; may on occasion be transferred to the GHQ pool as corps or army troops. Usually carry division auxiliary number.

b. GHQ units.—Classified according to their employment, GHQ engineer units may be divided into three groups: combat engineers, fortress engineers (Festungspioniere), and railway engineers (Eisenbahnpioniere).

(1) *Combat engineers* (including miscellaneous units).

(a) *Pionier-Lehr-Bataillon* (engineer instruction battalion).—Nos 1 and 2 are stationed at Engineer School No 1 (Pionierschule 1) at Dessau-Rösslau (Wkr. XI). There is also a Pioneer-Lehr-Bataillon z. b. V. at Offenbach am Main (Wkr. IX), which specializes in mining and similar activities. These units may also be found serving in the field.

(b) *Pionierregiment z. b. V.* (special engineer regiment) or *Pionierregimentsstab* (engineer regimental staff).—Used to control engineer battalions, bridge trains, and, if necessary, construction units of the GHQ pool under corps or army. Approximately twenty have been identified which have numbers selected from the series 501–700.

(c) *Pionierbataillon z. b. V.* (engineer battalion staff).—Staffs which control independent engineer units. Nos 300 and 750 have been identified.

(d) *Pionierlandungskompanie* (engineer landing company).—Equipped with assault boats with outboard motors. No 778 has been identified.

(e) *Sturmbootkompanie* (assault boat company) and *Sturmbootkommando* (assault boat detachment).—No companies have been identified as yet, but they are known to exist. The detachments carry numbers in the series 901–.

(f) *Brückenkolonne* or Brüko (bridge train).—Forms part of the division and GHQ engineer battalions. In addition there are two series of independent bridge trains in the GHQ pool. One series carries numbers in the 401–450 range and these consist of units of two trains (e. g. 1/403, 2/403) which operate independently. The other series, numbered in the 601–700 range, consists of single trains. All are fully motorized.

(g) *Technisches Bataillon* (technical battalion).—Intended for such specialized functions as the production and treatment of mineral oil, coal-mining, etc. They are supplied with personnel by the Technical Replacement Training Battalion at Pirna (Wkr. IV), and are numbered in series 1–50. Approximately twelve have been identified to date.

(h) *Stromsicherungsbataillon* (electric cable maintenance battalion).—No 503 identified.

(i) *Pionierpark* (enginner equipment park).—One to each army; numbered at random in the series 501–.

(j) *Pionierparkkompanie* (engineer park company).—Two per engineer park; also numbered in series 501–.

(k) *Pioniermaschinenzug* (engineer machine platoon).—One is included in each engineer park; likewise used independently under engineer battalion staffs z. b V., listed under (c) above.

(2) Fortress engineers (Festungspioniere) wear the letters "Fp" or "F" on their shoulder straps (Gothic "Fp" if the unit existed in peacetime; Latin "F" if it was formed on or after mobilization). The following units and staffs may be encountered:

(a) *Festungspionierkommandeur* (fortress engineer command staff).—Personnel wears Gothic "Fp" followed by the Roman numeral of a Wehrkreis. In effect, regimental Hq for fortress engineer units in the military district concerned.

(b) *Festungspionierstab* (fortress engineer staff).—Wears Gothic "Fp" or Latin "F" followed by an Arabic number in series 1–50. A regimental staff; normally controls two sector groups.

(c) *Festungspionierabschnittsgruppe* (fortress engineer sector group.)—Numbered I and II followed by the Arabic number of the controlling staff (e. g. Fest. Pi. Abs. Gr. II/21). Equivalent in status to a battalion staff.

(d) *Festungsstammbataillon* (fortress cadre battalion).—A training unit in Germany where personnel from basic training units receive further training while awaiting transfer.

(e) *Festungspionierpark* (fortress engineer equipment park).—One for each area in which fortress engineers are employed extensively.

For fortress signal, transport, and construction units, see paragraphs 18, 19, and 24.

(3) *Railway engineers* wear a Gothic letter "E" on the shoulder strap if the unit existed in peacetime, otherwise a Latin "E". They are not always easy to distinguish from railway troops (Eisenbahntruppen), for which see paragraph 19. The following types may be encountered:

(a) *Eisenbahnpionierregiment* (railway engineer regiment).—Consists of a Hq and two battalions of four companies each numbered consecutively (e. g. 7/Eisb.Pi.Rgt. 3-3d Co. II Bn. 3d Ry. Engr. Regt.); received personnel from five railway replacement training battalions (Nos 1–5), as do the independent companies listed below. Eight exist (Nos 1–8).

(b) *Eisenbahnpionierstab* z. b. V. (special railway engineer staff).—One unnumbered example has been identified.

(c) *Eisenbahn (Pionier)-Baukompanie* (railway (engineer) construction company).—Specialist companies. Their function may be defined by a further title: Eisb. Pfeilerbaukp. (railway pier construction company); or, in other cases the special title replaces Bau: Eisb. Fernsprechkompanie (railway telephone (construction) company). On the other hand, the Eisenbahnbaubataillon (railway construction battalion) belongs to the category of construction troops (paragraph 19).

(d) *Eisenbahnpionierpark* (railway engineer equipment park).—Nos 402 and 403 have been identified. In addition there is a Heimateisenbahnpionierpark at Rehagen-Klausdorf (Wkr. III), where the Railway Engineer School is situated.

c. Distinguishing color.—Black is the color of the engineer arm. As stated above, the special branches of this arm wear distinguishing letters on the shoulder strap.

d. Tactical signs.

The following figures show the tactical signs of the engineer units:

18. Signal troops.

a. Organic units.

(1) *Nachrichtenregiment* (signal regiment).—Assigned to army groups (Heeresnachrichtenregiment) or armies (Armeenachrichtenregiment); numbered in series 1–4, 10, and 501–.

(2) *Korps-Nachrichtenabteilung* (corps signal battalion).—One per army corps; numbered in series 41–53, 60, 66, 70, 420–480.

(3) *Nachrichtenabteilung* (signal battalion).—Ordinarily one to a division. Consists of headquarters, telephone company, and radio company.

b. GHQ units.

(1) *Nachrichten-Lehr-Regiment* (Signal Instruction Regiment).—Stationed at the Army Signal School at Halle (Wkr. IV). This regiment, like other instruction units, is potentially available for service in the field.

(2) *Kommander der Nachrichtentruppen* (signal troops commander).—Controls both training and army communications within his Wehrkreis; has the status of a regimental commander. A Roman numeral with yellow piping denotes the staff of the signal officer in a particular Wehrkreis. Officers of the same title may also be found in the field.

(3) *Nachrichtenregimentsstab z. b. V.* (special signal regiment staff).—Special regimental staff to command independent battalions and other units in special situations.

(4) *Nachrichtenführer z. b. V.* (special signal commander), *Nachrichtenabteilungsstab z. b. V.* (special signal battalion staff).—Special battalion staffs formed to control independent signal companies in the field. Numbered mainly in the series 651–700.

(5) *Feldnachrichtenkommandantur* (field signal command).— Static signal Hq for a sector of occupied territory or in rear areas of the zone of operations. The personnel wear a Latin "K" followed by the Arabic number of the unit (series 1–60) on the shoulder strap.

(6) *Führungsnachrichtenregiment* (command signal regiment).—Provides and maintains signal communications between GHQ, army group, and army Hq, as well as between the services. Nos 40 and 601 in the main series have this classification.

(7) *Heeresnachrichtenregiment* (GHQ signal regiment).—Provides and maintains communication nets of lesser importance than those of the Führungsnachrichtenregiment, or is allotted to army groups as army group signal regiment. Numbered in the series 501–700.

(8) *Propagandakompanie* (propaganda company).—Normally allotted to armies; personnel mainly journalists, press photographers, or film cameramen in civil life; their main function is front-line reporting. Replacements are provided from the Propaganda Replacement Training Battalion, Berlin (Wkr. III). Propaganda companies include No 501 and at least fifteen with numbers selected from the series 601–700. There are unnumbered battalions and companies in addition ("Frankreich" allotted to the Commanding General, former occupied France; "Belgien", under the CG, Belgium and Northern France; "Afrika", under Africa Panzer Army).

(9) *Independent signal companies, etc.*—The following are the principal types of independent signal companies which may be encountered (all numbered in series 601–):

(a) *Fernsprech-Baukompanie* (telephone construction company).

(b) *Fernsprechbetriebszug* (telephone operating platoon).

(c) *Fernschreibkompanie* (telegraph company).

(d) *Horchkompanie* (interception company).

(e) *Nachrichtenaufklärungskompanie* (signal reconnaissance company).

(f) *Funküberwachungskompanie* (radio supervision company).

(10) *Festungsnachrichtenkommandantur* (fortress signal command), *Festungsnachrichtenkommandanturstelle* (fortress signal command station).—The command carries the same number as the Festungspionierstab to which it is attached (see par. 17); the principle for numbering the stations is unknown.

(11) *Nachrichtenhelferinneneinsatzabteilung* (female signal operations battalion).—Probably administers the women signal assistants (largely telephone operators) throughout a large area such as former occupied France. No 52 is the only unit of this type identified.

(12) *Armeenachrichtenpark* (army signal equipment park).—One to each army; numbered in the series 501–.

c. Distinguishing color.—Lemon yellow is the distinguishing color of signal units. It should not be confused with the gold yellow of the cavalry.

d. Tactical signs.—The following figures show the tactical signs for signal units:

19. Transport and supply troops (*Nachschubtruppen* and *Fahrtruppen*).

a. Organic units.—Every unit normally has its own organic supply and transport echelon whose composition and organization varies according to the size and type of the unit which it serves. In divisions and higher organizations this echelon is under the command of officers designated as follows:

(1) *Kommandeur der Armeenachschubtruppen* (commander of army services of supply).—Formerly known as Armeenachschubführer; commands organic army supply units.

(2) *Kommandeur der Korpsnachschubtruppen* (commander of corps services of supply).

b. GHQ units.—Classified according to their organization and employment, GHQ transport units may be divided into three groups: transport units (Fahrtruppen), supply units (Nachschubtruppen), and railway units (Eisenbahntruppen).

(1) *Transport units.*

(*a*) *Kraftwagentransportregiment* (motor transport regiment).—Used primarily for moving non-motorized units, but may also be used for the transport of supplies. About twenty have been identified in the 300, 500, 600, and 900 series.

(*b*) *Kraftwagentransportabteilung* (motor transport battalion).—Independent battalions similar in function to the above units. About twenty have been identified in the 500, 600, 700, and 900 series.

(*c*) *Kraftwagentransportkolonne* (motor transport column or train).—Independent columns numbered in the series 601–.

(*d*) *Kraftfahrzeuginstandsetzungsabteilung* (motor vehicle repair battalion).—Twelve identified.

(*e*) *Panzerinstandsetzungsabteilung* (tank repair battalion).—Three identified.

(*f*) *Kraftfahrzeuginstandsetzungskompanie* (motor vehicle repair company).—Independent companies numbered in the series 101–200 and 301–.

(*g*) *Panzerinstandsetzungskompanie* (tank repair company).—No 122 identified.

(*h*) *Kraftwagenwerkstattzug* (motor maintenance workshop platoon).—Independent platoon; Nos. 37, 212, and 612 identified.

(*i*) *Werkstattkompanie (mot.)* (motorized workshop company).—Numbered in the series 1–300; about 12 identified.

(*j*) *Feldwerkstatt* (field workshop).—Normally one per army or Panzer army; numbered arbitrarily in the series 501–.

(*k*) *Feldwerkstattzug* (field workshop platoon).—Independent platoons, Nos 573, 604, and 607 identified.

(*l*) *Armeekraftfahrpark* (army motor transport park).—One per army or Panzer army; numbered arbitrarily in the series 501–.

(*m*) *Heereskraftfahrpark* (GHQ motor transport park).—Numbered concurrently with army motor transport park above.

(n) *Kraftfahrparkkompanie* (motor transport park company).—Component unit of 12 and 13 above and carrying the same number.

(2) Supply units.

(a) *Nachschubbataillon* (supply battalion).—Two series exist: 1–200 (non-motorized) of which about six have been identified; 501–700 (fully motorized) of which 26 have been identified. Both types serve as army troops.

(b) *Nachschubstab z. b. V.* (special supply staff).—Numbered in series 671–750 (18 identified). When employed as loading or unloading staffs at a seaport they are called Verladestab or Entladestab.

(c) *Nachschubkolonnenabteilung* (supply column or train battalion).—Some horsedrawn and some have motor transport; assigned to armies as required, and no standard allotment can be given. Approximately 40 have been noted carrying numbers between 501 and 950. Their component columns are distinguished by an Arabic number preceding that of the battalion (e. g. 10/N. K. A. 529).

(d) *Nachschubkolonnenabteilung z. b. V.* (special supply column battalion staff).—For control and administration of independent supply columns. Nos 671, 672, 788, 792, and 798 identified.

(e) *Independent supply columns.*—These include the following types (all numbered in the series 501–999):

    1. *grosse Kraftwagenkolonne* (heavy motor transport column).—Capacity 60 tons.

    2. *kleine Kraftwagenkolonne* (light motor transport column).—Capacity 30 tons.

    3. *Betriebsstoffkolonne* (fuel and lubricant column) (heavy or light).—Capacity 50 or 25 cubic meters (11,000 or 5,500 gallons).

    4. *Kesselwagenkolonne für Betriebsstoff* (tank truck column for fuel and lubricants).

    5. *Filterkolonne* (filter column).—Believed to be a water column.

6. *Kombinierte Kolonne* (combined column).—Function not known.

7. *Fahrkolonne* (horsedrawn column).

(3) *Railway units.*

(a) *Operating staffs.*—The following railway operating staffs, numbered concurrently in the series 1-, have been identified:

(i) *Feldeisenbahndirektion* (field railway command station).

(ii) *Feldeisenbahnbetriebsamt* (field railway operations office).

(iii) *Feldeisenbahnmaschinenamt* (field railway workshop office).

(iv) *Feldeisenbahnwerkstättenamt* (field railway workshop office).

The various offices are believed to be subdivisions of the command stations which carry the same number.

(b) *Operating units.*—Two series identified as follows:

(i) *Eisenbahnbetriebskompanie* (railway operations company).—Series 201-.

(ii) *Feldbahnkompanie* (field railway company).—301 -.

It is possible that some of the independent companies noted under paragraph 17 may come under the control of railway operating staffs, although their personnel are railway engineers and wear black piping accordingly.

c. *Distinguishing color.*—The distinguishing color of these units is light blue.

d. *Tactical signs.*—The following figures show the principal tactical signs for transport and supply troops:

20. Medical units (Sanitätseinheiten).

a. *Organic units.*—*Sanitätsabteilung* (medical detachment).—One per division; consists of one or two medical companies, field hospital detachment, and two or three ambulance platoons; carries division auxiliary number.

b. GHQ units.

(1) *Heeres-* or *Armeesanitätsabteilung* (GHQ or army medical battalion).—Some fully, others partly, motorized; numbered at random in the series 501–700.

(2) *Kriegslazarettabteilung* (station hospital detachment, communications zone).—Fully motorized; numbered in the same series as the foregoing.

(3) *Reserve-Kriegslazarettabteilung* (auxiliary station hospital detachment, communications zone).—Non-motorized; numbered in the same series as the foregoing but with a different war establishment.

(4) *Armeefeldlazarett* (army field hospital).—Units of this type carry the number of the army medical battalion preceded by 1, 2, 3, or 4 (e. g. A. Feldlaz. 3/542). The prefix Armee- is often dropped, but the type can be recognized by its double numbering.

(5) *Feldlazarett* (field hospital).—Independent field hospitals, some motorized; numbered in the series 601–700.

(6) *Feldhalblazarett* (field half-hospital).—No. 716 identified.

(7) *Kriegslazarett* (station hospital, communications zone).—Units of this type carry the number of the station hospital detachment preceded by 1, 2, 3, or 4 (e. g. Kriegslaz. 4/571) or single numbers in the series 901–.

(8) *Leichtkrankenkriegslazarett* (station hospital for minor cases, communications zone).—Some motorized; principles of numbering not yet known.

(9) *Krankentransportabteilung* (ambulance battalion).—Allotted to armies; numbered in the series 501–700.

(10) *Krankenkraftwagenzug* (motorized ambulance platoon).—Numbered in the series 501–800.

(11) *Lazarettzug* (hospital train).—Numbered in the series 501–700.

(12) *Leichtkrankenzug* (hospital train for minor cases).

(13) *Truppenentgiftungskompanie* (personnel decontamination company).—Definitely medical units, not to be confused with chemical warfare troops like decontamination and road-decontamination battalions; Nos 617, 620, 622 identified.

(14) *Armeesanitätspark* (army medical park).—Numbered in the series 501–700. Both officers and other ranks wear dark blue with the Arabic number of the park.

c. *Distinguishing color.*—Dark blue is the distinguishing color for medical units.

d. *Tactical signs.*—The following figures show the tactical signs for medical units:

21. Veterinary units (Veterinäreinheiten).

a. *Organic units.*—*Veterinärkompanie* (veterinary company).—One per infantry and mountain division; carries division auxiliary number.

b. *GHQ units.*

(1) *Heeres- or Armeepferdelazarett* (GHQ or army veterinary hospital).—Numbered in the series 501–700.

(2) *Pferdetransportkolonne (mot.)* (motorized horse transport column).—Numbered in the same series as the foregoing.

(3) *Armeepferdepark* (army horse park).—One assigned to each army (excluding Panzer armies); numbered in the same series as 1 and 2 above.

(4) *Armeeveterinärpark* (army veterinary park).—Numbering and allocation the same as for paragraph 3. Both officers and other ranks wear carmine with the Arabic number of the park.

c. *Distinguishing color.*—Carmine is the distinguishing color of veterinary units.

d. *Tactical signs.*—The following figures show the tactical signs for veterinary units:

22. Military police units (Feldgendarmerieeinheiten).

a. *Organic units.*—*Feldgendarmerietrupp* (military police detachment).—Several identified in corps and divisions, carrying their service number.

b. *GHQ units.*

(1) *Feldgendarmerieabteilung* (military police battalion).—One allotted to each army or Panzer army; thirteen identified in the series 501–700.

(2) *Feldgendarmerietrupp* (military police detachment).—Detachments allocated to the military administration of an occupied country are believed to carry the number of the Kommandantur to which they are attached (see paragraph 25).

(3) *Verkehrsregelungsbataillon* (traffic control battalion).—A battalion or a company may be allocated for as long as neces-

sary to an army on the move; seven units of this type identified which are numbered in the series 751–760.

(4) *Geheime Feldpolizei* (field security police).—Gruppen (groups) may be assigned impartially to army or air force organizations; normally one Gruppe per army and one or more attached to the military administration of each occupied country. Numbered in the series 501–800.

c. Distinguishing color and insignia.—Military police units wear orange piping and carry no number. On the left upper arm they wear the Nazi eagle and swastika surrounded by an oak wreath; on the lower arm a brown band inscribed with the word "Feldgendarmerie" in silver.

d. Tactical signs.—The following figures show the tactical signs for military police units:

23. Local defense units (Landesschützeneinheiten).

a. Organic units.—There are no organic local defense units.

b. GHQ units.

(1) *Landesschützenregiment* (Landesschützen regimental staff).—A regimental headquarters controlling a varying number of battalions. Some are designated z. b. V. and have a special type of organization. In the case of two-figure numbers the first, and in the case of three-figure numbers the first two figures give the Wehrkreis of origin (e. g. Lds. Schtz. Rgt. 115 comes from Wkr. XI).

(2) *Transportbegleitregiment.*—A staff controlling Landesschützen battalions which accompany trains. Identified at large railway centers such as Wien and Krakau.

(3) *Landesschützenbataillon* (Landesschützen battalion).—Comprise from two to six companies; some are designated z. b. V. and have a special organization. Within Germany they are employed for guard duties at prisoner of war camps and vulnerable points. In occupied territories they provide the main support for the military administration. In rear areas they may be used to guard dumps, parks, etc. Some 600 battalions have been identified, numbered according to the Wehrkreis of origin as follows:

Wkr.	Series	Wkr.	Series
I	201–250	IX	601–650
II	251–300	X	651–700
III	301–350	XI	701–750
IV	351–400	XII	751–800
V	401–450	XIII	801–850
VI	451–500	XVII	851–900
VII	501–550	XVIII	901–950
VIII	551–600	Various	951–1001

Recently a number of these units have been made more mobile and designated Sicherungsbataillone.

The air force also has Landesschützen units. These, however, may be distinguished from army Landesschützen units since they wear double numbers—Roman for the Luftgau (air district) of origin and Arabic for the particular unit.

(4) *Wachregiment* (guard regiment).—Two have been identified: Wachrgt. Clüwer (named after its commander) and Wachrgt. Paris.

(5) *Wachbataillon* (guard battalion).—Two main types: Heimatwachbataillon, serving in Germany, and Wachbataillon, serving with the armies in the field, numbered in two series: 1–500 and 501–800. The former type includes bridge guard battalions (Nos 58, 99, 122, and 143 identified) and cyclist guard battalions (Nos 45, 50, 326, and 614 identified). Units of the latter type are assigned to armies to provide guards for army parks, etc. (Sixteen identified to date.)

(6) *Grenzwacht* (frontier guard).—Regular units stationed in the frontier districts were reinforced in peacetime by a frontier guard organization, with the following chain of command:

(*a*) *Grenzschutzabschnittskommando* (sector command—regimental Hq).

(*b*) *Grenzschutzunterabschnitt* (sub-sector—battalion Hq).

(*c*) *Grenzwachtkompanie* (frontier guard company).

Each sector has a signal company, one or more fixed battalions of artillery, and other units. On mobilization, the sector commands were renamed regiments and numbered on the same principle as the Landesschützen regiments in (1) above (e. g. 122d Lds. Schtz. Regt. is probably the former 122d Frontier Guard Regiment from Wkr. XII, renamed).

c. Distinguishing color.—Local defense units wear white piping with the Latin "L" followed by an Arabic number in the case of Landesschützen regimental staffs and battalions. Various other types of unit fall under the same heading in the German classification although they are not specifically described as Landesschützen and lack the distinguishing "L". Some Landesschützen units have been reported to wear green piping, the color of mountain rifle and rifle (Jäger) units. The reason for this is not known.

d. Tactical signs.—The tactical signs for Landesschützen units are the same as those for the comparable infantry units, with the addition of the Letter L.

24. Construction units (Baueinheiten).

a. Organic units.—There are no organic construction units.

b. GHQ units.—

(1) *Oberbaustab* (superior construction staff).—Equivalent in status to a brigade staff; numbered in series 1–20.

(2) *Kommandeur der Bautruppen* (construction troops command staff).—Regimental commander and staff; two series, 1–50 and 101–150 (about twenty identified).

(3) *Baubataillon* (construction battalion).—Numbered in series 1–500 (about 100 identified, most of which are below 300), excluding bridge building, fortress, and railway construction battalions, which are numbered concurrently.

(4) *Brückenbaubataillon* (bridge building battalion).—Numbered in series 1–500 (sixteen identified) and 501–800 (twenty identified). The battalions in the higher series usually serve with the armies in the field and operate as engineers. The lower series is more likely to be employed in the rear areas.

(5) *Festungsbaubataillon* (fortress construction battalion).—Operate under the direction of fortress engineer staffs (paragraph 17); seventeen identified numbered between 8 and 314 inclusive.

(6) *Strassenbaubataillon* (road construction battalion).—May be designated as leichte or schwere (light or heavy), but it is not known how the two types differ. Numbered in the series 501–700 (shared with field army bridge building battalions); about thirty identified including seven cyclist battalions (series 501–510) intended to accompany spearhead formations.

(7) *Eisenbahnbaubataillon* (railway construction battalion).—Nos 83, 111, 116, 139, 511, 512, 513, and 515 identified. It is believed their function is to provide less specialized labor than that of the construction companies described in paragraph 17.

(8) *Marinebaubataillon* (naval construction battalion).—Nos 311, 312, and 323 in the main series are described thus. They are presumably intended to carry out construction works for the German Navy, though their personnel are provided by the army. (The coast defense units belong to the German Navy).

(9) *Kreigsgefangenenbau- und Arbeitsbataillon* (PW construction and labor battalion).—The German cadre personnel acts as guards to PW employed within Germany or in the rear areas. Numbered in series 1–50; six identified.

(10) *Landesbaubataillon* (regional construction battalion).—A series 1–8 has recently been identified.

c. Distinguishing color.—Light brown is the distinguishing color of construction units, but railway construction battalions wear black piping, as do bridge building battalions (with the possible exception of those carrying numbers below 501) and fortress construction battalions.

d. Tactical signs.—The following figures show the tactical signs for construction units:

25. Administrative units (Verwaltungseinheiten).

a. Organic units.—Each division has a bakery company, slaughter unit, and field post office, generally carrying the services number of the division. Armies and corps also have field post offices.

b. GHQ units.—For convenience these units are here grouped approximately according to their functions and to their place in the German war establishment as follows:

(1) *Administration of supplies.*—Units mainly staffed by civilian officials (Beamten) who wear dark green piping; officers wear the color of their original arm of the service.

(*a*) *Bäckereikompanie, Grossbäckereikompanie* (bakery company, large bakery company).—Allotted random numbers in the series 501–700.

(*b*) *Schlächterei-Einheiten* (animal slaughter units).—Vary in size and description and range of numbering as follows:

1. Abteilung (battalion)—Nos 201, 204, and 619 identified; principles for allocation not known.
2. Kompanie (company)—No 287 and seven in series 501–650 identified; allocated to armies.
3. Zug (platoon)—ten identified in series 550–700; principles for allocation unknown.

(c) *Eisenbahnküchenwagenabteilung* (railway kitchen-car detachment)—Nos 1 and 2 identified.

(d) *Heeresbetreuungsabteilung* (army welfare battalion)—series 1–54 identified.

(e) *Armeeverpflegungsamt* (army ration supply depot)—several available for each army in the field; numbered from the series 501–800.

(f) *Heeresverpflegungsamt* (GHQ ration supply depot)—numbered concurrently with those listed in (e) above.

(g) *Feldpostamt* (field post office)—army and GHQ field post offices carry numbers selected from the series 501–. In addition to its proper number, each post office (including corps and division offices) for all open correspondence uses a Kenn-Nummer (code number) selected at random from the series 1–999. Thus, K 943 might be the code number for 571st Army FPO; hence, it is necessary to exercise particular care in studying identifications of FPO's.

(h) *Armeebriefstelle* (army postal station)—branches of the army field post office for the collection and delivery of the field post; numbered in the same series as establishments in (g) above.

(i) *Armeebekleidungsamt* (army clothing depot).—Numbered same as in (e) above.

(2) Administration of ordnance stores.—Officers wear the color of their original arm; enlisted personnel wear light blue piping; distinguished by the letters "FZ" on shoulder straps (Latin for all except those in (a) below).

(a) *Feldzeugkommando* (ordnance command).—One or two in each Wehrkreis in Germany (the Gothic letters "FZ" followed by a Roman numeral give the identification); some in occupied countries (Belgium and Northern France). The officer appointed to this post has the status of a brigade commander. In the theater of operations there is no comparable post.

(b) *Oberfeldzeugstab* (higher ordnance staff).—Numbered in series 1–. The commander has the status of a regimental commander.

(c) *Feldzeugstab* (ordnance staff).—Equivalent in status to battalion headquarters; numbered in series 1–50 (twelve identified).

(d) *Feldzeugbataillon* (ordnance battalion).

(e) *Zentral-Ersatzteillager* (central spare parts depot).—Numbered in series 1–300.

(f) *Munitionsverwaltungskompanie* (ammunition administration company).—Numbered in series 500–.

(g) *Betriebsstoffsverwaltungskompanie* (fuel and lubricant administration company).—Numbered in series 971–980.

(3) Administration of occupied territory.

Enlisted personnel belonging to units of the following types wear white piping with the Latin letter "K" followed by the Arabic number of their unit.

(a) *Oberfeldkommandantur* (administrative area headquarters).—Headquarters of this type in the theater of operations come under the Commander of Army or Army Group Rear Area. In occupied territory outside the theater of operations they come under the general officer in command of the military administration, and in such cases they are distinguished by the addition of "V"— for Verwaltung—to their title. Nos 365, 372, 379, and 393 were formed in Poland from the staffs of divisions disbanded in 1940 and continue to carry the same numbers. They are to be classified as administrative divisions. All other identified units carry numbers in series 501–.

(b) Subordinate administrative headquarters.—The following headquarters carry numbers in the same series, in which the lowest number yet identified is 178 and the highest 928. Their relative importance may be deduced from their designation or from the rank of the officer in command, but there is no system discoverable in the allocation of numbers to them. About 150 identified, the majority numbered above 500.

1. *Feldkommandantur* (administrative sub-area headquar-

ters).—Approximately equivalent in status to a recruiting sub-area command of a Wehrkreis (see Section II). The term may also be loosely used to describe one of the following special types.

2. *Ortskommandantur* (town headquarters).—Major's command in a small town.
3. *Stadtkommandantur* (city headquarters)—major's command in a city or large town.
4. *Kreiskommandantur* (district headquarters)—major's command in a rural district.

(4) Administration of PW camps—following types all numbered in series 1–400. Personnel wear the color of their original arm. A PW camp located in a Wehrkreis also carries (and in all open correspondence uses) the Roman numeral of the Wehrkreis followed by a letter of the alphabet (e. g. Stalag XXI A).

(a) *Frontstalag* (forward PW camp)—twenty-five identified.

(b) *Dulag* (PW transit camp)—twenty identified.

(c) *Oflag* (camp for officer PW)—numbered in series 1–100; ten identified.

(d) *Stalag* (camp for enlisted PW)—numbered in series 301–400; forty identified.

26. Special mission unit.

There is one unit which defies classification, namely Lehr-Regiment Brandenburg z. b. V. 800 (800th Brandenburg Special Mission Demonstration Regiment). This unit was formed on the outbreak of war as Bau-Lehr-Bataillon 800 (800th Construction Demonstration Battalion), and expanded to a regiment during the summer of 1940. Its home station is at Brandenburg (Wkr. III), where its recruits are trained, but detachments from it may be encountered wherever German forces are operating. Its primary function is sabotage (whether by companies, platoons, or individuals). Its personnel contains a high proportion of Germans who have lived abroad and speak foreign languages fluently. Different companies of the regiment specialize in preparation for operations in specific countries. Its members often operate in civilian clothes, in some cases dropping by parachute into enemy-occupied country. Though they hold military rank the unit is under the direct control of the Intelligence Branch of the High Command (O. K. W./Abwehr) as regards its policy and organization.

27. Antiaircraft units of the Air Force.

All units are numbered in the series 1–1000. In some cases one number is carried by two or more units of different types. The following are the principal groups in the main series:

1–70—regiments consisting of Hq, I and II Battalions, each of three heavy and two light gun batteries, III Battalion of three searchlight batteries, and a personnel replacement battalion carrying the regimental number without qualification. Most of these units existed in peacetime.

71–99—light battalions of three light batteries each; also a number of independent regimental staffs carrying numbers in this series. Most of these units existed in peacetime.

100–997—units formed on or after mobilization; numbered according to no deducible system; including regiments, regimental staffs, and independent battalions (heavy, mixed, light, or searchlight). Army AAA batteries receive numbers in the same series. Naval batteries are numbered in a separate series, as are transport, balloon barrage, and plotting units (which belong to the same branch of the air force). The term "Reserve" prefixed to units in this group indicates that they have a special war organization (with a lower allocation of motor transport). It does not mean that the units in question were necessarily formed on mobilization.

The tactical unit is the battalion (Abteilung) and not the regiment. In action, battalions whether regimental or independent rarely operate under a regimental staff of the same number.

Antiaircraft artillery serving with the armies in the field is fully motorized. Units intended to cooperate with the spearhead of the attack are equipped for cross-country operation. Luftwaffe (air force) antiaircraft organizations and units operating with an army are subordinated operationally and for command purposes to the army units concerned, and administratively (for replacements, etc.) to a parent air force ground unit. There is no fixed allotment of units to higher formations, but the following range has been noted:

    To Flakkorps (AAA corps)—two to four AA divisions.
    To Flakdivision (AAA division)—two to five regiments.
    To Flakregiment (AAA regiment)—three to five battalions.

In general, the AAA corps controls the area of an army group, and the AAA division the area of an army. Allotment of units varies according to the estimated needs, but an army corps commonly has an AAA battalion attached to it during operations, and a light or mixed battalion will often be found attached to a Panzer division. An infantry division is not likely to be allotted more than an AAA battery.

The primary function of antiaircraft artillery in the field is to furnish antiaircraft protection to the field forces, such as antiaircraft protection of troop columns and concentrations, supply dumps and lines of communication, airdromes, and even to army units especially in front-line areas. It should be remembered, however, that mobile antiaircraft units regularly operate in the spearhead of the attack, being employed in this role not only for defense against air attack, but also against tanks and in some cases against strong points such as pill-boxes and troop concentrations. For this latter purpose the 88 mm gun with which the heavy antiaircraft battery is normally equipped has proved conspicuously successful.

28. Other Air Force units.

Apart from the Air Force ground troops described in paragraph 33, the following are the principal types of Air Force units likely to be found cooperating with army units in land operations:

  a. Parachute Troops (Fallschirmtruppen)—formations and units concerned are the following:

    (1) *XI Fliegerkorps* (XI Air Corps)—controls air-borne operations.

    (2) *7th Fliegerdivision* (7th Air Div)—containing units marked with an asterisk below.

    (3) *Fallschirmjägerregiment* (parachute rifle regiment)—Nos 1–3*, 4 and 5 have been identified.

(4) *Fallschirmartillerieregiment* (parachute artillery regiment)—No. 1* identified.

(5) *Fallschirmpanzerjägerabteilung* (parachute antitank battalion)—unnumbered*.

(6) *Fallschirm-Maschinengewehrbataillon* (parachute machine gun battalion)—unnumbered*.

(7) *Fallschirmnachrichtenkompanie* (parachute signal company)—No 7*.

(8) *Fallschirmfla-Bataillon* (parachute antiaircraft battalion)—unnumbered.

(9) *Fallschirmpionierbataillon* (parachute engineer battalion)—unnumbered.

(10) *Fallschirmsanitätskompanie* (parachute medical company)—unnumbered.

(11) *Sturmregiment* (glider-borne assault regiment)—No 1 identified.

b. Reconnaissance squadrons (Staffeln) attached to army ground force units. Squadrons (of nine aircraft) used for tactical reconnaissance missions are designed as H. Staffeln; those used for long range reconnaissance missions are designated as F. Staffeln. The addition of Pz indicates that a Staffel is trained to cooperate with Panzer units. The H Staffeln are operationally independent sub-units of Gruppen (groups), of which the following have been identified: 10–14, 21–23, 31–33, and 41. Each Gruppe may contain up to seven Staffeln.

c. Luftnachrichtenabteilung (Heer) motorisiert (motorized air signal battalion (army)). It cooperates with army ground force units and is allocated on the basis of one per army. Numbered in the series 1–.

d. Auxiliary units.—In addition to the above, air force construction, supply, or transport units may be encountered. These can readily be distinguished because, like air force Landesschützen units (see paragraph 23), they carry a double number: Arabic for the particular unit, and Roman for the Luftgau (air force administrative district) in which it was formed.

The tactical signs for the units in paragraphs 2 and 3 above and for air force AAA units are given in the following figures:

Section VII. TABLES OF IDENTIFIED UNITS

50. Introduction.

Whereas the foregoing pages (section VI) have contained data on all units of the German Army from the division upward, including those whose existence or composition can only be surmised, the present section VII records only those units, from armies down to battalions, which have actually been identified. These are listed in tabular form with details as to their component elements and the higher units to which they belong, so far as these are known.

It should be noted that in the case of armies and army corps the only component elements given are the special units (such as the Armee-Nachrichtenregiment and the field police units) which are organically attached to the staffs of these large organizations. The divisions which make up the combat strength of armies and corps are not included, since they are usually only allocated to them on a temporary basis for a specific operation or series of operations.

The German abbreviations used in the tables are explained in the list of abbreviations at the end of the book, and the character and functions of the various smaller units are described in the appropriate paragraphs of section III.

Where a blank (_____) is left in the tables, it means that the unit may exist but has not been identified. A dash (—) indicates that the unit is believed not to exist. Gaps in the numerical sequence of units are indicated by dotted lines and may be filled in later as information is received regarding such missing units.

Under the divisions, the column headed "small units" gives the number which is assigned to the various auxiliary units, such as the medical and veterinary. The last column indicates whether the division in question is considered to be offensive, defensive, or administrative, respectively.

51. Armies and Panzer armies (Armeeoberkommandos, Panzeroberkommandos).

ORDER OF BATTLE OF THE GERMAN ARMY

A. O. K.	Wkr.	A. N. R.	A. N. F.	Korück	F. G. A.	G. F. P.	F. P. A.	P. K.
1	IX	596	579		591	590	591	
Pz. 1		Pz. 1					422	691
2	XIII?	563?		550?				
Pz. 2	XVII	Pz. 2					419	
3**								
Pz. 3	IX	Pz. 3			551			
4	VI	589		580		721?	580	
Pz. 4	III	Pz. 4	571					697
5**								
Pz. 5								
6****	IV	549		585?	541?		540	637
7	V	*531	551		690?			
8**								
9		520?						
10**								
11***		558		521?	683?		554?	649
12***	XVII	521	530		501	611	530	690
14**								
15		*509				625?		698
16	I?	501?				616?		
17		596					550	666
18								
20		550					537	
Pz. Afrika****	III	Pz. 10	585	556	498	741	639	Libyen
Norwegen	XXI	*463	463			629	531	

*Bn only.
**Disbanded after the Polish campaign.
***Believed disbanded in 1942.
****Possibly disbanded early in 1943.

52. Corps and corps commands (Armeekorps, Panzerkorps, Gebirgskorps, Höhere Kommandos z. b. V., Reservekorps).

No.	Type	Wkr.	Nachr. Abt.	Services*	Home station
I	A. K.	I	41	---	Königsberg
II	A. K.	II	42	---	Stettin
III	Pz. K.	III	Pz. 43	403	Berlin
IV	A. K.	IV	44	404	Dresden
V	A. K.	V	45	---	Stuttgart
VI	A. K.	VI	46	406	Münster
VII	A. K.	VII	47	---	München
VIII	A. K.	VIII	48	---	Breslau
IX	A. K.	IX	49	409	Kassel
X	A. K.	X	50	410	Hamburg
XI	A. K.	XI	51	411	Hannover
XII	A. K.	XII	52	412	Wiesbaden
XIII	A. K.	XIII	53	413	Nürnberg
XIV	Pz. K.	XI	Pz. 60	---	Magdeburg
XV	Converted to Third Pz. Army				
XVI	Converted to Fourth Pz. Army				
XVII	A. K.	XVII	66	417	Wien
XVIII	Geb. K.	XVIII	Geb. 70	418	Salzburg
XIX	Converted to Second Pz. Army				
XX	A. K.	XX	420	---	Danzig
XXI	Converted to Army of Norway				
XXII	Converted to First Pz. Army				

*These include the Korpsnachschubführer, Feldgendarmerietrupp, and Feldpostamt, all bearing the same number.

53. Infantry, motorized, light, and miscellaneous divisions (Infanteriedivisionen, Infanteriedivisionen (mot.), Jägerdivisionen).

0304 ORDER OF BATTLE OF THE GERMAN ARMY

Div.	Type	Grenadierregimente	A. R.	Aufkl. Abt.	Pi. Btl.	Nachr. Abt.	Pz. Jg. Abt.	Krd.-S. Btl.	Small Units	Wkr.	Home station	Class
1	Inf	1 22 43	1	1	1	1	1		1	I	Insterburg	off
2	Mtz	Converted to 12th Pz Div										
3	Mtz	8 29	3	53	3	3	3	53	3	III	Frankfurt/O	off
4	Inf	Converted to 14th Pz Div										
5	Lt.	#56 #75 —	5	5	5	5	5		5	V	Konstanz	off
6	Inf	18 37 58	6	6	6	6	6		6	VI	Bielefeld	off
7	Inf	19 61 62	7	7	7	7	7		7	VII	München	off
8	Lt.	#38 #84 —	8	8	8	8	8		8	VIII	Neisse	off
9	Inf	36 57 116	9	9	9	9	9		9	IX	Giessen	off
10	Mtz	20 41 —	10	10	10	10	10	40	10	XIII	Regensburg	off
11	Inf	2 23 44	11	11	11	11	11		11	I	Allenstein	off
12	Inf	27 48 89	12	12	12	12	12		12	II	Schwerin	off
13	Mtz	Converted to 13th Pz Div										
14	Mtz	11 53 — 7/61	14	14	14	14	14	54	14	IV	Leipzig	off
15	Inf	Converted to 27th Pz Div/15										
*16	Mtz	60 156 —	146	341		228		59?	66	VI	Rheine	off
**17	Inf	21 55 95	17	***17	17	17	17		17	XIII	Nürnberg	off
18	Mtz	30 51 —	18	18	18	18	18	38	18	VIII	Liegnitz	off
19	Inf	Converted to 19th Pz Div										
20	Mtz	76 90 45	20	20	20	20	20	30	20	X	Hamburg	off
21	Inf	3 24 45	21	21	21	21	21		21	XX	Elbing	off
22	Inf	16 47 65	22	22	22	22	22		22	X	Oldenburg	off
23	Inf	Converted to 26th Pz Div										
24	Inf	31 32 102	24	24	24	24	24		24	IV	Chemnitz	off
25	Mtz	35 119 —	25	25	25	25	25	25	25	V	Ludwigsburg	off
26	Inf	39 77 78	26	26	26	26	26		26	VI	Köln	off
27	Inf	Converted to 17th Pz Div										
28	Lt.	#49 #83 —	28	28	28	28	28		28	VIII	Breslau	off
****29	Mtz	15 71 —	29	29	29	29	29	29	29	IX	Erfurt	off
30	Inf	6 26 46	30	****30	30	30	30		30	X	Lübeck	off
31	Inf	12 17 82	31	31	31	31	31		31	XI	Braunschweig	off
32	Inf	4 94 96	32	32	32	32	32		32	II	Köslin	off
33	Inf	Converted to 15th Pz Div										
34	Inf	80 107 253	34	34	34	34	34		34	XII	Heidelberg	off
35	Inf	34 109 111	35	35	35	35	35		35	V	Karlsruhe	off
36	Mtz	87 118 —	36	36	36	36	36	36	36	XII	Wiesbaden	off
38	Inf	68? 106? —	138	139	139				138?			off
39	Inf	113 114 —	139						139?			off
44	Inf	131 132 134	96	44	80	64	46		44	XVII	Wien	off
45	Inf	130 133 135	98	45	81	65	45		45	XVII	Linz	off
46	Inf	42 72 97	114	46	88	76	52		46	XIII	Karlsbad	off
50	Inf	121 122 123	150	150	150	150	150		150	XXI	Posen	off
52	Inf	163 181 205	152	152	152	152	152		152	IX	Kassel	off
56	Inf	171 192 234	156	156	156	156	156		156	IV	Naumburg	off

ORDER OF BATTLE OF THE GERMAN ARMY

57	Inf	179			157	157	157	157	VII	Bad Reichenhall	Off
58	Inf	154	199	217	158	158	158	158	X	Rendsburg?	Off
†60	Mtz	92	209	220	160	160	160	160	XX	Danzig	Off
61	Inf	151	120		161	161	161	161	I	Königsberg	Off
62	Inf	164	162	176	162	162	162	162	VIII	Glatz	Off
65	Inf	145	183	190	165			165			Off
68	Inf	169	146		168	168	168	168	III	Guben	Off
69	Inf	159	188	196	169	169	169	169	VI	Soest	Off
71	Inf	191	†193	236	171	171	171	171	XI	Hildesheim	Off
72	Inf	105	194	211	172	172	172	172	XII	Trier	Off
73	Inf	170	124	266	173	173	173	173	XIII	Würzburg	Off
75	Inf	172	186	213	175	175	175	175	II	Neustrelitz	Off
76	Inf	178	202	222	176	176	176	176	III	Berlin	Off
78	Inf	195	203	230	178	178	178	178	V	Tübingen	Off
79	Inf	208	215	238	179	179	179	179	XII	Koblenz	Off
81	Inf	161	212	226	181	181	181	181	XIII		Off
82	Inf	158	174	189	#182	182	182	182	IX	Frankfurt/M?	Off
83	Inf	251	166	168	183	183	183	183	X	Hamburg	Off
86	Inf	167	257	277	186	186	186	186	IV		Off
87	Inf	173	184	216	187	187	187	187	VII		Off
88	Inf	245	185	187	188	188	188	188	III	Berlin	Off
90	Lt	155	246	248	190	190	190	190	IX		Off
93	Inf	270	200	361	580	900	193	193	XI		Off
94	Inf	267	271	272	193	193	194	194	XIII		Off
95	Inf	278	274	276	195	195	195	195			Off
96	Inf	283	279	280	81			196	XVII		Off
97	Lt	#204	284	287	97			97	V		Off
98	Inf	282	#207		198			198	VIII		Off
99	Lt		289	290	Converted to 7th Mtn. Div				VI		Off
100	Lt	#54	#227		100	100	100	100	X	Oldenburg	Off
101	Lt	#228	#229		101	101	101	101	III		Off
102	Inf	232	233	235	?104	102		102	XII	Darmstadt	Off
106	Inf	239	240	241	107	106	106	106			Off
110	Inf	252	254	255	120	110	110	110			Off
111	Inf	50	70	117	?117	111	111	111			Off
112	Inf	110	256	258	86	120	112	112			Off

\# Jägerregiment.
\#\# Cyclist Co only.
* Also contains Pz. Abt. 116.
** Possibly now converted to a motorized division.
*** Cyclist Bn.
**** Also contains Pz. Abt. 129.
† Also contains Pz. Abt. 160.
‡ Possibly now under command of 210th Inf Div.
¶ Now designated Light Africa Division; Inf Regts are Panzer-Grenadier-Regimente; also contains 190th Pz Bn and 190th Fla Co.

ORDER OF BATTLE OF THE GERMAN ARMY

Div.	Type	Grenadierregimente				A. R.	Aufkl. Abt.	Pi. Btl.	Nachr. Abt.	Pz. Jg. Abt.	Krd.-S. Btl.	Small Units	Wkr.	Home station	Class
113	Inf.	260	405	261	268	87	113	113	113	113	---	113	XIII	---	Off
121	Inf.	405	409	407	408	121	121	121	121	121	---	121	X	---	Off
122	Inf.	409	415	411	?414	122	122	122	122	122	---	122	II	---	Off
123	Inf.	415	419	416	418	123	123	123	123	123	---	123	III	---	Off
125	Inf.	419	422	420	421	125	125	125	---	125	---	125	V	---	Off
126	Inf.	422	427	424	426	126	126	126	---	126	---	126	VI	---	Off
129	Inf.	427	431	428	430	129	129	129	129	129	---	129	IX	Fulda	Off
131	Inf.	431	436	432	434	131	131	131	131	131	---	131	XI	---	Off
132	Inf.	436	439	437	438	132	---	132	132	132	---	132	XII	---	Off
134	Inf.	439	447	445	446	134	134	134	134	134	---	134	IV	---	Off
137	Inf.	447		448	449	137	137	137	137	137	---	---	XVII	---	Off
141	Mob.												I	Königsberg	Adm
143	Res.												III	Frankfurt/O.	Def
147	Mob.												VII	Augsburg	Adm
148	Res.												XII	Metz	Def
151	Mob.												I	Allenstein	Adm
152	Mob.												II	Stettin	Adm
153	Res.												III	Potsdam	Def
154	Res.												IV	Dresden	Def
155	Mob.												V	Ulm	Adm
156	Res.												VI	Köln	Def
157	Res.												VII	München	Def
158	Res.												V	Strassburg	Def
159	Res.												IX	Frankfurt/M	Def
160	Mob.												X	Copenhagen	Adm
161	Inf.	336	303	364	371	241	*241	241	241	241	---	241	I	Rostock?	Off
162	Inf.	303	307	314	329	236	236	236	236	236	---	236	II	Berlin	Off
163	Inf.	307	125	310	324	234	*234	234	234	234	---	234	III	Leipzig	Off
164	Inf.	125		382	433	220	220	220	220	220	---	220	V	Epinal	Off
165	Res.												VI	Bielefeld	Def
166	Mob.														Adm
167	Inf.	315	417	331	339	238	238	238	---	238	---	238	VII	---	Off
168	Inf.	417	378	429	442	248	248	248	248	248	---	248	VIII	---	Offm
169	Inf.	378	391	379	392	230	---	230	---	230	---	230	IX	Bremen	Off
170	Inf.	391		399	401	240	---	240	---	240	---	240	X	Hannover	Off
171	Res.												XI	Mainz	Def
172	Mob.												XII	Würzburg	Adm
173	Mob.												XIII	Leipzig	Adm
174	Res.												IV	Wien	Def
177	Mob.												XVII	Liegnitz	Adm
178	Mob.												VIII	Weimar	Adm
179	Mob.												IX	Bremen	Adm
180	Mob.												X		Adm

ORDER OF BATTLE OF THE GERMAN ARMY

No.	Type										Wkr	Location	Status
181	Inf	334			222	222	222	222	222	222	XI	Nancy	Off
182	Res		349								XII		Def
183	Inf	330	343	350	219	219	219	219	219	219	XIII	Linz	Off
187	Res			351							XVIII	Salzburg	Def
188	Mob										XVII	Kassel?	Adm
189	Res										IX	Neumünster	Def
190	Res M&E.										X	Braunschweig	Def
191	Res										XI	Rostock	Def
192	Mob										II	Regensburg	Adm
193	Mob										XIII	Bielefeld?	Adm
196	Inf	340	345	362	233	233	233	233	233	233	VI	Speyer	Off
197	Inf	321	332	347	229	229	229	229	229	229	XII		Def
198	Inf	305	308	326	235	235	235	235			V	Düsseldorf	Off
199	Inf	341	357	410	199	*199	199	199			VI		Off
201	Sich	406											Def
203	Sich												Def
205	Inf	335	353	358	205	*205	205	205	205	205	V	Ulm	Off
206	Inf	301	312	413	206	*206	206			206	I	Gumbinnen	Off
207	Sich	322	368			*207	207	207			II	Stargard	Def
208	Inf	309	337	338	208	*208	208	208	208		III	Cottbus	Off
209	Inf	Disbanded in late summer 1940											Off
210	Inf	193?	388										Off
211	Inf	306	317	365	211	211	211	211	211	211	VI	Köln	Off
212	Inf	316	320	423	212	*212	212	212	212	212	VII	München	Off
213	Sich	318	354			213	213	213	†213		VIII	Glogau	Def
214	Inf	355	367	#388	214	214	214	214	214	214	IX	Hanau	Off
215	Inf	380	390	435	215	215	215	215	215	215	V	Heilbronn	Off
216	Inf	348	396	398	216	216	216	216	216	216	XI	Hamelin?	Off
217	Inf	311	346	389	217	217	217	217	217	217	I	Allenstein	Off
218	Inf	323	386	397	218	218	218	218	218	218	III	Spandau	Off
221	Sich	350	360			221	221	221	211	211	VIII	Breslau	Def
223	Inf	344	385	425	223	*223	223	223	223	223	IV	Bautzen	Off
225	Inf	333	376	377	225	225	225	225	225	225	X	Hamburg	Off
227	Inf	328	366	412	227	**227	227	227	227	227	VI	Düsseldorf	Off
228	Inf	Disbanded in late summer 1940										I	Lötzen	Def
231	Mob	Disbanded in late summer 1940										XIII		Def
***233	Mob											III	Frankfurt/O	Adm

*Cyclist Co only.
**Cyclist Bn.
***Division Nr. 233 (mot.); controls training of all Panzer and motorized units in Wkr. III.
#Now under command of 210th Inf Div.
##Now designated Light Africa Division; Inf Regts are Panzer-Grenadier-Regimente.
†Co only.

0308 ORDER OF BATTLE OF THE GERMAN ARMY

Div.	Type	Grenadierregimente			A. R.	Aufkl. Abt.	Pi. Btl.	Nachr. Abt.	Pz. Jg. Abt.	Krd.-S. Btl.	Small Units	Wkr.	Home station	Class
239	Inf	404	313	352								VIII	Oppeln	Off
246	Inf	689	263	269	246	#246	246	246	246		246	XII	Trier	Def
250	Inf	262			250	20					250		Spanish Blue Div.	Off
251	Inf	451	459	471	251	251	251	251	251		251	IX	Hanau	Off
252	Inf	452	461	472	252	252	252	252	252		252	VIII	Neisse	Off
253	Inf	453	464	473	253	253	253	253	253		253	VI	Aachen	Off
254	Inf	454	474	484	254	254	254	254	254		254	VI	Dortmund	Off
255	Inf	455	465	475	255	255	255	255	255		255	IV	Löbau	Off
256	Inf	456	476	481	256	256	256	256	256		256	IV	Meissen?	Off
257	Inf	457	466	477	257	257	257	257	257		257	III	Frankfurt/O.	Off
258	Inf	458	478	479	258	258	258	258	258		258	III	Rostock?	Off
260	Inf	460	470	480	260	260	260	260	260		260	V	Karlsruhe	Off
262	Inf	462	482	486	262	262	262	262	262		262	XVII	Wien	Off
263	Inf	463	483	485	263	263	263	263	263		263	XII	Idar-Oberstein	Off
267	Inf	467	487	497	267	267	267	267	267		267	XI	Hannover?	Off
268	Inf	468	488	499	268	268	268	268	268		268	VII	München	Off
269	Inf	469	489	490	269	269	269	269	269		269	X	Delmenhorst	Off
270	Inf	Formed and disbanded in summer 1940										V		
271	Inf	Formed and disbanded in summer 1940										II		
272	Inf	Formed and disbanded in summer 1940												
273	Inf	Formed and disbanded in summer 1940										III		Def
276	Inf	Formed and disbanded in summer 1940										VII		Def
277	Inf	Formed and disbanded in summer 1940												Def
281	Sich													Def
285	Sich													
286	Sich													
290	Inf	501	502	503	290	290	290		290		290	X		Off
291	Inf	504	505	506	291			291	291		291	I	Insterburg	Off
292	Inf	507	508	509	292		292		292		292	II		Off
293	Inf	510	511	512	293	293	293	293	293		293	III		Off
294	Inf	513	514	515	294		294	294	294		294	IV		Off
295	Inf	516	517	518	295		295	295			295	XI		Off
296	Inf	519	520	521	296		296	296	296		296	XIII	Nürnberg?	Off
297	Inf	522	523	524	297		297	297	297		297	XVII	Wien	Off
298	Inf	525	526	527	298		298	298			298	VIII		Off
299	Inf	528	529	530	299		299		299		299	IX	Weimar	Off
302	Inf	570	571	572	302		302	302			302	II	Schwerin?	Off
304	Inf	573	574	575	304		304		304		304	IV		Off
305	Inf	576	577	578	305		305				305	V	Konstanz?	Off
306	Inf	579	580	581	306		306		306		306	VI		Off
311*							311							Adm
319	Inf	582	583	584	319		319		319		319	IX		Off

ORDER OF BATTLE OF THE GERMAN ARMY 0309

Div	Type								WK	Location	Status
320	Inf	585	586	587		320	320	320	X		Off
321	Inf	588	589	590		321	321	321	XI		Off
323	Inf	591	592	593		323	323	323	XIII		Off
326	Inf	~~594~~ ~~762~~ ~~758~~									Off
327	Inf	595	596	597		327	327	327	XVII		Off
328	Inf	547	548	549		328	**328			IX		Off
329	Inf	551?	552?	553?	329	329		329	VI		Off
330	Inf	554	555	556	†330	330			V		Off
331	Inf	557	558	559	331	331	331	331	XVII		Off
332	Inf	676	677	678		332	**332	332	VIII		Off
333	Inf	679	680	681	#333	333	**333	333	III	Berlin	Off
334	Inf	754	755	##756	***334	334	**334	334	XIII		Off
335	Inf	682	683	684		335	**335	335	V		Off
336	Inf	685	686	687		336	**336	336	IV		Off
337	Inf	688	689	690		337	**337	337	VII		Off
339	Inf	691	692	693		339	**339	339	IX	Jena	Off
340	Inf	694	695	696		340	340	340	I	Königsberg	Off
342	Inf	697	698	699	#342	342	**342	342	XII	Kaiserslautern	Off
343	Inf					343		343	XIII	Grafenwöhr	Off
344	Inf										Adm
347	Inf										Def
358	Inf	Disbanded in 1940									
365	##										Off
369	Inf	369	370						Div	Croatian	Off
370	Inf	666	667	668		370	370	370	IV		Adm
371	Inf	669?	670	671?		371		371	VI		Off
372	##								IV		Adm
376	Inf	672	673?			376		376	VII?		Off
377	##	768	769	770	#377	377	377	377	IX		Off
379	##										Adm
383	Inf	531	532	533		383	383	383	III		Off
384	Inf	534	535?	536?		384		384	IV		Off
385	Inf	537	538	539		385	385	385	VI		Off
386	Inf	Disbanded, probably late in 1941							VII		
387	Inf	541	542	543		387	387	387	VII		Off

*Classification uncertain.
**Co. only.
***Schnelle Abt. (combined Aufkl. and Pz. Jg.).
#Cyclist Co. only.
##Gebirgsjägerregiment.
###Disbanded as a division in 1940 but now acting as Oberfeldkommandantur in Poland.
†Cyclist Bn.

ORDER OF BATTLE OF THE GERMAN ARMY

Div.	Type	Grenadierregimente			A. R.	Aufkl. Abt.	Pi. Btl.	Nachr. Abt.	Pz. Jg. Abt.	K rd.-S. Btl.	Small Units	Wkr.	Home station	Class
389	Inf	544	545	546	389				389		389	IX		Off Adm
*393	Inf	Disbanded in autumn 1940												Adm
395	Inf	Disbanded in autumn 1940												Adm
399	z. b. V.**											I	Königsberg	Adm
401	z. b. V.**											III	Stettin	Adm
402	z. b. V.**											III	Berlin	Def
403	z.b. V.** *Alchz.*											IV	Dresden	Adm
404	z. b. V.**											V	Stuttgart	Adm
405	z. b. V.**											VI	Münster	Adm
406	z. b. V.**											VII	München	Adm
407	z. b. V.**											VIII	Breslau	Adm
408	z. b. V.**											IX	Kassel	Adm
409	z. b. V.**											X	Hamburg	Adm
410	z. b. V.**											XI	Hannover	Adm
411	z. b. V.**											XII	Wiesbaden	Adm
412	z. b. V.**											XIII	Nürnberg	Adm
413	z. b. V.**													Def
416	Inf†	930	931?									XVII	Wien	Adm
417	z. b. V.**											I		Adm
421	z. b. V.**											XX	Danzig	Adm
428	z. b. V.**											XXI	Posen	Adm
429	z. b. V.**											XXI	Gnesen	Adm
430	z. b. V.**											XXI	Litzmannstadt	Adm
431	z. b. V.**											VIII	Neisse	Adm
432	z. b. V.**													Adm
442	Sich													Def
444	Sich											XII		Def
454	Sich													Def
461	z. b. V.¶													Adm
526	Grenzwach											VI	Aachen	Def
537	Grenzwach											XVIII	Innsbruck	Def
538	Grenzwach											XVIII	Klagenfurt	Def
539	Grenzwach											Prot.	Prag	Def
540	Grenzwach											Prot.	Brünn	Def
554	Disbanded late in 1940											IV		
555	Disbanded late in 1940											VI		
556	Disbanded late in 1940											XII		
557	Disbanded late in 1940											V		
702	Inf	722	742		#662		##704	##702			702	II		Def
704	Inf	724	734		#654		##707	##704			704	IV		Def
707	Inf	727	747		#657			##707			707	VII		Def
708	Inf	728	748				##708	##708				VIII		Def
709	Inf	729	739				##709	##709				IX		Def

ORDER OF BATTLE OF THE GERMAN ARMY

710	Inf	730	740		##710		710	X	Def
711	Inf	731	744		##711		711	XI	Def
712	Inf	732	745	#652	##712		712	XII	Def
713	Inf	733	746		##713		713	XIII	Def
714	Inf	721	741	#661	##714		714	I	Def
715	Inf	725	735		##715		715	V	Def
716	Inf	726	736		##716			VI	Def
717	Inf	737	749	#670	##717		717	XVII	Def
718	Inf	738	750	#668				XVIII	Def
719	Inf	723	743				719	III	Def

*Disbanded as a division in 1940 but now acting as Oberfeldkommandantur in Poland.
**Varying attached units.
***Acting as a Sicherungs division.
†Formerly 416 z. b. V.
‡Formerly z. b. V. Bialystok.
#Bn only.
##Co only.
There are also the following unnumbered divisions:
a. Infanterie-Division (mot.) Grossdeutschland, in which units carry the name Grossdeutschland (abbreviated GD) in place of a number, the two infantry regiments are known as Panzer-Grenadier-Regt. GD and Fusilier-Regt. GD respectively.
b. Division von Broich, composite division.

54. Cavalry divisions (Kavalleriedivisionen).

The 1st Cavalry division, which was the sole cavalry division in the German Army, was converted to the 24th Panzer Division during the winter of 1941–42. (For the SS Kavalleriedivision see paragraph 57.)

55. Panzer divisions (Panzerdivisionen).

Div	Pz. R.	Pz. Gr. R.	Pz. Gr. R.	A. R.	Aufkl. Abt.	Pi. Btl.	Nachr. Abt.	Pz. Jg. Abt.	Beob. Bttr.	Krd-S. Btl.	Small Units	Wkr.	Home Station	Class
1	1	1	113	73	4	37	37	37		1	81	IX	Weimar	Off
2	3	2	304	74	5	38	38	38	320	2	82	XVII	Wien	Off
3	6	3	394	75	1	39	39		327	3	83	III	Berlin	Off
4	35	12	33	103	7	79	79	49	324	34	84	XIII	Würzburg	Off
5	31	13	14	116	8	89	85?	53		55	85	VIII	Oppeln	Off
6	11	4	114	76	57	57	82	41		6	57	VI	Wuppertal	Off
7	25	6	7	78	37	58	83	42	325	7	58	IX	Gera	Off
8	10	8	28	80	59	59	59	43		8	59	III	Cottbus	Off
9	33	10	11	102	9	86	81	50		9	60	XVII	Wien	Off
10	7	69	86	90		49	90	90		10	90	V	Stuttgart	Off
11	15	110	111	119	231		341			61	61	VIII	Görlitz	Off
12	29	5	25	2	2	32	2	2		22	2	II	Stettin	Off
13	4	66	93	13	13	4	13	13		43	13	XI	Magdeburg	Off
14	36	103	108	4	40	13	4	4	326	64	4	IV	Dresden	Off
15	8	115		33	33	33	78	33			33	XII	Kaiserslautern	Off
16	2	64	79	16	16	16	16	16		16	16	VI	Münster	Off
17	39	40	63	27	27	27	27	27		17	27	VII	Augsburg	Off
18	18	52	101	88	88	209	88	88		18	88	IV	Hannover	Off
19	27	73	74	19	19	19	19	19	335	19	19	XI	Gotha	Off
20	21	59	112	92	92	92	92	92		20	92	IX	Berlin	Off
21	5	104		155	3	200	200	39			200	III		Off
22	204	129	140	140		140	140	140		24	140			Off
23	201	126	126	128		128	128	128		23	128			Off
24	24	21	26	89		40		40			40?	I		Off
25		146		*91								VI		Off
26	202	9	67	23		23	23	23			23	III	Potsdam	Off
27		81	88	15		15	15	15			15	IX		Off

There is also the Division Hermann Göring, in which units carry the name Hermann Göring in place of a number.
*Bn only.

56. Mountain divisions (Gebirgsdivisionen).

Div.	Geb. Jg. R.	Geb. Jg. R.	A.R.	Aufkl. Abt.	Pi. Btl.	Nachr. Abt.	Pz. Jg. Abt.	Small Units	Wkr.	Home Station	Class
1	98	99	79	*54	54	54	44	54	VII	Garmisch	Off
2	136	137	111	*67	82	67	47	67	XVIII	Innsbruck	Off
3	138	139	112	*68	83	68	48	68	XVIII	Graz	Off
4	13	91	94	*94	94	94	94	94	V	Ulm	Off
5	85	100	95	*95	95	95	95	95	XVIII	Salzburg	Off
6	141	143	118		91	91	55	91	XVIII	Klagenfurt?	Off
7	206	218	82	*99	*99	*99	*99	*99	XIII		Off
8	142?	144							XVIII		Off

*Cyclist Bn.

57. Waffen-SS units.—*a. Corps.*—The SS-Panzerkorps, of uncertain composition and with no further known designation, was formed in 1941. Its home station is in Wehrkreis XI.

b. Divisions.—These are of several varieties but are believed to be roughly similar in composition to the corresponding Army divisions. The SS Panzer divisions may have special features, such as an allotment of assault artillery. The following have been identified:

Division	Class	Component regiments
SS-Pz. Gr. Div. Leigstandarte Adolf Hitler	Pz	SS-Pz. Gr. Rgt. Wisch, SS-Pz. Gr. Rgt. Witt (named for their commanders)
SS-Pz. Gr. Div. Das Reich	Pz	SS-Pz. Gr. Rgt. Deutschland, SS-Pz. Gr. Rgt. der Führer
SS-Pz. Gr. Div. Theodor Eicke*	Pz	SS-Pz. Gr. Rgt. 1, SS-Pz. Gr. Rgt. 3
SS-Pz. Gr. Div. Wiking	Pz	SS-Pz. Gr. Rgt. Germania, SS-Pz. Gr. Rgt. Nordland, SS-Pz. Gr. Rgt. Westland
SS-Pz. Gr. Div. 9	Pz	
SS-Pz. Gr. Div. 10	Pz	
SS-Div. Prinz Eugen	Mtn	
SS-Gebirgsdivision Nord	Mtn	SS-Geb. Jg. R. 6 and 7
SS-Kavalleriedivision	Cav	
SS-Polizeidivision	Inf	Polizeischützenrgt. 1, 2, and 3

*Previously SS-Totenkopf Division.

c. Brigades.—These are independent organizations, of which the following have been identified:

Brigade	Component regiments
1st SS-Panzerbrigade	SS-Gr. R. 8, SS-Gr. R. 10
1st SS-Infanteriebrigade (mot.)	
2nd SS-Infanteriebrigade (mot.)	

d. Regiments.—The following SS infantry regiments have been identified:

SS Regt.	Home Station	Allotted to
Pz. Gr. 1	Berlin	Theodor Eicke
Pol. 1		SS-Polizeidiv.
2		
Pol. 2		SS-Polizeidiv.
3	Berlin	Theodor Eicke
Pol. 3		SS-Polizeidiv.
4		
5		
Geb. Jg. 6*	Trautenau	Nord
Geb. Jg. 7	Trautenau	Nord
Gr. 8		1st SS Inf. Brigade
9		
Gr. 10		1st SS Inf. Brigade
11		
Pz. Gr. Wisch	Berlin	Leibstandarte Adolf Hitler
Pz. Gr. Witt	Berlin	Leibstandarte Adolf Hitler
Pz. Gr. Deutschland	München	Das Reich
Pz. Gr. Der Führer	Wien	Das Reich
Pz. Gr. Germania	Hamburg	Wiking
Pz. Gr. Nordland	Klagenfurt	Wiking
Pz. Gr. Westland	Klagenfurt	Wiking

*Also called SS-Geb. Jg. R. "Reinhardt Heydrich."

58. Brigades.—In the German Army the brigade is no longer used as a tactical or administrative unit except in the following special cases:

a. Motorized infantry brigades in Panzer divisions, hitherto called Schützenbrigaden, now Panzer-Grenadier-Brigaden. These have hitherto comprised the two motorized infantry regiments and a motorcycle battalion. In recently formed Panzer divisions, however, the motorcycle battalion is no longer a part of the brigade. The bridages always carry the same number as the division.

There is also an independent motorized infantry brigade 999, which has appeared in Tunisia as a unique formation. It contains infantry regiments 961 and 962.

b. Panzer brigades.—These were used to comprise the two Panzer regiments which each Panzer division had in peacetime. The brigade staffs sometimes, but not always, carried the same number as the division. Under the present system of one Panzer regiment to a Panzer division, such brigade staffs are no longer needed and may have been disbanded.

There are also some Panzer brigades which have been known to operate independently. Their component regiments are not known and may vary from time to time. Of this type, Panzerbrigaden 4, 18, 100, and 101 have been identified. (Panzerbrigade 100 is apparently a training command only.)

c. Cavalry brigades.—Since the conversion of the 1st Cavalry Division to the 24th Panzer Division, it is probable that there are no longer any cavalry brigades in the German Army. SS cavalry brigades may continue to exist.

d. Sicherungs brigades.—Used for rear area duties.

e. Lehrbrigade 900.—Probably an infantry training organization.

(For SS brigades see paragraph 57.)

59. Infantry, motorized infantry, and mountain rifle regiments (Grenadierregimente, Panzergrenadierregimente, Jägerregimente, Gebirgsjägerregimente).

Gr. R.*	Wkr.	In Div	Gr. R.	Wkr.	In Div
1	I	1 Inf	44	I	11 Inf
Pz. Gr 1 Mtz	IX	1 Pz	45	XX	21 Inf
2	I	11 Inf	46	X	30 Inf
Pz. Gr 2 Mtz	XVII	2 Pz	47	X	22 Inf
3	XX	21 Inf	48	II	12 Inf
Pz. Gr 3 Mtz	III	3 Pz	Jg 49	VIII	28 Lt
4	II	32 Inf	50	III	111 Inf
Pz. Gr 4 Mtz	VI	6 Pz	51 Mtz	VIII	18 Mtz
Pz. Gr 5 Mtz	II	12 Pz	Pz. Gr 52 Mtz	IV	18 Pz
6	X	30 Inf	53 Mtz	IV	14 Mtz
Pz. Gr 6 Mtz	IX	7 Pz	Jg 54	XVII	100 Lt
7**	VIII		55	XIII	17 Inf
Pz. Gr 7 Mtz	IX	7 Pz	Jg 56	V	5 Lt
8 Mtz	III	3 Mtz	57	IX	9 Inf
Pz. Gr 8 Mtz	III	8 Pz	58	VI	6 Inf
Pz. Gr 9 Mtz	III	26 Pz	Pz. Gr 59 Mtz	IX	20 Pz
10**	IV		60 Mtz	VI	16 Mtz
Pz. Gr 10 Mtz	XVII	9 Pz	61	VII	7 Inf
11 Mtz	IV	14 Mtz	62	VII	7 Inf
Pz. Gr 11 Mtz	XVII	9 Pz	Pz. Gr 63 Mtz	VII	17 Pz
12	XI	31 Inf	Pz. G 64 Mtz	VI	16 Pz
Pz. Gr 12 Mtz	XIII	4 Pz	65	X	22 Inf
Geb. Jg 13	V	4 Mtn	Pz. Gr 66 Mtz	XI	13 Pz
Pz. Gr 13 Mtz	VIII	5 Pz	Pz. Gr 67 Mtz	III	26 Pz
14**	V		68	III	38 Inf?
Pz. Gr 14 Mtz	VIII	5 Pz	Pz. Gr 69 Mtz	V	10 Pz
15 Mtz	IX	29 Mtz	70	III	111 Inf
16	X	22 Inf	71 Mtz	IX	29 Mtz
17	XI	31 Inf	72	XIII	46 Inf
18	VI	6 Inf	Pz. Gr 73 Mtz	XI	19 Pz
19	VII	7 Inf	Pz. Gr 74 Mtz	XI	19 Pz
20 Mtz	XIII	10 Mtz	Jg 75	V	5 Lt
21	XIII	17 Inf	76 Mtz	X	20 Mtz
22	I	1 Inf	77	VI	26 Inf
23	I	11 Inf	78	VI	26 Inf
24	XX	21 Inf	Pz. Gr 79 Mtz	VI	16 Pz
Pz. Gr 25 Mtz	II	12 Pz	80	XII	34 Inf
26	X	30 Inf	Pz. Gr 81 Mtz	IX	27 Pz
27	II	12 Inf	82	XI	31 Inf
Pz. Gr 28 Mtz	III	8 Pz	Jg 83	VIII	28 Lt
29 Mtz	III	3 Mtz	Jg 84	VIII	8 Lt
30 Mtz	VIII	18 Mtz	Geb 85	XVIII	5 Mtn
31	IV	24 Inf	Pz. Gr 86 Mtz	V	10 Pz
32	IV	24 Inf	87 Mtz	XII	36 Mtz
Pz. Gr 33 Mtz	XIII	4 Pz	Pz. Gr 88 Mtz	IX	27 Pz
34	V	35 Inf	89	II	12 Inf
35 Mtz	V	25 Mtz	90 Mtz	X	20 Mtz
36	IX	9 Inf	Geb 91	V	4 Mtn
37	VI	6 Inf	92	XX	60 Mtz
38	VIII	8 Lt	Pz. Gr 93 Mtz	XI	13 Pz
39	VI	26 Inf	94	II	32 Inf
Pz. Gr 40 Mtz	VII	17 Pz	95	XIII	17 Inf
41 Mtz	XIII	10 Mtz	96	II	32 Inf
42	XIII	46 Inf	97	XIII	46 Inf
43	I	1 Inf	Geb 98	VII	1 Mtn

*Unless qualified by Pz. Gr., Jg., or Geb. Jg.
**Possibly re-formed under a new number.

ORDER OF BATTLE OF THE GERMAN ARMY

Gr. R.	Wkr.	In Div	Gr. R.	Wkr.	In Div
Geb 99	VII	1 Mtn	167	VI	86 Inf
Geb 100	XVIII	5 Mtn	168	IX	82 Inf
Pz. Gr 101 Mtz	IV	18 Pz	169	III	68 Inf
102	IV	24 Inf	170	XIII	73 Inf
Pz. Gr 103 Mtz	IV	14 Pz	171	IV	56 Inf
Pz. Gr 104 Mtz	XII	21 Pz	172	II	75 Inf
105	XII	72 Inf	173	IV	87 Inf
106	IX	38 Inf?	174	VIII	81 Inf
107	XII	34 Inf	...		
Pz. Gr 108 Mtz	IV	14 Pz	176	I	61 Inf
109	V	35 Inf	...		
110	XII	112 Inf	178	III	76 Inf
Pz. Gr 110 Mtz	VIII	11 Pz	179	VII	57 Inf
111	V	35 Inf	...		
Pz. Gr 111 Mtz	VIII	11 Pz	181	IX	52 Inf
Pz. Gr 112 Mtz	IX	20 Pz	...		
113		39 Inf	183	VIII	62 Inf
Pz. Gr 113 Mtz	IX	1 Pz	184	VI	86 Inf
114		39 Inf	185	IV	87 Inf
Pz. Gr 114 Mtz	VI	6 Pz	186	XIII	73 Inf
Pz. Gr 115 Mtz	XII	15 Pz	187	IV	87 Inf
116	IX	9 Inf	188	III	68 Inf
117	III	111 Inf	189	VIII	81 Inf
118 Mtz	XII	36 Mtz	190	VIII	62 Inf
119 Mtz	V	25 Mtz	191	XI	71 Inf
120 Mtz	XX	60 Mtz	192	IV	56 Inf
121	XXI	50 Inf	193	VI	69 Inf
122	XXI	50 Inf	194	XI	71 Inf
123	XXI	50 Inf	195	V	78 Inf
124	XII	72 Inf	196	III	68 Inf
Pz. Gr 125 Mtz	IV	164 Lt	...		
Pz. Gr 126 Mtz		23 Pz	198		
Pz. Gr 128 Mtz		23 Pz	199	VII	57 Inf
Pz. Gr 129 Mtz		22 Pz	Pz. Gr 200 Mtz	III	90 Lt
130	XVII	45 Inf	201*		
131	XVII	44 Inf	202	II	75 Inf
132	XVII	44 Inf	203	III	76 Inf
133	XVII	45 Inf	Jg 204	VII	97 Lt
134	XVII	44 Inf	205	IX	52 Inf
135	XVII	45 Inf	Geb 206	XIII	7 Mtn
Geb 136	XVIII	2 Mtn	Jg 207	VII	97 Lt
Geb 137	XVIII	2 Mtn	208	XII	79 Inf
Geb 138	XVIII	3 Mtn	209	X	58 Inf
Geb 139	XVIII	3 Mtn	210*		
Pz. Gr 140 Mtz		22 Pz	211	XI	71 Inf
Geb 141	XVIII	6 Mtn	212	XII	79 Inf
Geb.? 142	XVIII?	8 Mtn?	213	XIII	73 Inf
Geb 143	XVIII	6 Mtn	...		
Geb 144	XVIII	8 Mtn?	215	V	78 Inf
145		65 Inf	216	VI	86 Inf
146		65 Inf	217	VII	57 Inf
Pz. G 146 Mtz	VI	25 Pz	Geb 218	XIII	7 Mtn
151	I	61 Inf	...		
154	X	58 Inf	220	X	58 Inf
Pz. Gr 155 Mtz	III	90 Lt	...		
156 Mtz	VI	16 Mtz	222	II	75 Inf
...			...		
158	IX	82 Inf	...		
159	VI	69 Inf	...		
...			226	XII	79 Inf
161	VIII	81 Inf	Jg 227	XVII	100 Lt
162	I	61 Inf	Jg 228	V	101 Lt
163	IX	52 Inf	Jg 229	V	101 Lt
164	VIII	62 Inf	230	III	76 Inf
...			...		
166	IX	82 Inf	232	VIII	102 Inf

*Disbanded late in 1940.

Gr. R.	Wkr.	In Div	Gr. R.	Wkr.	In Div
233	VIII	102 Inf	Pz. Gr 304 Mtz	XVII	2 Pz
234	IV	56 Inf	305	V	198 Inf
235	VIII	102 Inf	306	VI	211 Inf
236	VI	69 Inf	307	III	163 Inf
...			308	V	198 Inf
238	V	78 Inf	309	III	208 Inf
239	VI	106 Inf	310	III	163 Inf
240	VI	106 Inf	311	I	217 Inf
241	VI	106 Inf	312	I	206 Inf
242*	XX		313	XII	246 Inf
243*	XX		314	II	162 Inf
244*	XX		315	VII	167 Inf
245	VII	88 Inf	316	VII	212 Inf
246	VII	88 Inf	317	VI	211 Inf
...			318##	VIII	213# Sich
248	VII	88 Inf	319*	XIII	
...			320	VII	212 Inf
251	X	83 Inf	321	XII	197 Inf
252	X	110 Inf	322#	II	207 Sich
253	XII	34 Inf	323	III	218 Inf
254	X	110 Inf	324	III	163 Inf
255	X	110 Inf	325*	I	
256	XII	112 Inf	326	V	198 Inf
257	X	83 Inf	327###		
258	XII	112 Inf	328	VI	227 Inf
...			329	II	162 Inf
260	XIII	113 Inf	330	XIII	183 Inf
261	XIII	113 Inf	331	VII	167 Inf
262	**	250 Inf	332	XII	197 Inf
263	**	250 Inf	333	X	225 Inf
264*	IV		334	XI	181 Inf
265*	V		335	V	205 Inf
266	XII	72 Inf	336	I	161 Inf
267	IV	94 Inf	337	III	208 Inf
268	XIII	113 Inf	338	III	208 Inf
269	**	250 Inf	339	VII	167 Inf
270	III	93 Inf	340	VI	196 Inf
271	III	93 Inf	341	VI	199 Inf
272	III	93 Inf	342¶	XIII	
...			343	XIII	183 Inf
274	IV	94 Inf	344	IV	223 Inf
...			345	VI	196 Inf
276	IV	94 Inf	346	I	217 Inf
277	X	83 Inf	347	XII	197 Inf
278	IX	95 Inf	348	XI	216 Inf
279	IX	95 Inf	349	XI	181 Inf
280	IX	95 Inf	350†	VIII	221 Sich
...			351	XIII	183 Inf
282	XIII	98 Inf	352	XII	246 Inf
283	XI	96 Inf	353	V	205 Inf
284	XI	96 Inf	354†	VIII	213 Sich
...			355	IX	214 Inf
287***	XI	96 Inf	356¶	I	
288#	III		357	VI	199 Inf
289	XIII	98 Inf	358	V	205 Inf
290	XIII	98 Inf	359	XI	181 Inf
...			360†	VIII	221 Sich
301	I	206 Inf	Pz. Gr 361 Mtz	III	90 Lt
302*	XIII		362	VI	196 Inf
303	II	162 Inf			

*Disbanded late in 1941.
**Spanish.
***Also carrying this number is Pz. Gr. Btl. 287, known as "Verband 287."
#"Panzer-Gr.-Rgt. Afrika," a special independent brigade group formerly called "Verband 288.
##Reinforced regt.
###Probably disbanded late in 1941.
¶Disbanded late in 1940.
†Reinforced regt.

ORDER OF BATTLE OF THE GERMAN ARMY

	Gr. R.	Wkr.	In Div		Gr. R.	Wkr.	In Div
	364	I	161 Inf		427	IX	129 Inf
	365	VI	211 Inf		428	IX	129 Inf
	366	VI	227 Inf		429	VIII	168 Inf
	367	IX	214 Inf		430	IX	129 Inf
	368**	II	207 Sich		431	XI	131 Inf
	369	***	369 Inf		432	XI	131 Inf
	370	***	369 Inf	Pz. Gr	433 Mtz	IV	164 Lt
	371	I	161 Inf		434	XI	131 Inf
	372				435	V	215 Inf
	...				436	XII	132 Inf
	374**	II			437	XII	132 Inf
	375**##	VIII			438	XII	132 Inf
	376	X	225 Inf		439	IV	134 Inf
	377	X	225 Inf		440	IV	
	378	IX	169 Inf		441		
	379	IX	169 Inf		442	VIII	168 Inf
	380	V	215 Inf		443		
	...				444*		
Pz. Gr	382 Mtz	IV	164 Lt		445	IV	134 Inf
	...				446	IV	134 Inf
	385	IV	223 Inf		447	XVII	137 Inf
	386	III	218 Inf		448	XVII	137 Inf
	...				449	XVII	137 Inf
	388	IX	214 Inf		450**		
	389	I	217 Inf		451	IX	251 Inf
	390	V	215 Inf		452	VIII	252 Inf
	391	X	170 Inf		453	VI	253 Inf
	392	IX	169 Inf		454	VI	254 Inf
	...				455	IV	255 Inf
Pz. Gr	394 Mtz	III	3 Pz		456	IV	256 Inf
	...				457	III	257 Inf
	396	XI	216 Inf		458	II	258 Inf
	397	III	218 Inf		459	IX	251 Inf
	398	XI	216 Inf		460	V	260 Inf
	399	X	170 Inf		461	VIII	252 Inf
	400*	I			462	XVII	262 Inf
	401	X	170 Inf		463	XII	263 Inf
	402				464	VI	253 Inf
	403				465	IV	255 Inf
	404	XII	246 Inf		466	III	257 Inf
	405	X	121 Inf		467	XI	267 Inf
	406**	VIII	201 Sich		468	VII	268 Inf
	407	X	121 Inf		469	X	269 Inf
	408	X	121 Inf		470	V	260 Inf
	409	II	122 Inf		471	IX	251 Inf
	410	VI	199 Inf		472	VIII	252 Inf
	411	II	122 Inf		473	VI	253 Inf
	412	VI	227 Inf		474	VI	254 Inf
	413	I	206 Inf		475	IV	255 Inf
	414	II?	122 Inf?		476	IV	256 Inf
	415	III	123 Inf		477	III	257 Inf
	416	III	123 Inf		478	II	258 Inf
	417	VIII	168 Inf		479	II	258 Inf
	418	III	123 Inf		480	V	260 Inf
	419	V	125 Inf		481	XIII	256 Inf
	420	V	125 Inf		482	XVII	262 Inf
	421	V	125 Inf		483	XII	263 Inf
	422	VI	126 Inf		484	VI	254 Inf
	423	VII	212 Inf		485	XII	263 Inf
	424	VI	126 Inf		486	XVII	262 Inf
	425	IV	223 Inf		487	XI	267 Inf
	426	VI	126 Inf		488	VII	268 Inf

* Disbanded late in 1940.
** Reinforced regt.
Includes a Walloon battalion.

ORDER OF BATTLE OF THE GERMAN ARMY

Gr. R.	Wkr.	In Div	Gr. R.	Wkr.	In Div
489	X	269 Inf	553	VI	329 Inf
490	X	269 Inf	554	V	330 Inf
...			555	V	330 Inf
492***	Prot.		556	V	330 Inf
493***	Prot.		557	XVII	331 Inf
494***	Prot.		558	XVII	331 Inf
...			559	XVII	331 Inf
496***	Prot.		...		
497	XI	267 Inf	570	II	302 Inf
...			571	II	302 Inf
499	XVII	268 Inf	572	II	302 Inf
500***			573	IV	304 Inf
501	X	290 Inf	574	IV	304 Inf
502	X	290 Inf	575	IV	304 Inf
503	X	290 Inf	576	V	305 Inf
504	I	291 Inf	577	V	305 Inf
505	I	291 Inf	578	V	305 Inf
506	I	291 Inf	579	VI	306 Inf
507	II	292 Inf	580	VI	306 Inf
508	II	292 Inf	581	VI	306 Inf
509	II	292 Inf	582	IX	319 Inf
510	III	293 Inf	583	IX	319 Inf
511	III	293 Inf	584	IX	319 Inf
512	III	293 Inf	585	X	320 Inf
513	IV	294 Inf	586	X	320 Inf
514	IV	294 Inf	587	X	320 Inf
515	IV	294 Inf	588	XI	321 Inf
516	XI	295 Inf	589	XI	321 Inf
517	XI	295 Inf	590	XI	321 Inf
518	XI	295 Inf	591	XIII	323 Inf
519	XIII	296 Inf	592	XIII	323 Inf
520	XIII	296 Inf	593	XIII	323 Inf
521	XIII	296 Inf	594	VIII	
522	XVII	297 Inf	595	XVII	327 Inf
523	XVII	297 Inf	596	XVII	327 Inf
524	XVII	297 Inf	597	XVII	327 Inf
525	VIII	298 Inf	...		
526	VIII	298 Inf	601**	V	
527	VIII	298 Inf	602**		
528	IX	299 Inf	603†	IV	
529	IX	299 Inf	606†	III	
530	IX	299 Inf	607†	I?	
531	III	383 Inf	608†	III	
532	III	383 Inf	609†		
533	III	383 Inf	610†		
534	IV?	384 Inf	611†		
535	IV?	384 Inf	612†		
536	IV?	384 Inf?	613†	IV	
537	VI	385 Inf	614†	IV	
538	VI	385 Inf	...		
539	VI	385 Inf	616†	IV	
540*			617†		
541	VII	387 Inf	618†	III	
542	VII	387 Inf			
543	VII	387 Inf			
544		389 Inf			
545		489 Inf	621¶	V	
546		389 Inf	622¶	V	
547	IX	328 Inf	623¶		
548	IX	328 Inf	624¶	VI	
549	IX	328 Inf	625¶	VI?	
550*			626¶	VI	
551	VI	329 Inf	...		
552	VI	329 Inf			

*Probably disbanded late in 1941.
**Bn only.
***Replacement training battalion only.
†Replacement training or field training regiment.
¶Probably disbanded late in 1940.

ORDER OF BATTLE OF THE GERMAN ARMY 0323

Gr. R.	Wkr.	In Div	Gr. R.		Wkr.	In Div
628**	XII		Pz. Gr	692	IX	339 Inf
629**	XII			693	IX	339 Inf
630**	XII			694	I	340 Inf
...				695	I	340 Inf
632**	IV			696	I	340 Inf
633**				697	XII	342 Inf
634**	XVIII			698	XII	342 Inf
...				699	XII	342 Inf
638***				...		
639**				721	I	714 Inf
640**				722	II	702 Inf
641**				723	III	719 Inf
642**	XII			724	IV	704 Inf
643**				725	V	715 Inf
644**				726	VI	716 Inf
645**				727	VII	707 Inf
646**				728	VIII	708 Inf
647**				729	IX	709 Inf
648**				730	X	710 Inf
649**				731	XI	711 Inf
...				732	XII	712 Inf
655**	IX			733	XIII	713 Inf
...				734	IV	704 Inf
657**				735	V	715 Inf
...				736	VI	716 Inf
...				737	XVII	717 Inf
660**				738	XVIII	718 Inf
661**				739	IX	709 Inf
662**				740	X	710 Inf
663**				741	I	714 Inf
664**				742	II	702 Inf
...				743	III	719 Inf
666	X?	370 Inf		744	XI	711 Inf
667	X?	370 Inf		745	XII	712 Inf
668	X?	370 Inf		746	XIII	713 Inf
669	VI?	371 Inf?		747	VII	707 Inf
670	VI	371 Inf		748	VIII	708 Inf
671	VI?	371 Inf?		749	XVII	717 Inf
672	VII	376 Inf		750	XVIII	718 Inf
673	VII	376 Inf?		...		
674**	I					
675**	I			754	XIII	334 Inf
676	VIII	332 Inf		755	XIII	334 Inf
677	VIII	332 Inf	Geb. Jg.	756	XIII	334 Inf
678	VIII	332 Inf		...		
679	III	333 Inf				
680	III	333 Inf		758	IX	377 Inf
681	III	333 Inf		769	IX	377 Inf
682	V	335 Inf		770	IX	377 Inf
683	V	335 Inf		...		
684	V	335 Inf				
685	VI	336 Inf		930		416 Inf
686	VI	336 Inf		931?		416 Inf
687	VI	336 Inf		...		
688	VII	337 Inf				
689	VII	337 Inf		961		999 Mtz Brig
690	VII	337 Inf		962		999 Mtz Brig
691	IX	339 Inf				

**Probably disbanded late in 1940.

There is also an Infanterie-Lehr-Regiment.

60. Cavalry regiments (Reiterregimente and Kavallerieregimente).

Rgt.	Wkr.	Allotted to
R. R. 1	I	Formerly 1 Cav Div; now possibly converted to units in 24 Pz Div
R. R. 2	I	Same as R. R. 1
K. R. 3*	IX	Training Command
R. R. 4	I	Same as R. R. 1
K. R. 5*	II	Training Command
K. R. 6*	XII	Training Command
K. R. 7	----	GHQ trs?
K. R. 8*	VIII	Training Command
K. R. 9*	III	Training Command
K. R. 10*	IV	Training Command
K. R. 11*	XVII	Training Command
K. R. 12	----	GHQ trs?
K. R. 13*	X	Training Command
K. R. 14*	XI	Training Command
K. R. 15*	VI	Training Command
K. R. 16*	XII	Training Command
K. R. 17*	XIII	Training Command
K. R. 18*	V	Training Command
K. R. 21	VIII	GHQ trs?
R. R. 22	IX	GHQ trs?
K. R. 23	X?	GHQ trs?
R. R. 24	I?	Same as R. R. 1

In addition to the above, there is a Kavallerie-Lehr-Abteilung.

*Now converted to a training unit (Kavallerie-Ersatz-Abteilung) which provides replacements for division reconnaissance units of the field army.

61. Motorcycle battalions (Kradschützenbataillone).

Btl.	Wkr.	In Div	Btl.	Wkr.	In Div
1	IX	1 Pz	34	XIII	4 Pz
2	XVII	2 Pz	...		
3	III	3 Pz	36	XII	36 Mtz
...			...		
6	VI	6 Pz	38	VIII	18 Mtz
7	IV	7 Pz	...		
8	III	8 Pz	40	XIII	10 Mtz
9	XVII	9 Pz	...		
10	V	10 Pz	43	XI	13 Pz
...					
15*	XII	15 Pz	53	III	3 Mtz
16	VI	16 Pz	54	IV	14 Mtz
17	VII	17 Pz	55	VIII	5 Pz
18	IV	18 Pz	...		
19	XI	19 Pz	59	VI	16 Mtz
20	IX	20 Pz	...		
...			61	VIII	11 Pz
22	II	12 Pz	...	IV	14 Pz
23		23 Pz	64	IV	14 Pz
24		22 Pz			
25	V	25 Mtz	160	XX	60 Mtz
...					
29	IX	29 Mtz	165		65 Inf
30	X	20 Mtz			
...					

*Now III./Pz. Gr. R. 104.

62. Panzer regiments and battalions (Panzerregimente, Panzerabteilungen).

Pz. R.	Wkr.	Allotted to*	Pz. R.	Wkr.	Allotted to*
1	IX	1 Pz Div	...		
2	IX	16 Pz Div	60**		
3	XVII	2 Pz Div	...		
4	XVII	13 Pz Div	100**	XII	(Flame thrower tks)
5	III	21 Pz Div	101**	IX	(Flame thrower tks).
6	III	3 Pz Div	102**		(Flame thrower tks)
7	V	10 Pz Div			
8	V	15 Pz Div	103**		(Flame thrower tks)
9	I				
10	III	8 Pz Div	116**	VI	16 Mtz Div
11	VI	6 Pz Div	129**	IX	29 Mtz Div
...			160**	XX	60 Mtz Div
14	V?		190**	III	90th L Div
15	VIII	11 Pz Div	...		
16			201	V	23 Pz Div
17	XVII		202	III	26 Pz Div
18	IV	18 Pz Div	203		
...			204	V	22 Pz Div
21	XIII	20 Pz Div	...		
...			211**		
23	XII		212**	XVII	
24	I	24 Pz Div	213**		
25	XIII	7 Pz Div	214**		
...			217**		
27	VI	19 Pz Div	...		
...			300**		
29	III	12 Pz Div	301**		
...			...		
31	VIII	5 Pz Div	500**		
...			501**		
33	XVII	9 Pz Div	502**		
...			503**		
35	XIII	4 Pz Div			
36	XIII	14 Pz Div			
37					
...					
39	XVII	17 Pz Div			

*Unallotted units probably belong to the GHQ pool.
**Pz. Abt.

There is also a Panzer-Lehr-Regiment.

63. Reconnaissance battalions (Aufklärungsabteilungen, Panzeraufklärungsabteilungen).

A. A.	Wkr.	In Div	A. A.	Wkr.	In Div
1	I	1 Inf	Pz 88 Mtz	IV	18 Pz
Pz 1 Mtz	I	3 Pz	...		
Pz 2 Mtz	II	12 Pz			
Pz 3 Mtz	III	21 Pz	Pz 92 Mtz	IX	20 Pz
Pz 4 Mtz	IX	1 Pz	...		
5 Mtz	V	5 Lt	94*	V	4 Mtn
Pz 5 Mtz	XVII	2 Pz	95*	XVIII	5 Mtn
6	VI	6 Inf	...		
7	VII	7 Inf	97*	VII	97 Lt
Pz 7 Mtz	XIII	4 Pz	...		
8*	VIII	8 Lt	99*	XVIII	7 Mtn
Pz 8 Mtz	VIII	5 Pz	100*	XVII	100 Lt
9	IX	9 Inf	101	V	101 Lt
Pz 9 Mtz	XVII	9 Pz	102	VIII	102 Inf
Pz 10 Mtz	XIII	10 Mtz	106	VI	106 Inf
11	I	11 Inf	...		
12*	II	12 Inf	110	X	110 Inf
Pz 13 Mtz	XI	13 Pz	...		
Pz 14 Mtz	IV	14 Mtz	113	XIII	113 Inf
Pz 15 Mtz	IX	27 Pz	117	III	111 Inf
Pz 16 Mtz	VI	16 Pz	120	XII	112 Inf
17*	XIII	17 Inf	121	X	121 Inf
Pz 18 Mtz	VIII	18 Mtz	122	II	122 Inf
Pz 19 Mtz	XI	19 Pz	123	III	123 Inf
Pz 20 Mtz	X	20 Mtz	125	V	125 Inf
21	XX	21 Inf	126	VI	126 Inf
22	X	22 Inf	Pz 128 Mtz		23 Pz
Pz 23 Mtz	III	26 Pz	129	IX	129 Inf
24	IV	24 Inf	...		
Pz 25 Mtz	V	25 Mtz	131	XI	131 Inf
26	VI	26 Inf	...		
Pz 27 Mtz	VII	17 Pz	134	IV	134 Inf
28	VIII	28 Lt	...		
Pz 29 Mtz	IX	29 Mtz	137	XVII	137 Inf
30*	X	30 Inf	139		39 Inf
31	XI	31 Inf	Pz 140 Mtz		22 Pz
32	II	32 Inf	150*	XXI	50 Inf
Pz 33 Mtz	XII	15 Pz	152	IX	52 Inf
34	XII	34 Inf			
35	V	35 Inf	156	IV	56 Inf
Pz 36 Mtz	XII	36 Mtz	157	VII	57 Inf
Pz 37 Mtz	IX	7 Pz	158	X	58 Inf
...					
Pz 40 Mtz	IV	14 Pz	Pz 160 Mtz	XX	60 Mtz
...			161	I	61 Inf
44	XVII	44 Inf	162*	VIII	62 Inf
45	XVII	45 Inf	165		65 Inf
46	XIII	46 Inf	168	III	68 Inf
...			169*	VI	69 Inf
Pz 53 Mtz	III	3 Mtz	171	XI	71 Inf
54*	VII	1 Mtn	172	XII	72 Inf
...			173*	XIII	73 Inf
Pz 57 Mtz	VI	6 Pz	...		
...			175*	II	75 Inf
Pz 59 Mtz	III	8 Pz	176	III	76 Inf
...			...		
67*	XVIII	2 Mtn	178	V	78 Inf
68*	XVIII	3 Mtn	179	XII	79 Inf
...			...		

*Cyclist battalion.

A. A.	Wkr.	In Div	A. A.	Wkr.	In Div
182*	IX	82 Inf	250	***	250 Inf
...			251	IX	251 Inf
186	VI	86 Inf	252	VIII	252 Inf
187	IV	87 Inf	253	VI	253 Inf
...			254	VI	254 Inf
193	III	93 Inf	255	IV	255 Inf
...			256	IV	256 Inf
195	IX	95 Inf	257	III	257 Inf
...			258	II	258 Inf
199*	VI	199 Inf	...		
...			260	V	260 Inf
205*	V	205 Inf	...		
206*	I	206 Inf	262	XVII	262 Inf
207*	II	207 Sich	263	XII	263 Inf
208*	III	208 Inf	...		
			267	XI	267 Inf
211	VI	211 Inf	268	VII	268 Inf
212*	VII	212 Inf	269	X	269 Inf
213	VIII	213 Sich	287*	III	287 Verband
214	IX	214 Inf	290	X	290 Inf
215	V	215 Inf	293	III	293 Inf
216	XI	216 Inf	296	XIII	296 Inf
217	I	217 Inf	...		
218	III	218 Inf	297	XVII	297 Inf
219	XIII	183 Inf	298	VIII	298 Inf
220	IV	164 Lt	299	IX	299 Inf
221	VIII	221 Sich			
222**	XI	181 Inf	312		
223*	IV	223 Inf			
225	X	225 Inf	329	VI	329 Inf
227**	IV	227 Inf	330**	V	330 Inf
...			331	XVII	331 Inf
229	XII	197 Inf	...		
...			333***	III	333 Inf
Pz 231 Mtz	VIII	11 Pz	334##		334 Inf
...			Pz 341 Mtz	VI	16 Mtz
233**	VI	196 Inf	342***	XII	342 Inf
234*	III	163 Inf	...		
235	V	198 Inf	377**		377 Inf
238	VII	167 Inf	...		
241*	I	161 Inf	402**		GHQ trs
			403**		GHQ trs
246*	XII	246 Inf	...		
...			580	III	90 Lt
248	VIII	168 Inf	615		
...					

*Co only.
**Cyclist battalion.
***Cyclist Co only.
"Schnelle Abt.", combined Rcn and AT unit.

64. Artillery regiments, battalions, and batteries (Artillerieregimente, Artillerieabteilungen, Artilleriebatterien).

A. R.	Wkr.	Allotted to	A. R.	Wkr.	Allotted to
1	I	1 Inf Div	59*	III	GHQ trs
Pz 2 Mtz	II	12 Pz Div	60*	IV	GHQ trs
3 Mtz	III	3 Mtz Div	61*	V	GHQ trs
Pz 4 Mtz	IV	14 Pz Div	62*	VI	GHQ trs
5 Mtz	V	5 Lt Div	63*	VII	GHQ trs
6	VI	6 Inf Div	64*	VIII	GHQ trs
7	VII	7 Inf Div	65*	IX	GHQ trs
8	VIII	8 Lt Div	66*	X	GHQ trs
9	IX	9 Inf Div	67*	XI	GHQ trs
10 Mtz	XIII	10 Mtz Div	68*	II	GHQ trs
11	I	11 Inf Div	69*	XII	GHQ trs
12	II	12 Inf Div	70*	XII	GHQ trs
Pz 13 Mtz	XI	13 Pz Div	71*	V	GHQ trs
14 Mtz	IV	14 Mtz Div	72*	XII	GHQ trs
Pz 15 Mtz	IX	27 Pz Div	Pz 73 Mtz	IX	1 Pz Div
Pz 16 Mtz	VI	16 Pz Div	Pz 74 Mtz	XVII	2 Pz Div
17	VIII	17 Inf Div	Pz 75 Mtz	III	3 Pz Div
18 Mtz	VIII	18 Mtz Div	Pz 76 Mtz	VI	6 Pz Div
Pz 19 Mtz	XI	19 Pz Div	77 Mtz	V	GHQ trs**
20 Mtz	X	20 Mtz Div	Pz 78 Mtz	IX	7 Pz Div
21	XX	21 Inf Div	Geb. 79	I	1 Mtn Div
22	X	22 Inf Div	Pz 80 Mtz	II	8 Pz Div
Pz 23 Mtz	III	26 Pz Div	81	VII	97 Lt Div
24	IV	24 Inf Div	Geb. 82	XIII	7 Mtn Div
25 Mtz	V	25 Mtz Div	83	XVII	100 Lt Div
26	VI	26 Inf Div	84 Mtz	IV	GHQ trs***
Pz 27 Mtz	VII	17 Pz Div	85	V	101 Lt Div
28	VIII	28 Lt Div	86	XII	112 Inf Div
29 Mtz	IX	29 Mtz Div	87	XIII	113 Inf Div
30	X	30 Inf Div	Pz 88 Mtz	IV	18 Pz Div
31	XI	31 Inf Div	89		
32	II	32 Inf Div	Pz 90 Mtz	V	10 Pz Div
Pz 33 Mtz	XII	15 Pz Div	Pz 91#	VI?	25 Pz Div
34	XII	34 Inf Div	Pz 92 Mtz	IX	20 Pz Div
35	V	35 Inf Div	93 Mtz	XIII	GHQ trs
36 Mtz	XII	36 Mtz Div	Geb. 94	V	4 Mtn Div
37*	I	GHQ trs	Geb. 95	XVIII	5 Mtn Di
38*	II	GHQ trs	96	XVII	44 Inf Div
39*	III	GHQ trs	97*	XVII	GHQ trs
40*	IV	GHQ trs	98	XVII	45 Inf Div
41*	V	GHQ trs	99*	XVII	GHQ trs
42*	VI	GHQ trs	100##	II	Training Comd (Bn only)
43*	VII	GHQ trs	101 Mtz	XII	
44*	VIII	GHQ trs	Pz 102 Mtz	XVII	9 Pz Div
45*	IX	GHQ trs	Pz 103 Mtz	XIII	4 Pz Div
46*	XIII	GHQ trs	104	III	102 Inf Div?
47*	I	GHQ trs	105 Mtz	XII	(Bn only)
48*	II	GHQ trs	106 Mtz	XII	(Bn only)
49*	XI	GHQ trs	107	VI	106 Inf Div
50*	IV	GHQ trs	108	XII	GHQ trs
51*	IX	GHQ trs	109 Mtz	XVII	GHQ trs
52*	VI	GHQ trs	110 Mtz	XVIII	GHQ trs
53*	XIII	GHQ trs	Geb. 111	XVIII	2 Mtn Div
54*	VIII	GHQ trs	Geb. 112	XVIII	3 Mtn Div
55*	XI	GHQ trs	Geb. 113	XVIII	GHQ trs
56*	X	GHQ trs	114	XIII	46 Inf Div
57*	XX	GHQ trs	115*	XIII	GHQ trs
58*	X	GHQ trs	Pz 116 Mtz	VIII	5 Pz Div

*Hq and 2d Bn are mechanized GHQ troops; 1st Bn is usually horse-drawn and attached to a divisional artillery regiment in place of a 4th Bn.
**150-mm Hows.
***240-mm Hows.
#Bn.
##Replacement training battalion for all railway artillery.

A. R.	Wkr.	Allotted to	A. R.	Wkr.	Allotted to
117	XI	111 Inf Div?	178	V	78 Inf Div
Geb. 118	XVIII	6 Mtn Div	179	XII	79 Inf Div
Pz 119 Mtz	VIII	11 Pz Div	...		
120	X	110 Inf Div	181	VIII	81 Inf Div
121	X	121 Inf Div	182	IX	82 Inf Div
122	II	122 Inf Div	183	X	83 Inf Div
123	III	123 Inf Div	184 Mtz		(Assault gun Bn)
...			185 Mtz		(Assault gun Bn)
125	V	125 Inf Div	186	VI	86 Inf Div
126	VI	126 Inf Div	187	IV	87 Inf Div
127 Mtz		GHQ trs?	188	VII	88 Inf Div
Pz 128 Mtz		23 Pz Div	189 Mtz		(Assault gun Bn)
129	IX	129 Inf Div	190 Mtz	III	90 Lt Div*
...			191 Mtz		(Assault gun Bn)
131	XI	131 Inf Div	192 Mtz		(Assault gun Bn)
132	XII	132 Inf Div	193	III	93 Inf Div
133 Mtz		GHQ trs?	194	IV	94 Inf Div
134	IV	134 Inf Div	195	IX	95 Inf Div
...			196	XI	96 Inf Div
136?	VI?	GHQ trs?	197 Mtz		(Assault gun Bn)
137	XVII	137 Inf Div	198	XIII	98 Inf Div
138		38 Inf Div	199	VI	199 Inf Div
139		39 Inf Div	200 Mtz	XIII	(Assault gun Bn)
Pz 140 Mtz		22 Pz Div	201 Mtz		(Assault gun Bn)
...			202 Mtz		(Assault gun Bn)
142	XII	(Btry)	203 Mtz		(Assault gun Bn)
143		(CD Bn)	204 Mtz		(Assault gun Bn)
144	VI	(CD Bn)	205	V	205 Inf Div
145		(CD Bn)	206	I	206 Inf Div
146 Mtz	VI	16 Mtz Div	207	II	CD Regt Staff
147		(CD Bn)	208	III	208 Inf Div
148	VI	(CD Bn)	209 Mtz		(Assault gun Bn)
149	XI	(CD Bn)	210 Mtz		(Assault gun Bn)
150	XXI	50 Inf Div	211	VI	211 Inf Div
151	I	(Bn only)	212	VII	212 Inf Div
152	IX	52 Inf Div	213**	VIII	213 Sich Div
153	XIII	(Bn only)	214	IX	214 Inf Div
154 Mtz	VIII	(Bn only#)	215	V	215 Inf Div
Pz 155 Mtz	III	21 Pz Div	216	XI	216 Inf Div
156	IV	56 Inf Div	217	I	217 Inf Div
157	VII	57 Inf Div	218	III	218 Inf Div
158	X	58 Inf Div	219	XIII	183 Inf Div
...			220	IV	164 Lt Div
160 Mtz	XX	60 Mtz Div	221**	VIII	221 Sich Div
161	I	61 Inf Div	222	XI	181 Inf Div
162	VIII	62 Inf Div	223	IV	223 Inf Div
...			...		
...			225	X	225 Inf Div
165		65 Inf Div	226 Mtz		(Assault gun Bn)
167	VII	(Bn only##)	227	VI	227 Inf Div
168	III	68 Inf Div	228***	I	(228 Inf Div)
169	VI	69 Inf Div	229	XII	197 Inf Div
...			230	IX	169 Inf Div
171	XI	71 Inf Div	231***	XIII	(231 Inf Div)
172	XII	72 Inf Div	...		
173	XIII	73 Inf Div	233	VI	196 Inf Div
...			234	III	163 Inf Div
175	II	75 Inf Div	235	V	198 Inf Div
176	III	76 Inf Div	236	II	162 Inf Div
177 Mtz		(Assault gun Bn)	...		

#150 mm Hows.
##Replacement training battalion only.
*Also an assault gun Bn of this number.
**Hq is GHQ trs; the Bns are attached to reinforced Inf Regts.
***Disbanded or transferred to GHQ trs late in 1940 (1941 for 239).

ORDER OF BATTLE OF THE GERMAN ARMY

A. R.	Wkr.	Allotted to	A. R.	Wkr.	Allotted to
238	VII	167 Inf Div	300 Mtz		(Assault gun Bn)
239***	VIII	239 Inf Div	...		
240	X	170 Inf Div	302	II	302 Inf Div
241	I	161 Inf Div	...		
242 Mtz		(Assault gun Bn)	304	IV	304 Inf Div
243		(Bn only)	305	V	305 Inf Div
244 Mtz		(Assault gun Bn)	306	VI	306 Inf Div
...			...		
246	XII	246 Inf Div	309	IX	(Repl Tng Bn)
...			...		
248	VIII	168 Inf Div	311		
249 Mtz		(Assault gun Bn)	...		
250	#	250 Inf Div	313		(CD Btry*)
251	IX	251 Inf Div	...		
252	VIII	252 Inf Div	315		
253	VI	253 Inf Div	...		
254	VI	254 Inf Div	318		CD troops
255	IV	255 Inf Div	319	IX	319 Inf Div
256	IV	256 Inf Div	320	X	320 Inf Div
257	III	257 Inf Div	321	XI	321 Inf Div
258	II	258 Inf Div	...		
...			323	XIII	323 Inf Div
260	V	260 Inf Div	327	XVII	327 Inf Div
...			328	IX	328 Inf Div
262	XVII	262 Inf Div	329	VI	329 Inf Div
263	XII	263 Inf Div	330	V	330 Inf Div
...			331	XVII	331 Inf Div
			332	VIII	332 Inf Div
267	XI	267 Inf Div	333	III	333 Inf Div
268	VII	268 Inf Div	334	XIII	334 Inf Div
269	X	269 Inf Div	335	V	335 Inf Div
...			336	VI	336 Inf Div
271			337	VII	337 Inf Div
272			338		(CD Bn)
273	III	(Bn only)	339	IX	339 Inf Div
274		(CD Btry)	340	I	340 Inf Div
...			...		
277			342	XII	342 Inf Div
...			...		
279			351		(Bn)
...			...		
281			353		
			354		(CD Btry)
283		(CD Bn)	355	VI	(CD Btry)
284		(CD Bn)	356	VI	(CD Btry)
285		(CD Bn)	361	III	(Bn)
286					
287	VII	(CD Bn)			
288	VIII	(CD Bn)	Unit**	Wkr.	Remarks
289		(CD Bn)			
290	X	290 Inf Div			
291	I	291 Inf Div	362	XII	CD Btry
292	II	292 Inf Div	363	XIII	CD Btry
293	III	293 Inf Div	364	XIII	CD Btry
294	IV	294 Inf Div	...		
295	XI	295 Inf Div	370		In 370 Inf Div
296	XIII	296 Inf Div	371	VI	In 371 Inf Div
297	XVII	297 Inf Div	...		
298	VIII	298 Inf Div	...		
299	IX	299 Inf Div	376		In 376 Inf Div

#Spanish.
*There is also a replacement training Bn of this number in Wkr. XIII.
**For type, where known, see remarks column.
***Disbanded or transferred to GHQ trs late in 1940 (1941 for 239).

Unit	Wkr.	Remarks	Unit	Wkr.	Remarks
377	IX	In 377 Inf Div	...		
...			452		CD Bn Staff
383	III	In 383 Inf Div	...		
384	IV	In 384 Inf Div	...		
385	VI	In 385 Inf Div	456		Bn
387	VII	In 387 Inf Div	...		
...			462		CD Btry
389		In 389 Inf Div	463		CD Btry
392		Bn	...		
...			468	III	CD Btry
...			...		
...			470		CD Btry
...			471		CD Btry
398		Bn	472		CD Btry
400 Mtz	III	Bn	474	X	CD Bn
401	VI	CD Bn	475		CD Bn
...			...		
...			477##		Regt
405		Bn	478		CD Bn
...			479		CD Bn
408 Mtz	VII	Bn*	480	XIII	Bn
...			...		
412			482		
413		Bn	484	VI	CD Bn
...			485	VI	CD Bn Staff
422 Mtz	X	Bn**	486	VI	CD Bn Staff
423		Bn	487		CD Bn Staff
...			488		CD Bn Staff
427 Mtz		Bn***	...		
428			490		CD Bn Staff
...			491		CD Bn Staff
430 Mtz		Bn	492		CD Bn Staff
431		CD Btry***	493	III	CD Bn Staff
432		CD Btry***	494		CD Bn Staff
433 Mtz		Bn	495		CD Bn Staff
434		CD Btry***	...		
436 Mtz		Bn***	497		CD Bn Staff
437		CD Regt Staff	498		CD Bn
438		CD Bn Staff	499		CD Bn Staff
439		CD Bn Staff	500		CD Bn
441		CD Bn	501 Mtz		Regt Staff
442		CD Bn	502		CD Btry
443		Bn	503		CD Btry
...			504		CD Bn
445		Bn	505	VI	CD Bn Staff
446 Mtz	XI	Bn*	506	I	Bn
447		CD Bn	507		CD Btry
			508		CD Btry
			509		CD Regt Staff
			510	XIII	CD Bn
			511	I	Bn###

*Reorganized under a new number.
**150-mm Hows.
***105-mm guns.
##Believed to have been disbanded.
###Also a Mtz Regt staff of this number.

ORDER OF BATTLE OF THE GERMAN ARMY

Unit	Wkr.	Remarks	Unit	Wkr.	Remarks
512		CD Btry*	569		CD Btry###
...			570		CD Btry###
514		CD Btry	571		CD Btry###
515		CD Btry	572		CD Btry###
516		CD Btry	573		CD Btry###
...			574		CD Btry###
			575		CD Btry###
519		CD Btry*	576		CD Btry###
520		CD Bn	577		CD Btry###
521			578		CD Btry###
...			579		CD Btry###
523	III	CD Bn**	580		Bn
...			...		
526	I	Bn	585		CD Btry####
527		CD Bn***	...		
528	XII	CD Bn#			
529	IX	CD Bn	588		CD Btry####
...			589		CD Btry####
531		CD Bn	590		CD Btry
532			591		CD Btry####
533	XII	CD Bn***	592		CD Btry###
534		CD Btry	593		CD Btry###
...			...		
536 Mtz	I	Bn*	...		
537		CD Btry	596		CD Btry
538		CD Btry	...		
...			...		
541		CD Btry	600 Mtz		Assault gun Bn staff
...			601 Mtz	II	Bn
543		CD Btry	602 Mtz	XVIII	Bn
...			603 Mtz		Regt staff
547		CD Btry	604 Mtz	XVII?	Bn
...			605 Mtz	IV	Bn
549		CD Btry	606 Mtz		Regt staff
550		CD Btry	607 Mtz	IV	Bn
551			...		
...			609 Mtz	III	Regt staff
553		Bn	610 Mtz		Regt staff
...			611 Mtz	XIII	Bn###
555##	VI?	Regt	612 Mtz		Regt staff
556##	XII	Regt	613 Mtz		Regt staff
557##	XVIII	Regt	614 Mtz		Regt staff
...			615 Mtz	V?	Bn
			616 Mtz	VI	Bn x
560	XVIII	Regt	617 Mtz		Regt staff
...			618 Mtz		Regt staff
563		CD Bn	619 Mtz		Regt staff
...			620 Mtz		Bn*
...					

*150-mm Hows.
**Now III Bn of Afr. A. R. 1.
***Also a Mtz Regt staff of this number.
#155-mm Hows.
##Now disbanded.
###105-mm guns.
####150-mm.
x210-mm Hows.

Unit	Wkr.	Remarks	Unit	Wkr.	Remarks
621 Mtz	VI?	Bn	672		Btry
622 Mtz		Regt staff	...		
623 Mtz		Regt staff	674 Mtz		Btry
624 Mtz	VIII	Bn	...		
625 Mtz	XI	Bn	676 Mtz	IV	Bn staff#
626 Mtz	V	Bn*	677 Mtz	IX	Regt staff
627 Mtz		Regt staff	...		
628 Mtz	III	Btry	679 Mtz		Bn staff
629 Mtz	IV	Bn	680 Mtz	IX	Bn
630 Mtz	IV	Bn*	681 Mtz	IX	Bn staff
631 Mtz		Bn***	...		
...			685		Btry
633 Mtz	IX	Bn	686		Btry
634 Mtz	X	Bn***	687		Btry
635 Mtz		Bn x	688		Btry
636 Mtz		Bn x	689		Btry
637 Mtz		Bn x	690		Ry Btry##
638 Mtz		Bn	694	III	Bn
...			695		
...			696		Ry Btry##
641 Mtz		Bn xx	697	V	CD Regt staff
642 Mtz		Bn xx	...		
643 Mtz	IX	Bn			
644 Mtz	IX	Bn	701		Btry
645 Mtz		Bn	702	IV	Bn staff
646 Mtz	V	Bn	...		
647 Mtz	XII	Bn*			
648 Mtz	XII	Bn*	705	XII	Bn
649 Mtz	XIII	Bn*	706		CD Bn
650		Bn	707		CD Bn
651		Bn	708		CD Bn
652	XII	Bn-In 712 Div	709 Mtz	III	Bn
...			710		Btry
654	IV	Bn-In 704 Div	711	IV	Bn
655		Ry Btry xxx	712		Btry
656	VI	Bn-In 716 Div	713		Btry
657	VII	Bn-In 707 Div	714	V	Bn
658		Bn	...		
			716 Mtz	IX	Bn
661	I	Bn-In 714 Div	717		Btry
662	II	Bn-In 702 Div	718		Btry
663			...		
			720 Mtz		Regt staff
665		Assault gun Btry	721		
666		Bn	722		Btry
667		Assault gun Btry	...		
668	XVIII	Bn-In 718 Div	724		
...			725	VIII	Ry Bn
670	XVII	Bn-In 717 Div	726		Btry
671		Bn	727	V	CD Bn

*Disbanded late in 1940.
***105-mm guns.
x 210-mm Hows.
xx 210-mm and 300-mm Hows.
xxx 280-mm Hows.
Also a replacement training Bn of this number.
280-mm Ry guns.

ORDER OF BATTLE OF THE GERMAN ARMY

Unit	Wkr.	Remarks	Unit	Wkr.	Remarks
728		CD Bn staff	780	IV	Ry Bn
729		Bn	781 Mtz		Regt staff
730 Mtz	VI	Bn	782 Mtz		Regt staff
731 Mtz	VIII	Bn*	783 Mtz		Regt staff
732 Mtz	X	Bn	784 Mtz		Btry
733 Mtz	XII	Bn**	785 Mtz		Regt staff
...			786 Mtz		Bn
735 Mtz	XI	Bn	787 Mtz		Regt staff
736 Mtz	XIII	Bn**	788 Mtz		Regt staff
737 Mtz	XVII	Bn*	789	IV	CD Bn***
738		CD Bn	...		
...			793		Bn
740	VII	Bn	...		
741		Bn	797		
742		CD Btry	...		
...			799	X	CD Bn
745	VI	Bn	800 Mtz		Bn
746	VI	CD Bn	801	II	Bn
...			802		Regt
...			803 Mtz		Regt staff
749	XI	Bn	804	XVIII	Bn
...			805	VIII	CD Bn
752	II	CD Regt staff	...		
753	IV	Bn	808		Bn
...			809		Bn
			810 Mtz		Btry
756		Bn	...		
757 Mtz		Bn	812		
			813	VI	CD Btry
			814 Mtz	IX	Regt#
759		Bn	815 Mtz	III	Bn##
			816 Mtz		Bn
761			817 Mtz	IV	Bn
762		Bn	818 Mtz	XI	Regt
...			...		
765		Btry	820		Bn
...			821		CD Bn?
767 Mtz		Bn	...		
768	VII	Bn	823		CD Bn###
769	VI	CD Bn staff	824		CD Regt staff
770	XI	CD Bn	825		CD Regt staff
			826	VI	CD Bn###
772	XII	CD Bn	827	VII	CD Bn###
773		CD Bn***	828		CD Bn
774	VII	CD Bn	829	VI	CD Bn
...			...		
...			831	VII	CD Bn
777	VI	Bn**	832	IX	CD Bn
778		CD Bn	833	III	Bn
779 Mtz		Btry	834	XII	CD Bn

* 150-mm Hows.
** 210-mm Hows.
*** 105-mm guns.
\# 240-mm Hows.
\#\# 300-mm Hows.
\#\#\# 150-mm guns.

ORDER OF BATTLE OF THE GERMAN ARMY

Unit	Wkr.	Remarks	Unit	Wkr.	Remarks
835		CD Bn	894	IX	CD Btry**
836	VI	CD Regt staff	895		CD Btry**
837		CD Regt staff	896		CD Btry
838		CD Bn	897		CD Btry
839		CD Regt staff	898		CD Btry
...			...		
841 Mtz		Bn	900	III	Bn
842 Mtz	VI	Bn	901	V	CD Bn
843 Mtz	VI	Bn	902		Btry***
844		Bn	903	III	CD Bn
845 Mtz		Bn	...		
846	II	Bn	905		Btry
847	V	Bn	906	VI	CD Bn
848 Mtz		Bn	907		CD Btry
849 Mtz		Bn	...		
850		Bn	909		
851 Mtz	XII	Bn	910	X	CD Bn
852		Bn	911	IV	Bn
853	III	CD Regt Staff	912	V	Bn
854	III	Bn	...		
855		Bn	914		CD Bn
856	VI	Bn	...		
857	XII	Bn			
858 Mtz		Bn			CD Btry
859 Mtz		Bn	927	V	CD Bn
860 Mtz	X	Bn	928	XII	CD Bn
861	XX	Bn	929		CD Btry
862		Bn	930		CD Btry
863	IX	Bn	931		
...			...		
865 Mtz	XIII	Bn	938		CD
866	V	Bn	---		
...			940		CD Regt staff
869		CD Btry	942		CD Btry
...			946		CD Btry x
...			947		CD Btry x
877		CD Btry	948		CD Btry x
...			949		CD Btry x
880		CD Btry	950		CD Btry xx
...			...		
...			952		CD Btry xx
884	XVIII	CD Btry	953		CD Btry
...			954		CD Btry xx
...			...		
887		CD Btry	956		CD Btry xx
888		CD Btry*	957		CD Btry xx
889		CD Btry*	958		CD Btry xx
890		CD Btry	959		CD Btry xx
...			960		CD Btry x
...			961		CD Btry x
893			962		CD Btry x

*120-mm guns.
**75-mm guns.
***175-mm guns.
x 105-mm guns.
xx 210-mm guns.

Unit	Wkr.	Remarks	Unit	Wkr.	Remarks
963		CD Btry*	982		CD Btry*
964		CD Btry	983		CD Btry*
...			984		CD Btry*
966		CD Btry	...		
967		CD Btry	987		CD Btry*
...			988		CD Btry
970		CD Btry*	989		CD Btry
971		CD Btry*	990		CD Btry
972		CD Btry*	991		CD Btry
973		CD Btry*	992		CD Btry
974		CD Btry*	993		CD Btry
975		CD Btry*	...		
976		CD Btry*	995		CD Btry
977		CD Btry*	996		CD Btry**
978		CD Btry*	997		CD Btry**
979		CD Btry*	998		CD Btry**
980		CD Btry*			
981		CD Btry*			

*105-mm guns.
**155-mm guns.

There are also Artillerie-Lehr-Regimente 1, 2, and 3.

65. Artillery observation battalions and batteries (Beobachtungsabteilungen, Panzerbeobachtungsbatterien).

B. Abt.	Wkr.	Allotted to	Pz. Bb.	Wkr.	Allotted to
1	I	GHQ trs	320	XVII	2 Pz Div
2	II	GHQ trs	321		
3	III	GHQ trs	322	V	10 Pz Div
4	IV	GHQ trs	323		
5	V	GHQ trs	324	XIII	4 Pz Div
6	VI	GHQ trs	325	IX	7 Pz Div
7	VII	GHQ trs	326	III	15 Pz Div
8	VIII	GHQ trs	327	III	3 Pz Div
9	IX	GHQ trs	328	VIII	
10	XIII	GHQ trs	...		
11	I	GHQ trs	333		
12	II	GHQ trs	...		
13	XI	GHQ trs	335	IX	20 Pz Div
14	IV	GHQ trs	...		
15	IX	GHQ trs	337		
16	VI	GHQ trs	...		
17	XIII	GHQ trs	339		
18	VIII	GHQ trs	...		
19	XI	GHQ trs			
20	X	GHQ trs			
21	XX	GHQ trs			
22	X	GHQ trs			
23	III	GHQ trs			
24	IV	GHQ trs			
25	V	GHQ trs			
26	VI	GHQ trs			
27	VII	GHQ trs			
28	VIII	GHQ trs			
29	IX	GHQ trs			
30	X	GHQ trs			
31	XI	GHQ trs			
32	II	GHQ trs			
33	XII	GHQ trs			
34	XII	GHQ trs			
35	V	GHQ trs			
36	XII	GHQ trs			
...					
Geb. 38	XVIII	GHQ trs			
...					
40		GHQ trs			
41		GHQ trs			
...					
44	XVII	GHQ trs			
...					
555		GHQ trs			
556		GHQ trs			

66. Antitank battalions (Panzerjägerabteilungen).

Pz. Jg. Abt.	Wkr.	In Div.	Pz. Jg. Abt.	Wkr.	In Div.
1	I	1 Inf	92	IX	20 Pz
2	II	12 Pz	...		
3	III	3 Mtz	Geb. 94	V	4 Mtn
4	IV	14 Pz	Geb. 95	XVIII	5 Mtn
5	V	5 Lt	...		
6	VI	6 Inf	97	VII	97 Lt
7	VII	7 Inf	...		
8	VIII	8 Lt	Geb. 99	XIII	7 Mtn
9	IX	9 Inf	100	XVII	100 Lt
10	XIII	10 Mtz	101	V	101 Lt
11	I	11 Inf	102	VIII	102 Inf
12	II	12 Inf	106	VI	106 Inf
13	XI	13 Pz	110	X	110 Inf
14	IV	14 Mtz	111	III	111 Inf
15	IX	27 Pz	112	XII	112 Inf
16	VI	16 Pz	113	XIII	113 Inf
17	XIII	17 Inf	...		
18	VIII	18 Mtz	122	II	122 Inf
19	XI	19 Pz	123	III	123 Inf
20	X	20 Mtz	125	V	125 Inf
21	XX	21 Inf	126	VI	126 Inf
22	X	22 Inf	...		
23	III	26 Pz	128		23 Pz
24	IV	24 Inf	...		
25	V	25 Mtz	131	XI	131 Inf
26	VI	26 Inf	132	XII	132 Inf
27	VII	17 Pz	...		
28	VIII	28 Lt	134	IV	134 Inf
29	IX	29 Mtz	...		
30	X	30 Inf	137	XVII	137 Inf
31	XI	31 Inf	138	XII	
32	II	32 Inf	...		
33	XII	15 Pz	140		22 Pz
34	XII	34 Inf	...		
35	V	35 Inf	150	III	50 Inf
36	XII	36 Mtz	...		
37	IX	1 Pz	152	IX	52 Inf
38	XVII	2 Pz	...		
39	III	21 Pz	156	IV	56 Inf
40	I	24 Pz	157	VII	57 Inf
41	VI	6 Pz	158	X	58 Inf
42	IX	7 Pz	...		
43	III	8 Pz	160	XX	60 Mtz
Geb. 44	VII	1 Mtn	161	I	61 Inf
45	XVII	45 Inf	162	VIII	62 Inf
46	XVII	44 Inf	...		
Geb. 47	XVIII	2 Mtn	168	III	68 Inf
Geb. 48	XVIII	3 Mtn	169	VI	69 Inf
49	XIII	4 Pz	...		
50	XVII	9 Pz	171	XI	71 Inf
...			172	XII	72 Inf
52	XIII	46 Inf	173	XIII	73 Inf
53	VIII	5 Pz	...		
54?			175	II	75 Inf
Geb. 55	XVIII	6 Mtn	176	III	76 Inf
56	X		...		
...			178	V	78 Inf
67			179	XII	79 Inf
...			...		
72	IV		181	VIII	81 Inf
...			182	IX	82 Inf
88	IV	18 Pz	183	X	83 Inf
...			...		
90	V	10 Pz	186	VI	86 Inf
...			187	IV	87 Inf

Pz. Jg. Abt.	Wkr.	In Div.	Pz. Jg. Abt.	Wkr.	In Div.
188	XVII	88 Inf	262	XVII	262 Inf
...			263	XII	263 Inf
190	III	90 Lt	...		
...			267	XI	267 Inf
193	III	93 Inf	268	VII	268 Inf
194	IV	94 Inf	269	X	269 Inf
195	IX	95 Inf	...		
196	XI	96 Inf	290	X	290 Inf
...			291	I	291 Inf
198	XIII	98 Inf	292	II	292 Inf
...			293	III	293 Inf
205	V	205 Inf	294	IV	294 Inf
206	I	206 Inf	...		
207	II	207 Sich	296	XIII	296 Inf
208*	III	208 Inf	297	XVII	297 Inf
211	VI	211 Inf	...		
212	VII	212 Inf	299	IX	299 Inf
213*	VIII	213 Sich	...		
214	IX	214 Inf	304	IV	304 Inf
215	V	215 Inf	...		
216	XI	216 Inf	306	VI	306 Inf
217	I	217 Inf	...		
218	III	218 Inf	320	X	320 Inf
219	XIII	183 Inf	...		
220	IV	164 Lt	323	XIII	323 Inf
221	VIII	221 Sich	...		
222	XI	181 Inf	327	XVII	327 Inf
223	IV	223 Inf	329	VI	329 Inf
...			331	XVII	331 Inf
225	X	225 Inf	332	VIII	332 Inf
...			333	III	333 Inf
227	VI	227 Inf	...		
228	I	228 Inf**	335	V	335 Inf
229	XII	197 Inf	336	IV	336 Inf
230	IX	169 Inf	337	VII	337 Inf
233	VI	196 Inf	...		
234	III	163 Inf	339	IX	339 Inf
...			340	I	340 Inf
236	II	162 Inf	...		
238	VII	167 Inf	342	XII	342 Inf
239	VIII	239 Inf**	...		
240	X	170 Inf	354		
...			...		
241	I	161 Inf	360		
246	XII	246 Inf	...		
...			370		370 Inf
248	VIII	168 Inf	371	VI	371 Inf
...			376	VII	376 Inf
251	IX	251 Inf	377	IX	377 Inf
252	VIII	252 Inf	...		
253	VI	253 Inf	383	III	383 Inf
254	VI	254 Inf	385	VI	385 Inf
255	IV	255 Inf	387	VII	387 Inf
256	IV	256 Inf	389		389 Inf
257	III	257 Inf	463	V	
258	II	258 Inf	...		
...					
260	V	260 Inf			
...					

*Company only.
**Division disbanded; unit may still exist.

ORDER OF BATTLE OF THE GERMAN ARMY 0341

Pz. Jg. Abt.	Wkr.	Remarks	Pz. Jg. Abt.	Wkr.	Remarks
511	I	GHQ trs	...		
...		GHQ trs	611	II	GHQ trs
521		GHQ trs	...		
522		GHQ trs	616	XI	GHQ trs
...			...		
525			624		
...			625		GHQ trs
529	VI		...		
...			628		
539			...		
...			635		
541			...		
543	III	GHQ trs	643	XII	GHQ trs***
...			645	XII	GHQ trs
545	XII	GHQ trs	...		
...			652	XI	GHQ trs
552			654	X	GHQ trs
...			...		
559	III	GHQ trs*	670	VII	GHQ trs
560		GHQ trs	...		
561	IV	GHQ trs	672		GHQ trs
563		GHQ trs	...		
...			900		
605	II	Africa Army**			
...					
607	III	?			

* On SPM.
** 75 mm on SPM.
*** 47 mm on SPM.

67. Motorized machine gun and antiaircraft battalions (Maschinengewehrbataillone (mot.), Flugabwehrbataillone (mot.)).

M. G. Btl.	Wkr.	Remarks	Fla. Btl.	Wkr.	Remarks
1	VI		48*	VIII	
2	XII	Now III./Pz. G. R. 115	...		
3	XII		52*	X	37 mm guns on SPM
4	V		...		
5	V	20 mm guns	55*	V	20 mm guns on SPM
6	XIII	Now disbanded	...		
7	IV		59*	IX	20 mm guns on SPM
8	III	Now I./Pz G. R. 104	...		
9	I	20 mm guns	66*	XII	20 mm guns on SPM
10	XII		...		
11	V	Now 36th Mtrcl Bn	190***	III	In 90th Lt Div
...			...		
13	XII		601**	VI	
14	XII		602**	XII?	
15	VIII	20 mm guns on SPM	603**		
16	XII		604**		
17	VI		605**		
...			606**	XIII	
			607**	VI	
			608**		
Fla. Btl.	Wkr.	Remarks	609**	I	
			610**	X?	
...			611**		
22			612**		
...			613**	XII	
31*	I		614**		
...			615**	XI	
33		37 mm guns on SPM	616**		
...			617**	XIII	
46*	VI		618**		
47*	XIII		619**	II?	
			...		

*Composed of six Cos which operate independently.
**Bns in this series consist of three Cos and operate normally as Bns.
***Company only.

68. Engineer regiments, battalions, etc. (Pionierregimente, Pionierbataillone, Brückenkolonnen).

	Pi. Btl.	Wkr.	Allotted to		Pi. Btl.	Wkr.	Allotted to
	1	I	1 Inf Div		70 Mtz	XVII	GHQ trs
	2 Mtz	II	32 Inf Div?		71	III	
	3 Mtz	III	3 Mtz Div		...		
Pz	4 Mtz	XI	13 Pz Div		73	XII	
	5 Mtz	V	5 Lt Div		74	XII	
	6	VI	6 Inf Div		...		
	7	VII	7 Inf Div	Pz	79 Mtz	XIII	4 Pz Div
	8	VIII	8 Lt Div		80	XVII	44 Inf Div
	9	IX	9 Inf Div		81	XVII	45 Inf Div
	10 Mtz	XIII	10 Mtz Div	Geb.	82	XVIII	2 Mtn Div
	11	I	11 Inf Div	Geb.	83	XVIII	3 Mtn Div
	12	II	12 Inf Div	Geb.	84***	XVIII	
Pz	13 Mtz	IV	14 Pz Div	Geb.	85	XVIII	GHQ trs
	14 Mtz	IV	14 Mtz Div	Pz	86 Mtz	XVII	9 Pz Div
Pz	15 Mtz	IX	27 Pz Div		88	XIII	46 Inf Div
Pz	16 Mtz	VI	16 Pz Div	Pz	89 Mtz	VIII	5 Pz Div
	17	XIII	17 Inf Div		...		
	18 Mtz	VIII	18 Mtz Div	Geb.	91	XVIII	6 Mtn Div
Pz	19 Mtz	XI	19 Pz Div	Pz	92 Mtz	IX	20 Pz Div
	20 Mtz	X	20 Mtz Div	Geb.	94	V	4 Mtn Div
	21	XX	21 Inf Div	Geb.	95	XVIII	5 Mtn Div
	22 Mtz	X	22 Inf Div		...		
Pz	23 Mtz	III	26 Pz Div		97	VII	97 Lt Div
	24	IV	24 Inf Div	Geb.	99	XIII	7 Mtn Div
	25 Mtz	V	25 Mtz Div		100	XVII	100 Lt Div
	26	VI	26 Inf Div		101	V	101 Lt Div
Pz	27 Mtz	VII	17 Pz Div		102	VIII	102 Inf Div
	28	VIII	28 Lt Div		106	VI	106 Inf Div
	29 Mtz	IX	29 Mtz Div		...		
	30	X	30 Inf Div		110	X	110 Inf Div
	31	XI	31 Inf Div		111	III	111 Inf Div
Pz	32 Mtz	II	12 Pz Div		112	XII	112 Inf Div
Pz	33 Mtz	XII	15 Pz Div		113	XIII	113 Inf Div
	34	XII	34 Inf Div		...		
	35	V	35 Inf Div		121	X	121 Inf Div
	36 Mtz	XII	36 Mtz Div		122	II	122 Inf Div
Pz	37 Mtz	IX	1 Pz Div		123	III	123 Inf Div
Pz	38 Mtz	XVII	2 Pz Div		...		
Pz	39 Mtz	III	3 Pz Div		125	V	125 Inf Div
Pz	40 Mtz	I	24 Pz Div		126	VI	126 Inf Div
	41 Mtz	I	GHQ trs		...		
	42 Mtz	II	GHQ trs	Pz	128 Mtz		23 Pz Div
	43 Mtz**	III	GHQ trs		129	IX	129 Inf Div
	44 Mtz	IV	GHQ trs				
	45 Mtz	V	GHQ trs		131	XI	131 Inf Div
	46 Mtz	VI	GHQ trs		132	XII	132 Inf Div
	47 Mtz	VII	GHQ trs		...		
	48 Mtz	VIII	GHQ trs		134	IV	134 Inf Div
Pz	49 Mtz	V	10 Pz Div				
	50 Mtz	X	GHQ trs		137	XVII	137 Inf Div
	51 Mtz	XI	GHQ trs		139		39 Inf Div
	52 Mtz	XII	GHQ trs	Pz	140 Mtz		22 Pz Div
Geb.	54	VII	1 Mtn Div		...		
	...				144 Mtz		
Pz	57 Mtz	VI	6 Pz Div		145	V	
Pz	58 Mtz	IX	7 Pz Div		146 Mtz	VI	16 Mtz Div
Pz	59 Mtz	III	8 Pz Div		...		
	60 Mtz	XI	GHQ trs		152	IX	52 Inf Div
	62 Mtz	IV	GHQ trs				
	...						

** Assault Engineer Bn.
*** Possibly now disbanded.

Pi. Btl.	Wkr.	Allotted to	Pi. Btl.	Wkr.	Allotted to
156	IV	56 Inf Div	234	III	163 Inf Div
157	VII	57 Inf Div	235	V	198 Inf Div
158	X	58 Inf Div	236	II	162 Inf Div
160 Mtz	XX	60 Mtz Div	...		
161	I	61 Inf Div	238	VII	167 Inf Div
162	VIII	62 Inf Div	239	VIII	239 Inf Div*
...			241	I	161 Inf Div
168	III	68 Inf Div	246	XII	246 Inf Div
169	VI	69 Inf Div	...		
...			248	VIII	168 Inf Div
171	XI	71 Inf Div	251	IX	251 Inf Div
172	XII	72 Inf Div	252	VIII	252 Inf Div
173	XIII	73 Inf Div	253	VI	253 Inf Div
...			254	VI	254 Inf Div
175	II	75 Inf Div	255	IV	255 Inf Div
176	III	76 Inf Div	256	IV	256 Inf Div
...			257 Mtz	III	257 Inf Div
178	V	78 Inf Div	258	II	258 Inf Div
179	XII	79 Inf Div	...		
			260	V	260 Inf Div
181	VIII	81 Inf Div	...		
182	IX	82 Inf Div	262	XVII	262 Inf Div
183	X	83 Inf Div	263	XII	263 Inf Div
...					
186	VI	86 Inf Div	267	XI	267 Inf Div
187	IV	87 Inf Div	268	VII	268 Inf Div
188	VII	88 Inf Div	269	X	269 Inf Div
...					
193	III	93 Inf Div	290	X	290 Inf Div
194	IV	94 Inf Div	...		
195	IX	95 Inf Div	292	II	292 Inf Div
196	XI	96 Inf Div	293	III	293 Inf Div
...			294	IV	294 Inf Div
198	XIII	98 Inf Div	295	XI	295 Inf Div
199	VI	199 Inf Div	296	XIII	296 Inf Div
Pz 200 Mtz	III	21 Pz Div	297	XVII	297 Inf Div
205	V	205 Inf Div	298	VIII	298 Inf Div
206	I	206 Inf Div	299	IX	299 Inf Div
207	II	207 Sich Div	300		(Bn staff only)
208	III	208 Inf Div	...		
Pz 209 Mtz	IV	18 Pz Div	302	II	302 Inf Div
211	VI	211 Inf Div	...		
212	VII	212 Inf Div	304	IV	304 Inf Div
213	VIII	213 Sich Div	305	V	305 Inf Div
214	IX	214 Inf Div	306	VI	306 Inf Div
215	V	215 Inf Div	...		
216	XI	216 Inf Div	311	I	311 Div**
217	I	217 Inf Div	...		
218	III	218 Inf Div	319	IX	319 Inf Div
219	XIII	183 Inf Div	320	X	320 Inf Div
220	IV	164 Lt Div	321	XI	321 Inf Div
221	VIII	221 Sich Div	323	XIII	323 Inf Div
222	XI	181 Inf Div	...		
223	IV	223 Inf Div	327	XVII	327 Inf Div
...			328	IX	328 Inf Div
225	X	225 Inf Div	329	VI	329 Inf Div
...			331	XVII	331 Inf Div
227	VI	227 Inf Div	332	VIII	332 Inf Div
228	I	228 Inf Div*	333	III	333 Inf Div
229	XII	197 Inf Div	334	XIII	334 Inf Div
230	IX	169 Inf Div	335	V	335 Inf Div
231	XIII	231 Inf Div*	336	IV	336 Inf Div
...			337	VII	337 Inf Div
233	VI	196 Inf Div	...		

*Division now disbanded; unit may still exist, possibly renumbered.
**It is possible that both the division and the unit have now been disbanded.

ORDER OF BATTLE OF THE GERMAN ARMY

Pi. Btl.	Wkr.	Allotted to	Pi. unit*	Wkr.	Remarks
339	IX	339 Inf Div	545		
340	I	340 Inf Div	...		
342	XII	342 Inf Div	...		
343	XIII		...		
...			...		
...			...		
370		370 Inf Div	...		
371	VI	371 Inf Div	...		
377	IX	377 Inf Div	591 Mtz		Regt staff
...			592		
383	III	383 Inf Div	593		Bn
385	VI	385 Inf Div	...		
387	VII	387 Inf Div	601 Mtz		Regt staff
			602 Mtz		Br Clm
			603 Mtz		Br Clm
Pi. unit*	Wkr.	Remarks	604 Mtz		Regt staff
			605 Mtz		Regt staff
			606 Mtz		Br Clm
400 Mtz		Br Clm	...		
401 Mtz		Br Clm	610 Mtz		Br Clm
...			...		
403 Mtz	III	Br Clm	612 Mtz		Br Clm
404 Mtz		Br Clm	...		
405			614 Mtz		Regt staff
...			...		
407 Mtz		Br Clm	616 Mtz		Br Clm
...			617 Mtz		Regt staff
409 Mtz		Br Clm	...		
410 Mtz			620 Mtz		Regt staff
411 Mtz		Br Clm	...		
412 Mtz		Br Clm	622		
413 Mtz		Br Clm**	...		
415 Mtz		Br Clm	624 Mtz		Br Clm
422 Mtz		Br Clm	...		
...			626 Mtz		Br Clm
427 Mtz		Br Clm	627 Mtz	III	Bn
...			628 Mtz		Regt staff
430 Mtz		Br Clm	...		
...			630 Mtz	X	Bn
442 Mtz	I	Br Clm	632 Mtz		Bn
501			...		
504 Mtz		Regt staff	633		
505		Bn	634		
...			635 Mtz		Bn
507 Mtz		Regt staff	636 Mtz		Br Clm
508		Bn	...		
...			639 Mtz		Br Clm
510			...		
511 Mtz		Regt staff	643		
512 Mtz		Regt staff	644 Mtz		Br Clm
515 Mtz		Regt staff	...		
517 Mtz	XII	Regt staff	...		
519		Regt staff	649 Mtz		Br Clm
520 Mtz		Regt staff			
521	XVII	Park Bn	651 Mtz	III	Bn
...			652 Mtz	VI	Bn
525			653 Mtz		Bn
...			654 Mtz	III	Bn
531			655 Mtz		Bn
532			656 Mtz	III	Bn
533		Br Clm	657 Mtz	VII	Bn
534		Br Clm	658 Mtz		Bn
538			659 Mtz		Bn
541 Mtz		Regt staff	660 Mtz		Bn
...			661 Mtz		Br Clm

*For type see Remarks column.
**There is also a Regt staff of this number.

Pi. unit	Wkr.	Remarks	Pi. unit	Wkr.	Remarks
662 Mtz	II	Bn	713 Mtz	XIII	Co, 713 Div
663 Mtz		Br Clm	714	I	Co, 714 Div
664			715	V	Co, 715 Div
...			716	VI	Co, 716 Div
666 Mtz	VI	Bn	741	III	Bn
667 Mtz		Regt staff	742 Mtz		Bn
668 Mtz		Br Clm	743 Mtz		Bn
...			744 Mtz		Bn
671 Mtz	VI	Bn	745 Mtz		Bn
672 Mtz	IX	Bn	746 Mtz		Bn
673 Mtz		Regt staff	747 Mtz		Bn
675 Mtz		Bn	...		
676 Mtz	XVII	Bn	750 Mtz		Bn
677 Mtz		Regt staff	751 Mtz	III	Bn
678 Mtz	XVII	Regt staff	752 Mtz	VI	Bn
...			753 Mtz		Bn
680 Mtz		Regt staff	754 Mtz	VI	Bn
...			...		
685 Mtz		Regt staff	770	XVII	Regt staff
...			...		
688			778		Landing Co
...			...		
690 Mtz		Regt staff	816 Mtz		Br Clm
...			817 Mtz		Br Clm
700 Mtz		Regt staff	843 Mtz		Br Clm
704	IV	Co, 704 Div	900 Mtz	III	Bn (90 Lt Div)
707	VII	Co, 707 Div	904		Assault boat unit
708	VIII	Co, 708 Div	905		Assault boat unit
709	IX	Co, 709 Div	906		Assault boat unit
710	X	Co, 710 Div			
711	XI	Co, 711 Div			
...					

69. Signal regiments, battalions, and companies (Nachrichtenregimente, Nachrichtenabteilungen, Nachrichtenkompanien).

	Nachr. Abt.*	Wkr.	Allotted to		Nachr. Abt.	Wkr.	Allotted to
	1	I	1 Inf Div		56 Mtz	IV	GHQ trs
N. R.	1 Mtz		1 Pz Army		57 Mtz	V	GHQ trs
Pz	2 Mtz	II	12 Pz Div				
N. R.	2 Mtz	XVII	2 Pz Army	Pz	59 Mtz	III	8 Pz Div
	3 Mtz	III	3 Mtz Div	Pz	60 Mtz	XI	XIV Pz Corps
N. R.	3 Mtz	IX	3 Pz Army		61	IX	(now Pz.A.N.R. 3)
Pz	4 Mtz	IV	14 Pz Div				
N. R.	4 Mtz	III	4 Pz Army		62	III	(now Pz.A.N.R. 4)
	5 Mtz	V	5 Lt Div				
	6	VI	6 Inf Div		63 Mtz		
	7	VII	7 Inf Div		64	XVII	44 Inf Div
	8	VIII	8 Lt Div		65	XVII	45 Inf Div
	9	IX	9 Inf Div		66 Mtz	XVII	XVII Corps
	10 Mtz	XIII	10 Mtz Div	Geb.	67	XVIII	2 Mtn Div
N. R.	10 Mtz	III	Pz Army Africa	Geb.	68	XVIII	3 Mtn Div
	11	I	11 Inf Div		...		
	12	II	12 Inf Div	Geb.	70	XVIII	XVIII Mtn Corps
Pz	13 Mtz	XI	13 Pz Div				
	14 Mtz	IV	14 Mtz Div		71	III	(renmbrd 150 ?)
Pz	15 Mtz	IX	27 Pz Div		72		
Pz	16 Mtz	VI	16 Pz Div		73	XII	(renmbrd 172 ?)
	17	XIII	17 Inf Div		74	IV	
	18 Mtz	VIII	18 Mtz Div		...		
Pz	19 Mtz	XI	19 Pz Div		76	XIII	46 Inf Div
	20 Mtz	X	20 Mtz Div		77 Mtz	VIII	Corps
	21	XX	21 Inf Div	Pz	78 Mtz	XII	15 Pz Div
	22	X	22 Inf Div	Pz	79 Mtz	XIII	4 Pz Div
Pz	23 Mtz	III	26 Pz Div		80 Mtz	XVII	(now Pz.A.N.R. 2)
	24	IV	24 Inf Div				
	25 Mtz	V	25 Mtz Div	Pz	81 Mtz	XVII	9 Pz Div
	26	VI	26 Inf Div	Pz	82 Mtz	VI	6 Pz Div
Pz	27 Mtz	VII	17 Pz Div	Pz	83 Mtz	IX	7 Pz Div
	28	VIII	28 Lt Div		84 Mtz		
	29 Mtz	IX	29 Mtz Div	Pz	85 Mtz	VIII ?	5 Pz Div ?
	30	X	30 Inf Div		86		
	31	XI	31 Inf Div	Pz	88 Mtz	IV	18 Pz Div
	32	II	32 Inf Div		...		
Pz	33	XII	(now disbanded)	Pz	90 Mtz	V	10 Pz Div
	34	XII	34 Inf Div	Geb.	91	XVIII	6 Mtn Div
	35	V	35 Inf Div	Pz	92 Mtz	IX	20 Pz Div
	36 Mtz	XII	36 Mtz Div		...		
Pz	37 Mtz	IX	1 Pz Div	Geb.	94	V	4 Mtn Div
Pz	38 Mtz	XVII	2 Pz Div	Geb.	95	XVIII	5 Mtn Div
Pz	39 Mtz	III	3 Pz Div		...		
N. R.	40 Mtz		OKW		97	VII	97 Lt Div
	41 Mtz	I	I Corps		...		
	42 Mtz	II	II Corps	Geb.	99	XIII	7 Mtn Div
	43 Mtz	III	III Pz Corps		100	XVII	100 Lt Div
	44 Mtz	IV	IV Corps		101	V	101 Lt Div
	45 Mtz	V	V Corps		...		
	46 Mtz	VI	VI Corps		106	VI	106 Inf Div
	47 Mtz	VII	VII Corps		...		
	48 Mtz	VIII	VIII Corps		110	X	110 Inf Div
	49 Mtz	IX	IX Corps		111	III	111 Inf Div
	50 Mtz	X	X Corps		112	XII	112 Inf Div
	51 Mtz	XI	XI Corps		113	XIII	113 Inf Div
	52 Mtz	XII	XII Corps		...		
	53 Mtz	XIII	XIII Corps		121	X	121 Inf Div
Geb.	54	VII	1 Mtn Div		122	II	122 Inf Div
					123	III	123 Inf Div

*Except where preceded by N. R.

ORDER OF BATTLE OF THE GERMAN ARMY

Nachr. Abt.	Wkr.	Allotted to	Nachr. Abt.	Wkr.	Allotted to
Pz 128 Mtz	XII	23 Pz Div	217	I	217 Inf Div
129	IX	129 Inf Div	218	III	218 Inf Div
...			219	XIII	183 Inf Div
131	XI	131 Inf Div	...		
132	XII	132 Inf Div	220	IV	164 Lt Div
...			221	VIII	221 Sich Div
134	IV	134 Inf Div	222	XI	181 Inf Div
...			223	IV	223 Inf Div
137	XVII	137 Inf Div	...		
...			225	X	225 Inf Div
Pz 140 Mtz		22 Pz Div	...		
150	XXI	50 Inf Div	227	VI	227 Inf Div
152	IX	52 Inf Div	228	VI	16 Mtz Div
156	IV	56 Inf Div	229	XII	197 Inf Div
157	VII	57 Inf Div	...		
158	X	58 Inf Div	231	XIII	231 Inf Div*
...			...		
160 Mtz	XX	60 Mtz Div	233	VI	196 Inf Div
161	I	61 Inf Div	234	III	163 Inf Div
162	VIII	62 Inf Div	235	V	198 Inf Div
165		65 Inf Div	236	II	162 Inf Div
168	III	68 Inf Div	...		
169	VI	69 Inf Div	239	VIII	239 Inf Div*
...			...		
171	XI	71 Inf Div	241	I	161 Inf Div
172	XII	72 Inf Div	...		
173	XIII	73 Inf Div	246	XII	246 Inf Div
175	II	75 Inf Div	...		
176	III	76 Inf Div	248	VIII	168 Inf Div
178	V	78 Inf Div	...		
179	XII	79 Inf Div	251	IX	251 Inf Div
181	VIII	81 Inf Div	252	VIII	252 Inf Div
182	IX	82 Inf Div	253	VI	253 Inf Div
183	X	83 Inf Div	254	VI	254 Inf Div
...			255	IV	255 Inf Div
186	VI	86 Inf Div	256	IV	256 Inf Div
187	IV	87 Inf Div	257	III	257 Inf Div
...			258	II	258 Inf Div
188	VII	88 Inf Div	...		
...			260	V	260 Inf Div
190 Mtz	III	90 Lt Div	...		
...			262	XVII	262 Inf Div
193	III	93 Inf Div	263	XII	263 Inf Div
194	IV	94 Inf Div	...		
...			267	XI	267 Inf Div
196	XI	96 Inf Div	268	VII	268 Inf Div
...			...		
198	XIII	98 Inf Div	269	X	269 Inf Div
			270**	X	270 Inf Div*
199	VI	199 Inf Div	271**	V	271 Inf Div*
Pz 200 Mtz	III	21 Pz Div			
			291	I	291 Inf Div
205	V	205 Inf Div	...		
206	I	206 Inf Div	293	III	293 Inf Div
...			294	IV	294 Inf Div
208	III	208 Inf Div	295	XI	295 Inf Div
209	IV	209 Inf Div*	296	XIII	296 Inf Div
...			297	XVII	297 Inf Div
211	VI	211 Inf Div	298	VIII	298 Inf Div
212	VII	212 Inf Div	...		
213	VIII	213 Sich Div	300		
214	IX	214 Inf Div	301		
215	V	215 Inf Div	302**	II	302 Inf Div
216	XI	216 Inf Div	303		

*Division now disbanded.
**Co only.

ORDER OF BATTLE OF THE GERMAN ARMY 0349

Nachr. Abt.	Wkr.	Allotted to	Nachr. Abt.	Wkr.	Allotted to
309			Pz 440 Mtz	X	XXXX Pz Corp
			Pz 441 Mtz	VIII	XXXXI Pz Corps
312					
313**		OKW	442 Mtz	III	XXXXII Corps
314			443 Mtz	XI	XXXXIII Corps
			444 Mtz	IV	XXXXIV Corps
320**	X	320 Inf Div	445 Mtz	XIII?	XXXXV Corps Cmd
321**	XI	321 Inf Div			
323	XIII	323 Inf Div	Pz 446 Mtz	X	XXXXVI Pz Corps
...					
327	XVII	327 Inf Div	Pz 447 Mtz	XX	XXXXVII Pz Corps
328	IX	328 Inf Div	Pz 448 Mtz	XXI	XXXXVIII Pz Corps
331	XVII	331 Inf Div			
332**	VIII	332 Inf Div	449 Mtz		XXXXIX Mtn Corps
333**	III	333 Inf Div			
334**	XIII	334 Inf Div	451 Mtz	XI	LI Corps
335**	V	335 Inf Div	452 Mtz	III	LII Corps
336**	IV	336 Inf Div	453 Mtz	XII	LIII Corps
337**	VII	337 Inf Div	454 Mtz		LIV Corps
			455 Mtz		LV Corps
339**	IX	339 Inf Div	Pz 456 Mtz	VI	LVI Pz Corps
340	I	340 Inf Div	Pz 457 Mtz	II	LVII Pz Corps
Pz 341 Mtz	VIII	11 Pz Div			
342**	XII	342 Inf Div	459 Mtz		LIX Corps
...			460 Mtz		LX Corps Cmd
369****			...		
370		370 Inf Div	463 Mtz	II	Army of Norway
			464 Mtz		LXIV Res Corps?
377	IX	377 Inf Div			
...					
380			467 Mtz		LXVII Corps Cmd?
...			...		
383	III	383 Inf Div	470 Mtz		
400			Pz 475 Mtz	III	Afrika Corps
420 Mtz	XX	XX Corps	480 Mtz		LXX Corps Cmd
...			...		
423 Mtz	VI	XXIII Corps	N. R. 501 Mtz	I	16 Army?
Pz 424 Mtz	XII	XXIV Pz Corps			
425 Mtz	V	XXV Corps	N. R. 503 Mtz		An army?
426 Mtz	I	XXVI Corps	...		
427 Mtz	VII	XXVII Corps	509 Mtz		15 Army
428 Mtz	III	XXVIII Corps	...		
429 Mtz	IV	XXIX Corps			
430 Mtz	XI	XXX Corps	N. R. 511 Mtz	III	An army?
431 Mtz	X?	XXXI Corps Cmd	512 Mtz		An army?
			513**		
432 Mtz		XXXII Corps Cmd	...		
			N. R. 514 Mtz		Railway trs
433 Mtz	VI	XXXIII Corps Cmd	N. R. 520 Mtz		9 Army?
434 Mtz***	III	XXXIV Corps Cmd	N. R. 521 Mtz	XVII	12 Army?
			N. R. 522 Mtz		
435 Mtz	VIII	XXXV Corps Cmd	...		
			525		
436 Mtz	II?	XXXVI Res Corps	526		
			...		
437 Mtz***	XVII	XXXVII Corps Cd	531 Mtz		7 Army?
			...		
438 Mtz	VIII?	XXXVIII Corps	536		
Pz 439 Mtz	IX	XXXIX Pz Corps	N. R. 537 Mtz		Army Gp
			...		

**Co only.
***Except where preceded by N. R.
****Telephone construction unit.

Nachr. Abt.	Wkr.	Allotted to	Nachr. Abt.	Wkr.	Allotted to
540*			635	III	
542			638***		
543**			N.R. 639 Mtz	IX	Army Gp
N. R. 549 Mtz	IV	6 Army	N.R. 642 Mtz		GHQ trs
N. R. 550 Mtz		20 Army	N.R. 643 Mtz****		GHQ trs
557*			N.R. 644 Mtz****		GHQ trs
N. R. 558 Mtz	V	An Army?	N.R. 645 Mtz****	V	GHQ trs
			646		
N. R. 563 Mtz	III	2 Army?	647**		
N. R. 564 Mtz			N.R. 649 Mtz		
N. R. 570 Mtz	VII	An army	660***		
N. R. 589 Mtz	VI	4 Army	665		
			666 Mtz**		
592			668**		
594			670**		
			671**		
N. R. 596 Mtz	XII	17 Army	672**		
N. R. 597 Mtz			673		
			682 Mtz***		
N. R. 601 Mtz		OKW	685 Mtz***	III	
602					
N. R. 603 Mtz		An army Gp	693***	IV	
N. R. 604 Mtz			694***		
605 Mtz**		(radio co)	696***		
610 Mtz**		(radio co)	697***		
			698 Mtz***		
612 Mtz**		(radio co)	702**	II	702 Inf Div
613 Mtz**		(radio co)			
614 Mtz**		(radio co)	704**	IV	704 Inf Div
N. R. 616 Mtz		GHQ trs	707**	VII	707 Inf Div
617 Mtz**			708**	VIII	708 Inf Div
N. R. 618 Mtz			709**	IX	709 Inf Div
619			710**	X	710 Inf Div
620 Mtz**			711**	XI	711 Inf Div
			712**	XII	712 Inf Div
621 Mtz**	IX	Alloted Africa Army	714**	I	714 Inf Div
622 Mtz**			717**	XVII	717 Inf Div
623 Mtz**					
627			721**	XI	Crete Cmd
			722**		
633 Mtz***	IV		751		

*Disbanded.
**Co only.
***Bn staff only.
****Telephone operating regt.

ORDER OF BATTLE OF THE GERMAN ARMY 0351

Nachr. Abt.	Wkr.	Allotted to	Fachr. Abt.	Wkr.	Allotted to
756			902*****		
...			...		
761			904*****		
762			...		
...			906*****		
806**			...		
...			907*****		
810**			...		
811**			920*****		
821 Mtz***			921*****		
...			922*****		
824			...		
825			930*****		
826			...		
...			937*****		

There is also a Nachrichten-Lehr-Regiment.

**Co only.
***Bn staff only.
*****Telephone operating platoon only.

70. Small units (divisional services, field replacement training battalion, field post office, medical unit, and military police unit, all carrying the same number).

No.	In Div	No.	In Div
1	1 Inf	85	5 Pz
2	12 Pz	...	
3	3 Mtz	88	18 Pz
4	14 Pz	...	
5	5 Lt	90	10 Pz
6	6 Inf	91	6 Mtn
7	7 Inf	92	20 Pz
8	8 Lt	93	
9	9 Inf	94	4 Mtn
10	10 Mtz	95	5 Mtn
11	11 Inf		
12	12 Inf	97	97 Lt
13	13 Pz	...	
14	14 Mtz	99	7 Mtn
15	27 Pz	100	100 Lt
16	16 Pz	101	101 Lt
17	17 Inf	102	102 Inf
18	18 Mtz	...	
19	19 Pz	106	106 Inf
20	20 Mtz	...	
21	21 Inf	110	110 Inf
22	22 Inf	...	
23	26 Pz	111	111 Inf
24	24 Inf	112	112 Inf
25	25 Mtz	113	113 Inf
26	26 Inf	...	
27	17 Pz	121	121 Inf
28	28 Lt	122	122 Inf
29	29 Mtz	123	123 Inf
30	30 Inf	...	
31	31 Inf	125	125 Inf
32	32 Inf	126	126 Inf
33	15 Pz	...	
34	34 Inf	128	23 Pz
35	35 Inf	129	129 Inf
36	36 Mtz	...	
...		131	131 Inf
40	1 Cav*	132	132 Inf
...		...	
44	44 Inf	134	134 Inf
45	45 Inf		
46	46 Inf	137	137 Inf
...		...	
54	1 Mtn	140	22 Pz
...			
57	6 Pz	150	50 Inf
58	7 Pz	...	
59	8 Pz	152	52 Inf
60	9 Pz		
61	11 Pz	156	56 Inf
...		157	57 Inf
66	16 Mtz	158	58 Inf
67	2 Mtn	...	
68	3 Mtn	160	60 Mtz
...		161	61 Inf
81	1 Pz	162	62 Inf
82	2 Pz		
83	3 Pz	168	68 Inf
84	4 Pz	169	69 Inf

*Now converted to 24 Pz Div.

ORDER OF BATTLE OF THE GERMAN ARMY 0353

No.	In Div	No.	In Div
...		246	246 Inf
171	71 Inf	...	
172	72 Inf	248	168 Inf
173	73 Inf	...	
...		250	250 Inf
175	75 Inf	251	251 Inf
176	76 Inf	252	252 Inf
...		253	253 Inf
178	78 Inf	254	254 Inf
179	79 Inf	255	255 Inf
...		256	256 Inf
181	81 Inf	257	257 Inf
182	82 Inf	258	258 Inf
183	83 Inf	...	
...		260	260 Inf
186	86 Inf	...	
187	87 Inf	262	262 Inf
188	88 Inf	263	263 Inf
190	90 Lt	...	
193	93 Inf	267	267 Inf
194	94 Inf	268	268 Inf
195	95 Inf	269	269 Inf
196	96 Inf	270	270*
...		371	271*
198	98 Inf	272	272*
199	199 Inf	273	273*
200	21 Pz	276	276*
...		277	277*
205	205 Inf	...	
206	206 Inf	290	290 Inf
207	207 Sich	291	291 Inf
208	208 Inf	292	292 Inf
209	209 Inf*	293	293 Inf
...		294	294 Inf
211	211 Inf	295	295 Inf
212	212 Inf	296	296 Inf
213	213 Sich	297	297 Inf
214	214 Inf	298	298 Inf
215	215 Inf	299	299 Inf
216	216 Inf	...	
217	217 Inf	302	302 Inf
218	218 Inf	...	
219	183 Inf	304	304 Inf
220	164 Lt	305	305 Inf
221	221 Sich	306	306 Inf
222	181 Inf	...	
223	223 Inf	319	319 Inf
...		320	320 Inf
225	225 Inf	321	321 Inf
...		...	
227	227 Inf	323	323 Inf
228	228 Inf*	...	
229	197 Inf	327	327 Inf
230	169 Inf	328	328 Inf
231	231 Inf*	329	329 Inf
...		330	330 Inf
233	196 Inf	331	331 Inf
234	163 Inf	332	332 Inf
235	198 Inf	333	333 Inf
236	162 Inf	334	334 Inf
...		335	335 Inf
238	167 Inf	336	336 Inf
239	239 Inf#	337	337 Inf
240	170 Inf	...	
241	161 Inf	339	339 Inf
...		340	340 Inf

* Disbanded in 1940.
\# Disbanded late in 1941.

No.	In Div	No.	In Div
341	341 Inf*	399	399 Inf*
342	342 Inf	400	Grossdeutshland
343	343 Inf	...	
344	344 Inf	554	554 Inf*
358	358 Inf**	555	555 Inf*
365	365 Inf**	556	556 Inf*
369	369 Inf	557	557 Inf*
370	370 Inf	...	
371	371 Inf	702	702 Inf
372	372 Inf**	...	
376	376 Inf	704	704 Inf
377	377 Inf	...	
379	379 Inf*	707	707 Inf
...		708	708 Inf
383	383 Inf	709	709 Inf
384	384 Inf	710	710 Inf
385	385 Inf	711	711 Inf
386	386 Inf*	712	712 Inf
387	387 Inf	713	713 Inf
		714	714 Inf
389	389 Inf	715	715 Inf
...		716	716 Inf
393	393 Inf*	717	717 Inf
...		718	718 Inf
395	395 Inf*	719	719 Inf

* Disbanded late in 1940.
** Disbanded late in 1940.

71. Antiaircraft artillery regiments, battalions, and batteries (Flugabwehrregimente or Flakregimente, Flakbataillone, Flakbatterien—all air force troops. Heeresflak are army units. Marineflak are naval units).

Flak	L. G.*	Remarks**	Flak	L. G.*	Remarks**
1	VII	Regt	47		Regt
1		Slt Regt	48	VIII	Regt (105-mm)
2	VII	Regt	49	XII	Regt (40-mm)
2		Slt Regt	50		Regt
3	I	Regt	51	III/IV	Regt
4	VI	Regt	52	III/IV	Regt
4		Slt Regt	53	VII	Regt
5	VII	Regt	54	VI	Regt
5		Slt Regt	55	XII/XIII?	Regt
6	XI	Regt (40-mm)	...		
7	III/IV	Regt	57		Regt staff
8	XVII	Regt	58		Regt staff
9	XII/XIII	Regt	59		Regt
10	IV	Regt	60	XI	Regt
11	III/IV	Regt	61	III/IV	Regt
12	III/IV	Regt (105-mm)	62	XI	Regt
13	XVII	Regt	...		
14	VI	Regt	64	VI	Regt
15	XII/XIII	Regt	65		Regt staff
16	XI	Regt	66	XII/XIII	Regt
17	XI	Regt	...		
18	XVII	Regt	68	XVII?	Regt
19	III/IV	Regt	69	VI	Regt
20	VIII	Regt	...		
20		Naval Regt	71	I	Lt Bn
21	I	Regt	72 mtz	VI	Lt Bn
22	III/IV	Regt	73 mtz	III/IV	Lt Bn
22		Naval Regt	74	VI	Lt Bn
23	III/IV	Regt	74		Slt Regt Staff
24	XI	Regt	75	VI	Lt Bn
24		Naval Regt	76 mtz	XI	Lt Bn
25	XVII	Regt	77	VIII	Lt Bn
26	XI	Regt	78	III/IV	Lt Bn
27	XI	Regt	78		Regt Staff
28	XII/XIII	Regt	79		Regt Staff
29	XI	Regt	...		
30		Regt	81 mtz		Lt Bn
31		Regt	82	VI	Lt Bn
32	XVII	Regt (105-mm)	83 mtz	III/IV	Lt Bn
33	III/IV	Regt	83		Regt Staff
34	VI	Regt	84	VI	Lt Bn
35	XI	Regt	85 mtz	VII	Lt Bn
36	XI	Regt	85		Regt Staff
37	VIII	Regt	86	III/IV	Lt Bn
38	XVII	Regt	87?		Lt Bn
39	VI?	Regt	88		Lt Bn
40		Regt staff	89 mtz		Lt Bn
41		Regt staff	90		Lt Bn
42	III/IV	Regt	91	XVII	Lt Bn
43	III/IV	Regt	91		Regt Staff
44	VI	Regt (105-mm)	92	XVII	Lt Bn
45	VII	Regt staff	92		Regt Staff
46		Regt	93	XVII	Lt Bn

*L. G.=Luftgau (the air force district corresponding in function to the Wehrkreis); L. G. I=Wkr. I, L. G. VI=Wkr. VI, L. G. VII=Wkr. V and VII, L. G. VIII=Wkr. VIII, L. G. XI=Wkr. X and XI, L. G. XII/XIII=Wkr. XII and XIII, L. G. XVII=Wkr. XVII and XVIII.

**Light battalions are normally equipped with 37-mm and 20-mm guns, heavy battalions with 88-mm guns, and all other battalions are *mixed*, with 88-mm, 37-mm, and 20-mm guns. Where a unit is known to be equipped with other calibres such as 40-mm or 105-mm, a reference is given in this column.

ORDER OF BATTLE OF THE GERMAN ARMY

Flak	L. G.	Remarks	Flak	L. G.	Remarks
93		Regt Staff	143		Bn
94 mtz	VI	Lt Bn	144		Bn
95	XII/XIII	Lt Bn	145		Bn
95		Regt Staff	146		Bn
96	VI	Lt Bn	147		Bn
97	VII	Lt Bn	148		Slt Bn
98 mtz		Lt Bn	149		Regt Staff
99 mtz	XVII	Lt Bn	...		
99		Regt Staff	151		Bn
100		Regt Staff	151		Regt Staff
101		Regt	152		Bn
102		Regt Staff	152		Regt Staff
102		Balloon Bn	153		Bn
103		Regt	153		Regt Staff
104		Regt Staff	154		Bn
...			155		Bn
106		Regt Staff	156		Bn
...			157		Bn
108		Regt?	158		Slt Bn
109		Slt Regt	...		
110		Ry Regt	160		Ry Btry
111		Bn	160		Regt Staff
111		Regt Staff	160		Slt Regt
112?		Regt	...		
112		Ry Regt	162		Regt Staff
...			...		
114 trop		Bn	164		Bn
115		Bn	164		Regt Staff
116		Bn	164		Naval Bn
...			...		
118		Regt Staff	166		Bn
...			167		Bn
120		Regt Staff	168		
120		Slt Bn	...		
121		Lt Bn			
121		Regt	180		Regt
122		Bn	181	XVII	Bn
122		Ry Regt	181		Regt Staff
123		Bn	182		Bn
123		Regt Staff	182		Regt Staff
124		Bn	183		Bn
125		Bn	...		
125		Regt Staff	185		Bn (75-mm)
126		Naval Bn	186		Bn (75-mm)
126		Regt Staff	187	XVII	Bn
127		Bn	...		
...					
129		Regt Staff	191		Bn
130		Slt Bn	192		Bn
131 mtz		Bn	193		Bn
131		Regt Staff	194		Bn
132		Bn	...		
132		Regt Staff	196		Bn
133		Bn	197		Hv Bn
133		Regt Staff			
134	III/IV	Bn	199		Bn
134		Regt Staff	200		Naval Bn
135 trop		Bn	201	XVII	Regt Staff
136		Regt Staff	201		Balloon Bn
137		Bn	202		Regt Staff
138		Slt Bn	202		Balloon Bn
138		Regt Staff	203		Balloon Bn
...			204		Naval Bn
...			204		Balloon Bn
141 mtz		Lt Bn	205		Balloon Bn
142		Bn	206		Bn
142		Regt Staff	206		Balloon Bn

ORDER OF BATTLE OF THE GERMAN ARMY 0357

Flak	L. G.	Remarks	Flak	L. G.	Remarks
207		Bn	262		Naval Bn
...			263		Bn
...			264		Bn
210		Balloon Bn	264		Naval Bn
211		Bn	265		Bn
211		Slt Bn	266	XI	Bn
212		Naval Bn	266		Naval Bn
...			...		
214		Naval Bn	269		Slt Bn
...			...		
216		Naval Bn	271		Army Bn
...			272		Army Bn
221		Bn	272		Naval Bn
222		Bn	...		
222		Naval Bn	274		Army Bn
223		Bn	274		Naval Bn
224		Bn	275		Army Bn
224		Naval Bn	276 mtz		Army Bn
224		Ry Bn	277 mtz		Army Bn
225			278		Army Bn
226		Bn	279 mtz		Army Bn
226		Naval Bn	280		Army Bn
227		Ry Bn	280		Naval Bn
...			...		
229		Regt Staff			
230	VI	Hv Bn?	286		Hv Bn
231 mtz		Regt	...		
232		Regt			
232		Naval Bn	289		Army Bn
233		Naval Bn	290		Bn?
234		Bn	291 mtz		Bn
234		Naval Bn	292		Bn
235		Bn	...		
236		Bn	294		Naval Bn
236		Naval Bn	295		Bn
237		Bn	296		Bn
			297		Bn
239		Naval Bn	298		Slt Bn
240		Naval Bn	299		Slt Bn
241		Regt	300		Slt Bn
241		Naval Bn	301		Hv Bn
242		Bn	302		Bn
242		Naval Bn	303		Army Bn
243		Bn	304		Bn
244		Hv Bn	305		Bn
244		Naval Bn	306		Bn
245		Bn	306		Ry Btry
246		Bn	307		Ry Btry
246		Naval Bn	308	III/IV	Regt
...			308		Slt Bn
...			309		Slt Bn
249		Bn	310		Bn
...			310		Naval Bn
251	VII	Bn	311		Bn
252		Bn	312 mtz		Army Bn
252		Naval Bn	313 mtz		Army Bn
252		Slt Bn	...		
253		Bn	315		Bn?
254		Bn	316		Bn
254		Naval Bn	...		
255		Bn	321		Hv Bn
256		Bn	321		Ry Bn
257		Bn	322		Bn
258	XI	Bn	323		Bn
...			...		
260		Slt Bn	325		Bn

0358 ORDER OF BATTLE OF THE GERMAN ARMY

Flak	L. G.	Remarks	Flak	L. G.	Remarks
...			406	VI	Bn
329 trop		Slt Bn	407		Bn
330		Bn	407		Ry Btry
331	III/IV	Bn	408		Slt Bn
332		Hv Bn	...		
333		Bn	...		
334		Bn	411 mtz		Regt
335		Regt	...		
...			414		Bn
...			415		Bn
340		Bn	416		Ry Bn
340	Slt	Bn	...		
341		Bn	...		
342		Bn	421		Hv Bn
343		Hv Bn	...		
344		Bn	423		Bn
345		Bn	...		
346		Bn	425		Hv Bn
...			...		
...			427		Hv Bn
351		Bn	428		Bn?
352		Hv Bn	...		
353		Lt Bn	...		
354		Bn	431		Bn
355		Bn	432		Bn
...			433		Bn
357		Hv Bn (94-mm)	434		Bn
...			...		
...			...		
360		Bn	438		Slt Bn
361		Bn	...		
362		Bn	...		
363		Bn	441		Regt
364		Bn	...		
365		Bn	...		
...			445		Bn
...			...		
371	VIII	Bn	447		Bn
372		Hv Bn	448		Slt Bn
...			449		Slt Bn
374		Bn	...		
...			...		
...			455		Bn
381		Bn	...		
382		Bn	...		
382		Regt Staff	461		Bn
383	XVII	Bn	...		
384		Bn	...		
385		Bn	464		Bn
386		Bn	...		
387	XVII	Bn	...		
...			467		Bn
...			469		Bn
391		Bn	...		
...			...		
393		Lt Bn	...		
394	XII	Bn	491		Bn
...			493		Bn
397	XVII	Bn	494		Bn
...			...		
...			496		Hv Bn
401		Ry Lt Btry	497		Bn
402		Bn	...		
403		Hv Bn	...		
404		Bn	...		
405		Bn	501 mtz		Regt

ORDER OF BATTLE OF THE GERMAN ARMY

Flak	L. G.	Remarks	Flak	L. G.	Remarks
502	VII	Hv Bn	...		
...			620		Slt Bn
504		Bn	...		
504		Regt Staff			
505		Bn (ferries)	629		Regt
506		Bn	...		
507		Bn			
...			641		Hv Bn
509		Slt Bn	642		Bn
...			643		Bn
511		Bn	644		Bn
511		Naval Bn	645		Bn
512		Bn	...		
...			...		
514		Bn	649		Bn
515		Hv Bn	...		
516		Bn	...		
517		Bn	652		Regt Staff
...			653		Regt Staff
519		Slt Bn	654		Regt Staff
...			655		Regt Staff
			656		Regt Staff
522		Hv Bn	657		Regt Staff
523		Bn	...		
524		Bn			
525		Hv Bn	660		Hv Bn
526		Hv Bn	670		Bn
527		Hv Bn	671		Bn
528		Bn ?	672		Bn
...			673		Bn
...			674		Bn
532		Bn	675		Bn
...			676		Bn
...			677		Bn
541		Bn	678		Bn
...			679		Bn
			680		Lt Bn
550		Bn?	681		Bn
...			682		Bn
			683		Bn
573		Lt Bn	684		Bn
...			685		Bn
			686		Bn
582		Bn	687		Bn
...			688		Bn
			689		Lt Bn
591		Bn ?	690		Bn
...			691		Lt Bn
			691		Ry Bn
601	XI	Hv Bn (105-mm)	692		Bn
602		Bn	693		Bn
603		Bn	694		Bn
604		Regt	695		Bn
605		Bn	696		Naval Bn
606		Bn	...		
607		Bn			
608		Slt Bn	701		Regt
609		Slt Bn	701		Naval Bn
...			702		Bn
611 mtz	XI	Regt	702		Naval Bn
...			703		Lt Bn
613		Bn	703		Naval Bn
...			704		Regt
615		Bn	705		Naval Bn
616		Bn	706		Hv Bn
617		Hv Bn	707		Hv Bn
618	XI	Slt Bn	708		Slt Bn

0360 ORDER OF BATTLE OF THE GERMAN ARMY

Flak	L. G.	Remarks	Flak	L. G.	Remarks
708		Naval Bn	...		
...			781		Lt Bn
711		Bn	782		Hv Bn
711		Naval Bn	...		
712		Bn			
713		Lt Bn	793		Bn
...			...		
715		Lt Bn ?	797		Bn
...			...		
717		Lt Bn			
...			...		
			801		Bn
720		Lt Bn	802		Bn
720		Naval Bn	802		Naval Bn
			803		Naval Bn
722		Lt Bn (disbanded)	804		Bn (94-mm, 40-mm)
723		Bn	804		Naval Bn
724		Lt Bn	805		Bn
725		Lt Bn	805		Naval Bn
726		Lt Bn	806		Hv Bn
727		Lt Bn	806		Naval Bn
...			...		
729		Lt Bn			
...			809		Lt Bn
731		Lt Bn (50-mm)	809		Navel Bn
732		Lt Bn	810		Naval Bn
733		Lt Bn ?	811		Naval Bn
734		Bn	812		Naval Bn
735		Lt Bn	813		Naval Bn
736		Lt Bn	...		
737		Lt Bn	815		Bn
...			...		
739		Lt Bn			
740		Lt Bn	822		Ry Bn
741 mtz		Lt Bn	823		Lt Bn
742		Lt Bn	824		Lt Bn
			825		Ry Lt Bn
744		Lt Bn	826		Lt Bn
745		Lt Bn	...		
746		Bn	...		
...			830		Lt Bn
...			831		Bn
750		Lt Bn	832		Bn
751		Lt Bn	833		Bn
752		Lt Bn (50-mm)	...		
753		Lt Bn	835		Lt Bn
...			...		
755		Bn	837		Lt Bn
756		Lt Bn	...		
757		Bn	839		Lt Bn
...			...		
			841 mtz trop		Lt Bn
761 mtz		Lt Bn	842		Lt Bn
762		Bn	...		
763		Lt Bn	...		
764		Lt Bn	845		Bn
765		Bn	...		
767		Lt Bn	848 ?		Slt Bn
768		Bn	849		Lt Bn
769		Lt Bn	...		
...			851 mtz		Lt Bn
...			852		Lt Bn
772		Lt Bn	853		Lt Bn
773		Lt Bn	854		Bn
774		Lt Bn	...		
775		Lt Bn	856		Lt Bn

ORDER OF BATTLE OF THE GERMAN ARMY

Flak	L. G.	Remarks	Flak	L. G.	Remarks
...			925		Lt Bn
860			...		
861 mtz		Ry Lt Bn	928		Bn
862		Lt Bn	...		
863		Lt Bn	...		
864		Lt Bn	931		Lt Bn
865		Ry Lt Bn	932		Lt Bn
...		Ry Lt Bn	...		
...			...		
871		Lt Bn	941	XVII	Lt Bn
...			942		Lt Bn
873		Lt Bn	...		
874		Lt Bn	...		
875		Bn	952		Lt Bn
...			953		Lt Bn
...			...		
891		Lt Bn	...		
...			978		Lt Bn
...			979		Lt Bn
901		Bn	980		Lt Bn
902		Ry Hv Bn, (105-mm)	...		
			982		Lt Bn
903		Bn	983		Lt Bn
904		Bn	984		Lt Bn
905		Bn	985		Lt Bn (40-mm)
...			...		
909		Slt Bn	990		Lt Bn
...			991		Lt Bn
911		Lt Bn	992		Lt Bn
912		Lt Bn	...		
913		Lt Bn	994	XII	Lt Bn
914		Lt Bn	995		Lt Bn
...			...		
			997		Lt Bn
921		Lt Bn	998		Lt Bn
...			999		Lt Bn
923		Lt Bn	...		
...					

Also, Heeresflak-Lehrabteilung and Flak-Lehrregiment (Battalions I–III).

www.ingramcontent.com/pod-product-compliance
Lightning Source LLC
Chambersburg PA
CBHW080529170426
43195CB00016B/2510